AF517316

A Traveller in an Unknown Land

SECOND EDITION

A Traveller in an Unknown Land

SECOND EDITION

Jagadis Chandra Misra

Formerly, Professor & Head, Department of Mathematics,
I.I.T. Kharagpur, India
&
Pro Vice-Chancellor, SOA University, Bhubaneswar, India

ALLIED PUBLISHERS PVT. LTD.

Noida • Mumbai • Kolkata • Chennai • Bangalore

ALLIED PUBLISHERS PRIVATE LIMITED

D-5, Sector-2, **Noida**–201 301
Ph. Nos.: 0120-4320295/2542557/4352866
E-mail: delhi.books@alliedpublishers.com

17 Chittaranjan Avenue, **Kolkata**–700072
Ph.: 033-22129618 • E-mail: cal.books@alliedpublishers.com

15 J.N. Heredia Marg, Ballard Estate, **Mumbai**–400001
Ph.: 022-42126969 • E-mail: mumbai.books@alliedpublishers.com

No. 25/10, Commander-in-Chief Road, Ethiraj Lane (Next to Post Office)
Egmore, **Chennai**–600008
Ph.: 044-28223938 • E-mail: chennai.books@alliedpublishers.com

P.B. No. 9932, No. 15, 3rd Floor (Next to Vijaya Bank), 5th Cross, Gandhinagar,
Karnataka, **Bangalore**–560009. Ph.: 080-41530285/22386239
E-mail: bngl.books@alliedpublishers.com

Website: https//:alliedpublishers.in

First Published: 2023
Second Edition: 2025

ISBN: 978-93-48699-77-0

Published by Sunil Sachdev and printed by Ravi Sachdev
at Allied Publishers Pvt. Ltd., D-5, Sector-2, Noida–201 301

RAMAKRISHNA MATH, COSSIPORE

Sri Sri Ramakrishna Paramahansa Dev Sarani

(90, Cossipore Road, Kolkata – 700 002)

The Cossipore Udyanbati

Website: www.rkmcudyanbati.org **Email:** cossipore@rkmm.org

Mobile: 9433306107 Phone: (033) 2557-3605/ 2532-9348 Date 17/07/2025

Foreword

My beloved alma mater, Ramakrishna Mission Vidyamandira, Belur Math has produced many distinguished pioneers over the years. One such pioneer, Shri Jagadis Chandra Misra (our Jagadis Da), has requested me to write a 'Foreword' for his autobiography "A Traveller in an Unknown Land." Since he was a respected senior fellow-student of the Vidyamandira, I have agreed to write it, with great joy.

At first, I was a bit surprised. After all, Jagadis Da is one of the brightest gems of the nation in the field of mathematical sciences, and he is revered and respected in academic circles across the world. His name is adorned with a long list of academic degrees and honours. There are many eminent scholars, both in India and abroad, who are far more qualified to write the foreword for such a distinguished person's autobiography. Had he asked, they would have gladly accepted the offer. Yet, he chose me—why? It didn't take long for my surprise to fade. During my student days at Vidyamandira, I had noticed, how much affectionate this brilliant alumnus of Vidyamandira was to the monastic members and other faculty members of the institution. Years later, as a monk of the Ramakrishna Mission, I had the fortune of close association with him in Bhubaneswar. I visited Ramakrishna Math and Mission, Bhubaneswar during Kali Puja for several years, and each year, Jagadis Da would come to the Mission to meet me during my stay there. At that time, he had retired from IIT Kharagpur and was serving as the Pro Vice-Chancellor of SOA University in Bhubaneswar.

Through those conversations, I realized that despite being a globally respected scientist and holding a high administrative position in a university, the core of his discussions always revolved round Belur Vidyamandira, spiritual practices, the revered monks of the Mission—especially his guru, the seventh President of the Mission, Swami Shankaranandaji Maharaj, and the Principal of Vidyamandira, Swami Tejasanandaji Maharaj. These memories made it clear to me that while Vidyamandira nurtured Jagadis Da's intellectual brilliance and academic achievements, it was equally true that his life was deeply enriched and sanctified by the sacred spiritual atmosphere of Belur Vidyamandira, shaped by the ideals of Sri Ramakrishna and Swami Vivekananda. From that life perspective, it is only natural that he chose a monk of the Mission to pen the 'Foreword' for his autobiography.

But another surprise awaited me as I journeyed through the manuscript of the book "A Traveller in an Unknown Land." As I began reading his life story, just a few pages in, I was amazed. I discovered that even before coming to Vidyamandira, his upbringing—rooted in his ancestral home and joint family—was like living in a traditional hermitage, where life lessons were imparted continuously. His father, a high school teacher and the president of the local Union Board, rose through poverty and hardship. His mother, though simply educated, was affectionate and wise. His uncle, a homeopathic doctor and caretaker of household affairs, and his aunt, skilled in household work and loving in nature—all of them were like his first spiritual teachers. The foundation of their lives was India's timeless spiritual consciousness—the worship of household deities, and the flowing nectar of the Ramayana, Mahabharata, Gita, and Chandi.

Along with providing for their children's physical needs, they showed them the path to becoming true human beings. From them, the young traveller learned that the greatest wealth in human life is not material possessions, but character. The moral teachings from Bengali poems or Sanskrit slokas he learned then have remained with him throughout his life. They taught him that acquiring knowledge requires focus and perseverance, and maintaining society requires selfless love, service, simplicity, and good conduct. These were not mere words; they embodied these ideals in their daily lives.

His father was a living embodiment of the ideal "Atmano Mokshartham Jagat Hitaya Cha" (For one's own liberation and for the welfare of the world). He fought to establish himself in society and simultaneously dedicated himself to serving the school, students, and the local community. He hardly had time for family matters, yet before sleeping at night or during the oil massage before bathing, he ensured his son's and others' education was properly supervised.

Though his father and uncle were not biological brothers, the joint family was a model of harmonious, joyful social living. From his uncle, he learned life's brevity and the need to extract the essence from vast fields of knowledge, like the mythical swan separating milk from water. His uncle encouraged him to overcome laziness, lead a disciplined life, and mingle freely in society.

Even among relatives, he witnessed examples of a passion for knowledge and service to society. He saw firsthand the establishment of Sauri High School through the efforts of his maternal grandfather, a school from which student Narayan Chandra Rana later achieved global fame in astrophysics.

Thus, before even stepping foot into Vidyamandira, Jagadis Da had already been shaped as an ideal human being, blessed with a harmonious combination of worldly and spiritual knowledge. I believe that at Vidyamandira, under the influence of Sri Ramakrishna, Holy Mother Sarada Devi, and Swami Vivekananda's profound ideals, this foundation was further strengthened and consolidated. That became the ultimate provision for the fearless, global journey of the Traveller in the unknown land.

It may not be possible to establish Vidyamandira in every village, yet in every home, the infinite potential of the dormant Brahman awaits manifestation in countless child forms. To awaken them, every village needs families like the "Bagmari's united household"—and building such families is not impossible. All that is needed is the light of ideals.

Carrying that message of light, "A Traveller in an Unknown Land" will reach readers worldwide. Through his life's journey, present and future generations will discover the craftsmanship behind building a hermitage-like home, the key to personal accomplishment, and the secret of dedicating oneself to the welfare of the world.

Though this is an autobiography, the author humbly keeps himself in the background, shining a light instead on the supreme life ideals and the divine lamp illuminating the path of public welfare.

Therefore, I wish for this book's widespread circulation for the welfare of mankind. I pray that Jagadis Da and his family forever receive the blessings of Sri Ramakrishna, Holy Mother Sarada Devi, and Swami Vivekananda.

Swami Divyananda

Swami Divyananda
Vice President,
Ramakrishna Math and Mission, Belur Math

Foreword

It is both an honour and a privilege for me, as a junior colleague in the academic lineage of IIT Kharagpur and as its present Director, to pen a few words for the autobiography of Professor J. C. Misra. The very title of this book, *A Traveller in an Unknown Land*, is evocative, for it captures with rare elegance the spirit of a life that has continuously journeyed across the frontiers of knowledge, values, institutions, and inner awakening.

Professor Misra belongs to that vanishing class of scholar-saints of the academy—individuals for whom intellectual pursuit was never divorced from ethical depth, and professional distinction never detached from human sensitivity. Internationally acclaimed for his contributions to mathematical sciences, revered as a teacher, institution builder, and academic leader, he is also remembered by his students and colleagues for something far more enduring: his quiet grace, his unassuming conduct, and his unwavering commitment to truth, discipline, and service.

As one reads through the pages of this autobiography, it becomes abundantly clear that the foundations of such a life were laid much before the author entered the portals of great institutions. The narrative of his early years, shaped by a joint family steeped in learning, moral rectitude, simplicity, and spiritual consciousness, reads almost like the description of a modern-day *gurukul*. His parents, relatives, and elders emerge not merely as caregivers, but as the first teachers who demonstrated, through lived example, that character is the highest form of capital, and that education finds its true meaning only when aligned with compassion and social responsibility.

The imprint of the Ramakrishna Mission Vidyamandira, Belur Math, on Professor Misra's life forms a luminous thread through this book. Vidyamandira did not merely refine his intellectual acumen; it consolidated a worldview shaped by the eternal ideals of Sri Ramakrishna, Holy Mother Sarada Devi, and Swami Vivekananda—ideals that harmonize personal liberation with universal welfare. The Vedantic maxim " *Ātmano mokṣhārtham jagat hitāya cha*" was not, for him, a slogan, but a lived philosophy. It is this synthesis of rigorous scholarship and spiritual rootedness that empowered him to navigate the "unknown lands" of global academia with fearlessness, humility, and purpose.

At IIT Kharagpur, where he served with distinction for decades, and later in leadership roles beyond, Professor Misra exemplified what it means to be an academic institution-builder in the truest sense. He saw universities not merely as sites of instruction or administration, but as crucibles for nation-building—spaces where knowledge, values, and service must coalesce. His journey reminds us that excellence and empathy are not competing virtues, but complementary ones.

What makes this autobiography particularly remarkable is the author's self-effacement. Though it chronicles an extraordinary life, the narrative consistently places the spotlight on the ideals, institutions, mentors, family values, and spiritual influences that shaped him. In doing so, the book transcends the genre of personal memoir and becomes a guidebook for building meaningful lives—homes that resemble hermitages, careers anchored in conscience, and achievements consecrated to the common good.

In an age often driven by speed, spectacle, and self-promotion, *A Traveller in an Unknown Land* offers a quiet but powerful counterpoint. It reminds us that the most transformative journeys are inward as much as outward, and that the unknown becomes navigable when illuminated by ideals.

I earnestly hope that this book reaches a wide and diverse readership—students, teachers, parents, and seekers alike. May it inspire families to become the first sanctuaries of values, institutions to recommit to their civilizational role, and young minds to believe that it is possible to be globally accomplished while remaining deeply rooted.

I join the author's well-wishers in praying that Professor J.C. Misra and his family continue to be blessed with strength, peace, and fulfilment. May the grace of Sri Ramakrishna, Holy Mother Sarada Devi, and Swami Vivekananda ever guide this noble traveller, and through him, illuminate the paths of countless others.

Prof. Suman Chakraborty
Director & Sir J C Bose National Fellow
Indian Institute of Technology Kharagpur

Prof. Gautam Biswas
FNA, FASME, FAUTSE, FASc, FNAE, FNASc, FIE
Former Director, Indian Institute of Technology Guwahati
Senior Professor Emeritus
Department of Mechanical Engineering

Foreword

It is a bivalent state of mind while writing a forwarding note on the autobiography of Prof. J.C. Misra, entitled "A Traveller in an Unknown Land.". Prof. Misra has taught me at the Indian Institute of Technology Kharagpur. On one hand, I am definitely indebted to him for what I could learn under his excellent tutelage. On the other hand, it is a difficult task to make a meaningful interpretation of the experiences of illustrious and indefatigable Prof. J.C. Misra, who deserves our solemn tributes for his extraordinary achievements.

The book written by Prof. Misra is an impeccably articulated philosophy of a lifelong learner. The academic achievements and accomplishments of Prof. Misra at different stages of his multi-faceted life are truly noteworthy. We wholeheartedly admire his academic scholarship and research accomplishments. The social, cultural and spiritual aspects of this illustrious scholar are exceptionally nice and pleasant. From this book, one can learn how to work on various problems at the highest level of academic echelon yet remaining calm, well balanced and carrying out all the societal commitments with an ever-smiling face.

This book will serve as a fountain-head of several brilliant ideas to progress on the track of excellence and at the same time putting in efforts to make others happy and spreading peace and tranquillity in the surrounding ambience. I pray to Thakur Sri Ramakrishna, Maa Sarada and Swami-ji Maharaj for the wellness of Prof. J.C. Misra and the members of his family.

Gautam Biswas

(Gautam Biswas)

Birla Institute of Technology & Science, Pilani
K K Birla Goa Campus, Near NH 17B, Bypass Road
Zuarinagar 403726, Goa, India
E mail: gautamb@goa.bits-pilani.ac.in, gtm@iitk.ac.in

Foreword to the First Edition

Charaiveti (Keep Moving Forward)

Let us start the discussion by recalling a part of the conversation from 'Sri Sri Ramakrishna Kathamrita' recorded on September 7, 1883.

Sri Ramakrishna: Well, do I resemble anyone else?

Mani: No, Sir.

Sri Ramakrishna: With any 'Paramahansa'?

Mani: No, Sir. You have no comparison.

Sri Ramakrishna: (Smiling) Have you heard of 'the unknown tree'?

Mani: No, Sir.

Sri Ramakrishna: There is a kind of tree that cannot be recognized by anyone, merely by seeing.

Mani: Just like that, no one can fully comprehend you. The more someone understands you, the more elevated he feels.

Mani was quietly trying to contemplate. Thakur (Sri Ramakrishna) mentioned 'The Rising Sun' and 'The Unrecognized Tree'. Do these suggest the appearance of 'Avatar' (Incarnation)? In this what is called 'Naralila' (God's advent on earth in the shape of man)? Is 'Thakur' himself an 'Avatar'? Is this the cause why Thakur gave a clarion call to his disciples from his rooftop, saying 'Hey, where are you all, come to me soon.'

The call he gave out that time in his eagerness to see his disciples, still resonates in the sky and the air. Many have embarked on a journey in search of the 'Unknown Tree' after hearing this call. One such traveller, identifying himself as 'A Traveller in an Unknown Land' has beautifully narrated his journey for the benefit of future travellers. The truth of the statement "the more one understands the Unknown Tree, the more elevated they become spiritually"—How far this assertion made by Sri Mahendranath Gupta (who sometimes goes by the pseudonyms: Mani, Master or Sri M.) will be realized by any reader of the book 'A Traveller in an Unknown Land'.

The title of the book in question is 'A Traveller in an Unknown Land'. The author is Sri Jagadis Chandra Misra, our senior brother, whose name is accompanied by numerous titles such as Dr. J.C. Misra, Ph.D., D.Sc., FNASc., FNAE, FIMA (UK), FIThP, FIET (UK), FRSPH (London), FRSB (London), FASc.T, Adjunct Professor, Indian Institute of Engineering Science and Technology, Shibpur, Howrah, 711103, India; Formerly Pro Vice-Chancellor, SOA University, Bhubaneswar; Former Professor and Head, Department of Mathematics, IIT Kharagpur; Ex-President, Mathematical Sciences Section, Indian Science Congress; Recipient of INAE Outstanding Teachers Award and Ram Mohan Puraskar.

To one who has set out his journey on the path in search of the untitled 'unknown tree', titles are quite unnecessary. Only through the sacrifice of all titles one can attain the feet of the all repudiating Lord (the Tyagiswara). The person adorned with titles understands their futility and becomes ready to relinquish them. Our senior brother has embarked on this golden path since his birth, unknowingly. Therefore, the details of his journey are important to all, irrespective of whether they want to be achievers in materialistic life ('*Abhyudayakami*') or seekers of liberation ('*Muktikami*'). An '*abhyudayakami*' will find in the book ways to rise to the pinnacle of honour slowly, but steadily with honesty, dignity as well as with industry and nobility of the soul. A 'muktikami' (seeker of liberation) will be able to learn how to advance in the way of spiritual pursuits following steadily the path shown by Sri Guru.

The book is not just an autobiography. It vividly portrays the socio-economic conditions of the contemporary period, along with eternal scriptural and ethical teachings, and the histories of several institutions. Many verses from the Vedas, Upanishads, Puranas, and ethical texts have been quoted with their interpretations in the pages of the book. Here is an example to illustrate how even the simplest statements can be immensely significant. The author learnt cycling from someone named Radhamadhav. Radhamadhav, his student, said, "Sir, never try to overtake anyone." The Vedic mantra "*Sangachchhadhwam samvadadhwam...*" (Walk with altogether and chant with altogether) resonates like a *rishi's* voice to remind us to follow this principle in every aspect of life for peace. We forget this often, and that is why we suffer most in life. The author has attained peace by following this precept of his dear student in all aspects of life.

The ultimate goal of human life is Self-Knowledge or Self-Realization. Our wise ancestors structured life into four Ashramas (stages), each with a distinct purpose leading toward this ultimate realization:

1. *Brahmacharya Ashrama*: The student phase, dedicated to education.
2. *Grihastha Ashrama:* The householder stage, where one earns wealth ethically to support not only their family but also society and other beings.
3. *Vanaprastha Ashrama:* The stage of gradual withdrawal, where the responsibilities are passed on to the next generation, and preparation for renunciation begins.
4. *Sannyasa Ashrama:* The stage of complete detachment and spiritual pursuit.

It is mandatory for all to pass through the first three Ashramas before entering the Sannyasa Ashrama. However, if divine grace (*Sri Bhagavat Kripa*) bestows renunciation at any stage, one is entitled to take 'Prabrajya'(monastic vows). Only through sacrifice does one attain immortality—for immortality and self-knowledge are one and the same.

Our scriptures emphasize not only Nishreyas (liberation) but also Abhyudaya (worldly prosperity). They suggest that the spiritual seeker may reach the ultimate goal of life through either of the two paths:

1. Pravritti (engagement with the world)
2. Nivritti (withdrawal from the world)

The purpose of elaborating on these concepts is to highlight how the author's life aligns with these scriptural precepts—beautifully reflected in his autobiographical work, 'A Traveller in an Unknown Land.'

The book has been arranged in fifteen chapters, rich in meaningful contents. Each chapter reveals the eternal values of life through the description of different characters and events. In the first chapter 'Childhood Days' the exemplary character of the author's parents is brought out in such a way that it feels like reading the lives of any sage and his wife. At a far-flung village Bagmari in the district of East Medinipur, during the occasion of Mahanabami of Autumn festival of Durga Puja in 1350 B.S., a child saw the light of the earth, lying on the lap of Pramila Devi, the wife of the pious ideal teacher Ganes Chandra Misra. Little could anyone think then that the said child would become so famous a scholar as to be the guide of many research fellows in future. The sage-like father named the child Jagadis, so that the child would grow up to be famous like Acharya Jagadish Chandra Basu. For that he slowly prepared his son's nature and character, as he himself was a teacher. To him all his students were like his sons, and in reality he had proved it by keeping a fatherless destitute student named Tarak Pahari at his own house and raising him on an equal footing with his son Jagadis. Jagadis Chandra's mother used to tell him moral stories, having him on her lap in his childhood days. All parents should read this Chapter in educating their children properly. Nowadays the joint family is no longer seen. But from this Chapter we come to know how the child Jagadis grew up in the company of everyone in a joint family.

The Second Chapter deals with the boyhood and the period of receiving school education. The Chapter is named: Secondary Education. He has made the Chapter valuable referring to the character of some ideal teachers, and he has also shown how the students should renounce all happiness and make study a meditative act of student life. The only two students from Tikrapara Ambikamoyee High School who passed with First Division in the School Final Examination in 1959 were Jagadis Chandra Misra and Tarak Pahari.

The third and fourth chapters narrate his time at the Ramakrishna Mission Vidyamandira and Belur Math—an experience that opened new horizons in his life. The rare privilege of spending seven uninterrupted years in institutions run by the Ramakrishna Mission profoundly shaped his learning and enriched his understanding. It was there that his perception of life's purpose attained clarity. His youthful years were profoundly influenced by the spiritual companionship. Especially the blessings of his revered Guru, Srimat Swami Shankarananda and the affectionate guidance of other highly revered monks, like Swami Shantananda and Swami Premeshananda altered the course of his life. These chapters extensively discuss the true purpose of education and the means to achieve it, making them particularly valuable for any student. *The fourth chapter, in particular, is a must-read for spiritual aspirants.*

The fifth chapter paints a vivid picture of the education system and scientific research at the time through a detailed description of the academic environment at the University of Calcutta and particularly, the Rajabazar Science College. The holistic education he received while staying at the Calcutta Ramakrishna Mission Vidyarthi Ashrama is also mentioned in this chapter.

Thus, the book *'A Traveller in an Unknown Land' is not just the story of a life—it is a guide for all seekers, whether they walk the path of worldly success or spiritual awakening.*

The sixth chapter discusses his initiation into research, teaching, and lecturing, as well as his entry into the second stage of life, the Grihastha Ashrama (Domestic Ashrama). According to the Scriptural rule: "prajatantum ma byabachchetsih" keeping himself fully engaged in Brahmin's duties (study, teaching, doing worships and sacrifices), he diligently performed his responsibilities, as reflected in his students' memories.

The next Chapter describes his teaching, research, and the early years at IIT Kharagpur. The date 9th August, 1971 marks the second turning point in his life, with the first being his entry into the Ramakrishna Mission's educational institution as a student in 1959. Twelve years later he joined IIT Kharagpur as a faculty. A boy from a remote village had become a faculty in one of the most prominent institutions of learning of our country. The enormous effort he had to put in is reflected in his research papers. But to be satisfied with the achievement of a single Doctorate title was not the ultimate goal of Jagadis Chandra's life. Wherever he went to the famous universities in India and abroad, he learned much as well as taught others. A great number of scholars were immensely benefitted in their personal life coming to his contact. He heard in his childhood the saying: '*Vidwan sarbatra pujyate*' (Scholars are worshipped everywhere). He could directly feel it, when he went to visit a famous busy doctor in Europe, for his treatment. The doctor gave special instruction to his secretary that not a single valuable minute of the honourable Professor be wasted in the process of his treatment.

In the following Chapters there are ample information about his research, and many awards and honours. Details of his activities in the various educational institutions of the country and abroad are mentioned. Along with teaching he has adeptly handled administrative responsibilities. He has also skillfully written brief history of various educational institutions. He had a deep connection with the Ramakrishna Order. Wherever he went, whether in India or abroad, if he found a branch centre of the Ramakrishna Math and Mission, he visited and stayed there with the monks, and participated in their service activities, to the best of his ability both financially and physically. His father's instruction—"The country expects something from you", constantly resonated in his ears, keeping him engaged in the service of the Nation throughout his life. The wealth and comfort of foreign lands could never tempt his mind. He could raise his children with the same ideals. All this was possible with the cooperation of his wife. Quite naturally, the contributions of his wife and others of his family have been beautifully presented in a Chapter. Marriage is not a mere union of a man and a woman, it is also a union of a family with another family. As a result of the union of two families, the branches that develop there from make the next generation. The previous generation hands over to the next generation the key to the entrance of a beautiful and peaceful life. This is how human civilization spreads and develops.

Before entering the 'Vanprastha Ashrama' in the third Stage the householder shares all his experiences with his children and those like his children, so that they can proceed in their life, being enriched with such experiences. The book "A Traveller in an Unknown Land' contains within its covers invaluable gems and jewels. Whoever reads this book will immensely be benefitted by the essence of higher life.

It has been said earlier that Shri Jagadis Chandra Misra is my 'senior brother' (Satirtha). We got the opportunity to study under the same teachers. After completing education for five years in the Vidyamandira, named by Swami Vivekananda, when he entered the University, I started my study in Vidyamandira. Despite his busy schedule, he would occasionally come to the Vidyamandira, the first turning point of his life. We would then see how dear he was to the revered Vice-Principal and Hostel Chief of the Vidyamandira, Swami Gokulanandaji Maharaj, and how blessed his life was with the affection and how blessings of the revered Swami Shantanandaji Maharaj (of the Belur Math), direct disciple of the Holy Mother Sri Sri Sarada Devi. Seeing those heavenly scenes with amazed eyes, we received so much inspiration for a pure life!

Many years later, I once went to IIT Kharagpur to meet a friend. I heard that our respected brother was a renowned Professor there at that time. Actually, I lost touch with him for many years in between. When he came to know that I went to my friend's house, he himself came down to our friend's house and cordially invited me to receive alms (to have dinner) at his home. Going to his quarters, I had a feeling like entering the ashrama of a sage. The description of the ashramas of sages described in the Ramayana matched exactly with that place. The sage, his wife and their children had transformed the residence into a temple. We received the offered *prasad* at that temple. What satisfaction! The person with numerous titles before and after his name stood before us as the beloved elder brother of the Vidyamandira, devoid of all titles. He and his family exemplify the humility that education imparts. The ideal householder depicted by Swami Vivekananda in his *'Karma Yoga'* book is embodied in reality here! The scripturally prescribed lifestyle for humans is fully realized in this family. The book "*A Traveller in an Unknown Land*' is a testament to that.

With the boundless grace of god, after leading an ideal life in the Grihastha Ashrama, our elder brother with his wife has now handed over the responsibilities of the household to his worthy children and is living unattached in the Vanaprastha Ashrama.

There are no ancient forests now. They live at home, but reside in another realm. Gradually shedding, the burdens of all titles, he is advancing on the path of self-realization. With the help of internal renunciation through the Guru's grace, he will surely reach the ultimate goal of human life, find the 'unknown tree' and sitting at its base, make the rare human life fruitful. His life will be worthwhile to the men and women of the world at large. His forefathers exclaim in unison—"Blessed are you, accomplished are you, you have purified the lineage". (*Dhanyo'si kritakrityo'si pavitam te kulam tvaya*)

I pay my respect to our 'senior brother' and his wife. I pray for both of them for long healthy life, so that they can further enrich the atmosphere of noble thoughts in the world by remaining immersed in the meditation of 'Jagadish'.

Belur Math
Howrah-711202
31 October, 2023

Swami Devarajananda
Joint-Convener
Ramakrishna Vivekananda Bhav Prachar
Committee, Ramakrishna Math, Belur Math

Bow Down Again and Again

"He who can make the mute speak,
He who can make the lame cross mountains,
By whose grace all is possible—
I bow down to that Supreme Bliss, Madhava."

The author's journey began from a remote village, in a mud house thatched with straw. Throughout this long journey, there were many obstacles and uncertainties. By divine grace and with the help of many kind souls along the way, the rugged path became somewhat smoother. The author has been blessed with the sincere love and affection of many, which filled his life with joy.

It is not possible to mention everyone's name here, and for that the author seeks apology. However, after his parents some significant names mentioned are—the late *Srimat Swami Shakaranandaji*, *Swami Tejasananda*, *Swami Gokulananda*, *Swami Dhyanatmananda* of *Ramakrishna Lok*, and the late revered *Professor Bibhutibhushan Sen.*

To them and to all the well-wishers who have remained in the background the author offers deep reverence and heartful gratitude.

May the rest of his life's journey be always surrounded by the good will and love of those around—this is the author's earnest prayer at the lotus feet of *Sri Ramakrishna.*

Dedication

Dedicated to the lotus-feet of my revered father
Ganes Chandra Misra
&
My dear mother Pramila Devi,
whom I consider my God and Goddess on this earthly life
&
my next younger brother Dines Chandra,
who left for heavenly abode immaturely
despite all our sincere efforts of medical treatment.

Family Tree

Author's Paternal Side

(Gotra: Vatsya)

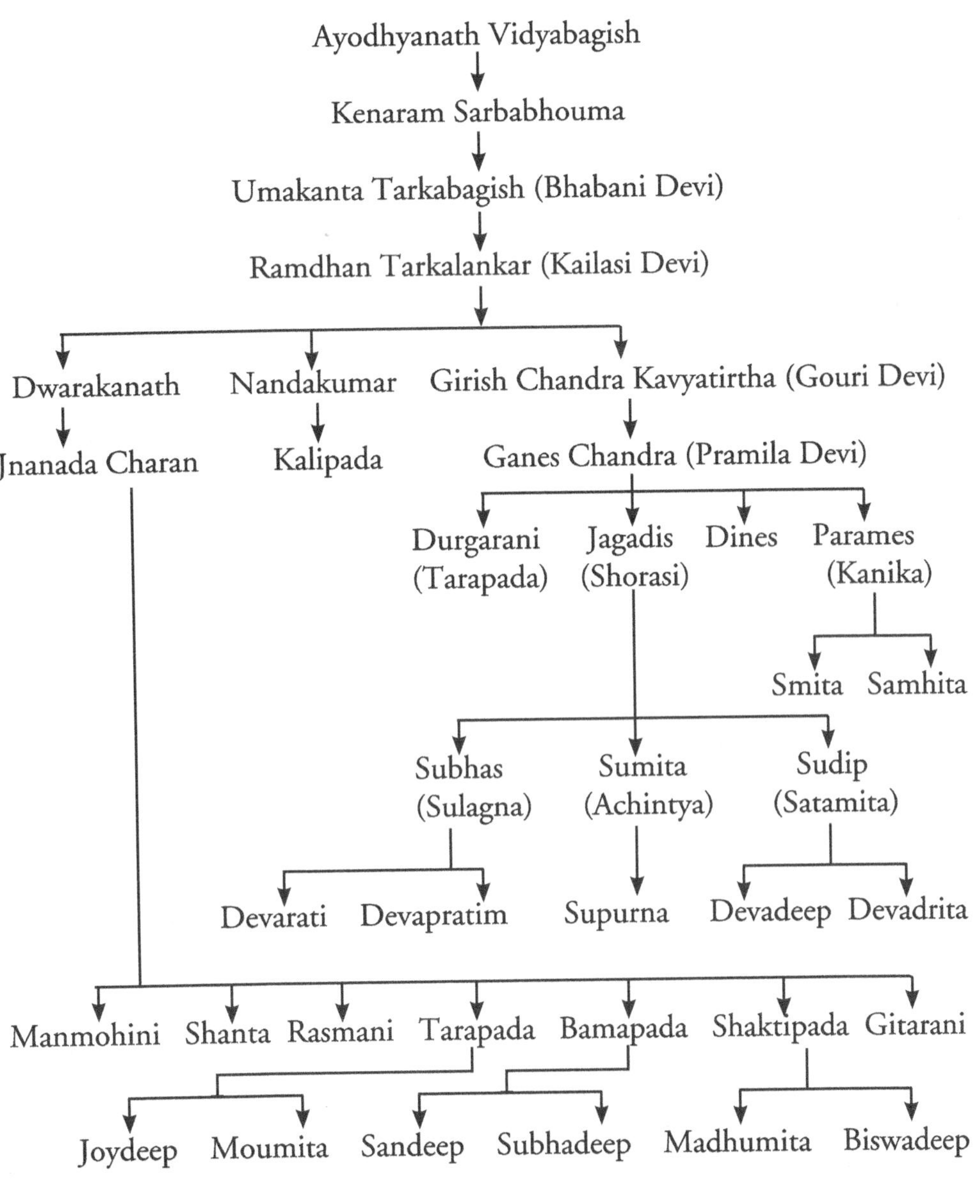

Author's Note

A few years ago, Dr. Haripada Maity, the former principal of Mugberia Gangadhar Mahavidyalaya in Purba Medinipur, visited the residence of Dr. Shantanu Dhara, a professor at the School of Medical Science and Technology, IIT Kharagpur. Dr. Dhara, an alumnus of IIT Kharagpur, had been known to me for a long time. Moreover, his wife, Smt. Nilanjana, is Dr. Maity's daughter and a close friend of my younger daughter-in-law, Satamita. Thus, they were more than acquaintances—they were our family friends.

After my retirement, I often stayed on the IIT Kharagpur campus, where Shantanu and Nilanjana treated us with great affection. One day, Nilanjana warmly invited me, saying, "Dear Uncle, my father is visiting us. You may not have met him before. But he knows all about you. He would love to meet you. Could you please join us for dinner at our home tonight?"

I have always enjoyed engaging with different people. So I accepted her invitation with pleasure. That evening, I visited their home and met Dr. Maity for the first time. Interestingly, his college, Mugberia Gangadhar Mahavidyalaya, was merely 17 km from my native village, Bagmari (near Pratapdighi). Though I had often been invited to various events held in the region on different occasions, I had never personally met Dr. Maity, although I heard of his eloquence as a speaker.

During our conversation, he repeatedly insisted, "You must write your autobiography—may not be necessary for yourself, but for the benefit of the future generations." I expressed reluctance at the first instance, as I was busy with some academic activities that time. However, as a seasoned professor and administrator, he knew how to persuade people. He urged me to reflect on the matter, and later, he continued to remind me through phone calls, saying, "Have you started writing your autobiography? Once you begin, you will find your way forward. One day, you'll realize it's complete. You may not feel the need for yourself, but for the younger generations, the book will be invaluable. Children of the future, along with their parents will find great inspiration in reading your autobiography. They will find you as an appropriate role model."

A few days later, my dear friend Manmatha Nath Das, a renowned teacher (retired) of Mugberia Gangadhar High School and a distinguished historian, along with my schoolmate Balai Lal Das, an esteemed and student-friendly teacher at a higher secondary school, encouraged me in various ways to embark on this journey. Yet, I remained hesitant. Doubts clouded my mind—was my life truly worth documenting? Would my experiences serve as a guide for future generations? And even if they did, would I be able to write about them with absolute honesty and detachment? Would not my personal biases overshadow the narrative?

I found myself in a dilemma, torn between my inner apprehensions and the persistent encouragement from Dr. Maity, Sri Manmathanath Das, and Sri Balailal Das. It felt as if I were caught between two forces, uncertain of which path to take.

During such moments of indecision, the words of Sri Ramakrishna would echo in my mind: "Not even a single leaf of a tree moves without God's will." Many times in life, I have found solace and direction in these words, and this time was no different. I gradually started believing that the writing of my autobiography was part of a greater divine plan.

In writing this book I had opportunity to relive and cherish the memories of my past—my childhood, adolescence, youth, and advancing age. Though my childhood years were brief, they were filled with joy and simplicity. In those days, there were no heavy academic pressure, no lofty ambitions, and no rigid class distinctions. Children played in the open ground, dressed only in shorts, free from the burdens of today's education system, which demands admission into kindergarten at the tender age of three. We attended primary school at five or six, wearing nothing more than half-shirts, half-pants and even at the high school level, students continued to wear the same attire.

As I recounted the various phases of my life, both in India and abroad, I found great joy in reliving those experiences. By God's grace, most of my memories are sweet and fulfilling. I was fortunate to have grown up in the environment of a loving joint family, nurtured by the care and affection of my parents, uncles, aunts, teachers, and villagers. Later I was fortunate to be shaped by the ideals of the Ramakrishna Mission.

It is my humble hope that the present and future generations will find some inspiration in my modest account of life's journey, which has been guided by the teachings of Sri Ramakrishna, Holy Mother Sarada Devi, and Swami Vivekananda.

This book also provides glimpses into various educational institutions across India and beyond. In writing it, I feel as if I have had the privilege of recording a few pages of history. Even if a handful of students and parents find it useful, I will consider my efforts well rewarded.

I feel highly indebted to Srimat Swami Divyananda, Vice-President, Ramakrishna Math and Ramakrishna Mission, Belur Math for the highly insightful 'Foreword' of the book. I want to express my deep sense of gratitude to Srimat Swami Devarajananda, Joint Convenor of the Ramakrishna-Vivekananda Bhav Prachar Committee and a highly respected senior monk of Belur Math, for writing the excellent 'Foreword' for the first edition of the book (Bengali version). His words of appreciation and thoughtful analysis will undoubtedly delight all the readers. I want to extend my heartfelt thanks to the distinguished educator and academic administrator, Srimat Swami Suparnananda, Secretary of the Ramakrishna Mission Institute of Culture at Golpark, Kolkata for his kind encouragement in respect of the early publication of the present Second Edition (English version) of the book and for providing invaluable suggestions during the preparation of the book. I offer my sincere thanks to Prof. Ranajit Kumar Nayek, former Professor of English at Mugberia Gangadhar Mahavidyalaya and Miss Sampurna Dan, JRF at SWAN Lab, IIT

Kharagpur for kindly reviewing the entire manuscript with utmost care and diligence, and for making proof corrections with all devotion. Thanks are due to Dr. Ayan Mondal (IIT Indore), Dr. (Mrs) Chandana Roy, Dr. Arijit Roy (IIT Patna), Miss Ruelia Saha (SRM University, AP) as well as Kumarjit, Rajdeep, Atonu, Biswajit, Aparesh, Shiv, Rukhshar, Sunanda and others for their help in different matters.

I am thankful to my maternal cousin Anup for his constant encouragement and timely help in bringing out this volume. I appreciate the steadfast support of my wife Shorasi in all my creative endeavours. The contributions of each of our children are highly appreciated. I am thankful to Subhas for his continuous encouragement towards publication of the present updated English version (Second Edition) of the book, which acted as a driving force towards preparation of the manuscript of the present book; to Sumita for her sincere concern about my all-round welfare and to Sudip for providing proper environment for continuing my literary/scientific activities. By the grace of Lord Sri Ramakrishna and Holy Mother Sri Sarada Devi, at the present phase of life the author along with his wife has always been fortunate to live under the loving care of someone who is blessed with the heart of an affectionate mother and the mind of a responsible father.

Finally, I sincerely thank Shri Jagdish Singh and his dedicated team at the Allied Publishers Pvt. Ltd., Noida, for their excellent work in producing and publishing this book with utmost efficiency.

15th December, 2025

Jagadis Chandra Misra

B-74, IIT Campus, Kharagpur-721302
Mobile: 8373843896

Contents

CHAPTER 1

Childhood Days

It was the year 1943. The independence of Mother India was on the horizon. Freedom fighters were relentlessly striving with all their might to liberate the nation from the humiliation of colonial subjugation. The non-violent movement, led by Mahatma Gandhi gathered immense strength, while Netaji Subhas Chandra Bose inspired the people with his bold call—*"Give me blood, and I will give you freedom."* The leading role of the two districts of undivided Bengal—Medinipur and Chattogram—in the freedom struggle is well known to all Indians. In the East Medinipur district the contributions of Tamluk and the then Contai (Kanthi) subdivisions were particularly noteworthy. Even remote villages like Srirampur and Pratapdighi under the Patashpur police station (now part of the Egra subdivision) also participated in the Salt Movement, symbolizing their commitment to the cause of freedom.

It was Thursday, the 20th of Ashwin, 1350 in the Bengali calendar (7th October, 1943), the auspicious day of Mahashtami during the Sharadiya Durga Puja. Everyone was immersed in the festive joy of the grand puja. The Sandhipuja rituals had just concluded when the author was born in the village of Bagmari, adjacent to Pratapdighi. His father, Ganes Chandra Misra, and mother, Pramila Devi, were deeply devout individuals with a strong sense of duty. However, October 1943 also marked a significant milestone in India's freedom struggle, as Netaji Subhas Chandra Bose formed the Azad Hind Fauz (Indian National Army) on the 21st of that month—just two weeks after the author's birth.

The year 1350 (1943–44) was a period of immense hardship in undivided Bengal under the British rule. The region experienced the devastating Bengal famine, often referred to as the 'Famine of 50', which resulted in severe food shortage and claimed the lives of approximately three million people. The Second World War (September 1, 1939 – September 2, 1945) was still ongoing, adding to the distress of the people of Bengal.

The village of Bagmari, where the author was born, was expansive and bordered by a canal to the east, called the Barochowka canal. The canal, with water year-round, was crossed by bamboo bridges, a common sight of rural areas of the time. Near the author's birthplace, the bridge remained made of bamboo for years before being upgraded to wood and later to concrete. The settlement of fishermen lay close to the canal, and on the way to the author's ancestral house, one would pass through a few Vaishnav households including those of Motilal Das, Charu Chandra Das and Baneswar Das. The fishermen's settlement included the Barman families of Haran Chandra (fondly called Haru babu), Khagen Chandra, Bhusan Chandra and others. Like other homes in the village in those days, the author's house was also constructed of mud but remarkably stood three stories tall. To the east of the author's house were the homes of his two uncles—Gurakes Babu and Bhutes Babu. To the west was the Dhara neighbourhood. A vibrant community was marked by mutual cooperation and warmth, with children playing together in the fields, next to the author's house and elders fostering a spirit of mutual trust and friendship among one another.

Author's Dilapidated House at Bagmari Village, East Midnapore, West Bengal

Father-Teacher

In 1913, the author's father, Ganes Chandra, was born in his maternal home in Mugberia village. Tragically, the author's grandfather, Girish Chandra, passed away at the young age of forty, leaving behind him, Gauri Devi and their three-year-old son, Ganes Chandra. Despite her immense grief, Gauri Devi raised her son with unwavering devotion, embodying both maternal affection and paternal responsibility. The author's grandmother was a deeply spiritual woman. She spent a lot of time every day in worship. During the scorching summer, she would stand by the roadside offering water and sweet to thirsty travellers. She used to find great joy and satisfaction in doing so.

Since the author's father was orphaned at a very young age, the author never had the fortune of meeting his grandfather, Girish Chandra. Even the memory of his grandmother, Gauri Devi, is quite faint. However, it is vividly remembered that the author's father was very devoted to his mother. When he used to go out of the house, he would bow to her. He personally attended to his mother's needs with all sincerity. All these indicate that he had profound respect and love for his mother. By God's grace, this quality has become somewhat hereditary. All three of the author's children—Subhas, Sumita, and

Sudip—have maintained this tradition. Each of them extends a helping hand to those in need, both within and outside the family.

The author's father began his primary education in the village school while living in a joint family. Later, through his mother's relentless efforts and dedication, young Ganes Chandra received support from Zamindar Gangadhar Nanda and got the opportunity to study at Mugberia Gangadhar High School where his education was highly subsidized.

Even when the author was a very young child, his father used to impart in him various moral lessons.

His father drew his attention to the following Sanskrit verse about the five characteristics of an ideal student:

> *Kako Chesta, Bako Dhyanam, ShwananidraTathaiva Cha*
> *Swalpahari, Grihatyagi Vidyarthi Pancha Lakshanam.*

This means, in student life, education should be regarded as penance. Students should have the perseverance of a crow, the concentration of a heron, the alertness of a dog, eat sparingly, and be willing to leave home—these are the five characteristics of ideal students. Even if they stay at home, they should not be concerned with petty household matters, and an appropriate environment for studying should be maintained.

Author's Father Ganes Chandra

During his academic journey, Ganes Chandra earned a little money by coaching students, utilizing which he used to buy his own books and notebooks. It is highly commendable that despite the hardships, he consistently ranked first in almost every class through hard work. According to the records of Mugberia Gangadhar High School, he passed with honor the Matriculation exam in 1933. The author's father would proudly and joyfully say, "I am a student of the renowned mathematics teacher Dharani Babu, who was a student of the famous mathematician Somesh Bose."

Poverty and hardship, however, never left his side throughout his student life. By simultaneously studying and coaching students, he passed the IA exam from P.K. College at Contai (Kanthi) with first division. Even later, while studying for a BA with honours in Sanskrit at Asutosh College in Kolkata, he also had to earn money by coaching students to cover his educational expenses.

Although he grew up amid so much want and scarcity, by God's grace, he could demonstrate the love of humanity both inside and outside the home. In later life, he also focused on religious practices and, along with his wife (author's mother), took mantra initiation from Sri Sri Sitaram Das Omkarnath. An institution was established around him. His contemporaries participated in his readings of the Gita and other religious texts. The author's mother, Pramila Devi, was not only his companion in religious practices but was also his true shadow companion everywhere.

Guidance and Legacy

As a father, Ganes Chandra instilled strong values in his children. At the high school level, the author's father could skillfully teach various subjects such as English, Mathematics, and Sanskrit. His teaching method was extraordinary. Along with bookish knowledge, he emphasized character building. One of his favourite maxims was *"If money is lost, nothing is lost; if health is lost, something is lost; but if character is lost, everything is lost."* He used to explain this by saying if someone loses money, there is no need to worry too much because they can soon earn money again. If health deteriorates, it causes some loss, but if a person loses character, it results in complete destruction. In childhood itself, the author's father advised him to be courageous and bold. He often said, *"Cowards die many times before their death."* This valuable saying still encourages the author to be fearless. These valuable teachings were imparted not only to the author but were shared with all the students during his classroom teaching. At home, while teaching the author, these valuable sayings, the father would first say the phrase in Bengali, then ask the author to translate it into English and Sanskrit. The author also clearly remembers that from a very young age, his father taught him not to leave any work undone out of laziness. He taught the Sanskrit translation of this saying—*'Shvah Karyam Adya Kurveeta'* and then the English translation—'Don't defer till tomorrow what you can do today.' Thus Ganes Chandra's approach to education extended much beyond the boundary of course curriculum.

Another characteristic of the author's father was the optimal use of time. When the author was a school student, his father was busy all the day with teaching activity in the school and social service. In the evening, he would also participate in judgement/conciliation meetings at someone's house in their own or neighbouring village, trying to resolve various people's issues. In those days, family or social issues were resolved in this way. People rarely went to court. Prominent people in the locality used to be called to resolve disputes. As a social worker and president of the Srirampur Union Board No. 11, the author's father often had to be engaged in such activities. Therefore, he had little opportunity to coach the author in the house at a fixed time every day. But as an ideal teacher he skillfully managed his time to oversee the author's studies. Before bathing, he would sit on a mat and thoroughly rub mustard oil on his body and coconut oil on his head. This process took about 25–30 minutes. During this time, he supervised the studies of both the author and his classmate, Tarak (who was given shelter in the author's house). Usually, he would ask them to translate a Bengali text into English or Sanskrit or solve all the problems from the chapter of a mathematics book in advance. The next day, while applying oil on his body, he would first check the previous day's work, make corrections, and then give the next assignment. Even if a translation or solution was correct, he would suggest better translations, discuss various alternative methods for solving the same problems of mathematics. The author would carefully make a note and write them down.

Ganes Chandra recounted an anecdote about the importance of proper understanding of English in problem-solving. In a casual storytelling manner, author's father once mentioned that when he was studying matriculation at Mugberia School, their headmaster, Sashi Bhushan Maiti, used to teach English, and the assistant headmaster, Dharani Dhar Mahapatra, used to take the maths class. They were good friends. Once, in some examination many students received low marks in maths. Headmaster Sashi Babu asked Dharani Babu why the students had done so poorly in his subject. Dharani Babu instantly replied that the students did not fail in his subject, but rather in Sashi Babu's subject. It turned out to be true; when the math questions were translated from English to Bengali, most of the students could solve the problems correctly.

For English grammar, in school life the author's father studied from Nesfield's Grammar book. He kept his own copy beautifully bound. He used the same copy of the book while teaching English grammar. He considered Nesfield's grammar to be authoritative. Following his instructions, the author maintained a bound notebook for English grammar. As his father would dictate, the author would write it down in that notebook, including examples with each definition of grammar. The father would randomly ask the author questions at any time, and if the answer was wrong, he would ask the same question again a few days later. Following his father's advice, the author also maintained a word-meaning book (a small notebook) to note down any new English words along with their Bengali meanings. This notebook used to be always in the author's pocket, and whenever he had time, he would glance through it. In this manner, he was gradually improving his English vocabulary. Thus his father's guidance greatly influenced the author's linguistic development. Also, following his father's advice, the author used to complete the mathematics books of higher classes in advance.

Notably, Ganes Chandra's guidance left a lasting legacy, not only in his family but also in the broader community. His teachings continue to inspire the author and his siblings to lead lives of integrity, compassion and dedication.

Primary Education

In his early years, the author attended Pratapdighi (Majna) Primary School with his elder sister. One of the teachers, Sri Basanta Kumar Sahu, was Bratachari-trained. He taught the students many Bratachari dances and songs. First, he would perform the dance and simultaneously sing himself, and then ask the students to imitate him. The author still remembers a few Bratachari songs, which when translated into English sound as below:

Primary School, Pratapdighi

"Let's wield the hoe, forget vanity's woe
Shake off lazy moods, the body will grow.

All ailments will flee, saying 'we cannot stay,'
Driven by hunger's fire, we'll feast on kheer and cream."

Bratachari Vow

"Whatever we do, we will do it well,
If the work is shoddy, we'll die of shame."

The scenes of Bratachari dances still float before the author's eyes. The Bratachari teacher Basanta Babu was known for his warm demeanor. He always bore a smiling face and treated his students with great affection.

Tikrapara High School

The author's father was a teacher at Tikrapara High School. In the initial years, this school functioned as an M.E. school. When it was upgraded to a secondary school, the author's father joined as the headmaster. At that time, the institution was financially very weak. During its early stages, the author's father along with a few of his colleagues nurtured the institution like their own child. They would serve the school sometimes without any salary or for a nominal honorarium and would visit the homes to house of wealthy patrons to collect funds for the school.

Some kind-hearted individuals even donated land for the school. Under the leadership of the author's father and with the cooperation of the local people, a two-storey building made of raw bricks was constructed in 1942. Unfortunately, shortly after its completion, a devastating cyclone that hit southern Bengal that year completely destroyed the newly built building. The following year, in 1943, as mentioned earlier a severe famine struck southern Bengal. Despite these disasters, the author's father, with his strong will and enthusiasm, successfully rebuilt the school building with the collective help of the local people. As said earlier, in the same year the author was born.

After serving as the headmaster for a few years, he handed over the responsibility to another person and as an assistant teacher, focused on the school's improvement. He was an ideal teacher, highly respected, and beloved by both the headmaster and his colleagues. This school was primarily for male students. Later, a girls' school was established in nearby Bagmari village, which is located in the vicinity of Tikrapara High School.

In his childhood, the author was not particularly attentive to his studies. Although he secured the highest marks in every subject in the fifth-grade exams, his father advised him not to be complacent as village schools often had only one or two strong students in a class.

His father heard of an intelligent orphan boy named Tarak Pahari from the nearby village of Bhairabdanri who had stopped his studies due to lack of opportunity. The author's father admitted Tarak to the sixth grade at Tikrapara School, providing accommodation and food at their home. From then on, the author and Tarak studied together, engaging in healthy competition that spurred them both to excel.

Father's Dedication

The author's father also accommodated several other students, not only relatives, but non-relatives too, in their home, ensuring equal attention and opportunities for all. He was equally conscious and caring regarding the education and employment, not only for his own children, but also for his nephews and nieces with equal emphasis, and arranging their marriages with equal care, thus elevating him to a high pedestal of humanity.

Although the author's father was always busy with various tasks, he would leave everything to take care of an ill person at home. He personally provided meticulous care to the sick. The author saw his father in various roles. In the joint family, when any child's milk teeth loosened, he would expertly extract them by hand, eliminating the need for a dental surgeon. He also personally cleaned garbage, drains, and surrounding roads, perhaps intending to teach the children of the house.

The father was very affectionate towards the children. During school examination days, there was always a provision of snacks for the teachers. The father would not eat, he would call the author and hand over the snacks to him.

The father heard from a friend of his that consuming a mixture of honey, ghee, and sugar (one teaspoon each) daily would enhance students' intellect. He prepared this mixture himself every morning and gave it to the author, along with a ripe banana and a glass of milk. Eating fruits was not very common in those days, especially in rural areas. The father encouraged eating local fruits like bananas, guavas, sapodillas, and pineapples. He would wash and cut various local fruits, sprouted chickpeas (chana), and mung beans, and tomatoes, serving them to the author right at his study place.

It is interesting that when the author became father, he followed the same practice for all his children.

Both the parents of the author set a rare example for today's youth.

Father at the IIT Campus, Kharagpur

The IIT Kharagpur campus environment and climate were very conducive to the health and mind of the author's father. He used to remain mentally relaxed, with no worldly worries, maintaining a joyful and peaceful disposition while residing at the IIT Campus. He spent most of his time engaged in worship, meditation, and reading scriptures. One morning, while brushing his teeth at the quarters (C1-63), the father told the author, "Since you have brought me here, I have been able to remain alive till now. If I weren't staying here, I would have passed away long ago." The author firmly believes that all the prosperities in their family today are due to the immense blessings of his parents, whose virtuous souls continue to protect them all the time.

The author's father suddenly left this mortal world in November 1994, on Shukla Chaturthi (two days after Bhai Dooj), merging with the lotus feet of Lord Vishnu. Initially admitted to the IIT hospital when he felt unwell, he was later transferred to the Railways Hospital at Kharagpur, following the advice of an external specialist doctor of cardiology. He breathed his last there. Those days because of inadequate communication system, and considering his poor health condition, it was not at all advisable to transfer him to an advanced health centre in Kolkata.

Last Rites

Following his father's wish/instructions, the author took his lifeless body to Tikrapara Higher Secondary School, where he had spent most part of his life, and then to institutions like Ramakrishna-Sarada Shiksha Sadan (Pratapdighi), which had largely benefitted from his financial help. Finally, the last rites were performed at the crematorium near their home in Bagmari village. On the day of the Shraddha ceremony, countless men and women, many of his students, and relatives were present. His colleagues like Lakshmikanta Misra and others paid their respect at both the crematorium and the Shraddha ceremony. More information about this exemplary person can be found in the book "Our Teachers" by Sri Manmatha Nath Das, first published at the Kolkata Book Fair in 1998.

My Father: A Small Tribute

Baba: Every now and then I am reminded of the values that you instilled in me with all care. Your guidance from the very childhood has acted as a guiding light throughout my journey. You, perhaps did not realize at that time the incredible impact of your acts of sharing your limited resources with many others. People remember your generosity of doing something meaningful for others and effectively shaping the destinies of future generations. It is heartening to see that the people whom you helped did well in life and moved towards more prosperity.

Being a teacher of a school located in a rural environment, you had to deal with children from different backgrounds. You demonstrated how to treat all the students in the classroom equally. You took every possible care to improve the quality of each and every student.

Mother's Teachings

The author's mother did not have much formal education, but she imparted wisdom to the author through her words and actions. Throughout different stages of life, the author's mother provided various advice, sometimes directly and sometimes indirectly. Many of these pieces of advice still resonate in his ears. She used to converse in Bengali; her words often carried deep meanings. She used to say, "I never lie because to cover one lie, one has to tell four more." She always treated everyone with simplicity and adhered to the truth, never showing any deceit or duplicity.

Mother Pramila Devi

Often, the author's mother would mutter to herself or recite rhymes, poems, or sing songs. When the author was very young, she would sometimes recite, "The palash flower, although very beautiful to look at, no one admires it because it has no fragrance." Today, the author wonders if his mother by this utterance, wanted to convey that even if someone looks beautiful, no one loves him, if he lacks virtues. Sometimes, she would recite.—*"Apnare baro bale, Baro sei noy. Loke jare baro bale, baro sei hoy. Sansarete baro hayoa, Kathin byapar…"*

That is,

> *"One who considers oneself great is not truly great,*
> *One whom others consider great is actually great.*
> *Becoming great in this world is a difficult task,*
> *One becomes great through great qualities.*
> *If you possess great qualities, everyone will call you great.*
> *If you want to be great, first become humble."*

Although the author's mother would recite Bengali version of this poem to herself, he sometimes felt that she was teaching him to be humble, modest, and polite from a very young age. She would also sometimes mutter to herself:

"A flower without fragrance, what kind of flower is it?
No bulbul is ever enchanted by it."

She would often recite from Ishwar Chandra Gupta's poem.

"The Value of Merit":

"The crow has never stolen anyone's wealth,
Nor has the cuckoo distributed any riches.
The crow's harsh call is unpleasant to the ear,
While the cuckoo's melodious song delights everyone.
Merit is respected everywhere,
Without merit, there is no honour anywhere."

Since his childhood, the author heard his mother recite the following poem (Bengali version) many times:

"As the fire flares up quickly,
Anger rises just as swiftly.

When the fire extinguishes, ashes remain,
When anger subsides, sorrow lingers in the mind."

Usually, when someone in the house or a neighbouring house was enraged, this poem would come from the mother's mouth like a soliloquy.

Her Spiritual Side

The author's mother never sat idle; she always found some work to do. In the afternoons and sometimes in the evenings, she would read the Ramayana, the Mahabharata, the Lakshmi Charitra, and other religious books. She would also read the Bengali version of Srimad Bhagavad Gita. In her later years, after bathing and performing her daily prayers, she would recite a couple of verses from Markandeya Chandi, such as:

"Prasida Bhagavati Amba, Prasida Bhakta Vatsale.
Prasadam Kuru Me Devi Durge Devi Namo'stute."

With perfect Sanskrit pronunciation, she would recite many such verses. It is noteworthy that the author's mother, father, uncle, and aunt had all received initiation mantra Diksha from Sri Sri Sitaramdas Omkarnath Deva. The author's wife, Shorosi, was blessed to receive initiation from the same Guru at a very young age.

My Mother: A Small Tribute

Ma: You were patience incarnate. You have demonstrated to us to remain calm and quiet under any circumstances. You have taught your children how to adjust with all others in a joint family. We have observed how you remained unperturbed in your advanced age, ignoring all sorts of physical difficulties and inconveniences.

You taught me in the childhood, the principle—'The more you give, the more you get.' You used to instill in me the idea of the proverb—'The more fruits are there on a tree, the more bent it is.' After saying this, you have emphasized, 'When you have achieved more, become humbler, not arrogant.'

My Parents

Baba o Ma: I fondly remember, when I started my journey as a primary school student, you emphasized on my being humble and respectful and stressed on discipline, honesty and human values.

You demonstrated to your children your unique quality to mix with different people and treat everybody with respect. All your children and grandchildren are highly thankful to you for passing on the rooted values both of you possessed, your exemplary life lesson, and your wisdom. These gifts have been immensely beneficial to me in performing my journey through ups and downs, in my professional as well as personal life.

The Ideal Joint Family

The joint family of the author's father Ganes Chandra and uncle, Jnanada Charan, was a role model not only for the author but also for the neighbours, relatives and villagers. Their cooperative work, harmonious behaviour and selfless mindset demonstrated a commitment to the family's collective well-being. Both of them took care to ensure that everyone stayed healthy and strong, and that all the children in the family received good education. Similarly, the author's mother and aunt worked together harmoniously in the household. The neighbours often used to be confused and used to think that the father and the uncle were biological brothers, hardly they could imagine that in reality, they were first cousins; their fathers were different, but grandfather was the same.

The author's father once shared that because his uncle took care of all the household affairs, he could focus on teaching job in the school, social service and other responsibilities. The father's dedication and honesty in managing the financial aspects of the joint family, taking care of the education of all the children, and arranging marriages were evident. A few days before passing away, the uncle once told the father, with tears of joy in his eyes, "Brother, you have done so much for me, my wife and children!"

The family's legacy of unity and scholarship was rooted in their ancestry. Their ancestors also lived in a joint family. They were all well-versed in Sanskrit scriptures. The author's grandfather, Girish Chandra Kavyatirtha, was a great scholar of poetry and had his own Sanskrit school (chatuspathi). He was so proficient in poetry that he could instantly compose Sanskrit verses. For his poetic talents, Gangadhar Nanda, the renowned philanthropist and zamindar from Mugberia, used to hold him in high esteem.

Girish Chandra's elder middle brother, Nandakumar was also a learned man. He was an Ayurvedic physician and used to himself manufacture Ayurvedic medicines at home using traditional methods with the help of a mortar and pestle.

Uncle's Marriages and Descendants

The uncle Jnanada Charan married twice. His first wife from Chakbhabani village, passed away at a young age leaving behind three daughters—Manmohini, Shanta and Rasmoni. The eldest, Manmohini was married to Dinabandhu Tripathi from Mugberia, who was a maternal cousin of the author's father. Later, they migrated to the Sundarbans (Gadamathura, 9th Plot). Shanta didi was married to Biswanath Misra from Srirampur village, while Rasmoni didi was married to Bisheswar Pahari from Barha Kumarda village. All the three were very jolly. The former two are no more. But Rasmoni didi is still alive.

The uncle's second marriage took place with Bhadrabati Devi from Argoal village. Her father was Pandit Aghore Acharya (a Sanskrit scholar). This marriage resulted three sons—Tarapada, Bamapada and Shaktipada as well as a daughter, Geetarani. Tarapada married to Gita, a sister-in-law of the author. They constructed a house in Krishnanagar of Nadia district and have been residing there. They have a son, Joydeep and a daughter, Moumita. Both of them are married.

Graduated with a degree in Electronics Engineering from Jadavpur University, Joydeep is currently working as an engineer in the USA. They live permanently in their own house there. His wife, Shrimanti, holds an engineering degree and is employed in that country. Their son, Sreedeep is a student of standard-V in a school there. Tarapada's daughter, Moumita is working as a Quality Analysis Engineer at an MNC. Her husband, Pritam is a manager at Central Medical Service under Govt. of India. Their son, Tamojit is in standard-V of a school located in Kolkata and daughter, Tannistha is 3 years old.

Geetarani, uncle's daughter from his second marriage, is married to Prabhat Nanda of the village of Tepurpara. She is very sweet-natured and extremely hardworking. Prabhat is a retired State Government employee and also a good-natured person as well as very friendly. They have two daughters, one son and several grandchildren, living quite happily. Their son, Bapi, graduated with honours in mathematics from Rahara Ramakrishna Mission College and is now a teacher at a school. Second cousin, Bamapada, got married to Renuka from the village of Balyagobindapur. They have two sons, Sandeep and Subhadeep. Sandeep and his wife Atashi have two daughters, Sreyasi and Tanusree. Subhadeep became a sannyasin. Shaktipada got married to Anima from Khargram. They have one son, Biswadeep and one daughter, Madhumita. Biswadeep and his wife Jaitri have a son, Yasojit. Madhumita and her husband Apurba have two daughters, Nandini and Nandita. Tarapada, Bamapada, and Shaktipada all worked for the government of West Bengal and are now retired.

Life and Discipline in the Joint Family

When the author was young, he was the only male child in the entire joint family. Possibly due to this reason, the elders used to shower all love and affection on him. Neighbours and relatives also gave him immense affection. Bishweshwar da (Rashmoni Didi's husband), loved the author very much. Whenever there were special occasions like making rice cakes, his father, Gobinda Babu, would personally come to take the author to their house. After a day or two, someone would bring him back home. In their house, they used to have Basanti Puja every year. Many of their relatives would also gather there on that occasion. The author used to have a few joyful days during that time.

In the joint family, life was fairly disciplined. Some household chores were done by author's father, while his uncle was responsible for daily worship of the deity, taking care of the cows, shopping, and overseeing the farming of paddy fields. The author's mother would clean all the utensils in the house, prepare puffed rice, serve breakfast, and prepare all the items for lunch. Preparing and serving meals on time for all the school-going children and others in the house was a tough task. The aunt used to prepare dinner, with both mother and aunt serving the meal together at night. Cleaning the house in the morning, boiling paddy for rice preparation, and collecting fuel from the garden were tasks done by the aunt. In those days, there was no gas for cooking, so collection of fuel daily was quite challenging.

The author fondly recalls, whenever the mother was cooking any fried food item, she would give it to him and in the evening, the aunt would give similar cooked items to him. Another special trait of the aunt was that whenever the author came home during holidays, she would present various news about relatives, neighbours and the village. She would have a beaming smile when delivering good news and would look very sad when delivering bad news.

Both father and uncle showed a great sense of unity through their work, behaviour, and attitude. The mother and aunt both also worked together harmoniously without much disagreement. The author's father even took out a life insurance policy for his uncle when he got one for himself. Thus the unity in the family extended to financial matters as well. The author notes with great pleasure that all his three children—Subhas, Sudip, and Sumita—have inherited this sense of love, affection as well as duties and responsibilities towards one another, despite living in different parts of India owing to their jobs at different locations.

In the joint family, private tutors were hired. They mostly stayed at the house all the time, teaching the children regularly and ensuring that they remained disciplined. Whenever necessary, a maid was also hired, who would stay at the house full-time. One such maid was called "Ramer Ma" (mother of Ram). She stayed with the family for many years. At one point, when the mother and the aunt were both unwell, a widow Brahmin lady was hired to help with the cooking. She and her young son Kedar lived with the family. She loved the author and his sister very much, often telling them stories at bedtime. Later, with the help of the author's father, Kedar da got a job at Tikrapara High School as a staff. Before getting the job, they had moved out of the author's house to their home.

Lessons Received from Uncle

The author's uncle was a repository of wisdom and life lessons. As a child, the author used to have dinner with his uncle daily but would sleep with his father, who would ask various questions, to which he would respond. When at home, the uncle would give him various pieces of advice. The uncle advised him to go to the marketplace instead of sitting idle at home, as it would help him meet and get to know various people. He also advised that when feeding guests, one should ensure they are satisfied rather than worrying about the expenditure. The uncle loved feeding people, often sitting close to them while they ate.

Uncle Jnanada Charan, Aunt Bhadrabati Devi with Cousin Sister, Gitarani

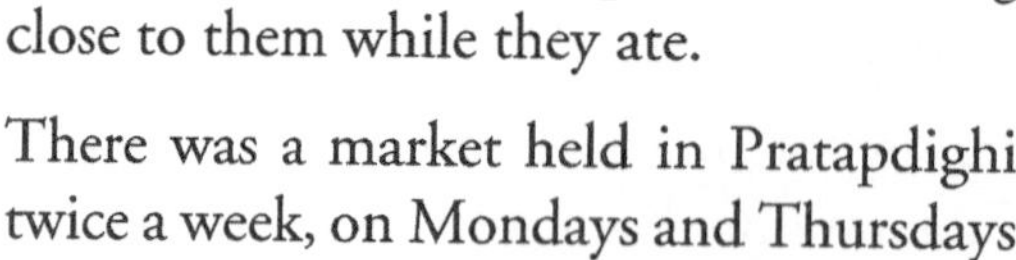

There was a market held in Pratapdighi twice a week, on Mondays and Thursdays afternoons. The uncle would go to the market and bring half a dozen bananas for the author, to be eaten one per day. The uncle also brought for him a mixture of fried snacks in a paper cone, costing four annas (25 paisa). On returning from the market, he would first find the author and hand over the packet of snacks, deriving immense satisfaction from seeing his joyous face.

The author fondly recalls the uncle's teachings during childhood, such as the importance of a disciplined routine: *"If you wish to be stout and strong, go to bed at nine, get up at five. Keep your teeth clean..."* The author also remembers a Sanskrit verse the uncle used to recite to emphasize the need to focus on the essence of any knowledge due to life's brevity and the many obstacles one faces during that limited life-period.

> *"Ananta shashtram bahu veditavyam, alpascha kalo bahavascha vighnah!*
> *Yatsarabhutam tadupasitavyam hamso yatha kshiramivambumishram!!"*

Explanation: The learning is as vast, as the sky. We cannot comprehend it with all our might and intellect. So much is there to learn that our entire life is not enough. The time at our disposal is very little. Many obstacles come on the way even in this little period of time. In view of this, one must focus on the essence of knowledge, just as a swan extracts milk from a mixture of water and milk.

This wonderful sloka teaches us that the milk of life, which is comparable with the essence of scriptures, needs to be extracted from the chaff of each type of information available at all corners of the world.

A Legacy of Love and Service

The author's uncle had a homeopathy dispensary at home, where he would personally give medicine to patients, despite not having any formal training in homeopathic medicine. However, the villagers found his medicines quite effective, and he did not charge any amount from them. Thus he tried to provide primary healthcare in the village. This way the uncle's selfless contributions to the family extended to the community.

The uncle also urged the author to avoid laziness, as it leads to a lack of education, wealth, friends, and ultimately, happiness.

> *"Alasasya kuto vidya, avidyasya kuto dhanam,*
> *Adhnanasya kuto mitram, amitrasya kuto sukham!!"*

Another lesson he tried to impart in the author was to keep certain things confidential, such as one's age, wealth, family secrets, and any insults received. To emphasize on this lesson, he used to recite:

> *"Ayurbittam grihashchhidram mantra maithuna bheshajam*
> *Tapodanamapamanascha nava gopyati yatnatam!!"*

One valuable lesson frequently shared by the uncle was about child-rearing:

> *"Lalayet panchavarshani, dashavarshani tadayet.*
> *Praapte tu shodashae varshe, putram mitravadacharet."*

'A child should be nurtured with love for the first five years, disciplined for the next ten, and treated as a friend after sixteen.'

When the author's sacred thread ceremony (upanayanam) was scheduled, his uncle taught him the meditation and prayer mantras for the five deities (Ganesh, Surya, Vishnu, Shiva, and Durga) and the family deity Vishnu Raghunath Shila's worship rituals. Although the author performed the worship for only a couple of days, the mantras taught by his uncle have been very useful throughout his life.

The author cherishes the lessons, love and discipline imparted by his uncle and fondly remembers their time together. The values of unity, selflessness, and responsibility upheld by the joint family continue to inspire generations.

Siblings

Sister: Durgarani

The author had two brothers and one sister (Didi). His sister, Durgarani, is about two years older than him. His middle brother, Dines, was about eight years younger, and the youngest brother is Parames. Because of the small age gap, the author and his sister would go to school and play together, sharing friendly conversations and stories. There were no girls' schools in the area back then, and the nearby schools did not allow co-education, limiting girls' education to the fifth grade. Thus, his sister could not pursue higher education despite being intelligent. A few years after leaving school, she married Tarapada Bhattacharya, the elder son of Dr. Navakanta Bhattacharya from Jabda village. After the marriage, his brother-in-law used to shower much affection towards the author.

Left to Right: Father, Elder Sister, Mother with middle brother Dines, the Author

The author fondly recalls, when his brother-in-law came to their house, he would sometimes stay for a day or two. He would sing various songs to pass the time, including popular songs of that era. Some of them were:

> *"Kajal nadiro jole, bhora dheu chhol chhole*
> *Prodeep bhasao kare smariya*

Sonar boroni meye, balo kar poth cheye
Ankhi duti othe jole bhoriya."

Another song he sang quite often was:

"Runner chhuteche tai jhumjhum ghonta bajche raate
Runner cholche khaborer bojha haate,

Runner, runner choleche runner!
Raater path-e path-e chole kono nishedh jane na manar
Digonte theke digonte chhote runner, runner
Kaj niyechhe se notun khabor anar, runner..."

Sometimes he sang:

"Bolechhile tai chithi likhe jai, katha ar sure sure
Mon bole tumi royechho je kachhe, ankhi bole koto dure!
Tumi aaj koto dure!"

The brother-in-law had no sisters, but had only one younger brother, Shyamapada (Khokada), who was about 2–3 years older than me, making our relationship more like friends. My father and brother-in-law's father, Dr. Navakanta Bhattacharya, shared a very cordial relationship. The father would occasionally visit my sister's in-laws' house, and my brother-in-law's father would also visit our house even if my sister wasn't there in our house. He usually arrived in the evening and left before sunrise to attend to the patients in his clinic. He was a compassionate doctor who would walk down to examine patients in their residence, particularly for those whose health did not permit to visit the doctor. It is to be noted that in remote villages, those days walking was the only available option, for those who could not ride a bicycle. His wife (my aunt) had asthma problem. Although she was a bit strict by nature, she was very affectionate towards the author. Owing to the acute health problem, she passed away at a premature age.

At the time of my sister's marriage, her husband was doing his diploma in Pharmacy in Jalpaiguri. After completing that programme, he got an employment in R.G. Kar Medical College. His residence was at Medini Chhatrabas at 90, Bipin Behari Ganguli Street in Central Calcutta. He also did D.M.S. from D.N. De Homeopathic Medical College (Night shift). Those days B.M.S. (bachelor's degree of Homeopathy) was not being offered. After passing D.M.S., he also used to practice as a homeopathic doctor, beyond office hours. Soon he earned reputation as a good physician. Like his father, he was very popular and kind hearted to the patients. During Durgapuja and other festive occasions, the author used to spend a few days in the house of his sister at Jabda village. Gradually the author gained popularity among the friends and relatives of his brother-in- law, both in his native village and in his Calcutta residence.

Through the initiative of Dr. Nabakanta Bhattacharya, the father-in-law of the author's sister, the great Ras Yatra festival started in Jabda village. Every year the festival used to continue for around one week. At his cordial invitation, the author's mother, aunt and later, sometimes Shorasi also used to visit the festival and spend a couple of days at his house.

After his retirement, author's brother-in-law used to spend most of his days at his native place. There used to be a good rush of patients from nearby and distant villages. Like his father, he was also very compassionate. He used to treat the patients without taking any remuneration, in deserving cases. In critical cases, sometimes he also used to accompany the rural patients to specialist doctors in Calcutta.

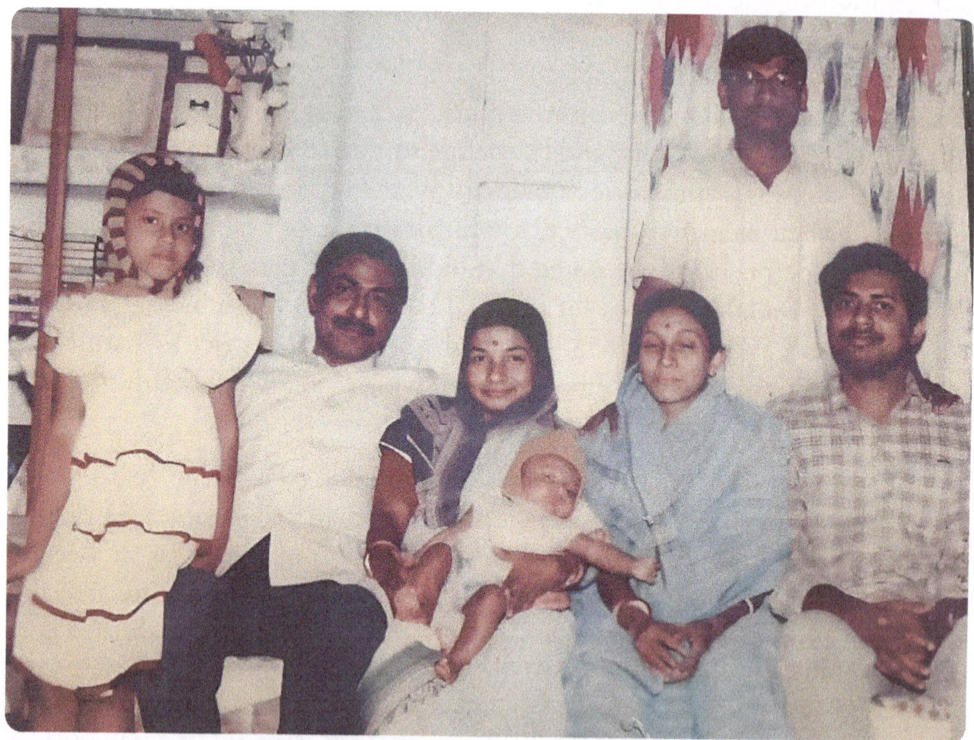

Elder Sister and Brother-in-law with their Relations

My sister has three daughters—Namita, Kabita, and Sumita as well as a son Debasis. All of them are married. All the spouses are good in all respects. Debasis is the youngest of all. He is very intelligent, very dutiful, honest and religious minded. He took initiation from Srimat Swami Ranganathananda of Belur Math. After doing his B.E. in Civil Engineering from Jadavpur University and M.E. from the National Institute of Technology Durgapur, he has been working as a faculty of Civil Engineering in an Engineering College of West Bengal. He has earned reputation as a very sincere teacher. His son Debarpan after doing B.E. in Electrical Engineering from Jadavpur University, Calcutta and M.E. from the Indian Institute of Science (I.I.Sc.), Bangalore, has now been pursuing his doctoral degree at the same Institute. Another grandson (niece Kabita's son) Dr. Santanu Kar after doing M.B.B.S. from P.G. College, Calcutta (IPGMER) and M.S. (Orthopedics) from Atal Bihari Vajpayee Institute of Medical Sciences and Dr. Ram Manohar Lohia Hospital, New Delhi, served the All India Institute of Medical Sciences (AIIMS), New Delhi as a Senior Resident Surgeon. He also did his DNB and is an MNAMS. Currently he is serving Subham Hospital, Cooch Behar as an orthopaedic surgeon and hospital superintendent. One of the grand daughters, Moumita (elder daughter of niece Sumita) did her B.E. (Instrumentation and electronics Engineering) from Jadavpur University and MBA from IIM Bangalore; currently she is working in Denmark for an MNC. Her younger sister, Sangita is a pharmacist and presently working in the Netherlands. Both of them are married. My sister's eldest son-in-law, Dr. Utpal Acharya was a veterinary surgeon under the Govt. of West Bengal. Her other two sons-in-law, Dr. Sukhendu Bikas Kar (Ph.D. in Maths) and Sri Pradeep Acharya (M.Sc.) were headmasters in higher secondary schools. All three of them are now retired.

My brother-in-law (sister's husband) breathed his last after a heart attack, only a couple of years after retirement. But he was quite active, even after retirement. So for sometime he used to go to Calcutta and take care of his chamber. On such a day, when he was in his Calcutta residence the said incident occurred. On getting this news I rushed from the IIT Campus to my sister, who was then living at Jabda village. Her son Debasis also reached home immediately and performed his father's last rites.

Afterwards, Didi (my sister) had to take charge of the household. Her son was unmarried at that time. So her first major responsibility was to find out a suitable match for him. By the grace of God, my sister got a very capable daughter-in-law, Suparna (Tusi). She is very talented, has made significant sacrifices when needed, worked hard, and properly raised her only child, Debarpan (Sayan). With Tusi's help, my sister bought a piece of land and constructed a house in Egra (which is now a sub-divisional town). Since my nephew works in another distant city, Tusi's contribution to household chores and child-rearing has been immense. Didi's brother-in-law, Khokada (Shyamapada), and other relatives also helped in various ways. However, her daughter-in-law Tusi has filled my sister's life with maternal love and affection, all the time taking care of her, not caring for her own comfort and rest. Whenever necessary, she also attends to her parents. She travels alone by bus and train and works tirelessly. May God bless every home with such a capable and hardworking girl.

Middle Brother: Dines Chandra

Dines, affectionately called Mantu, was about eight years younger than me. He was of the same age as cousin Tarapada. He was very sweet-natured. I fondly recall, when he was very young, I used to carry him on my lap when I was at home. I used to feed him milk, fruits, and fruit juices with a spoon. He also loved me very dearly right from his school days. He was a very simple boy with ever smiling face. He was always ready to help me. Since childhood, he had a problem with chronic asthma. Baba did not leave any stone unturned for his medical treatment. He was taken to Kolkata to visit good specialist doctors with the help of brother-in-law. All kinds of treatments—allopathy, homeopathy, and ayurvedic were tried—but no permanent cure was elusive.

Finally, arrangement was made for his treatment through yoga and pranayama. Contact was made with Swami Shivananda Saraswati, the author of the book "Yogabale Rogarogya" (Treatment of diseases by yogic practice) and a famous yoga guru of that time. He had a yoga ashrama/hospital near Palpaara bus stop in Kolkata, but his main ashrama was located in Guwahati (Assam), called "Umachal Yoga Ashram," where he treated many patients under his own supervision. Once, when the Swami came to Kolkata, we sent Dines to Guwahati for treatment by yogic methods. Through yoga and pranayama,

Left to Right: Middle Brother Dines, Father and the Author

health of Dines improved significantly at Guwahati. When he returned home after a few months, he appeared to have regained normal health. He said he was able to maintain good health by following a regimen of morning walks, pranayama, and vegetarian diet.

After passing his higher secondary examinations in the science stream, Dines studied DMS at Kharagpur Homeopathic Medical College. He stayed with us in our quarters on the IIT campus but again continued to suffer from occasional severe asthma attacks. During such times, he used to be taken to IIT hospital, where the doctors would manage with injections like Decadron/Deriphyllin and later with medications like Prednisolone. After Baba (author's father) got retired from service, as mentioned elsewhere, our parents permanently moved to the IIT Kharagpur Campus, making it convenient for all of us to stay together. They took care of household chores and personal needs of Dines to some extent.

In June 1975, the author was selected for a Humboldt Fellowship for advanced research, necessitating a two-year stay in Germany. Baba encouraged me a lot and urged that I should avail this rare opportunity, although there was quite a bit of apprehension about the health of Dines at the native place. In view of this apprehension, however, our parents took the final decision to take him to their ancestral place at Bagmari village along with their daughter-in-law, Shorasi and grandchildren. I used to send asthma medication from Germany for Dines, which used to provide him some relief. At that time, there were not many options for treating asthma in our country, especially in rural areas where doctors were scarce. Therefore, in late 1975, when one day Dines had a severe asthma attack and no doctor could be made available in the vicinity, Dines passed away at a very young age. The news of this promising life cut short was devastating for the author, who was in Hannover (Germany) at the time. The father found it very difficult to convey

Sitting Right to Left: Father, Mother, Elder Sister; Standing Left to Right: Younger Brother Parames, his wife Kanika

this tragic news to the author. However, he chose to inform the truth rather than conceal it or communicating false news for a long time. Baba did not send the letter directly through post, but through Mr. Amitabha Banerjee (Andu da), who lived in Uelzen, a small town near Hannover, where I was staying. Andu da was working as an engineer in Germany, and his wife Irene was a nurse. When I was teaching at Uluberia College, I was introduced to all the members of the Banerjee family. As soon as Andu da received the letter, he and his wife drove to Hannover, took me to their home in Uelzen for about a week, and provided great mental support. Their hospitality and friendship are unforgettable. Andu da and Irene even took me to Irene's parental place, where I enjoyed picking and eating cherries from their trees. Andu da and Irene had a son named Subhadra Sevastian Banerjee, a name given by Anduda's elder brother, Professor Ajay Banerjee (Jhintu da), who was the Head of the Department of Bengali at Uluberia College.

Youngest Brother: Parames

The youngest brother, Parames (Kanu), is very brilliant and much younger than me. When he was admitted to the school, Baba had reduced his activity of social service and focused more on coaching Parames. I remember, when he was very young, Baba himself would sometimes feed him by hand. Parames won a Government of India Merit Scholarship for studying in residential schools and secured a place at the Ramakrishna Mission Vidyapith in Purulia after excelling in the competitive examination. The government of India was bearing all his expenses. The list of prescribed schools, included several top residential schools, like Ramakrishna Mission Vidyalaya in Narendrapur, Ramakrishna Mission Vidyapith in Purulia and Patha Bhavana in Santiniketan etc. After consulting with Swami Satyaghanananda, an experienced monk from the Ramakrishna Mission at Belgharia, we took the decision to admit Parames to the Ramakrishna Mission Vidyapith in Purulia in the eighth grade. Though he studied in Bengali medium up to the seventh grade at Tikrapara High School, he switched over to English medium at the Ramakrishna Mission Vidyapith. Some teachers from Tikrapara High School also helped him prepare for the scholarship examination. Parames had to come to Kolkata twice, once for the written test and then for the viva voce. On the basis of his excellent performance in the tests Parames was fortunate to be selected for this lucrative scholarship.

I accompanied Parames to Purulia for admission. Since a couple of monks and teachers were known to me before hand, there was not much anxiety and uncertainty for his stay in the hostel, away from home for the first time. Studying at this esteemed institution, Parames received excellent education and developed human qualities inspired by Swami Vivekananda's ideals. English and Bengali handwritings of Parames have always been excellent. Although he is a distinguished engineer, his articles in both Bengali and English are of very high standard. Despite living abroad for most of his life, his simplicity is still evident. He leads a disciplined life, practising yoga, pranayama, and exercising regularly.

After passing his higher secondary examination in science, Parames studied BE in Electrical Engineering at Jadavpur University and then completed his MTech in Instrumentation Engineering from IIT Kharagpur. He worked for sometime at McNally Bharat in Kumardubi and later at Jawaharlal Nehru Port Trust in Navi Mumbai. He used to come to Kharagpur during Saraswati Puja, helping his nephews and niece, Subhas, Sumita and Sudip prepare for the Saraswati Puja in a gorgeous style.

Interestingly, Parames was initially not keen on going abroad. Even when some of his close friends got opportunities to go abroad, he did not feel interested. I encouraged him to go abroad for a few years and then return. He was also reluctant to marry. A few years later, he got married to Kanika, daughter of Mr. Shibaprasad Acharya, assistant headmaster of Egra Higher Secondary School. Mr. Acharya was an excellent teacher of English and Sanskrit and was a man of principles. Although Kanika, lived in Canada for a long time, she is still very respectful towards Indian culture and traditions.

Parames seemed to have developed interest in going abroad while working at Jawaharlal Nehru Port Trust in Navi Mumbai. First, he got a job in Bahrain, a Middle Eastern island country consisting of 36 islands in the western part of the Persian Gulf. At that time, he had two daughters. I advised him to move to an English- speaking country, keeping in view of his daughters' education. Fortunately, he got a job in Toronto, Canada, where he now works as a Section Manager for Ontario Power Generation. He lives with his family in his own house in Toronto. His elder daughter, Smita, did her Ph.D. from an American university and is an assistant professor at the University of Waterloo, Canada. She married Leon Latty, Discipline Head-Physiotherapy and Kinesiology, University Health Network, Toronto. They are blessed with a daughter named Isani Mya Misra-Latty. The younger daughter of Parames, Samhita, studied law at a Canadian University and works for a law firm in Canada.

Maternal Ancestry

Left to Right: Maternal Grandfather Brajendranath and his Younger Brother Asutosh

The author's maternal grandparents lived in a village named Sauri, located in between Egra and Belda. It is very close to the Digha-Kharagpur bus line. Earlier, the road to the village was made of gravel, but later it was converted into a paved road. The grandfather Brajendranath and grandmother, Basantakumari Devi were an ideal couple. Brajendranath worked as a teacher at Boro Mohanpur High School (Khakurdah). Both of them loved me very dearly. Grandmother's ever-smiling face is still vivid in my memory.

In my childhood, when my mother visited her paternal home, she usually travelled by bullock cart, as no other vehicles operated on that road. Occasionally, I and my sister would accompany her. After spending a few days at the maternal grandparents' house, our father would come to take us back home. The shortest route from village Bagmari to Sauri was via Kharui More and Lalat, the distance being approximately 12 kilometers. Several times in my childhood I walked down this distance with my father.

Maternal Relatives

Ma had seven siblings. Out of them there were two brothers, Pinakipada (the eldest) and Shaktipada (the youngest). Pinakipada had to start earning through business at a very young age due to family needs. However, he used to keep himself abreast of all news and current events, by reading newspapers everyday. He had interests in knowing different important events occurring in different parts of the world. He particularly enjoyed listening to the details of my journey to Germany and my stay in that country. The eldest aunt, Kiranbala, was very affectionate and a good homemaker, always providing proper hospitality to relatives. She had deep affection for me.

The youngest uncle, Shaktipada was the headmaster of Aragora Primary School, located two kilometers away from his home, and he used to travel there by bicycle. His first wife, Kanchanbala, passed away after prolonged illness. I fondly remember, attending the wedding ceremony in Kolaghat as a member of the groom's party. After her untimely death, the youngest uncle married Asita, a devoted wife and efficient homemaker.

Families of the Maternal Uncles

Elder Maternal Uncle's (Pinakipada) Family

Pinakipada had four sons—Tapas, Ashis, Ashok, and Manas—and two daughters—Tapati (Kajol) and Sutapa (Moni). Tapas worked as a teacher in a school but unfortunately a few years ago he passed away. He left behind two daughters, Saswati (Gopa) and Swatilekha, and a son, Sandeepan (Bappa). Saswati works as a nurse in a government hospital, and Sandeepan holds a high position at Coca-Cola Company. Saswati's husband is a doctor, and Swatilekha is a housewife.

Ashis, the second son, was an officer in the West Bengal government and is now retired. His only son, Kaushik (Pappu), is an engineer at IBM, and his daughter, Paramita (Piu), is an engineer at TCS. Ashok, the third son, runs a pharmaceutical business. His two daughters, Sayantani and Sancharini, are both engineers. The youngest son, Manas, and his son, Kaustav, are in business, while his daughter, Madhumita (Mou), is a housewife. Recently Manas passed away.

Younger Maternal Uncle's (Shaktipada) Family

Shaktipada had four sons and one daughter. His eldest son, Sanat (Santu), and his third son, Somesh (Bubu), are businessmen. The second son, Anup (Nantu) did his B.E. and worked as an engineer at the Tarapur Atomic Power Station and is now retired. His youngest son, Debashis (Madan), is an employee of the West Bengal government. Sanat has a son who teaches in a primary school and a daughter who did her Ph.D. from IIEST, Shibpur. Anup has a son and a daughter. Both are engineers. The son-in-law after completing his Ph.D. is doing job in Canada, while the daughter after doing masters is also employed in the same country.

My wife Shorasi and I have always received much love and blessings from both the uncles and the aunts. Shorasi sometimes used to visit them alone, and she has endeared herself to everyone there.

Author's Mother and Her Eldest Sister

The author's mother was the second of their five sisters. Her eldest sister, Urmila, was married to Shri Bidhubhusan Sarangi from Mugberia. She was very fond of reading books. Her husband was a cheerful person.

Contribution to Education

Those days, there was no high school in Sauri village and the surrounding areas. To address this need the maternal grandfather, Brajendranath, played a key role in establishing a high school in the village. He went from door-to-door, collecting donations for the school. At the time, the author was studying at Ramakrishna Mission Vidyamandira in Belur Math. His grandfather wrote, "When you come for the next summer vacation, I will get you associated with a noble endeavour. You will accompany me, when I go to collect funds for the school."

Thanks to the dedicated efforts of the local community. Sauri High School, named as Sauri Bholanath Vidyamandir, came into existence soon and started functioning. The school earned a good reputation in no time. One teacher, Mr. Manindra Narayan Lahiri, taught mathematics and science. He had problem with his neck (orthopaedic). Being a bachelor, he used to devote much time for the benefit of the school. He was deeply passionate about teaching. Astronomy was his hobby. He himself used to set up telescopes by using equipments brought from Kolkata and observed planets and stars. At the same time, he used to see that the students get interested in Astronomy. This earned him significant popularity.

In Sauri village, there is a monastery of the Vaishnavas. The author used to visit it when he used to visit his maternal grandparents' house. Especially during the evening prayers, the serene atmosphere created was very enjoyable. The nearby village of Kedar has a Shiva temple, where the local people can feel the presence of Lord Shiva.

The Legacy of Narayan Chandra Rana

One of Mr. Lahiri's students, Shri Narayan Chandra Rana was from Sauri village. He came of a very poor family. His father expired, when he was an infant. He studied in Sauri Bholanath Vidyamandir and developed a keen interest in celestial bodies under Manindranath's guidance. He ranked second in the West Bengal Secondary Examination from this school. Later, he studied Physics at Presidency College and earned an M.Sc. in Physics from the University of Calcutta. He did his Ph.D. in astrophysics under the supervision of the renowned professor Jayant Vishnu Narlikar at TIFR (Tata Institute of Fundamental Research), Bombay. He then conducted post-doctoral research at Durham University in the UK. Narayan served as a research professor at

IUCAA (Inter-University Centre for Astronomy and Astrophysics) in Pune, Maharashtra. One of his notable contributions was precise determination of the radius of the Sun, which he calculated to be 696,500 km on October 24, 1995. His groundbreaking work brought him widespread recognition. Tragically, Narayan passed away at the young age of 42 only. His achievements continue to inspire future generations of students.

CHAPTER 2

Secondary Education

After completing primary education, the author was enrolled in the fifth grade at Tikrapara Ambikamoyee High School. Those days, the region was highly underdeveloped. Of course there has been significant development of the area over the years. Although the school was located in a very remote village, most of the teachers used to teach with all devotion and the quality of their teaching was excellent. The depth of their knowledge was remarkable. The Headmaster, Shri Pramatha Nath Basu used to teach English in higher classes. His teaching skill was commendable. To reinforce vocabulary he would ask different students to construct different sentences using a particular word. This technique was very helpful to earn expertise in English language, at least at that level. Many years later, when the author went to Germany on Humboldt Fellowship for doing post doctoral research, in the beginning he took two Elementary German Courses (Grundstuffe I & II) at the Goethe Institute at Lüneburg during June-September 1975. To his utter surprise, the method of teaching German was fundamentally similar to that used by our English teacher Pramatha Babu for teaching English during 1957–1959. Of course, as expected the German teacher used to take the help of scientific advancements,

Tikrapara High School (Higher Secondary)

like use of tape recorders and headphones. To alleviate the monotony of lessons, Pramatha Nath Basu would occasionally tell engaging stories. He was not only an excellent teacher but also an efficient administrator. During his regime of headmastership, the school attained greater heights. He used to conduct special coaching classes for English during last 3–4 months before the Board Examination, absolutely free of any private tuition fee! He came from a village under Bhagawanpore Police Station. But in order to nurture the school properly, he along with his family used to live in the Headmaster's quarters, which was located very close to the school. When the students would visit his quarters, he would affectionately engage with them and share insightful stories. In course of time, he became a popular figure in the locality.

The assistant headmaster, Shri Sudhir Kumar Ghosh, taught science. His house was in Pariharpur village, very close to the school. Another teacher, Shri Lakshmikanta Basu, who was also from Pariharpur used to teach geometry in the fifth and sixth grades. While introducing the concepts of angles, opposite angles, etc., he would use relatable real-life examples. His teaching method was truly exceptional. In some cases, he taught across three generations. This was also true for our family. He once taught my father, later taught me, and when my eldest son Subhas was in the fifth grade at Tikrapara High School, he also taught him. This venerable teacher was very honest and idealistic, although his financial condition was not good. So, some students would bring vegetables from their gardens for him. He would then feel happy and bless the students.

From the seventh to the tenth grade, Shri Anil Krishna Bera used to teach mathematics. He paid special attention to the author. He also used to serve as a referee during football matches on the play ground of the School. On many occasions when he would be heading to the play ground with a whistle in hand, if the author approached him with a mathematics problem, he would solve/explain it first before reaching the football ground. The Sanskrit teacher was revered Pandit Joynarayan Acharya (Gunakar Babu). He was a conservative Brahmin and a dedicated teacher. He never sat down on the chair in the classroom, always standing while teaching. In the ninth and tenth grades, the author had two Sanskrit subjects—one compulsory and the other optional. During those days, it was mandatory to have one elective subject for the school final examination. Additionally, one could take an additional subject if desired. The author chose "Elective Sanskrit" as an elective subject and "Additional Mathematics" as the additional subject. He remembers, he was the only one in the class who took "Elective Sanskrit." Others chose different other subjects. However, revered Pandit Gunakar Babu used to attend each and every class with unwavering dedication. Even long after the author left the School, Gunakar Babu taught him two chapters from Srimad Bhagavad Gita on his request. This was obviously not a part of his duty, but *Pandit Masai* (our Sanskrit teacher) did this favour to the author out of affection. He loved the author like his son. His residence was in Samantakhanda village. Many a time, after leaving school, the author visited his house. He had a "chatuspathi" (traditional teaching center for Sanskrit) near his house. In the mornings and evenings, the Pandit taught Sanskrit poetry and grammar to students there. After studies, the students cooked their meals, and Panditji himself would help them. It was like a gurukul ashrama. He often imparted wisdom to the author, advising that one should always speak impartially and without any bias to maintain a clear conscience and gain respect from others. Always he used to have logical deliberations, on various matters inside/outside the classroom.

Another teacher, Shri Lakshmikanta Misra, was a native of Srirampur village. He was a distant relative of the author. The author used to have love and deep respect towards him and used to call him 'Lakshmikanta Da' (elder brother),

Headmaster Pramatha Nath Basu (second in the second row, from Right to Left) with his Colleagues

who also had deep affection towards the author. After becoming a teacher at Tikrapara High School, he constructed a house near Pratapdighi market place. He taught Bengali literature. His conversations and thoughts had a clear modern touch, free from conservative ideas. He was generous and open-minded. At various stages of the author's life, he gave quite valuable guidance and showered immense love and affection, just as somebody shows towards his own younger brother. During vacations, when the author used to come to his ancestral house in Bagmari, he would often visit his 'Lakshmikanta Da'. They used to have very lengthy discussions on various topics. The author had various types of encouragement and inspiration from him. Many a time, he invited the author to have dinner/lunch at his house. When once the author was suffering from hepatitis, caused by viral infection, while staying at the IIT quarters (C1-63), Lakshmikanta Da rushed to the author's quarters at the IIT Campus on having the information. He stayed there for 2–3 days and demonstrated how to prepare oil-free yet nutritious tasty meals. He suggested planting papaya trees from the gate of the compound right up to the house, saying they would look nice, and the whole family could use the unripe ones for vegetables and the ripe ones as fruit.

When the author was selected for a postdoctoral fellowship and got an opportunity to go to Germany, the teacher felt extremely happy and encouraged the author profusely. Upon his return, when they met, their joy knew no bounds. Lakshmikanta Da was very eager to hear stories about Germany.

Many years later, when the author became the Head of the Mathematics Department at IIT Kharagpur and organized several international conferences and news of all the events came out in various National/regional English and Bengali newspapers, teachers of Tikrapara School felt very happy. The headmaster, Pramathanath Basu, got retired by that time. He was then residing in his native place in Bhagawanpore. Reading the description/appreciation of activities of their student (the author) in the newspapers, Pramathanath became overwhelmed with joy and wrote to the author, "Had your father been alive today, he would have been so proud." Revered Lakshmikanta Da wrote, "If Kakababu (the author's father) were alive today, he would have been so happy!" After the author received the Ram Mohan Puraskar in 2004, he was invited to Tikrapara High School for a felicitation ceremony. At that time, Lakshmikanta Da had retired from his job and was living in his house in Pratapdighi. He wrote to the author, "On that day first come to our house in the morning and have lunch with us." The author fondly remembers with enormous pleasure and happiness, he made arrangement for lunch with varieties of fish, yogurt, sweets etc. So much genuine love and affection he possessed for the author!

The author also fondly remembers several other teachers, including Shri Kalipada Latua, Shri Ramjiban Misra, Shri Bimal Krishna Manna, Shri Benimadhav Mahesh, and Shri Amal Chandra etc. Their images are still vivid in his memory. When the author was a high school student, the monthly salary of a teacher used to vary between Rs. 40 and Rs. 60 only. Even then the teachers were taking the classes very regularly, used to teach with all sincerity and devotion. They were also quite thorough in their subjects. Many of them might have had specialized training/knowledge in one subject, but some of them had proficiency in teaching several different subjects at least in lower classes. Shortly after the author left the school, after passing the School Final Examination (Class-X) of the Board of Secondary Education, West Bengal, Shri Kalipada Latua and Shri Bimal Krishna Manna left the School and joined as faculty members of Palpara B.Ed. College. Shri Ramjiban Misra was an excellent teacher of Bengali Literature. He later became the Headmaster of Tikrapara High School.

Above all, the person whose contribution enriched me the most was undoubtedly my father, Ganes Chandra Misra. He has been my first teacher, mentor and guide. Much of the glory in my long teaching career owes to him. The knowledge he instilled in me during my high school days formed a robust foundation for my teaching career. I also feel very fortunate to have some of the very brilliant teachers. They were really outstanding. They played a significant role not only in cementing my educational foundation, but also in character-building.

In the school office, Shri Indu Bhusan Mahanti was the senior clerk, while Shri Narayan Chandra Nandi was his assistant. Niranjan Goswami and Kedar Dash used to lend their helping hand to the Headmaster and all teachers as well as the office clerks. The author remembers, under the leadership of Pramatha Nath, there was a good co-ordination among different people in the office. When some teachers were on leave, other teachers used to take extra classes, following the provisional time-table prepared by the Headmaster. The overall discipline of the school was good.

In 2016, Tikrapara High School's Platinum Jubilee kicked off with pomp and celebration. It was really a proud moment for the school, because the celebration gave an opportunity to reflect upon a rich legacy of 75 years dedicated to nurturing young minds and fostering a culture of academic excellence in a rural environment. Since its inception, the school served as a beacon of knowledge, guiding generations of students through the journey of education. The platinum jubilee marked in a modest way a significant milestone in the School's history and served as a testament to the unwavering commitment to contributing positively to a vast rural area. The Platinum Jubilee celebrations served as a moment to honour the dedication of educators, staff and students, who have been instrumental in building a community that thrives on learning and character building. Various events were organized throughout the year, and several new classrooms were inaugurated on this occasion. The new classrooms were, however, constructed by raising extra funds from the public. One of these rooms was named "Ganes Chandra Memorial Room." The author donated the total construction cost of this room. During the Platinum Jubilee celebrations, the author could meet several teachers from his time. Shri Bimal Krishna Manna and Shri Benimadhav Mahesh came from Bhagwanpur. Mr. Kamalakanta Misra came from Srirampur village. Another teacher, Shri Lakshmikanta Misra, was an elder relative who taught Bengali literature. This was really a golden opportunity and a very happy occasion for the author to meet them after a very long lapse of time. As the school looks back with some satisfaction regarding its alumni, it should look forward with a renewed sense of purpose and should have a vision of a future, where it can continue to inspire and empower generations to come. The present authorities of the school may keep an eye on this aspect.

The author strongly feels, the fundamental concepts of English grammar and Mathematics that he learned from his father are still relevant to him. My deep interest in Sanskrit was nurtured by both my father and Gunakar Babu. This helped me recite properly hymns to the deities and sing devotional songs during prayers. As a student, I maintained a notebook filled with Sanskrit *slokas*, the first one being:

> *"Vidvatvam cha nripatvam cha naivatulyamkadaachana*
> *Swadeshe pujyate raja vidwaan sarvatra pujyate."*

This translates to: 'A king is respected only in his kingdom, but a learned person is revered everywhere.'

Over time, the author realized the profound truth that lies behind this verse at various stages of his life, during travelling in India and abroad. A memorable instance was during an international conference on "Computational and

Applied Mathematics" in Brussels, the capital of Belgium in Western Europe. The author got an opportunity to deliver a lecture and preside over a session at the Conference. Those days the author was suffering from severe knee pain (arthritis). A professor friend at IIT Kharagpur had advised the author to consult a European doctor while attending the conference. Following his advice, the author had his knees examined by an orthopaedic surgeon in Brussels. What happened next is still vivid in his memory and worth remembering lifelong.

After medical examination and giving necessary advice, he called his secretary and said, "This gentleman is an esteemed professor from India. He is here to attend an International Conference. Please ensure he receives priority service." At that moment, the wisdom of the Sanskrit *sloka* resonated deeply in the mind of the author.

Moral Education from Father

The author's father was a man of unwavering integrity. He often said, "I have never told a lie in my lifetime" and expressed his pride that his children had also upheld this principle. He instilled in the author the values of honesty, discipline and wisdom, often quoting Sanskrit verses to reinforce life lessons.

The author's sage-like father taught him the definition of a true student: *"Gurordoshaavaranam Chhatram. Chhatraanaam jnaayate Chhaatrah."*—meaning, according to the scriptures, a student is recognized by his ability to cover up their teacher's faults. Here, "Chhatram" does not mean an umbrella in the literal sense. It signifies the act of concealing the teacher's shortcomings. Having spent all his life as a teacher, the author realizes how much significant this definition is. He has never heard this definition elsewhere. This single definition can have an important bearing on the society. If students were transformed following this brilliant concept, the current scenario of educational institutions, society, and the entire world would have been much different.

Both of the author's parents had exemplary lifestyle, which their children could easily emulate. Most of the school and college teachers of the author also lived lives worth emulating. However, nowadays, students face the problem that the lifestyle of their parents and teachers lives is rarely exemplary, leaving them without role models both at home and at educational institutions.

Another lesson my father instilled in me reads, *"Satyam bruyaat priyam bruyaat, ma bruyaat satyamapriyam."*—This means: "Speak the truth and do so pleasantly, but avoid speaking harsh truths unnecessarily".

Another important lesson my father used to repeatedly impress upon me, was:

> *"Shad doshah purushena iha haatavya bhutir ichhata, nidraa tandraa bhayam krodham aalasyam deergha sutrataa."*—He explained that a person seeking prosperity should diligently avoid these six faults: sleep, drowsiness, fear, anger, laziness, and procrastination. This philosophy shaped my work ethics and resilience.

Another of his teachings emphasized keeping one's word under any circumstances reads: *"Udayati yadi bhaanuh pashchime digviraaje, vikashati yadi padmam parvatanaam shikhaagre, ushnam bhavati shishirah sheetataam yaati vahnih, na talati khalu vaakyam sajjanaanaam kadaachit."*—meaning, even if the sun rises in the west, a lotus blooms on a mountain peak, snow becomes warm, or fire turns cold, a noble person's word remains unshaken. In other words, no matter how impossible an event, a noble person's word is never broken.

On appropriate occasions the author's father warned him, by saying, *"Durjano parihartavyo vidyayaalankrito'pi san, maninaa bhooshitah sarpah kim asau na bhayankarah."*—He explained, "a wicked person should be avoided, even if he is adorned with knowledge, just as a jewelled snake is still dangerous. This advice is highly relevant in the present world. The world being highly complex today, people should be very cautious during their journey in life.

He would often cite another *sloka*: *"Kimvaa swayambhuh shiva shakti vishnuh, kapaala duhkhah na karoti dooram. Atah para jeevah svakarma bhogah, kapaalah kapaalah kapaalah moolam."*—This verse translates to: Even though Brahma, Vishnu, and Maheshwara are omniscient and possess all powers of the three worlds, they could not avoid their own sufferings. Similarly, a living being must endure the fruits of their actions. None can escape his fate.

To emphasize the importance of doing the right thing at the right time, my father would occasionally quote a Sanskrit *sloka*: *"Nirvaana deepe kimu taila daanam, choureh gate kimu saavadhanam. Bayogate kim vanitaa vilaasah, payogate kim khalu setu bandhah."*—He used to explain: There is no use of pouring oil into a lamp after it has burnt out, it is of no use to become cautious after a theft has occurred, it is rather funny to be engaged, in pleasures after youth has passed, why to build bridges after the rainy season is over. Thus, all tasks should be done timely, as negligence can lead to inevitable trouble. Another maxim he used to frequently utter was, "A stitch in time saves nine."

Reflecting on these values, I am highly grateful for the solid foundation my father and teachers provided. Their teachings, which continue to guide me, have shaped my academic and personal life, allowing me to navigate challenges with wisdom and perseverance.

The author fondly remembers many of his school friends, such as Tarak Pahari, Balai Das, Pares Manna, Shrikanta Pahari, Bhargabendra Jana, Debakinandan Jana, Sudhir Jana, Tapan Bose, Atul Kamilya, Pashupati Raychowdhury, Sarveshwar Mishra and others. During their School Final (now Secondary) exams, the examination center was Egra High School. Several rooms were rented in Egra for the examinees during the exam period. The author's father stayed with him there during the whole period of the examinations.

In the ninth grade, the author took the first exam for Saraswat Grammar (Chandrika) and passed the examination with distinction. On that occasion, he had to memorize many *slokas* from the Amarakosha, the first being, *"Swaravyayam swarganakah tridivah tridasalayah..."* and so on. The Amarakosha contains synonyms for various Sanskrit words. The first *sloka* lists synonyms for "heaven." He also studied the Hitopadesha and Saraswat Grammar. Studying these books made the compulsory and additional Sanskrit subjects for the school final syllabus easier. The Hitopadesha (Beneficial Advice) contains beautiful stories about humans and animals, each ending with a moral. This book is very helpful for young children to grow up righteously. It provides many valuable lessons for navigating life correctly.

When the author was merely a child, his father during conversation with friends would tell that he named his son 'Jagadis' with the hope that he would grow up to be a great scientist like Sir Jagadish Chandra Bose. When the author was in the ninth or tenth grade, his father had a strong desire for him to study medicine (M.B.B.S.) in the future. Therefore, the author took biology as an additional subject while doing I.Sc. with Mathematics, Physics and Chemistry. However, due to a change in his interests, he did not pursue medicine or engineering later on and instead studied B.Sc. with Honours in Mathematics. Nevertheless, his father's wish was at least partially fulfilled, because a significant part of the author's research involved the application of mathematics in physiology and medicine. This might have given his father some satisfaction, even though the author did not become a great scientist like Jagadish Chandra Bose or a doctor.

Back then, since there was no internet, email, or mobile phones, after the West Bengal Board of Secondary Education published the School Final Exam results, someone from Tikrapara High School was sent to collect the results/mark sheets for all the students of the School, as waiting for them by postal service would take too long. The Headmaster Pramatha Babu assured the author that he would inform him immediately after the School Final Exam results were received at the School. In those days, passing the School Final in the first division was considered a significant achievement. In 1959, only Tarak Pahari and the author passed in the first division from Tikrapara High School. The author scored letter marks (over 80%) in Mathematics. There was a gap of about two months between the end of examinations and announcement of the results. During this period, following the Headmaster's advice, the author read several novels by Rabindranath Tagore and Sarat Chandra Chattopadhaya, specifically suggested by him.

Chapter 3 The Vidyamandira

A Prestigious Temple of Learning

In those days, after completing high school education, one had to enroll in a college for higher education. The first step in this journey was a two-year course: Intermediate of Arts (I.A.)/Intermediate of Science (I.Sc.)/ Intermediate of Commerce (I.Com.). The courses were run in colleges and managed by universities. They were equivalent to today's higher secondary education managed by Higher Secondary Council, and conducted in higher secondary schools.

The author's father had long cherished the dream of enrolling his son in I.Sc. at a reputed institution. He had heard from friends that the educational institutions of the Ramakrishna Mission focused on character building and physical development along with academics. Therefore, he obtained the application form and prospectus for admission to Ramakrishna Mission Vidyamandira (Belur College) near Belur Math by post. Ramakrishna Mission Vidyamandira is affiliated to the University of Calcutta. The prospectus stated that Belur College was a fully residential institution, meaning all students had to reside in the hostel. Here, special attention was given to character building along with studies. Not only character building but also physical fitness was emphasized. The college had a gymnasium, where students could perform physical exercise with/without equipments. The students were trained to be self-reliant, cleaning their own clothes and utensils, and keeping their rooms tidy. This institution was modelled on the *gurukul system* according to the ideals of Swami Vivekananda. The principal and hostel superintendents were all monks. These selfless renunciates had dedicated their lives to shaping ideal students for the welfare of the society/Nation. Inspired by these principles, the author's father was determined to secure his son's admission to this esteemed college. At that time, Belur College offered only intermediate courses—I.A. (Intermediate Arts) and I.Sc. (Intermediate Science).

Two days after the School Final results were announced, the author and his father embarked on a journey to Belur College with the marks sheet in hand. They were accompanied by Shri Sudhir Kumar Ghosh, the Assistant Headmaster of Tikrapara High School.

The Journey to Belur

Till that time the author never visited Howrah/Kolkata. This trip marked the author's first visit to Howrah Station/Kolkata. As a child, he had once expressed a desire to visit Kolkata, to which his father had replied, "You will study at a college in Kolkata when the time comes." Now, as they set foot on this journey, the author's heart swelled with excitement at the fulfillment of his father's promise.

In those days, travelling from their village to Howrah Station was a challenging task. First, they had to walk about 8 kilometers on a dirt road to Kharui More. During the rainy season, this path was highly inconvenient to walk on, with knee-deep mud in some places. One had to lift their clothes above the knees to cover some portions of the road. Some parts of the road used to be very slippery during the rainy season. Occasionally people would slip and their clothes would be muddy. Upon reaching Kharui More, they would wash the affected parts of their body at a hand pump, change clothes and board a bus, when available. The distance between Kharui More and Egra is about 7 kms. But on that segment, buses were quite infrequent. So often people had to wait for a long time to get a bus at Kharui More. After reaching Egra, they would have to take a different bus for going to Kharagpur station. If there were no vacant seats, people had to stand for the entire journey. Finally, they would take a steam-powered train from Kharagpur station to Howrah Railway junction. In those days, trains used to run by steam engine, a journey lasting approximately five hours.

Admission to Ramakrishna Mission Vidyamandira (Belur College)

Before departing, the author performed traditional rituals at home—offering prayers to the household deity and seeking blessings from the elders. In those days, buses on routes 54, 56 and 51 would ply from Howrah Station to Belur Math. After getting down at Belur Math Bus stop, we walked down to the Ramakrishna Mission Vidyamandira (Belur College). After entering into the college premises, we met a person dressed completely in white. We were attracted

Ramakrishna Mission Vidyamandira, Belur Math

by his smiling face and nice behaviour. We were told that he is Brahmachari Murari Chaitanya (Govinda Maharaj) and he is the person who was assisting the Principal, Swami Tejasananda in the matter of admission. However, we felt very disappointed to learn from him that admission process for the IA/I.Sc. programme was already over more than a month ago. Advertisement had been published in the newspaper more than four months ago. Then the shortlisted applicants had to write a written examination followed by interview. On the basis of the performance in the written test and interview, selection was done. It was highly competitive to get a seat there.

Despite this set back, Govinda Maharaj took us to the Principal's office, where we met the Principal, Swami Tejasananda. The author's father and Sudhir Babu explained that they had travelled from a remote village where newspapers are seldom available and so they were completely ignorant of all the above information. The Principal asserted, "Ours is a residential college. So all the students have to stay in the hostel. Since there is no more vacancy in the hostels, it is not at all possible to admit a single student further." The author and his

Swami Tejasananda

father again tried to impress upon their long-standing desire for admission to the Institution.

The Unexpected Admission Opportunity

Realizing the intensity of our eagerness, the Principal Maharaj said to his assistant, "Govinda, hold an examination for this boy and see how he performs." Govinda Maharaj asked the author to write an essay in English on the topic 'Aim of My Life'. Since the author studied in a Bengali medium school, until then, and that too in a remote village, it was unlikely that the quality of his English essay would be very good. Still the author was courageous to write the essay in English. He remembers, he wrote that he would like to be a doctor in the future. By the grace of the Lord, both Govinda Maharaj and Principal Maharaj were satisfied with the quality of his essay.

Swami Tejasananda then instructed, "Govinda, admit this boy."

By the grace of Lord Sri Ramakrishna, the author had got the rare opportunity to enroll in this great institution named after Him. It remained totally unknown how an additional seat was arranged in the hostel. Getting admission to this great institution was the first and the most important turning point in the author's life. For a student coming from a very remote and underdeveloped village, it was indeed a significant achievement. "*Mukam karoti vachalam pangum langhayate girim. Yat kripa tamaham vande paramananda madhavam.*"—With God's grace, a mute person can become an eloquent speaker, and a lame person can climb mountains. Swami Vivekananda said, "Have faith in yourself, have faith in God." With self-confidence and faith in God, one can attain any height.

It is interesting that the name '*Vidyamandira*' was given by none other than Swami Vivekananda himself in 1898 who had envisioned such an institution modelled on the ancient 'Gurukul' system. It is a fully residential college for boys affiliated to the University of Calcutta founded by the Ramakrishna Mission in 1941. Thus, the name of the esteemed institution was given 43 years before it came into existence. Swami Vimuktananda (Upen Maharaj) was the founder Secretary, while Swami Tejasananda was the founder Principal of the College.

Although it started as an Intermediate Arts College in 1941, it received affiliation in some commerce subjects in 1945 and in some science subjects in 1946. The institution was upgraded to a three-year degree College with effect from July 1960. In this College, students can interact closely with their teachers. Sincere attempt is made to impart all-round training to the students in a serene atmosphere with an emphasis on discipline and moral values, so that the students can grow up as worthy citizens of India.

After the Principal had approved the admission, the author observed an indescribable joy on his father's face. He felt, his long-cherished wish had been fulfilled and so he looked extremely happy and satisfied. The author strongly feels, this opportunity to study at this college acted as a great blessing for the entire life of the author in every way and made his human life meaningful.

The Prestigious Legacy of Vidyamandira

Due to the unique educational methods adopted in the Vidyamandira, 6–7 students consistently ranked in the top ten in the IA examinations of Calcutta University and 3–4 students in the top ten in the I.Sc. examinations every year. In the author's batch, Ashok Sarkar, who had topped the School final examinations from Oriental Seminary School in Kolkata, enrolled in IA course at Vidyamandira. He also secured the first position in IA examination of Calcutta University in 1961. After passing IA, Ashok graduated with honours in Economics from Presidency College, Kolkata and became a bank officer. The second rank holder in IA was Biswanath Das from the Tarakeswar region. Very humble and unassuming, he graduated with honours in Statistics from Presidency College, Kolkata, and later obtained his M.A. in Statistics from Calcutta University, followed by a Ph.D. degree. He later became the head of the Statistics Department at Presidency College.

In early July 1959, the new students including the author, became entitled to enter into the gate of the Ramakrishna Mission Vidyamandira, the educational institution envisioned by Swami Vivekananda, located very close to Belur Math. While entering into the gate with their luggage, the students experienced a mixed feeling of fear and joy. It was their first time living away from home, away from their parents. The environment here was entirely different, with a structured and disciplined lifestyle.

Infrastructure of the Vidyamandira in the Past

During that time, Vidyamandira was a much smaller institution. The general education system those days consisted of ten years of school final, two years of intermediate (IA/ISc/ICom.), two years of honours/pass courses, and two years of M.A./M.Sc./MCom. In those days, Vidyamandira had only one two-storey building (without a dome). The upper floor housed a large room called Vivekananda Hall, the Principal's office, the college office, and the common room for the professors. On the ground floor, there was a gallery-equipped classroom, a library, and 2–3 small classrooms. The Physics laboratory was on the first floor, with the Chemistry laboratory directly below it on the ground floor. Since the college offered only intermediate courses at the time, the number of students and professors was very small, fostering genuine trust and friendship among the students. They used to spend lot of time together. The second-year students loved the first-year students like their younger brothers, while the first year students used to have respect for the senior students as their elder brothers. The juniors used to address the seniors as 'Dada'. This has been a unique culture in all Ramakrishna Mission institutions.

On the way from the gate to the college building, there were open fields on both the left and right sides. There was also a small pond on the left side, where lilies bloomed. In those days, there were only two hostels: Ashananda Hostel (West Hostel) and another of similar size (East Hostel) beside it. The prayer room for both hostels was on the second floor. The kitchen and dining hall for West Hostel were attached to the hostel, while East Hostel's kitchen and dining hall were a bit further away, accessible by a paved path. During the rainy season, umbrellas had to be used for going from East Hostel to its dining hall.

To the left of the path from the East Hostel to the dining hall, there was a large pond, where students from both the hostels used to take bath. Separate arrangements were made for those who couldn't swim. Behind the college and in front of East Hostel, there is the gymnasium (now known as Vikas Bhavan), where students could perform exercises with/without instruments. Occasionally, various meetings and events like Saraswati Puja were held here. A few students were sometimes accommodated on the first floor of Vikas Bhavan.

Despite the simplicity, the disciplined and structured lifestyle of the students in the college and the hostel, laid the foundation for producing exceptional students, many of whom went on to make significant contributions to the society.

Teaching Methods and Curriculum at the Vidyamandira

As mentioned earlier, in those days the number of professors at the Vidyamandira was small. However, despite their limited numbers, they demonstrated exceptional dedication, sincerity and devotion to teaching. Many of them were full-time professors at different colleges in Kolkata and part-time professors at the Vidyamandira. The author recalls having some difficulty in the first few days of classes, since he had studied in Bengali medium up to the tenth grade. Similar was the case with many other students. At the Vidyamandira, professors of different science subjects lectured in English, and all the books were written in English. Some textbooks were written by English authors, such as S.L. Loney's Trigonometry, Co-ordinate Geometry, Statics and Dynamics as well as Algebra by H.S. Hall and S.R. Knight, and Higher Algebra by S. Barnard and J.M. Child. However, within a few days, the students became accustomed to it and did not find it as challenging any more.

One unique feature of the curriculum at this great educational institution was that Principal Maharaj Swami Tejasananda held a weekly "Religious Class." This subject was not a part of the university syllabus, but Principal Maharaj taught it with great care to cultivate moral values among the students. Like other subjects, examination was also held for this subject, and passing was mandatory. The curriculum of this subject included the history of the Ramakrishna Movement, selected writings and poems of Swami Vivekananda, and more. During the Religious classes, Principal Maharaj would caution the students about the ideals of the Vidyamandira and provide timely advice that would benefit them in their future lives. He beautifully narrated short biographies and teachings of Sri Ramakrishna, Holy Mother Sarada Devi, and Swami Vivekananda, as well as their influence and contributions in India and abroad. At the beginning of the religious class, all students as well as Maharaj would stand and collectively recite a mantra from the Taittiriya Upanishad of Krishna Yajurveda (2.2.2):

> *"Om sahanaavavatu sahanaubhunaktu, sahaveeryam karavaavahai. Tejasvinaavadheetamastu maa vidvishaavahai. Om shantih shantih shantih."*

Meaning,

"May He protect us both (teacher and student). May He nourish us both. May we work together with energy and vigour. May our study be enlightening and not give rise to hostility. Om peace, peace, peace."

The religious subject as well as Bengali, and English classes (which were large) used to be held together for all intermediate (IA and ISc) students. Thus, these classes were conducted in the Vivekananda Hall on the upper floor (or sometimes in the gallery-equipped room on the ground floor).

Bhratrivaran Ceremony: Embracing Brotherhood

About 8–10 days after classes started, a 'Bhratrivaran' (Brotherhood) festival was held on a holiday. This ceremony took place in the prayer hall on the second floor of the hostel. Initially, there would be special worship and homa (sacred fire ritual) for Sri Ramakrishna, Sri Sarada Devi, and Swami Vivekananda. All new students sat on one side, while the senior students sat separately.

The second-year students welcomed each first-year student by marking their forehead with white sandalwood paste and tying a *rakhi* (sacred thread) on their wrists, solidifying their journey at Vidyamandira. Thus began the author's transformative journey at the Vidyamandira, an institution dedicated to holistic education, discipline and self-reliance. After this, the 'Vidyarthi Homa' was performed. Each new student offered a mixture of *ghee* and *bel* leaves to the sacred fire while reciting the five resolutions, listed below.

Such Bhratrivaran ceremonies and Vidyarthi Homas are organized in every educational institution run by the Ramakrishna Mission. Considering the violent ragging practices of present times, in other educational institutions, this Bhratrivaran ceremony stands out as a beautiful tradition, filling the author's heart with joy as a teacher.

During the author's time, the entire ceremony was conducted by Swami Bodhatmananda Maharaj, the principal of the Brahmachari Training Centre of Belur Math. Every year, on this particular day, a distinguished guest would be invited to deliver a lecture, inspiring the new students. During our time at the Intermediate stage, the famous writer Shri Dakshinaranjan Basu was invited, who graced the auspicious occasion as a distinguished guest. His son Shri Kalyan Basu was then a second-year student at the Vidyamandira.

Five Resolutions of the *Vidyarthi Homa*

Resolution 1: Commitment to Health and Well-being

> *"Shariramadyam khalu dharmasadhanam iti nitivakyam avadharya shramaksha niroga shariraya svasthya vidhi palana paro bhavitum aham yathasadhyam yatishye."*

Following the scriptural (*Niti-Sastra*) advice that "the body is the foremost instrument for practicing Dharma, I will strive hard to follow health rules to maintain a healthy body suitable for doing hard work."

Prayer: *'O you are the vitality, bestow vitality upon me. You are the strength, bestow strength upon me. You are nourishment, nourish me. You are enthusiasm, inspire me. May my muscles be as strong as iron, my nerves be like steel, and my heart be as firm as a diamond. I offer my oblation to the Supreme Self, the abode of infinite energy, the source of limitless power.'*

Resolution 2: Dedication to Learning

"Chhatranam adhyayanam tapah, iti smritivakyam avadharya pratibha-vikasharthamachara-nirato adhyayanaparo bhavitum aham yathasadhyam yatishye."

Adhering to the advice from the scriptures (*smriti-sastra*) that *"Study is the penance for students,"* I will strive to devote myself to study for the development of my intellect.

Prayer: *May Indra endow me with intelligence, may the goddess Saraswati bless me with intelligence, may the Ashwini Kumars, garlanded with lotus flowers, bestow intelligence upon me. I offer my oblation to the Supreme Self, who eradicates all ignorance, embodies all knowledge, and bestows all achievements.*

Resolution 3: Upholding Truth

"Satyam eva jayate na anritam satyena pantha vitato devayanah—iti shrutivakyam avadharya kayena manasa vacha satyaparanah bhavitum aham yathasadhyam yatishye."

—'Truth alone triumphs, not falsehood. The path of the divine is spread out through truth,' I will strive to adhere to truth in body, mind, and speech following the concerned advice from the scriptures (*Shrutivakya*)

Prayer: *Take me from untruth to truth, from darkness to light, and from death to immortality. I offer my oblation to the Supreme Self, the embodiment of truth, the refuge of the true Dharma, who destroys all falsehood.*

Resolution 4: Service to Humanity

"Swartho yasya parartha eva sah pumaan ekah satyam agranee—iti manishivakyam avadharya neechatakruratadambhikatadi malinaswartha-santatirbbhihaya udaracheta vinayi shraddhavan deshabhakto naranarayana-sevanishtho bhavitumaham yathasadhyam yatishye."

—*'He whose self-interest is the welfare of others, he alone is the greatest among good men,'* keeping this wise- saying in mind, I will strive to be generous, humble, respectful, loving, and dedicated to serving humanity.

—Having heard and grasped the essence of Dharma: Do not do unto others what is harmful to oneself. Regard each of your mother, father, and guest as a deity. Only perform those actions that are praiseworthy and avoid those that are not. I offer my oblation to the Supreme Self, who eradicates the impurities of the mind, embodies compassion, and bestows the sweetness of love.

Resolution: 5: Commitment to Unity and Social Welfare

> *"Suparichalita sanghati shaktireva samajakalyanam nidhanam. Atah aikyapratishtha mulakam sanghati shakti jagaranaatmakam samgaccha-dhwam sambadadhwam sambo manansi janatam iti shrutyadesham avadharya sadupaya parah sannaham etadvidyapratishthanagoshti bhuktaih sarvairaikyabaddho bhavitum yathasadhyam yatishye."*

—*Well-managed collective strength is the foundation of social welfare.* Therefore, let us come together. Let us speak in unison. Let our minds be united in knowledge, I will strive to follow the righteous path and unify with all members of this educational institution.

—I offer my oblation to the Supreme Self, the embodiment of the universe, the eternal one, the refuge of all worlds. May the Supreme Self, through these mantras, assist me in these resolutions. May He bring me auspiciousness and peace. O Sun God, remove all my sins and grant me all that is auspicious.

—After this, the final oblation (*Purnahuti*) is offered.

In the Company of Senior Monks at Belur Math

From the neighbouring village, Pratapdighi, Dr. Ram Chandra Mahanti's elder middle brother had long ago become a monk of the Ramakrishna Mission, known as Swami Ajapananda (Purna Maharaj). He was in charge of the kitchen and pantry at Belur Math. I used to meet him almost every afternoon, during the first couple of months of my stay at the Vidyamandira.

Occasionally, he would give prasad (sanctified food) of Thakur (Sri Ramakrishna). He introduced me to many senior monks at Belur Math. Many of them would walk from the Mission Office to the main gate of Belur Math in the evening.

One of them was Swami Tyagishwarananda (Hem Maharaj). Due to old age, his leg muscles had shriveled, and he struggled to walk. With the help of a stick and assistance from others, he tried to walk. However, his mind was full of courage and enthusiasm. On the first day of meeting, he arranged for me to receive framed pictures of Sri Ramakrishna and Holy Mother Sarada Devi. Those pictures were in black and white, but the two photographs were very beautiful. I kept those pictures on my study table and offered flowers and incense to them every morning. Every evening I used to offer only incense. The sweet smell of the incense used to create a divine environment around the study table. The framed pictures prepared in 1959 are still preserved.

I heard that some of these senior monks of that time were revolutionaries of the fiery era (freedom fighters) before becoming monks. Another elderly monk, Dwarika Maharaj, would interact with the students and tell humorous stories. Therefore, he was known as 'Galpo Maharaj.' He was a very cheerful person and took care of the garden at Belur Math. I got a sapling of a *Nagalingam* flower tree from him, which I planted in the garden of our ancestral house at Bagmari in 1961. The tree's trunk is now quite thick and tall, and it is now 64 years old.

Swami Brahmananda, who was a direct disciple of Sri Ramakrishna and the first President of the Ramakrishna Math and Mission brought a Nagalingam sapling from Madras and planted it in Belur Math. The colour of Nagalingam flower is light pink. It has light sweet smell. The geometrical configuration of the petals of the flower resembles the hood of a snake and due to this reason, the name of the flower is 'Nagalingam'. If the deity is worshipped with these flowers, a divine fragrance is spread all over.

The Influence of Monastic Wisdom

In those days Srimat Swami Shankaranandaji was the President of the Ramakrishna Math and Ramakrishna Mission. He was the 7th President (1951–1962) of the Ramakrishna Order. He was a disciple of Swami Brahmananda, the Divine son (*Manas Putra*) of Lord Sri Ramakrishna. Swami Bishuddhananda, a disciple of the Holy Mother was the only Vice-President. Almost every afternoon with an ever smiling face he used to be found engaged in religious discourses with devotees in the verandah of Belur Math, facing the Ganga river. The author was fortunate to be present there during the discourse for a short while several times. Those days the General Secretary was Swami Madhavananda. There were two Asst. Secretaries of the Ramakrishna Mission—

Swami Vireshwarananda (Prabhu Maharaj) and Swami Saswatananda (Suresh Maharaj). Swami Madhavananda was the General Secretary of the Ramakrishna Mission for a long period of 24 years from 1938 to 1961. He went to New York in 1961 for medical treatment. As a student that time, the author was present in Belur Math and was one among those to see Swami Madhavananda off at that time. The author fondly remembers that Maharaj wore the European dresses (possibly, for convenience) at the time when he was leaving.

Suresh Maharaj had profound affection for the author. He used to interact with the author during evening walk in Belur Math premises and gave valuable guidance. Those days there was a monastic disciple of Swami Vivekananda, named *Jnan Maharaj*. He used to live in a room in the ground floor of the building, while in the first floor in one room towards Ganga river Swami Vivekananda used to live.

In the room adjacent to Swamiji's bed room, the President, Swami Shankarananda used to live. Although Jnan Maharaj was a monk, following the advice of his Guru Swami Vivekananda, he did not take 'Sannyasa' diksha. He led whole of his life as a 'Naishtika Brahmachari' (a person who takes a vow to remain celibate until death). Even when Swami Shankaranandaji was the President of the order, he used to behave very cordially with Jnan Maharaj. The author remembers another such 'Naishtika Brahmachari', named Brahmachari Akshay Chaitanya (1900–1997). He was initiated by the Holy Mother, Sri Sri Sarada Devi at her Baghbazar residence on 29.12.1918; subsequently he joined the Ramakrishna Mission at Varanasi Advaita Ashrama in 1922 and later, received the vow of brahmacharya from Swami Saradananda. He wrote the very first comprehensive biography of the Holy Mother Sri Sri Sarada Devi. The author was fortunate to meet Brahmachari Akshay Chaitanya once in the office of Govinda Maharaj.

Swami Shantananda (1883–1974)

When the author was a student of I.Sc. at the Vidyamandira, he was very fortunate to come in holy contact with another very senior monk, Srimat Swami Shantananda. Those days he was living in a small room at Premananda Bhavan (an old house in front of Vivekananda Temple). In his pre-monastic life, his name was 'Khagen'. He received initiation from Sri Sri Sarada Devi. The author heard that he was one of the very few monks, who was believed to be a 'Realized Soul' (Brahmajnani). The author used to visit him almost daily in the afternoon time and enjoy his holy company for sometime. But those days he was not keeping good health. He used to have severe hiccups almost in a non-stop manner. He was under the treatment of some famous clinicians from Calcutta. But they were unable to cure him. The doctors said, as the author heard, human life cannot survive for more than three days in that condition. But Swami Shantanandaji with that sort of acute health issue, survived for many years. The author feels, the Divine Mother Sarada Devi protected his life with special care/attention. The author used to observe that Swami Shantanandaji used to interact very little, possibly due to the fact that he used to live mostly in a Divine world doing *Japam* ceaselessly and thinking of Sri Sri Thakur and the Holy Mother in the heart. By seeing him, one could get at least some idea about Sri Ramakrishna and the State of Samadhi (a state of absorptive contemplation of the Absolute), which he used to attain every now and then, as described in the Ramakrishna Kathamrita. The author was fortunate that on rare occasion Swami Shantanandaji used to give him small pieces of religious advice. He advised the author, "Always do Japam."

The Author Standing Behind
Srimat Swami Shantananda Ji (1959)

Swami Shantanandaji was appointed a trustee of the Ramakrishna Math and a Member of the Governing Body of the Ramakrishna Mission in the year 1930. Although he was appointed the Head of the Ramakrishna Mission Advaita Ashrama, Varanasi he resigned from the post after sometime and felt more comfortable in the worship at the shrine. This work suited his meditative temperament better.

As indicated earlier, this monk was highly respected and loved for his spiritual attainments and sweet nature. From his face, it was apparent that his mind used to always remain engrossed in Sri Ramakrishna and Holy Mother Sarada Devi. Swami Shantananda's countenance used to attract monks and devotees, young and old alike. In his vicinity, all used to feel a sense of peace and joy.

How to Receive Holy Mother's Advice?

Swami Sridharananda (Salil Maharaj) was Swami Shantananda's sevak for a few years. He writes—Holy Mother Sri Sarada Devi had once told Shantanandaji how to receive her advice: "If there is any crisis in your life, remember me. Isolate yourself from others for a few days, and practice japa and meditation intensely. Pray whole heartedly and ask me 'Mother what shall I do?' During that period, eat less and keep your body and mind pure. Try to maintain silence and speak only if it is absolutely necessary. Don't let other people know what you are doing. Continue your prayers and *sadhana* in this way with a one-pointed mind. Never lose patience. *If you see that you are not receiving my command, still you should not give up. If you find that no response is coming, then know for certain that your mind has not risen high enough to receive my advice. You will* ***definitely*** *receive my advice if you call on me with a whole hearted faith and devotion."* Swami Shantanandaji also used to insist on doing japam along with breath (ceaselessly). This practice is called **'Ajapa japa.'**

Power of Prayer

In an attempt to validate the power of praying with intense longing (as demonstrated time and again by Lord Sri Ramakrishna and Holy Mother Sri Sarada Devi), in his article on "Power of Prayer" Swami Divyananda (one of the present Vice-Presidents of the Ramakrishna Math and Mission) narrates the following story, of which he was a witness (*Vivekvani.com/m5021*): "... One day a little before evening, Swami Santoshanandaji, Secretary of Belgharia Ramakrishna Mission came to pay respect to Swami Shantananda Maharaj. Swami Santoshananda too was a disciple of the Holy Mother Sri Sarada Devi; he was junior to Shantanandaji both in age and in sannyasa-diksha. After offering his pranamas, Santoshanandaji said—Maharaj, West Bengal is now in the grip of a terrible drought. If there is no rainfall soon, the poor people solely dependent on agriculture will starve to death. Why don't you pray to Mother for rainfall? Hearing these words, Shantanandaji with a smile on his face, turned to Santoshanandaji and sweetly replied—'You too are a child of the Holy Mother. Why don't you also pray to her? And then something extraordinary happened. These two sannyasi children of the Holy Mother started praying to Mother with the heart rending cry, 'Maa', 'Maa'; tears streamed down their faces. Speechless, we sat drinking in those divine moments of prayer.... As I was finally preparing to go to bed that night—lo and behold! ... O—rain started pouring down in torrents! It rained the whole night. All along, I felt that the tears of those two sannyasis were heavily coming down as streams of rain water. ..."

Conversation of Swami Shantananda with Holy Mother

It seems, Swami Shantanandaji sometimes used to converse with the Holy Mother even much after she returned to her heavenly abode. Once R.K. Mission Sanatorium Hospital at Ranchi was in a state of extreme hardship with finance and was about to close. On hearing this from the Secretary Swami Vedantananda (Anukul Maharaj), Swami Shantanandaji (who was staying there that time) had a conversation with Holy Mother. He informed Anukul Maharaj that he had talked to Holy Mother and that she had said that the Sanatorium need not be closed down and the required funds will come soon!

Shortly, a Bengali gentleman named Nirmal Kumar Dey (N.K. Dey) living in London expressed his interest to donate a substantial amount for the Ranchi Sanatorium. Mr N.K. Dey was a barrister practising in London.

Swami Atmasthananda (the then Asst. Secretary, who later became the President of Ramakrishna Mission) met the said gentleman, when he came to Calcutta. The gentleman handed him over a cheque of 15 lakh rupees! That was 1952. It was a huge sum those days. Thus the financial crisis of Ranchi Sanatorium was resolved. (cf. 'Consulting Holy Mother' written by Swami Vimokshananda, vivekvani.com/m5021)

Swami Suhitananda (another Vice-President of Ramakrishna Math and Mission) in his article entitled "Divine innocence" nicely narrates some incidents that he witnessed with Swami Shantanandaji. The incidents depict how much innocent of worldly matters the great Swami was (vivekvani.com/m 5021).

One monk, named Sushil Maharaj (Swami Indrananda) used to take care of the daily welfare (Sevak) of Swami Shantananda when the author was an I.Sc. student of the Vidyamandira. He was also very sweet natured. It was due to his help, the author could have the holy company of Shantanandaji on a regular basis. The foundation stone of a new hostel 'Vivek Bhavan' was laid by Swami Shantanandaji. After several months, when the construction of Vivek Bhavan was completed, it was inaugurated also by the great Saint. On both these occasions, the author had the fortune of remaining present beside Swami Shantananda.

Swami Nirvanananda

At that time, Swami Nirvanananda (Surya Maharaj) was the Manager of Belur Math. He occupied this responsible position for 26 years. Everyday he used to sit on a chair on the front verandah of the Math office. In order to meet Swami Ajapananda (Purna Maharaj) or any other monk, one had to first intimate him and then he used to ask an attendant to call the concerned monk. Swami Nirvanananda was a disciple of Raja Maharaj (Swami Brahmananda). During interactions he revealed that he had the opportunity to be a personal attendant to Raja Maharaj for sometime and for this he used to express great pleasure and satisfaction. Swami Nirvanananda played an important role in acquiring the house of Sri Balaram Bose in Kolkata (currently known as Balaram Mandir). He was also instrumental to founding a branch centre of the Ramakrishna Mission at Sikra-Kulingram, (on Taki Road, Barasat Postal Division, North 24 Parganas, West Bengal) the sacred birth-place of Swami Brahmananda. These were Swami Nirvanananda's two significant contributions to the Ramakrishna Order. He also told the author that in the youth he used to perform physical exercises, with special emphasis on 'don' for overall body conditioning. By saying this, he used to inspire the author to perform physical exercises and yoga daily. Here it is worth mentioning that our knees and back are so designed as to remain healthy for 100 years, but due to sedentary lifestyle, degeneration of these essential joints starts at early 40's. Swami Nirvanananda became Vice-President of Ramakrishna Math and Mission in 1966.

Other Senior Monks

In the office of Belur Math, another very senior monk used to be seen quite often those days. His name was Swami Abhayananda (Bharat Maharaj). But he used to talk much less. The author was also fortunate to get into a number of senior monks of the Order, like Swami Yatiswarananda, Swami Gahanananda, Swami Gambhirananda, Swami Ranganathananda, Swami Bhuteshananda, Swami Chandikananda, Swami Atmasthananda, and others. Some of them later became Presidents/Vice-Presidents of the Ramakrishna Math and Mission. The author is indebted to Swami Gokulananda for introducing him with most of the monks, mentioned above.

Agamani Songs

Every year from the first day (pratipada) after Mahalaya to the sixth day there is a long tradition of singing 'Agamani songs' at Belur Math in the early morning.

As a student of the Vidyamandira, the author attended several sittings of Agamani songs sung by the sannyasins and brahmacharis of Belur Math. He still remembers the event very fondly.

A Life of Discipline and Devotion at Vidyamandira

When I was admitted to the I.Sc. programme at the Vidyamandira, I was first allotted Ashananda Chhatrabas/West Hostel (now named as Vidya Bhawan). I was allotted a seat in a four-seated room in the first floor of the hostel, the other roommates being Mr. Dilip Dutta (Kalyani), Mr. Jyotiprakash Ghosh (Kanchrapara) and Mr. Dipankar Chatterji (Batanagar). The superintendent of the hostel was Anil Maharaj (named as Abheda Chaitanya after brahmacharya and Swami Adishwarananda after sannyasa). The assistant superintendent was Balaram Maharaj (who also was in-charge of the college library) and ever smiling Hrishikes Maharaj (Swami Srinivasananda). Hrishikes Maharaj used to guide the students in such a manner that they would prosper more in future. There were several very good customs in the hostel. After the morning prayer when the students came back to their respective rooms, one senior student would come to every room, and enquire if any of them has any health issue. Then he would arrange for sick diet in consultation with the Superintendent.

In the East Hostel, the Superintendent was Govinda Maharaj (Brahmachari Murari Chaitanya/Swami Gokulananda) and the assistant wardens were Lakshminarayan Maharaj (Swami Tathagatananda) and Arun Maharaj. Swami Gokulananda was a professor of Philosophy, while Arun Maharaj was a Professor of English. He was highly punctual in the class. As soon as the bell rang, he would immediately stop even if he was in the middle of a sentence. Keeping the sentence incomplete he would immediately leave the class. The author fondly remembers that once he mentioned in the class a teaching of Gautam Buddha that it is better to follow the middle path. The author has experienced in life the validity of this teaching of Gautam Buddha. His name was Arun Mukherjee in the pre-monastic life. Later, he decided to become a Sadhu and joined the Vidyamandira to teach English. But by that time, he crossed the age limit for becoming a brahmachari at Belur Math. However, he continued to lead the life of renunciation and service, and took 'sannyasa' from Kailas Math, established by Adi Sankaracharya. For this he got all help and cooperation from Belur Math.

Swami Gokulananda

Swami Gokulananda,
Superintendent, East Hostel

In later years, Swami Gokulananda (1929–2007) became the Vice-Principal and then the Principal of the Vidyamandira. After that he was bestowed upon the responsibility of managing several big schools of the Ramakrishna Mission in Cherrapunji, Meghalaya. There he could demonstrate his high calibre of management. Thereafter, he took charge of a large residential school run by the Ramakrishna Mission, Narottam Nagar, Arunachal Pradesh and succeeded in bringing about significant improvements in the school despite many adversities. Then he served as the Secretary of the Ramakrishna Mission, New Delhi for a long period of 21 years. There he became very popular among the devotees and the general public in Delhi. He used to conduct 'guided meditation' programmes. I had the opportunity to participate in one of those programmes. Whenever from IIT Kharagpur, I used to go to Delhi, for some academic work, many a time I used to visit revered Govinda Maharaj and receive his blessings. His affectionate guidance had a significant impact on my life.

Swami Adiswarananda

Swami Adiswarananda (1925–2007) became the Head (Minister & Spiritual Leader) of the Ramakrishna-Vivekananda Center, founded by Swami Nikhilananda in the year 1933 at 17 East 94 third Street, New York, NY101028, USA. It deserves a special mention that while staying in this center, Swami Nikhilananda translated "Sri Sri Ramakrishna Kathamrita" from Bengali to English, and published with the title "Gospel of Sri Ramakrishna" in the year 1942. This is considered to be the first complete and best English translation of the Kathamrita. The center has a temple in New York City and a summer cottage at Thousand Island Park, New York. Vivekananda cottage at Thousand Park on St. Lawrence River is the place, where Swami Vivekananda stayed and delivered 'Inspired Talks' to a group of selected disciples from mid-June to early August 1895. This is why this center is of historical importance to Ramakrishna-Vivekananda devotees. I had an occasion to meet Swami Adiswarananda at this center in the year 1981. I was amazed to see that several brahmacharis and sannyasins (all of whom were Americans) were singing '*Kali*

Kirtan'. They were chanting with all sincerity and devotion. As we know, *Kirtan helps to uplift the mind, open the heart and bring inner peace. It is the fastest and easiest way to achieve joy and peace of mind. Similarly mantras being universal mystical sounds seem to bear the potential to resonate with our chakras and to remove negative thoughts. Chanting of slokas from Sri Sri Markandeya Chandi and Srimad Bhagavad Gita is very helpful in improving the concentration of mind, restoring mental peace and enhancing memory. Occasionally chanting of Sanskrit slokas plays the role of 'pranayamas' in regulating breath to a good extent.*

Swami Tathagatananda

After his stay in Vidyamandira, Swami Tathagatananda (1923–2016) assumed the position of the Secretary of Ramakrishna Mission Ashrama, Baranagar in 1975. From 1977 to 2016 he was the Head of Vedanta Society of New York housed at 34 West 71st Street, New York, NY 10023, USA. This was the first Vedanta Society founded by the Indian Hindu Monk, Swami Vivekananda in New York in 1894.

I had the opportunity of meeting Swami Tathagatananda in the Vedanta Society of New York in 1981. He was a very simple minded monk, who developed some special affection towards me, when I was a resident of the Vidyamandira hostel. It is because of his generosity I could stay for 3–4 days in the Vedanta Society and visit Courant Institute of Mathematical Sciences, New York and Cornell Medical Center of New York in 1981.

Seminar Lectures at Courant Institute and Cornell Medical Centre, New York

On an invitation from Prof. Charles Peskin I had the opportunity to visit the Courant Institute of Mathematical Sciences, New York and deliver a seminar lecture on cardiovascular dynamics in 1981. On another invitation, I could visit Cornell Medical Center of the New York Hospital. Here I delivered a lecture on the biomechanics of bones.

Many years later, when Swami Tathagatananda visited Belur Math, he came to IIT Kharagpur. One morning he visited our residential quarters of IIT Kharagpur (Qrs. No. C1-63) and had breakfast on our invitation. The childlike conversations of the Swami with all the members of our family are still fresh in the mind. On hearing that my wife Shorasi knows a bit of Sanskrit, he asked her to recite a few Sanskrit verses from the lyric poem 'Meghduta' of Kalidasa. The theme in this famous poem concerns a piece of cloud which is carrying a message of hope to the wife from her husband, who was separated from his wife.

Daily Life in Vidyamandira (contd.)

Let us now return to the discussion on the hostel life in the Vidyamandira. As mentioned earlier, initially I was staying in the West Hostel after being admitted as a student of the Vidyamandira in 1959. Jagaddhatri Puja was celebrated in the Tattva Mandira in 1959, which is very close to our hostel. In the first year, due to the pressure of studies (possibly due to some upcoming examination), I did not go to visit the Puja pandal. When it came to the notice of the Superintendent Anil Maharaj, he gently scolded me and told that I should have definitely visited the Puja. This shows to what extent, revered Anil Maharaj used to try to take care of the mental health of the students. In the Tattwa Mandira, for many years Jagaddhatri Puja used to be performed by one sannyasi, named Gouri Maharaj. I was very affectionate to him as well.

Occasionally I used to meet Govinda Maharaj, superintendent of the East Hostel at his office. He used to offer guidance to a group of students, who had inclination towards spirituality. Most of them belonged to the East Hostel. So after taking approval of both Anil Maharaj and Govinda Maharaj, I moved to the East Hostel, so that I can stay with other like-minded students.

Life at the Vidyamandira followed a structured routine. Much before sunrise, the wake-up bell used to be given. This was followed by a bell for rushing to the prayer hall in proper dresses (*dhoti*) at 5 A.M., when it was still dark. All students of the East and West Hostels would go to the common Prayer Hall situated on the second floor. Usually a second-year student, who could play harmonium would take a leading role in singing the devotional songs during the prayer, both in the morning and in the evening. Usually two songs would be sung from the book 'Prarthana O Sangeet', compiled by the Principal, Swami Tejasananda and published by Ramakrishna Mission Saradapith. Different songs used to be sung on different days of the week; for example, hymns and songs of Lord Shiva on Mondays while hymns to the Mother Goddess on Saturdays and Tuesdays. Sometimes, on Tuesdays one song on Sri Ramachandra or Lord Hanuman used to be sung. On Wednesday, songs on Sri Ramakrishna would be sung, as Wednesday is the birthday of Ramakrishna Deva. On Thursdays/Fridays/Sundays, sometimes songs on Holy Mother Sarada Devi/Swami Vivekananda would be sung.

When our music teacher, Bishweshwar Chakraborty, used to be present, he would take the lead in the Prayer Hall. The original Bengali version of the following song composed by Manomohan Chakraborty, which used to be sung during prayer time, in our student life, still resonates in my mind quite often and gives a sense of indescribable joy and reliance on the Mother Goddess, bringing peace to the mind:

"Mother is here and so am I,
What worry do I have?
I eat and wear by Mother's hand,
She has taken my burden."

In my memory, the following Bengali song written by Swami Vivekananda and sung on Shivaratri is still vivid:

"Tathaiya Tathaiya Nache Bhola, Bam Bab Baje Gal,
Dimi Dimi Dimi Damaru Baje Dulichhe Kapala-Mal."

And the song "Madhura Chhandhe Paramanande Nache Brajagopal" still evokes a divine feeling. I also remember the following song composed by Swami Premeshananda about Sri Ramakrishna and his disciples sung during their birth-tithis:

"Joya Joya Ramakrishna Bhuvan-Mangala
Joya Mata Shyamasuta Oti Niramala."

When certain devotional songs reveal in the mind of the author, even today his mind is elevated to a different dimension. For example,

"Come, O Lord, come, O compassionate one,
Accept today my body, mind, and life,
Kindly give your blessings,
So that my life may go in your service."

Daily Routine

After morning prayer, there was a bell for breakfast. There was a gap of about half an hour. Some of us would go to Belur Math during this time to offer prayers and walk all the way round the temples of Sri Ramakrishna, Holy Mother Sarada Devi, Swami Vivekananda, Swami Brahmananda as well as the Old Temple of Belur Math and Swami Vivekananda's bed room. Then, we would quickly return to the hostel, have breakfast, and start studying during the study hours. Each student of the hostels had a separate table, but there were no chairs; we had to sit on the bed and study at the table. Morning study hours were from 7 to 9 AM, and evening study hours would also extend until 9 PM. During these hours, there was complete silence. The warden and assistant wardens kept a strict watch to ensure no one talked in any room. Occasionally, Principal Swami Tejasananda would make a surprise visit. If someone was found drowsy, the Principal Maharaj would tell him to wash his face with water.

At 9 AM, there was a bell for taking bath, and at 9:30 AM, there would be another indicating that the students should proceed for taking lunch. After morning study hours, students had to perform temple duties by rotation—cleaning the temple utensils, collecting flowers for worship in the shrine, preparing sandalwood paste, and mopping the floor of the shrine. At 10 AM, the college bell used to ring. Classes used to run one after another from 10 AM to 4:30 PM. After returning from college in the evening, there used to be heavy snacks with a different menu on different days. After taking snacks, some students used to proceed to the gymnasium for exercises, some would play football or cricket, while some others would go to visit Belur Math and enjoy the riverside view.

In the evening, when the prayer bell rang, all the students had to go to the prayer hall. The students themselves took turns performing the aarti. Mostly, Brahmin students used to get this opportunity. The five offerings used to be made—lamp (pancha-pradeep), conch, cloth, flower, and hand-fan (chamar). During this time, a bell had to be rung with the left hand while performing the offerings with the right hand. It wasn't easy for those who were not accustomed, requiring some practice. I was fortunate to be chosen for performing the aratrikam for a long time in the Vidyamandira and also later at the Ramakrishna Mission Kolkata Vidyarthi Ashrama, Belgharia. Typically, a senior student led the evening bhajan, with everyone else following in chorus. The evening bhajan was composed by Swami Vivekananda:

> *"Khandana Bhava Bandhana Jaga Bandana, Bandi Tomay.*
> *Niranjana Nara-Rupadhara Nirguna Gunamoy."*

Then, the *Narayani Stuti*:

> *"Sarva Mangala Mangalye Shive Sarvarthasadhike,*
> *Sharanye Trambake Gauri Narayani Namostute."*

After the evening *bhajan*:

> *"Joy Shri Guru Maharaj Ki Joy!*
> *Joy Mahamayi Ki Joy!*
> *Joy Swamiji Maharaj Ki Joy!"*

(Sri Ramakrishna is referred to as *Guru Maharaj* and Swami Vivekananda as *Swamiji* in the Ramakrishna Math and Mission Centres.)

The disciplined yet spiritually enriching atmosphere at the Vidyamandira cultivated a deep sense of purpose, shaping my life and academic endeavours. The unique traditions of the Vidyamandira and Belur Math instilled in us a sense of discipline, devotion and service. The influence of the revered monks and the structured routine provided a foundation that shaped our academic and spiritual lives. These experiences continue to inspire me, reinforcing the values of truth, service and unity in every aspect of life.

Shyama Sangeet by Pannalal Bhattacharya (1930–1966)

On some evenings, after the evening bhajan, a renowned singer arranged by Govinda Maharaj would perform a few devotional songs in the prayer hall. I remember, one evening the famous Shyama Sangeet singer Pannalal Bhattacharya performed a few Shyama Sangeet songs (composed in Bengali). He was from Bally, a town near Belur Math. I was fortunate to sit close to Sri Pannalal Bhattacharya and listen to his songs. He sang the following songs:

1. *"Amar Sadh Na Mitilo, Asha Na Purilo, Sakali Furaye Jaye Maa"*
2. *"Amar Mayer Payer Jaba Hoye Oth Na Phute Mon"*
3. *"Tui Naki Maa Doyamoyi"*
4. *"Sakali Tomari Ichchha, Ichchhamoyee Tara Tumi"*
5. *"Amay De Ma Pagol Kore"*
6. *"Muchhiye De Ma Amar E Duti Noyon"*

Visit of Other Luminaries

One evening during study hours, we had the opportunity to listen to a lecture by the famous economist of those days V.K.R.V. Rao in the hostel's prayer hall. At that time, he was the Vice-Chancellor of Delhi University. Later, he held distinguished positions, including being a member of the Planning Commission and the Education Minister of the Government of India.

Once, revolutionary Hemchandra Ghosh visited Vidyamandira on Independence Day and narrated several incidents of India's freedom struggle and shared some thrilling memories with the students.

For the annual sports event at the Vidyamandira, Principal Maharaj Swami Tejasananda would invite renowned athletes. The author remembers when he was an intermediate student, Mr. Pankaj Gupta, who was the then President

Some Fellow Students of the Intermediate College (1959-61)

of the Indian Olympic Association, visited the college on the Sports Day and was present as the Chief Guest.

Hostel Life

After the evening bhajan, study hours began immediately. At 9 PM, the dinner bell rang. The quality of all meals was excellent. On Thursdays, the entire day's food was vegetarian but included delightful items like jackfruit curry (enchorh), banana blossom curry (mocha), and *payesh* (rice pudding). On Wednesdays and Sundays, the dinner included mutton curry. During dinner, students used to serve food turn by turn.

Before starting principal meals (lunch/dinner), following the practice at all Ramakrishna Math/Mission centres, all the students together had to recite the following mantra (prayer), which is a sloka from Srimad Bhagvad Gita:

"Om Brahmarpanam Brahma Havir Brahmagnau Brahmanaahutam,
Brahmaiva Tena Gantyavyam Brahma Karma Samadhina."

—Hari Om Tatsat

Meaning: The act of offering is Brahma, the oblation is Brahma. By Brahma it is offered into the Fire of Brahma. Brahma is that which is to be attained by him, who performs pertaining to Brahma.

Brief explanation: For those who are completely absorbed in God-consciousness, the oblation is Brahman, the ladle with which it is offered is Brahman, the act of offering is Brahman, and the sacrificial fire is also Brahman. Such persons, who view everything as God, easily attain Him.

At the end of taking the food (before leaving the seat), together we used to pronounce,

"Jai Shri Guru Maharaj Ji ki Jai!
Jai Mahamayi ki Jai!
Jai Swamiji Maharaj Ji ki Jai!
Jai Ganga Mayi ki Jai!'

("Guru Maharaj" refers to Lord Shri Ramakrishna, "Mahamaya" refers to Holy Mother Sri Sarada Devi, "Swamiji Maharaj" refers to Swami Vivekananda and "Ganga Mayi" means River Ganga).

After dinner, various programmes were held in the common room of each hostel separately on different days, including antakshari competitions, literary discussions, scientific discussions, word-making competitions, quiz competitions, group discussions, impromptu speech competitions, debates, etc. The emphasis on cleanliness, orderliness, punctuality, and harmony with others, which are essential qualities for a healthy life style deserves special mention. Every week, evaluations were made, and a list of rooms graded as 'A,' 'B,' or 'C' was posted on the notice board. Needless to say, this system significantly helped the residents for their upliftment in the future.

Memorable Visit to Swami Vivekananda's Ancestral Home

In the early days of the author's time at Vidyamandira in 1959, Govinda Maharaj took a few of us to Swami Vivekananda's ancestral home on Simla Street in Kolkata (now a branch of the Ramakrishna Mission). At that time, Swami Vivekananda's younger brother Bhupendranath Dutta (4.9.1880–25.12.1961) was still alive. Hence, we were fortunate to meet the younger brother of a rare personality like Swami Vivekananda. He was a bachelor and lived in their ancestral home, which was then in a state of disrepair as the Ramakrishna Mission had not yet acquired it. As Swami Vivekananda had passed away at the age of 39 on July 4, 1902, we felt a profound connection to him through our meeting with his younger brother. For this reason, we felt highly fortunate to meet Bhupendranath and hear his voice, giving us a glimpse of Swami Vivekananda's charismatic personality. The author remembers, when we visited, Bhupendranath was lying on a bed. We sat around him, and he continuously spoke about Swamiji. He signed and wrote blessings in the notebooks of a few of us. Unfortunately, the notebook was lost subsequently.

Volunteering Service at Belur Math

On the birthdays Sri Ramakrishna, Sri Sarada Devi, Swami Vivekananda, and Swami Brahmananda, some of us used to serve as volunteers at Belur Math to manage the crowd near the temples and Math premises, serve *prasad*, and ensure discipline. Since the author knew the monastic names of many monks, he was most of the times entrusted with the responsibility of distributing invitation letters to the monks for various events at the Vidyamandira.

With the inspiration of the hostel superintendent Swami Gokulananda, some of us occasionally took part in Durga Puja and Kali Puja held at the *Natmandira* of Sri Ramakrishna Temple of Belur Math. Durgapuja being held according to Vedic rules and customs, used to be performed by a Brahmacharin, but the role of *Tantradharak* used to be played by a senior sannyasin. Most of the time Swami Dhyanatmananda from R.K. Mission, Belgharia used to be seen as *Tantradharak*. Some of us had the opportunity of being present during Shivaratri Puja, which also used to be held at the said *Natmandira*. One attraction of the Shivaratri festival at Belur Math was '*Shiva Nritya*', performed by a sadhu at the end of Puja in all the four '*praharas*'. However, a divine environment used to prevail during the Shiva Nritya, which used to be very much enjoyed by the devotees present.

Literary Pursuits

Each hostel maintained beautifully curated wall magazines with pictures and writings, published monthly. Once, an article written by the author titled "The Heroic Monk Vivekananda" was published in a wall magazine. Additionally, the college magazine "Vidyamandira Patrika" was published annually. The various editions of the wall magazines and issues of the "Vidyamandira Patrika" demonstrated the creative writing abilities of the students on a variety of topics.

Transition to a Degree College

During 1959–61, the Intermediate programme (IA and ISC) at Calcutta University was in its final regular phase. In 1960, the Vidyamandira was transformed into a degree college, along with other colleges of Calcutta

University. From then on, the number of students and faculty members at the Vidyamandira (Belur College) increased significantly.

Faculty Members at the College

Mathematics Department

During the Intermediate period, there were only two mathematics faculties: Prof. Phanigopal Chatterjee and Prof. Ashwini Kumar Lahiri. Phani Babu would often tell humorous stories to entertain the students during his lectures. One day, while teaching, the bell rang. He said, "Today, we don't have time for a roll call. If you're absent, please stand up." If he caught two students talking during class, he would say, "I'll send you out of the class." Sometimes he would say, "See me after the period, when the class is over." Once, he scolded a student for failing to solve a mathematics problem. Another student mentioned, "Sir, he was first in our batch in the school final." Phani Babu retorted, "I've seen so many first boys that my eyes are rotten. Don't show me any more first boys." The funniest thing he would say was, "In my time, I was the second in the first-class in M.Sc. final. But the one who was first is no longer alive, so now I am the first-class first in our batch." The entire class would burst into laughter on hearing such faulty sentences. Of course, he used to say such things to make us laugh.

In contrast, the other Mathematics faculty, Prof. Ashwini Kumar Lahiri had a very grave personality. His age seemed to be between 60 and 70 years. He was the Principal of Mymensingh College in the then East Pakistan. He used to speak in the *Bangal* dialect with Mymensingh accent, even in the class-room while teaching. He used to teach Algebra in the first year and Statics in the second year of Intermediate.

After the Vidyamandira switched over to a degree college, a few more faculty members joined the Mathematics department—Amiya Bhushan Roy, Pranranjan Sengupta, Sachindra Nath Baksi, Hrishikesh Sen, and Dhirendra Nath Sarkhel. They were all excellent teachers and very affectionate towards the author. Each of them used to take special care for him. Much later, the author occasionally used to talk to Professor Baksi on the phone and receive his blessings until he expired on 26th January 2025. We also had two more Mathematics Professors for a short period—Dr. Samir Ranjan Majumdar (who later became a Professor at the University of Calgary, Canada) and Dr. Rabindranath Chatterjee (who subsequently became the

Dean of Science at Visva-Bharati University). Dr. Amiya Bhushan Roy later became a Professor at Jadavpur University, Dr. Dhirendra Nath Sarkhel and Dr. Pranranjan Sengupta both became faculty members at Kalyani University, and Dr. Hrishikesh Sen held a faculty position at Burdwan University. They all helped the author a lot during his undergraduate studies at the Vidyamandira.

Bengali Department

During the Intermediate phase at Belur College, we had two Professors of Bengali language and literature: Professor Shital Prasad Bhattacharya and Professor Pulin Das. Professor Das was very precise in his lectures and never went outside the context. But Professor Bhattacharya would tell engaging stories during his lectures. One day, he said, "Do you know how busy people are nowadays? A gentleman was travelling on a bus, occupying a seat. His friend boarded the bus after him. The first friend asked, 'How are you?' The second friend replied, "I'm going through a very tough time. My father passed away two months ago, and after having long illness, my mother died 15 days ago. Now I'm in great distress. ..." The first friend said, "That's great, great!" Prof. Bhattacharya then asserted that people are so busy nowadays that they assume their friend is saying "I'm fine". Without even listening to the reply, they often give the second response. Later, Shital Babu became the Principal of a College in the Medinipur district, and Pulin Babu joined as a Professor at Contai Prabhat Kumar College.

English Department

The memories of several Professors from the English department remain vivid in the author's mind—Professors Sudhamoy Ganguly, Chittaranjan Maitra, Sunanda Sanyal, and Aravinda Poddar. Professor Ganguly would start almost every class with the assertion, "Write less, get more; write more, get less." He warned us that writing more in examinations would result in fewer marks, while writing less would yield more marks. Another famous quote of his was, "Common sense is a sense which is uncommon to a common man." Professor Maitra was a simple man with a simple mind but somewhat absent-minded. His teaching of English poetry and the rhetoric and prosody of the English language was quite entertaining to the students. Professor Aravinda Poddar's Bengali book 'Bankim Manas' was held with high esteem. He was also popular as a Professor of English. We enjoyed quite a bit on Professor Sunanda Sanyal's teaching as well.

Chemistry Department

In the Chemistry Department, Professor Priyanath Chakraborty and Professor Jagjiban Ray were excellent teachers. Another chemistry Professor, K.M. Sen, seemed somewhat frail due to his age, but his teaching was very engaging. He would demonstrate some chemistry experiments in the classroom itself with great enthusiasm. For example, when hydrogen gas combines with oxygen to produce water with a loud sound, he would humorously say that hydrogen and oxygen got married and celebrated with fireworks.

Physics Department

Physics professors Santosh Kumar Sengupta and Neelkamal Dutta were very proficient in their teaching. Professors Gouranga Chakraborty and Jagadish Chandra Pal were straightforward and simple by nature.

Biology Department

During I.Sc, the author's fourth subject (additional) was biology. Botany Professor Atin Basu would flawlessly utter the Latin names of various plants, which amazed the students. Zoology Professor Sudeb Bhusan Ghosh taught various topics in an engaging manner. The author still remembers the practical classes involving the dissection of frogs, guinea pigs and plant stems and examining them under microscope in the biology laboratory. Second-year student Ajitda (Maiti), the son of lawyer Kartik Maiti from Contai, gave the author his biology book (written by Mukherjee & Mukherjee) and biology box. Ajit Da later studied Medicine and subsequently became a famous cardiologist.

Vision of Swami Tejasananda and the Glory of the Vidyamandira

On July 4, 1941, "Ramakrishna Mission Vidyamandira" was established near Belur Math. As mentioned previously, this fully residential college was modelled following the concept of the ancient Gurukul system of India, as envisioned by no other than Swami Vivekananda, who himself selected the name "Vidyamandira" in 1898 and indicated to his spiritual brothers, where this great institution should be established.

Swami Tejasananda (1896–1971) was the founder Principal of the Vidyamandira. This institution is a significant constituent of the Ramakrishna Mission Saradapitha, adjacent to Belur Math. At the time of Vidyamandira's establishment, Swami Vimuktananda (Upen Maharaj) was the Secretary of the Saradapitha, making him the founder secretary of the Vidyamandira. Swami Tejasananda and Swami Vimuktananda worked together from the very inception of Vidyamandira to advance this sacred institution with a steady progress. We saw Vimuktanandaji as a truly free-spirited, ever smiling, and hardworking individual. During the construction of new buildings, he personally supervised the work in bright sunshine, by holding an umbrella in hand.

Following Swami Vivekananda's ideology, Swami Tejasananda and the authorities of the Vidyamandira strived tirelessly to produce good citizens for our motherland, not merely academically proficient youth. To achieve this goal, they followed the path shown by Swami Vivekananda to ensure the balanced development of body, mind, and intellect. The selfless efforts of the ever-dedicated monk, Swami Tejasananda, and the monastic superintendents of the hostels made this possible. This tradition continues to this date.

Swami Tejasananda's Tireless Efforts

Mention may be made of a few incidents about the Principal, Swami Tejasananda, which will give an insight into how he worked tirelessly, day and night, to elevate the Vidyamandira to its peak of glory within just a few years of its journey. He succeeded in establishing it as an institution providing the "man-making education" as per the dream of Swami Vivekananda. Of course, the journey of the Vidyamandira was not always smooth; there were many ups and downs, but this self-sacrificing monk nurtured Vidyamandira with all his might. He fostered the institution with maternal affection and love.

In those days, there was no College Service Commission (C.S.C.), so the college authorities could appoint teachers on their own. Swami Tejasananda, after talking for a while, could understand who among the candidates was the most qualified and most suitable to be a teacher at the Vidyamandira. He possessed keen intuitive power. Besides, being a residential college and an institution for man-making education, Maharaj could easily detect the most suitable candidate. The Mission authorities always accepted his chosen person without any hesitation.

He would identify some students during their student days as future teachers. Immediately after they completed their M.A./M.Sc., he would call them and appoint them as teachers at Belur College. Many of these teachers, with a spirit of service, helped advance Vidyamandira as an ideal seat of learning.

Attracted by the ideals of Sri Ramakrishna and Swami Vivekananda as well as the towering personality of Swami Tejasananda, many distinguished Professors continued to teach selflessly at the Vidyamandira for long periods even after retirement.

His Daily Routine and Discipline

Every moment of his day, from waking up early in the morning to going to bed at night, was bound by a strict routine. He tried to spend as much time as possible with the students. It is heard that in the early days of Vidyamandira, he himself would ring the bell early in the morning to wake up the students. He would wake up before everyone else. He would ensure that all students turned off their lights and went to sleep after the designated time. Although several others were responsible for supervision, Tejasanandaji himself kept an eye on whether everyone was following the routine.

During morning and evening prayers, Swami Tejasananda would be the first to enter the prayer hall. He would sit in the front but look back to see if all the students were present for the prayer. If there was any announcement to be made, immediately after the prayer, he would make it himself. He was never busy with any other task during prayer time.

In physical exercise, too, he would be present in the gymnasium, demonstrating various exercises to the students so that they could perform them correctly. His presence on the playground and encouragement would change the atmosphere of the games. Sometimes, he would arm wrestle with the students, treating them as friends at that point of time.

Apart from university-specified studies, he encouraged students to engage in various extracurricular activities like recitation, drama, and debate. He taught recitation in Bengali, English, and Sanskrit. Many who learned recitation from this monk later gained fame as reciters. Some became famous actors after learning acting from him. He considered acting an "art." Along with studies, the seeds of debate, mock parliament, essay reading, and delivering speeches that he sowed in Vidyamandira's students made the alumni quite popular in their workplaces at a later stage. To outsiders, students, and colleagues, he might have seemed strict, but after spending some time with him, one would be able to realize his inner softness. Sometimes, he would scold someone harshly by mistake. But as soon as he would realized his own mistake, he would feel repentant.

A Testament to His Affection

Once, the son of the music teacher Sri Bireswar Chakraborty, Siddheshwar Da, who studied at the Vidyamandira from 1958 to 1960 (one year senior to the author in Intermediate), performed poorly in a college examination. His father went to his room in the hostel and slapped him hard, making Siddheshwar Da weep a lot. When Tejasanandaji heard about this incident, he called Bireswar Babu and told him that it was not right for him to hit his son on the college campus. He reminded him that as long as the students were at the Vidyamandira, they are to be considered as sons of the Principal Maharaj. Such was the paternal affection of the self-less monk Swami Tejasananda! His life was molded by the ideals of Swami Vivekananda. He never considered any task inferior. If a worker was absent, he would hang the volleyball net himself. He even marked the football field's boundaries with lime powder. There were times when he stayed up all night by a sick student's bedside, applying cold compresses to his forehead. He had an indomitable enthusiasm and remarkable dedication for every task. To ensure the "all-round development" of Vidyamandira's students according to Swami Vivekananda's ideals, he used to personally demonstrate various tasks. Observing his working style, one could clearly realize how deeply he cared for this rare institution.

Even after retiring from college, he was seen in a wheelchair, going around the hostels and the college, inquiring about possible difficulties and giving necessary advice. It was only natural, as he had nurtured the Vidyamandira with paternal affection from its very inception.

The Everlasting Legacy

The tremendous success of the Vidyamandira and its worldwide fame today are primarily due to Swami Tejasanandaji's unparalleled efforts. Alongside him, significant contributions were made by Swami Vimuktanandaji and the subsequent Secretaries of Saradapith, as well as Tejasanandaji's successors as Principals and Vice-Principals. The hostel wardens and assistant wardens also played a crucial role. The dedicated service of Vidyamandira's Professors and their affection towards the great institution have undoubtedly been instrumental in the Vidyamandira's towering success.

Later, when the author visited Belur Math, he had the opportunity to meet some of the subsequent principals and hostel wardens of Vidyamandira. At this moment, various memories of the Vidyamandira are crowding the mind of the author.

A Bright Memory

By the grace of Sri Ramakrishna, the author received the Ram Mohan Award in 2004 for 'outstanding contributions to the field of Mathematics'. At that time, he was a Professor in the Mathematics Department at IIT Kharagpur. The then Principal of the Vidyamandira, Swami Atmapriyananda, informed him that the Vidyamandira would hold a felicitation in his honor. He was invited to attend the ceremony with his wife, and arrangements were made for them for stay at the Guest House of Belur Math. The author felt very happy to get this additional opportunity to visit Belur Math. On the designated day, the author went to Vidyamandira with his wife. Many alumni of Vidyamandira were present at the felicitation ceremony. In addition to other items, the author was presented with several books as gifts. Shortly before this event, the book entitled '*Mathematics and Mathematicians at IIT Kharagpur*', edited by the author had been published by the renowned publisher Allied Publishers of New Delhi. On the occasion of IIT Kharagpur's Golden Jubilee, the author had published a mathematical series of books on behalf of the Mathematics Department through various well-known publishing houses in India and abroad like World Scientific, Singapore and Narosa, New Delhi, etc. The above-mentioned book was one of them.

At that time, revered Srimat Swami Ranganathananda Maharaj was the President of Ramakrishna Math and Ramakrishna Mission. Since he was very enthusiastic about education, I visited Belur Math with my wife the day after the felicitation to seek Swami Ranganathananda's blessings. After doing Pranama at the temples of Thakur, Ma, and Swamiji, we went to offer a copy of the above-titled book to revered President Maharaj at 11 o'clock. However, his secretary informed them that they could meet the President Maharaj in the evening. I requested the secretary to hand over the said book to President Maharaj. Later that day, at the appointed time, we went to pay our respect to Swami Ranganathananda. First, we met the then Manager of Belur Math (later one of the Vice-Presidents), Swami Prameyananda (Ramgopal Maharaj). When we offered our respect to him, he informed them that Swami Ranganathananda had already read the book and had shown it to him with great delight.

At the appointed time, when I and my wife stood in line to meet Maharaj, he called me closer. This was far beyond my expectation. With a divine smile, Maharaj placed both the hands on the author's head in a gesture of blessing, filling him with a profound sense of joy. I felt as if my life had been blessed by the divine touch of the Sangha Guru. Such incidents are very scarce. I realized that the Maharaj had been very pleased by reading the book. It was a moment of unparalleled spiritual fulfillment affirming that all my efforts had been worthwhile.

It may be reiterated that the legacy of the Vidyamandira remains intertwined with the dedication of its mentors and the success of its students, continuing to shine as a beacon of knowledge and values, just as Swami Vivekananda envisioned.

Swami Ranganathananda (1908–2005): Life and Contributions

Srimat Swami Ranganathananda Maharaj was the thirteenth President of the Ramakrishna Math and Ramakrishna Mission. Renowned for his extraordinary intelligence and memory, he was a profound scholar of Hindu scriptures and Puranic literatures. His deep interest extended to the study of texts of other religions which he approached with great attention and respect. Known for his humility and amiability, he never sought personal recognition.

Swami Ranganathananda Ji

Between 1956 and 1972, he travelled to various countries around the world over fifty times as an ambassador of religion and Indian culture, delivering lectures. These countries included nations in North and South America, Asia, Europe, and Africa. He even lectured on Vedanta and Ramakrishna-Vivekananda in then- communist countries like the Soviet Union, Poland, and Czechoslovakia. The Indian government sponsored most of his lecture tours. He could deliver lectures proficiently in many languages. He played a pioneering role in opening many new branch centers of the Ramakrishna Math and Mission. The author first had the fortune of listening to Swami Ranganathananda's inspiring and informative lecture when he was an intermediate student at the Vidyamandira. At that young age, he was deeply moved by Maharaj's lecture. In 2000, the Indian government selected Maharaj for the Padma Vibhushan award. However, since the award was intended for him personally and not for the Ramakrishna Mission, he declined it. However, he did accept the Indira Gandhi Award for National Integration in 1987 and the Gandhi Peace Prize in 1999, as both of them were awarded in the name of the Ramakrishna Mission. He was the author of over fifty valuable books, with notable titles including "Eternal Values for a Changing Society" and "Science and Religion."

Other Recognition Received by the Author from the Vidyamandira

In 2020, Stanford University in the USA published a list of the world's top 2% scientists, which included the author's name. Seeing this list on the internet, the authorities of the Vidyamandira were very pleased and published on the college notice board detailing his various achievements in the field of education and research, a copy of which was sent to the author. Vidyamandira's Principal, Swami Mahaprajñananda (Devarsi Maharaj), personally conveyed his congratulations. At that time, he was the the Vice-Principal of Vidyamandira.

In December of that year, the Vidyamandira authorities sent to the author an appointment letter, designating him as an 'Honourary Visiting Faculty' in the Mathematics Department of the Vidyamandira, an honour that held great significance for him as an alumnus.

The Legacy of the Vidyamandira Alumni

Over the years, alumni of the Vidyamandira have held distinguished positions in various fields. Many have become eminent doctors, engineers, administrators, and academicians, while others have chosen the path of renunciation, dedicating their lives to the Ramakrishna Order. Swami Suhitananda Maharaj, the former General Secretary and current Vice President of the Ramakrishna Math and Mission, is one such illustrious alumnus.

One of our class-mates of B.Sc., Saroj Bandhu became a sannyasi of Belur Math. His sannyas name was Swami Bhaktirupananda. For several years he was the headmaster of Ramakrishna Mission Vidyabhawan, a reputed higher secondary school at Midnapore.

Several of the author's juniors from the Vidyamandira have taken up significant responsibilities of the Order. Swami Medhasananda (Gananath Maharaj), a former Principal of the Vidyamandira, later became the head of the Vedanta Society of Japan. Swami Shantarupananda (Biswanath Maharaj) served as the Principal of the Vidyamandira before leading the Vedanta Society in Portland, USA. He was so affectionate to the author that he sent gifts from USA to the author, a couple of times as a token of their divine affection/respect towards each other.

Swami Devarajananda (Haranath Maharaj), who was three years junior to the author served as the Principal of the Brahmachari Training Center at Belur Math and as the head of various branches of the Ramakrishna Mission.

Currently, he holds the significant responsibility of Joint Convenor of the Ramakrishna-Vivekananda *Bhav Prachar* Committee across India. The talented singer of devotional songs, Swami Sarvagananda, is also an alumnus of the Vidyamandira. Senior monks like Swami Divyananda, Swami Vimalatmananda (Tapas Maharaj), and Swami Animeshananda have been involved in significant roles within the Ramakrishna Math and Mission after completing their studies at the Vidyamandira. Swami Divyananda (Amal Maharaj) was the author's junior in the Vidyamandira family. He has served as the Vice-Principal of the Vidyamandira, the Principal of Vivekananda Centenary College, Rahara and the Secretary of Ramakrishna Mission branch centers at Agartala and Malda, as well as the Secretary of the Ramakrishna Mission Saradapitha. Currently, he is one of the Vice-Presidents of Belur Math.

The author cherishes the five formative years (1959–1964) he spent at the Vidyamandira, which provided him with the company of many revered monks of the Ramakrishna Math and Mission. These experiences shaped his life, instilling in him a deep sense of devotion and discipline.

Further Experience at Vidyamandira

As already mentioned, since the author had the fortune of being a student at the Vidyamandira for a long period of five years, he had the opportunity to get the company of many senior monks of the Ramakrishna Math and Mission. Whenever they visited Belur Math from other branch centers, he got a chance to be in touch with them, often with the help of revered Govinda Maharaj. He also had the opportunity to interact with the monks from the Ramakrishna Mission Vedanta Centres abroad when they visited Belur Math. This is how he met Swami Prabhavananda, the head of the Vedanta Society in Hollywood, USA, who was blessed by Sri Sarada Devi and a disciple of Swami Brahmananda. He shared insights about the activities of Vedanta Societies abroad to the students of the Vidyamandira.

The author also had an opportunity to listen to a lecture by Swami Nikhilananda (1895–1973), who was the founder of the Ramakrishna-Vivekananda Center in New York City, USA, and a disciple of Sri Sri Ma Sarada Devi. He translated Mahendranath Gupta's Sri Sri Ramakrishna Kathamrita into English, which was published as "The Gospel of Sri Ramakrishna." This book was considered one of the 100 most important religious books of the 20th century in America.

From time to time, Swami Chandikananda would sing various devotional songs for the students of the Vidyamandira when he used to stay at Belur Math. Most of these songs were his own compositions. He wrote many songs about Thakur, Ma, and Swamiji, which were very popular among the devotees of the Ramakrishna Order. Many of these songs can be found in the book "Prarthana O Sangeet" compiled by Swami Tejasananda and published by Ramakrishna Mission Saradapith. He also translated many devotional songs into Khasi language. Through these songs, he was able to spread the ideas of Sri Ramakrishna, Sri Ma Sarada Devi, and Swami Vivekananda among the Khasi community.

Physical Education

Our physical education teacher was Mr. Bimal Das. Under his supervision, we practiced PT in the morning and perform exercises in the evening. As mentioned earlier, most of the time, Principal Swami Tejasananda Maharaj used to remain present in order to ensure that these activities were taken seriously by the students. He often attended the football and volleyball matches, and to encourage the boys, he would sometimes join them in the games, rolling up his garments. He was, as if, meditating on the all-around development of the Vidyamandira. On Sunday mornings and Wednesday afternoons, the students used to have NCC. Occasionally, all the students of the hostel would go on excursions to nearby places of interest. Various competitions were held annually at the college level—carrom, table tennis, high jump, long jump, and games like football and volleyball. Besides these, there were competitions in drawing, music, drama, and recitation.

Recitation

The Principal Maharaj himself directed all these activities. He personally taught recitation in Sanskrit, Bengali, and English. For Sanskrit recitations, he usually selected verses from Sri Sri Chandi. During that time, the author had the opportunity to learn the recitation of the Chandi with proper pronunciation from Swami Tejasananda.

Swami Gokulananda advised the author to chant one chapter of the Srimad Bhagavad Gita every day. Consequently, the author could memorize many chapters of the Gita during that time. Swami Gokulananda would occasionally read out special parts of other scriptures to the students.

Other Proficiencies of Vidyamandira Students

Renowned reciter Pradeep Da (Ghosh) passed away some time ago. He was a year senior to the author in the Intermediate. We used to see him as a rising star. Swarup Da (Dutta) later gained fame as a film actor. While studying at the Vidyamandira, he used to be a very good table tennis player and showed great skill in presenting his arguments in debates in flawless English. Our classmate, Tapan Saha Mandal was also good at debating.

Influences and Teachings

While studying at the Vidyamandira, a Professor of English, Arun Maharaj once mentioned a teaching of Lord Buddha, which is still vivid in the author's memory. It is very beneficial in mutual dealings within society and is mentioned here for that reason. If someone, in a fit of anger, speaks offensive words to another, but the second person remains silent and undisturbed, then those words return to the first person. The author believes this has a scientific basis.

Most of the students from our Intermediate batch passed IA/ISc and left the Vidyamandira for higher education elsewhere. Three students—Kamalesh (Bhowmik), Nimai, and the author—stayed on to study the three-year degree course at the Vidyamandira. Kamalesh enrolled in Physics Honours. Since the author had good marks in all subjects in ISc—Physics, Chemistry, Mathematics, and Biology—he could have taken Honours in any subject. Principal Swami Tejasananda asked him, "Which subject will you take Honours in?" When he remained silent, Maharaj asked, "How much marks did you get in each subject?" As the author had letter marks in Mathematics (more than 80%), Maharaj said, "Take Honours in Mathematics." After that, the author did not think of anything else and pursued higher studies in Mathematics. It is worth mentioning that in those days, most science students opted for Physics Honours, and some for Chemistry Honours. At that time, job opportunities in Mathematics were relatively less. Besides, the results of Mathematics Honours students at Calcutta University were usually not very impressive. Influenced by these notions, very few were interested in pursuing Mathematics Honours. In the first year of the three-year degree course, the author had many new classmates, some of whom had passed ISc from other colleges, while the rest had passed Higher Secondary and joined the Vidyamandira for the degree course. During the long five years (1959–1964) at the Vidyamandira, many of them remain fresh in the author's memory.

Swami Jagadishwarananda

Swami Jagadishwarananda was a renowned senior monk of the Ramakrishna Math and Mission. He took sannyasa from Srimat Swami Shivananda (Mahapurush Maharaj), the second President of the Ramakrishna Math and Mission. He was born in Chhota Udaypur village (near Argoal) under Patashpur police station in the East Midnapore district. His pre-monastic name was Bhuvan Mohan. His father's name was Chhaku Mohan Maiti and mother was Sitamoni Devi. He translated the Srimad Bhagavad Gita and Sri Sri Chandi into Bengali. These two books have been highly appreciated in Bengali society and are very suitable for daily use for chanting.

In his later years, for some reason completely unknown to the author, he broke off his ties with the Ramakrishna Mission and established a separate ashrama named *Ramakrishna Dharma Chakra.* This ashrama was established at a place near the bank of the Ganges in Belur. After establishing this new ashrama, he performed the very popular Ramayana songs of Belur Math, "*Shuddha Brahmaparātpara Rām, Kālātmakaparamēśvara Rām,...*" in various places to perhaps raise some funds for the new ashrama. When he performed the Ramayana songs at Pratapdighi, the author was in the ninth grade at Tikrapara High School. He went to attend that event with his father. He remembers, Swami Jagadishwarananda's very melodious singing of the Ramayana songs. He had vast erudition and was skilled in oratory and storytelling. While he was a student at the Vidyamandira, the author once visited the *Ramakrishna Dharma Chakra* in Belur and met him. The author recalls that Swami Jagadishwarananda was very pleased to see him and gifted him a few of his books, including *Bina Chashmay Ksheen Drishtir Pratikar* (Treatment of Poor Vision without spectacles) and *Sahaj Yougik Byayam* (Simple Yougik Exercises). The musical event, referred to above was organized and managed by Sri Barenda Patra.

Self-Analysis Chart for Self-Improvement

During student life, as per the advice of revered Govinda Maharaj, the author used to maintain a Self Analysis Chart every night before going to bed. He himself used to award for each of the items—speaking the truth for the whole day, not hurting anyone's feelings, focusing on studies, self-restraint, yoga practice, and japam & meditation, etc. The aim was to ensure that the score in various items was higher than that on the previous day. This method is very suitable for transforming oneself into an ideal person. *Maintaining a Self-analysis chart on a regular basis is a very effective method for self-improvement.*

The author still remembers that on Govinda Maharaj's table at his office, there was a framed quote: "Preetih Parama Sadhanam"—which suggests that love is the highest spiritual practice. This philosophy guided his interactions with others, fostering an attitude of kindness and service that remained with him throughout his life. According to the perception of the author, that quote suggests that 'Love' is the best among various kinds of spiritual practices which can lead to perfection. Maintaining loving relationships with everyone was considered the highest penance. This quote left a significant impression in the author's mind. He used to make sincere attempts to avoid harbouring any ill will towards anyone, refrained from harming anyone as far as possible and helping others as much as it was possible. By the grace of Sri Ramakrishna and Ma Sarada Devi, this attitude has made a permanent place in the author's mind, since those days.

Daily Routine and Spiritual Practices

Every day, the author practised free hand exercises and some yoga postures, including 15–20 push-ups (Don), 50–100 squats (Baithak), *Padmasana, Sarvangasana, Matsyasana, Gomukhasana, Gorakshasana,* and *Shirshasana.* After each posture, he would rest in *Shavasana* for 2–3 minutes. Usually, he used to perform these practices in the evening after returning from the college, sometimes in the morning before breakfast. After morning prayer, he would walk to Belur Math, pay respect and do *pranama* at the temples of Lord Ramakrishna, Sri Sri Sarada Devi, Swami Vivekananda and Swami Brahmananda, and then do meditation for a while in the old shrine at Belur Math before returning to the hostel. His mind would then be filled with divine joy. Since at that time, the then President Srimat Swami Shankarananda Maharaj resided in the room next to Swamiji's bedroom, he would mentally offer respect to him as well.

Pilgrimages and Notable Associations

We visited various pilgrimage sites with revered Govinda Maharaj, such as Swami Vivekananda's birthplace (Simla, Kolkata), Ramakrishna Mahasamadhi Smashan at Cossipore, Baranagar Monastery, the Hanseswari Temple in Bansberia (Adi Saptagram), the birthplace of Swami Brahmananda in Shikrakulin gram, the birthplace of Swami Shivananda in Barasat, and the birthplace of Swami Premananda (Baburam Maharaj) in Antpur. Additionally, we visited Puri, Kashi, and some other places.

Swami Premeshananda (1884–1967)

Srimat Swami Premeshananda Ji

Swami Premeshananda (popularly called Premesh Maharaj) was a highly respected monk of the Ramakrishna Math and Mission. He was an initiated disciple of the Holy Mother Sarada Devi. He possessed an outstanding capability to motivate/encourage many people, men and women, householders and monastics, to lead lives dedicated to spirituality and service. His letters, full of mind-opening deep spiritual ideas, present a picture of a man of great spiritual realization and also a unique angle of vision on the Ramakrishna movement.

We visited the Sargachhi Ashrama of the Ramakrishna Mission in Murshidabad district several times. Swami Premeshananda Maharaj (pre-monastic name Indradayal Bhattacharya), a disciple of Sri Sri Ma Sarada Devi was residing there those days. Known for his deep spiritual wisdom, Swami Premeshananda was revered as an enlightened monk. His book *Atmavikash*, proved invaluable in guiding students toward self-development. *Atmavikash* (Manefestation of the self) is very helpful for the overall development of students. The author was fortunate to receive immense affection from revered Premeshananda Maharaj, who used to call him *Puruta* (priest), possibly because he was born in a Brahmin family, was trying to lead a disciplined life and had inclination towards performing Puja and meditation. He gave the author a lot of advice for leading a virtuous life. At that time, respected Sanatanda (Swami Suhitananda, who is now one of the Vice Presidents of the Ramakrishna Math and Mission) was a sevak of Premesh Maharaj. He had not formally joined the Ramakrishna Order at that time but was living a life of a renunciant.

Upon hearing that the author practiced yoga, revered Premesh Maharaj said, "Then I will tell Sanatan also to practice yoga every day."

Many of the songs composed by Swami Premeshananda evoke deep spiritual feelings in the hearts of devotees. Many young students have joined the Ramakrishna Mission as monks after coming into his contact. Even those who have not renounced the world have led exemplary household lives. Premeshananda Maharaj probably had some issues with his vocal cords, so he always spoke very softly in a very low voice. At that time, Swami Sukhadananda was the head of the Sargachhi Ramakrishna Mission, and his assistant was Swami

Anamayananda. The headmaster of the Mission-run high school at Sargachhi was respected Ranen Maharaj (later known as Swami Shivamayananda).

Pointed Gourd (also called parwal) and other vegetables were grown in the fields of the Sargachhi Ashram, and we greatly enjoyed the taste of fresh parwal.

Many incidents from that time have recently been published by Swami Suhitananda Maharaj in his series of articles *'Sadhusanga'* in the Udbodhan magazine.

Achievement of Contemporary Students of the Vidyamandira

Many of those who studied at the Vidyamandira from 1959–64 have become renowned in their respective fields. Ajitda (Maiti) became a famous cardiologist, serving as a doctor at SSKM Medical College and Hospital. He used to attend former Chief Minister Jyoti Basu. Uday Da (Chattopadhyay) and Bimlendu Da (Shashmal) were Professors in the Metallurgical Engineering Department at IIT Kharagpur. When the author joined the Mathematics Department at IIT, he met them, and a close friendship developed with them. Dhiman (Ganguly), the author's classmate at the Vidyamandira, later became a renowned pulmonologist (Chest Specialist, MD (Cal), MRCP (UK)). Our Intermediate classmate Chandranath De later became the General Manager of Howrah Motors Company. Chandranath possessed a very generous nature but unfortunately passed away at a young age. Chandrakanta Ghosh and Sabyasachi Sarkar, contemporaries from the Vidyamandira, both passed Chemistry (Hons) and later obtained their M.Sc. degrees from Calcutta University's Pure Chemistry Department. Chandrakanta Ghosh later became a Professor & Head of that department, while Sabyasachi Sarkar became a Professor & Head of the Chemistry Department at IIT Kanpur and received the Humboldt Fellowship. Haradas Bandyopadhyay, who completed his Physics (Hons) at the Vidyamandira, later became a Professor in the Material Science Department at IIT Kharagpur.

Impact of the Vidyamandira on the Author's Life

During his student years, the author received immense affection from his teachers and community members. His journey from Tikrapara High School to the Vidyamandira, and later into academic and spiritual life, was shaped by the guidance of eminent monks and educators. The principles he imbibed at the Vidyamandira continue to guide his life and professional pursuits.

The experiences, teachings, and associations from the Vidyamandira have played a crucial role in the author's intellectual, spiritual and personal growth, leaving a lasting impact on his journey.

Thus, the author's journey—from being a student of the Vidyamandira to becoming a recognized mathematician—has been deeply intertwined with the blessings and teachings of the Ramakrishna Math and Mission. The values he imbibed during those years have shaped his character, and the divine grace he received has been the most cherished treasure of his life.

Community Affection and Support

From his early school days at *Tikrapara High School*, the author was blessed with the love and affection of his teachers. This warmth extended beyond school, as the respected elders in his native *Bagmari-Pratapdighi* region held him in high affection/regards.

Upon passing his *School Final Examination* and securing admission to *Ramakrishna Mission Vidyamandira at Belur Math*, public admiration for him increased further. Several eminent individuals, like Sri Prasanna Kumar Tripathi (Saradabarh village), Sri Rakhal Chandra Sahu (Bagmari), Sri Kedar Chandra Das (Pratapdighi), Dr. Nripen Jana (Mathura), Sri Manoranjan Roy (Mechheda), Sri Krishnadas Roy (Bagmari), Sri Suresh Chandra Mitra (Kashimpore), Sri Bimal Nandy (Argoal) and Pandit Nilmani Goswami (Jabda) treated the author with great affection.

During his *summer and Durga Puja vacations*, whenever he visited home, Rakhal Babu would invite him for a feast and after serving him, would offer a small monetary gift as a token of appreciation. The author cherished those moments. Later, this tradition was continued by *Rakhal Babu's nephew, Ishwar babu (Rajendra Nath Sahu's son)*, and his two sons, *Parameshwar and Maheshwar.*

Recently, upon hearing about Parameshwar's illness, the author visited him at his house in Bagmari. Overwhelmed with emotion, Parameshwar said, "Jagadis Da, I have been very ill for several years, often bed ridden. But seeing you makes me feel completely healthy." His sincere joy deeply touched the author. Reflecting on this, the author felt immense gratitude for having been able to bring even a moment of happiness to him.

The love and affection extended by the people from a large area surrounding his native village remain deeply cherished memories for the author.

CHAPTER 4

Spiritual Initiation at Belur Math

Srimat Swami Shankarananda (9 March – 13 January 1962)

Srimat Swami Shankaranandaji Maharaj, 7th President of the Ramakrishna Math & Mission

Swami Shankarananda, the seventh President of the Ramakrishna Math and Mission was born on Tuesday, 9 March 1880 at his maternal uncle's house at Baje Pratappur in Hooghly district of West Bengal on the auspicious day of Shivaratri. In the pre-monastic life Swami Shankarananda's name was Amritalal Sengupta. His ancestral home was at Bamunmura in the district of 24 Parganas of West Bengal. His father Navinkrishna Sengupta was an engineer. Due to his posting at various places, Amritalal had to move about frequently with his parents.

During his student years at the Medical College, he had the privilege of attending the inspiring lectures of Swami Vivekananda and got the inspiration for a monastic life from his distantly related maternal uncle, in his pre-monastic life, Swami Sadananda, the first monastic disciple of Swami Vivekananda. As a child, Amritalal (alias Amulya) got an opportunity to have a glimpse of Swami Vivekananda after he returned from the West. From his very childhood, Amulya was very energetic, yet possessed a gentle disposition. His gentleness developed substantially in his monastic life. Amulya discontinued his studies and joined the Ramakrishna Math in the year 1902. In 1906, he got initiation from the first President of the Ramakrishna Math and Mission, Swami Brahmananda (Raja Maharaj) who is regarded as the spiritual son of Lord Sri Ramakrishna.

Raja Maharaj had developed great liking for the boy and fondly called him 'Amulya'. He moulded his life under the active guidance of Swami Brahmananda. Being a beloved disciple of Swami Brahmananda and his personal attendant for several years, Amulya Maharaj had the rare opportunity of living with Sri Sri Thakur's spiritual son and visiting with him various places of pilgrimage all over India as well as many centres of the Ramakrishna Math and Mission. Visits of Amulya Maharaj to various places in India with sister Nivedita and a visit to Japan with Swami Sadananda, helped him gather educational experiences related to culture, region and architecture. Later, he also visited China.

Since Swami Shankarananda had a sound knowledge of building construction, he could personally supervise the construction of Holy Mother temple and Swami Brahmananda temple at Belur Math and also Ramakrishna Math in Bhubaneswar (narrated briefly elsewhere in this book). Swami Shankarananda was well versed in *Puranic* literatures. He had the capacity to quote verses on specific points of spiritual practice. He was appointed as one of the Vice-Presidents of the Ramakrishna Math and Mission in 1947 and as the President on 19th June 1951. He was a very simple person and an embodiment of punctuality, self-reliance and austerity.

Swami Shankarananda was meditative by nature and took up spiritual discipline at several places, including Darjeeling, Bhubaneswar and Puri. (cf. rkmathharipada.org.our-centre/important-personalities)

An Important Day in the Author's Life

April 9, 1960, a Saturday, stands as one of the most significant day in the author's life. On this auspicious day, he received initiation (*mantra diksha*) from the seventh president of the Ramakrishna Math and Mission. Srimat Swami Shankaranandaji Maharaj (referred to as 'Maharaj' in the rest of this chapter) had ceased public appearances due to ill health for quite some time. However, at the beginning of 1960, he resumed meeting with the devotees. Before the evening aratrikam in the temple of Sri Ramakrishna, devotees and monks would line up to offer their respect and bow down to Maharaj. Along with a few students from the Vidyamandira, the author also had the privilege of paying respect to Maharaj almost every day.

Maharaj would sit solemnly near the door of his bedroom and the devotees would bow down in front of him (usually two at a time). One day, the author had the rare opportunity to hear him speak, when he was standing a few people behind Upuda Maharaj (Swami Yogishwarananda). The author witnessed a profound exchange that time. Maharaj, in his deep and solemn voice, called out, "Upuda, today!" Upuda responded, "Maharaj, I am your servant."

Without hesitation, Maharaj replied, "Upuda, I am also your servant." Upuda, with his characteristic gesture, nodded his head and kept repeating, "Maharaj, I am your servant, I am your servant." This display of humility and mutual respect between the two senior monks filled the hearts of all present with joy.

The Initiation Ceremony

Due to his frail health, Swami Shankaranandaji had stopped initiating disciples for a long time. However, he resumed the practice by initiating a few students from the Vidyamandira. The author was fortunate to be one of them.

On the above-mentioned date, the initiation seekers entered Maharaj's room (adjacent to Swami Vivekananda's bedroom) one by one and sat in a semicircle on the floor before him, each holding a plate of offerings. Maharaj sat on his bed, facing the east, with a small table in front of him holding a copper vessel, utensils, and a flower vase.

Maharaj gazed intently at each seeker before beginning the ritual. He instructed us to perform *achaman* (a purification ritual) with Ganges water provided by his attendant (*Sevaka*). He himself performed *achaman* and arranged offerings with *bel* leaves, sandalwood, *durva* grass, raw rice, and flowers, which he then offered several times. Among the flowers, the author recalls, there were some cannonball flowers (*Nagalingam*), *giloy* (Gulancha), and hibiscus.

Holding the flowers in his right hand and placing them in his left hand in *kurma mudra* (a sacred hand gesture), Maharaj, with closed eyes, offered the flowers into the copper vessel. We watched his divine meditative posture intently. Then, taking his *rudraksh mala* (rosary), he began to chant, his lips moved gently. He spent about 5 to 7 minutes in this absorbed state.

Teachings and Spiritual Guidance

After the initiation ceremony, Maharaj imparted profound spiritual wisdom. **He emphasized that God alone is the ultimate truth in this world, and the supreme purpose of human life is to realize Him.** The initiation is a means to attain this realization. Through initiation, the body and mind become pure and sanctified. The primary purpose of initiation is to surrender oneself at the lotus feet of the Lord. For spiritual practice and advancing towards God, one needs support; that unwavering support is the *Guru.*

Maharaj further elaborated that after wandering through 84 lakhs (8.4 million) life forms, one attains a human body, and it is only in this human form that one can realize God. Therefore, after having this rare human life if one does not strive for God-realization, the human life is a waste. After the initiation, Maharaj shared a verse from the *Hitopadesha* with us:

> *"Ajaramarabat prajna vidyamarthancha chintayet*
> *Grihita iba kesheshu mrityuna dharmam acharet."*

Explanation: Wise persons should study and earn wealth as if they are immortal. But when practicing dharma, they should act as if death is pulling them by the hair. This means one should remember that death can come at any moment. Hence, from a young age, one should strive for God-realization. However, while acquiring knowledge and wealth, thinking about death would deter one from enthusiasm. Thus, during such pursuits, people should think they are free from old age and death.

Thus, the author's initiation by Srimat Swami Shankaranandaji became a turning point, marking the beginning of an earnest and spiritual journey under the guidance of an enlightened *Guru*.

Instructions on Meditating Upon the *'Ishta'*

Maharaj provided detailed guidance on meditating upon the *Ishta* (chosen deity). He instructed:

Visualize the Guru seated upon your head, radiating serenity and wishing only the best for you.

In your heart, envision Sri Sri Thakur (Sri Ramakrishna) seated with a smiling countenance, alive and luminous, sitting upon a thousand-petalled lotus.

Gradually, visualize the Guru descending from the head and merging with the *Ishta*, Sri Ramakrishna, in your heart.

Finally, see Mother Sarada Devi residing in Thakur's heart, representing the eternal union of the masculine and feminine divine principles.

Maharaj likened this visualization to the depiction of Sri Ramachandra residing in Hanuman's heart, emphasizing that the *Ishta* guides the devotee's mind, intellect and senses.

He then clearly pronounced the *initiation mantra* three times and explained the meaning of the *seed mantra* in the middle. The meaning is that Sri Sri Thakur embodies all deities, encapsulating the divine essence of all gods and goddesses.

Spiritual Revelations and Divine Visions

To reinforce this truth, Maharaj narrated several incidents illustrating Thakur's divine manifestations:

1. *Mathur Babu*, the son-in-law of Rani Rasmani, saw simultaneous forms of Shiva and Kali in Thakur at Dakshineswar.
2. On another occasion, Thakur asked Swamiji (Swami Vivekananda) if he wanted to see the divine form of *Sri Radha*. Swamiji replied that he could, if Thakur graciously showed him. Swamiji then saw an extraordinary beauty and form manifest in Thakur's body, and it seemed to him that Sri Radha herself was standing before him.
3. At the *Kashipur garden house*, Thakur told Swamiji, "The Rama and Krishna of the past are now Ramakrishna of the present. But not from the standpoint of your Vedanta," as Advaita Vedanta does not accommodate idol worship or any rituals; it acknowledges only Brahman as the ultimate reality.

Maharaj concluded by affirming that worshiping any deity is equivalent to worshiping Sri Ramakrishna and the *Guru*, the *Ishta*, and *mantra* are fundamentally inseparable.

Instructions on *Japam* and Mental Worship

Every day, in the morning and evening, sit on a designated seat facing north or east and chant the *Ishta* mantra at least 108 times. It is advisable to take a bath beforehand, if possible.

The seat used for *japa* should not be used for any other purpose.

Besides morning and evening, *japa* and meditation can be done at any other convenient time without using the seat, even while sitting on the bed.

However, morning and evening japam and meditation should be done properly, sitting on the seat (*asana*) and counting with hands.

Maharaj demonstrated the method of counting on the right hand and how to keep track of the number of japas on the left hand.

During the period of *Ashoucha* (*sutaka*), one should do mental *japa* without going to the Shrine (worship room) or using the *japa* seat.

Mental Worship (*Manas Puja*)

Before starting *japa*, perform mental worship (*manas puja*). Visualize that Sri Sri Thakur is seated on the lotus of your heart.

Mentally offer him *padya* (water for washing feet), clothes, *arghya* (offering), flowers, *naivedya* (food offering), etc.

While performing manas puja, think that Sri Sri Thakur has accepted your offerings with a joyful heart.

Offering fruits and sweets mentally is preferable, as it requires no help from others. However, if convenient, fruits and sweets can be physically offered to Sri Sri Thakur during morning and evening *japa* and meditation.

As part of *manas puja*, mentally perform *arati* with five lamps and fan Thakur with a *chamara* (yak-tail fan).

Importance of the Ishta Mantra and Preservation of its Confidentiality

Maharaj emphasized the sacred nature of the *Ishta* Mantra:

He said that the *Guru* and the *Ishta* are inseparable.

In spiritual practice, the scripture (*Bhagavata*), the devotee, and God are one and the same.

Once a disciple advances spiritually, the purified mind itself acts as the *Guru*, guiding what is right and what is wrong.

Maharaj mentioned that Sri Sri Thakur himself gives the *mantra* through the *Guru*. He has imparted the *mantra* as the representative of Sri Sri Thakur.

The confidentiality of the *Ishta mantra* must be maintained. It should not be revealed to anyone or written down anywhere.

The scriptures state that the *Ishta mantra* is like the embryo in a mother's womb, kept secretly until the child is ready to be born. Similarly, the disciple must protect the *Ishta mantra* in the heart until God-realization is attained. Sri Guru said "The *Ishta mantra* is living and powerful. This *mantra* alone bears the potential to clear all doubts in the disciple's mind and to answer all questions."

Sri *Guru* further said, "From today, Sri Sri Thakur has taken all responsibility for you and will guide you from within your heart. Never feel disappointed, thinking that there is no spiritual advancement. The *Ishta mantra* will protect you."

Maharaj advised us to read *Sri Sri Ramakrishna Kathamrita* (Gospel of Sri Ramakrishna) daily, saying that all instructions and advice for leading a life properly are depicted there. Finally, all of us had to go close to him and bow down. That time he touched the head of each of us with a shield (*kabach*) attached to his *Rudraksh Mala* (sacred necklace). Then all of us did *Sashtang Pranama* to Sri Guru and came out of his room. After that we went to bow down to Sri Sri Thakur, Sri Sri Ma, Swami Vivekananda and Swami Brahmananda. Lastly we went to the Old Shrine of Belur Math and did Japam and meditation for a while there. We then returned to our college hostel after taking noon *prasadam* (lunch) at Belur Math.

After this day, whenever there has been any opportunity to have *'Darshana'* of Sri Guru, we tried to avail it. Although he had a grave personality, after doing *pranama*, the author used to occasionally notice that Sri Guru used to look at him with a smiling face for a while. It appeared to the author that Sri Guru used to shower his blessings on him.

Appointment with Swami Shankaranandaji

When the author passed the I.Sc. examination in 1961, Guru Maharaj Srimat Swami Shankaranandaji advised him to pursue a three-year B.Sc. (Honours) at the Vidyamandira, even though it would take an additional year. By that time, the author had been selected to study two-year B.Sc. with Honours in Mathematics at the Presidency College, Kolkata, and secured a seat at the *Ramakrishna Mission Kolkata Vidyarthi Ashrama*. Naturally, his father wanted him to enroll at Presidency College. The author then sought an appointment to discuss all this with Sri Guru. On hearing that the author would have to study for an extra year at the Vidyamandira, Maharaj remarked that parents often overemphasize on the loss of a year but do not value the opportunity to study in a good environment. However, when he learned that the author had got an opportunity to stay at the Ramakrishna Mission Vidyarthi Ashram at Belgharia, Maharaj reassured him, saying, "Alright, we have our monks there too." He agreed to the author's studying at Presidency College, but the author felt that Maharaj believed studying the three-year B.Sc. (Honours) at the Vidyamandira would be better for him. Ultimately, he decided to enroll in the three-year course at the Vidyamandira. When he informed Srimat Swami Shankaranandaji of this decision, the author noticed an expression of relief and joy on his face. The author firmly believes, this omniscient saint realized that this decision would be more beneficial for the author in future.

Mahasamadhi

On Saturday, January 13, 1962, at 3:10 AM, Swami Shankaranandaji attained Mahasamadhi. Within a few minutes, the news reached the Vidyamandira by phone from Belur Math. Revered Govinda Maharaj immediately informed us, and we quickly made our way to Belur Math as soon as possible. We had the opportunity to see Maharaj for the last time and pay our respects. We saw Maharaj lying on his bed, his face still bearing a calm, divine expression with no sign of distortion. A few monks were taking impressions of Maharaj's feet together. They placed two pillows under his feet to get the footprints. One person was cutting cloth into pieces, while another brahmachari was applying red sandalwood, white sandalwood, and *alta* (red dye) under his feet. Another brahmachari placed those pieces of cloth on a pillow and took impressions of Maharaj's feet. The author was fortunate to receive one such impression of Maharaj's feet and a shawl he had used. Later, when he left Vidyamandira, he entrusted these precious relics to a monk. However, he could not collect those invaluable mementos from that monk later on.

Swami Shankaranandaji was an exemplary monk, unassuming and reserved. It was learnt that his nerves became very sensitive due to deep spiritual practices, making it difficult for him to endure loud noises. He advised us, "Never indulge in idle gossip." Once, during a visit to the Vidyamandira, he gave a speech to the students and shared some invaluable insights. On that occasion, Maharaj made an observation, "In contemporary times, young people lack role models. The conduct of most parents at home is not exemplary. Even among the teachers at schools/colleges, there are few who can be considered ideal. However, having a role model makes it easier to shape oneself by emulating that person."

CHAPTER 5

University of Calcutta
College of Science and Technology—A Great Centre for Higher Education

After completing B.Sc. with Honours in Mathematics in 1964, the author applied for doing M.Sc. at the University of Calcutta in Applied Mathematics. The study of Applied Mathematics was conducted at the Science College on Acharya Prafulla Chandra Road, commonly known as Raja Bazar Science College. Pure Mathematics was offered at the Ballygunge Science College. Those interested in pursuing an M.Sc. in Pure Mathematics had to attend classes at Ballygunge Science College. At that time, there were only 36 seats available for the M.Sc. programme in Applied Mathematics. With admission typically granted to the top 36 students based on their Honours results. Given the author's good performance in Mathematics Honours, securing a place in the M.Sc. Applied Mathematics programme was not very challenging.

It is relevant to highlight the prestige of this esteemed university and its Applied Mathematics department. The University of Calcutta was established on January 24, 1857, during the tenure of Governor-General Lord Canning (1856–1862). The first Vice-Chancellor of the University was Sir James William Colvile, who served from January 1857 to January 1859. Several other Europeans succeeded him in the role of Vice-Chancellor.

Sir Gurudas Banerjee was the first Indian Vice-Chancellor of the university. He held office from January 1, 1890, to December 31, 1892. Among the University's most influential leaders was Sir Ashutosh Mukherjee, who served as the Vice-Chancellor twice, from 1906 to 1914 and from 1921 to 1923. During his tenure, he made substantial development of the affiliated colleges, significantly reformed the school education and a complete restructuring of the University's academic framework. His efforts led to the substantial expansion of post-graduate programmes. Eminent lawyers, Sir Tarak Nath Palit and Sir Rash Behari Ghosh made substantial financial contributions to the growth of the university. With their donations, Sir Ashutosh could construct large buildings, purchase necessary equipments, and establish a grand library for research at the Science College. Additional financial support from Maharaja Rameshwar Singh of Darbhanga, Maharaja Manindra Chandra Nandi, Nilaratan Sircar, Premchand Roychand, and Jnanendra Chandra Ghosh, helped transform the University of Calcutta into a leading centre for higher education and knowledge dissemination. The Institute of Nuclear Physics and the Department of Radio Physics and Electronics at the Science College played a crucial role in advancing applied sciences education in India.

University of Calcutta: College of Science and Technology (Rajabazar Campus)

Under the visionary leadership of Sir Ashutosh Mukherjee, the University of Calcutta gained international recognition for pioneering research in arts and sciences. Distinguished researchers from the university include the world-renowned scientists such as Jagadish Chandra Bose, Satyendra Nath Bose, Meghnad Saha, Sir C.V. Raman, Jnan Chandra Ghosh, and Biresh Chandra Guha. The teaching and research in various subjects of arts and fine arts at the University of Calcutta also received global acclaim.

The Department of Applied Mathematics was established in 1914 by Vice-Chancellor Ashutosh Mukherjee himself. Initially named as the Department of Mixed and Applied Mathematics, it produced several illustrious alumni, including Satyendra Nath Bose, Meghnad Saha, Nikhil Ranjan Sen, and Ganesh Prasad. Many of these distinguished scholars later became faculty members of the Department, significantly contributing to its development. The author held deep respect and admiration for this prestigious university and its Applied Mathematics department, along with a sense of apprehension. Consequently after enrolling in the M.Sc. programme, the author devoted himself delightedly to his studies from the outset. The curriculum emphasized the practical application of mathematics to solve problems in engineering science, physical science, life sciences, environmental science, and commerce, while also covering key topics in pure mathematics.

Academic Environment in the Department of Applied Mathematics

As previously mentioned, during the author's time (1964–66), only 36 students were admitted to the M.Sc. programme in Applied Mathematics at the University of Calcutta. In contrast, the Pure Mathematics Department enrolled approximately 150–200 students in the M.A./M.Sc. programmes.

The Applied Mathematics Department at that time was led by Professor S.K. Chakrabarti (Subodh Kumar Chakrabarti), a reserved and serious personality who commuted from Khardah. Previously, he was a Professor at the Bengal Engineering College, Shibpur, Howrah. He maintained a strict demeanor that instilled fear in students. Even among faculty members, he kept a considerable distance. His presence was so imposing that the sound of his boots could be heard from a distance as he walked.

Department of Applied Mathematics

In those days, almost all departments at the University of Calcutta faced space constraints. The Applied Mathematics department occupied a few rooms on the second floor of the main building of the Raja Bazar Science College. There was a separate, albeit small, office for the head of the department while other faculty members shared a common room. There were two dedicated classrooms for the first-year and second-year students. The blackboards on the walls were of the rolling type, allowing teachers ample writing space without erasure.

The departmental library housed several books suited for the M.Sc level, alongside a vast collection of academic journals, neatly bound and organized. These journals were primarily used for research purposes. Researchers would sit in the library and take notes on the necessary sections. Since photocopying machines and computers were unavailable at the time, and the internet had yet to be invented, students and researchers had to spend long hours in the library, meticulously taking notes from reference materials.

Another room in the department was designated for Numerical Analysis practicals, adjacent to the departmental office. At the far end of the corridor was the office of the Indian Chemical Society. There were two assistant staff members, both Hindi-speaking, one of whom was named Dhyan Singh. On the same floor, the neighbouring department was Applied Psychology.

Unlike today, where female students are well represented in the Department, our batch, had only three: Indrani Dasgupta (B.Sc. from Lady Brabourne College), Usha Adhikari (B.Sc. from Scottish Church College), and Himani Sur. However, Himani Sur did not continue beyond the first year.

During our time, the curriculum and syllabi for the Applied Mathematics Department underwent significant revisions, and we were the first batch under the newly implemented curriculum. As a result, only 21 students out of 36 successfully completed the final examinations. By God's grace, the author completed the examinations on the first attempt. During those days, examinations of all subjects were held together at the end of the two years. Later, an annual examination system was introduced, with exams held at the end of the first year covering half the subjects, and the remaining subjects at the end of the second year. The final results based on the cumulative scores of both years, easing the burden of a single comprehensive examination. Nowadays, like many other universities, the University of Calcutta has adopted the semester system, dividing two years into four semesters, with four examinations, significantly reducing academic pressure.

In our time, Prof. S.K. Chakrabarti taught Hydrodynamics. His strict and serious demeanor extended into the classroom. He travelled from Khardah in his own car; so even if he had the first period, it was not a problem for him.

Prof. Parimal Kanti Ghosh

Prof. Parimal Kanti Ghosh's home was in Serampore, Hooghly district. He was unmarried and commuted by train from Serampore. He had extensive knowledge across multiple fields of mathematics and was proficient in Russian language besides English, allowing him to study the works of prominent Russian mathematicians. Subjects like Topology and Functional Analysis were not widely popular at that time, but Professor Ghosh had a good grasp over these subjects. Therefore, although some topics of these subjects were included in the syllabus for Real Analysis during our time, he had no difficulty in teaching them. He did not hold a doctorate himself, but several students earned their doctorates under his guidance.

Prof. Amritava Gupta

Prof. Amritava Gupta was known for his willingness to teach new subjects. In the first year of our postgraduate programme, he instructed us in Complex Analysis as well as Ordinary and Partial Differential Equations. Later, when Automata Theory was introduced into the curriculum of the Department, he played a leading role in offering this course. In the second year, he taught us Probability and Statistics. He authored two books: "Introduction to Mathematical Analysis" and "Groundwork of Mathematical Probability and Statistics," which were quite popular at the time. Despite having health issues he never let his condition hinder his academic commitments, continuing his lectures with the aid of medication. In a certificate he gave me, he wrote, "...Jagadis C. Misra has a good grasp over the fundamentals of Mathematics. ... He bears a pleasing personality". Those days, since the size of the class was quite small, the teachers used to have idea of the merits/weaknesses of individual students.

Prof. Subhas Chandra Bose was a distinguished educator who taught Particle Dynamics and the Special Theory of Relativity. He was the youngest faculty in the Applied Mathematics department during our time and was known for his affectionate nature. I perceived him as a cheerful individual. We always saw him in a cheerful mood. He was unmarried and lived in a rented house in Barrackpore, commuting daily by train or bus. Occasionally, we would travel to Science College from Sealdah station on the same bus. Whenever he saw me, he would often insist on paying my fare as well, never allowing me to cover the cost. Once, the author suggested to him that he might consider purchasing an apartment, but he said that his family migrated from Bangladesh as refugees and so he had initial family responsibilities. Later, the sharp increase in real estate prices made it impossible for him to afford a home.

Prof. Subhas Chandra Bose

Prof. Prafulla Prasun Chatterjee and Prof. Jnan Gopal Chakrabarti taught Mechanics of Deformable Bodies. The author received useful guidance from both these teachers, which was very beneficial in his life in later years.

Prof. Rabindranath Bhattacharya from Jadavpur University taught Rigid Dynamics, while Prof. S. Ganguly from BE College instructed Theory of Electricity and Magnetism. They were guest professors. In the second year, students had to choose a Special Subject. During the author's time, the options were Theory of Elasticity and Plasticity, Fluid Mechanics, Geodesy and Geophysics, and Quantum Mechanics. The author opted for Elasticity and Plasticity as his Special Subject. Each special subject used to have two papers, each worth 100 marks, totalling 200 marks. However, significant changes were introduced to the syllabus and examination structure during the author's time. Under the old system, the special subject had a written examination worth 200 marks. Under the new system, it was 2 × 75, or 150 marks for the written examination, and 50 marks for a dissertation. Each student, under the guidance of a supervisor, would select a topic in their specialized subject, study some research papers in-depth, and then do something new on the chosen topic in consultation with the supervisor. The goal was to do something akin to a research paper, but due to time constraints, original work was not always possible. Nevertheless, the process provided the students with essential research training. An external expert would come to evaluate the dissertation. The title of my dissertation was "Thermal Stresses in an Elastic Medium with a Spherical Cavity." The external expert for our group was Prof. Devendranath Mitra, who was a recipient of both Ph.D. and D.Sc. degrees. At that time, he was a professor in the Mathematics Department at the Regional Engineering College (now National Institute of Technology), Durgapur. We had to give a presentation in English on our chosen topics. At that time, students were not accustomed to giving presentations in English. Although we did not have much time, we practiced and rehearsed our presentations in front of our supervisors. The supervisor, Prof. Prafulla Prasun Chatterjee, was satisfied with the author's presentation but advised him to practice a bit more to be more confident on the final day. After the presentation, the external expert, Prof. Mitra, asked a few questions. Later, Prof. Devendranath Mitra (the external expert that day) joined IIT Kharagpur as a Professor in the Mathematics Department. Therefore, when the author joined IIT, Kharagpur, in 1971, he became Prof. Mitra's junior colleague. Eventually, Prof. Mitra became the Head of the Mathematics Department at IIT Kharagpur.

Faculty Members Teaching Other Special Papers

It will not be out of place to give some brief information about the faculty teachers of the other special subjects. Fluid Mechanics was taught by Prof. Durgadas Mallik (D.D. Mallik) and Prof. Ambarish Ghosh, who was a professor of Applied Mathematics at the Indian Statistical Institute (ISI) in Kolkata. Geodesy & Geophysics was taught by Prof. S.K. Chakrabarti (Head of the department) and Prof. S. Ganguly (BE College). Quantum Mechanics was taught by Prof. Mithil Ranjan Gupta and Prof. Tapen Roy (Physics Department, Jadavpur University). Ambarish Ghosh, Tapen Roy, and S. Ganguly were part-time professors in the Applied Mathematics department. There was a Fluid Mechanics Laboratory within the Raja Bazar Science College campus, supervised by Ambarish Ghosh. It seems this was the first Fluid Mechanics Laboratory of India and it was established by Prof. Nikhil Ranjan Sen from the Department of Applied Mathematics of Calcutta University. Although the author was never a student of the Pure Mathematics Department at Ballygunge Science College, some professors of that department were renowned for their distinguished teaching methods and research contributions. Mention may be made here of just one former professor of Pure Mathematics. His name was Prof. Manindra Chandra Chaki (M.C. Chaki). He had profound expertise in various branches of geometry. Once, the author went with a friend to visit him at his residence. He was unmarried and lived in a rented room in a hotel in Central Kolkata. That time he was over 90 years old. Although the author had met him only 2–3 times, Prof. Chaki had very high opinion about the author's contributions to the field of Mathematics. He authored several books suitable for postgraduate studies. His book "Tensor Calculus" was very useful for mathematics honours students and served as a textbook in several universities.

Sir Ashutosh Mukherjee's Contribution

Sir Ashutosh Mukherjee was widely recognized as an exceptional Vice-Chancellor of the University of Calcutta. He also officiated as the Chief Justice of the Calcutta High Court for sometime in the year 1920. People referred to him as the "Tiger of Bengal". He was the first president of the Calcutta Mathematical Society. However, few may be aware that he was also a mathematician.

After the establishment of the Indian Science Congress, Sir Ashutosh Mukherjee became its first General President. Despite his multifaceted talents, his primary passion was Pure Mathematics. In 1885, he earned his M.A. degree in Mathematics. Interestingly, as previously mentioned, it was Sir Ashutosh Mukherjee himself who established the Department of Applied (Mixed) Mathematics at the University of Calcutta. As a student of this Department, the author took great pride in this legacy.

Postgraduate Classmates and their Career Paths

The author's postgraduate classmates were involved in both teaching and research. A few joined industrial sectors. However, the author does not have complete information about everyone. Ashesh Roy Choudhury taught and conducted research in the Physics Department at Jadavpur University. Birendra Nath Mondal taught and conducted research in the Applied Mathematics Department at the University of Calcutta before joining the Physics and Applied Mathematics Unit at the Indian Statistical Institute (ISI) as a Professor. The author worked as a Professor and researcher at IIT Kharagpur; details to be followed. His classmates Charugopal Chakrabarti and his junior, Anil Pramanik, were Professors and for sometime heads of the Applied Mathematics Department. Tarapada Mondal taught at Medinipur College, and Bhavesh Ranjan Pal at Dinabandhu Andrews College. Partha Pratim Chakrabarti joined an industrial organization, and Ashok Bhowmik gained reputation as the headmaster of Sodepur Higher Secondary School.

The author visited the Applied Mathematics Department many times in later years and always received great encouragement and warmth from the faculty. There used to be an annual conference of CASAMCU (Centre for Advanced Studies in Applied Mathematics, Calcutta University). The author participated in many of these conferences and delivered lectures on his research.

As his research gained reputation, the author was invited as a chief guest to various events of the Department. During one such event where he was the Chief Guest, Professor Suranjan Das (who was the Vice-Chancellor of Jadavpur University) was present as a Dean of Calcutta University. The author also attended some of the reunion ceremonies of the department. On some occasions he shared his views on several matters and suggested some changes for the betterment of the department.

Alumni of the Department

Former students of this department have held/are holding teaching and other responsible positions in various institutions across India. The senior alumni, Dr. Phulan Prasad and Dr. Alok Chakrabarti, were renowned professors in the Mathematics Department at the Indian Institute of Science, Bangalore, and are now retired. Many alumni have taught and conducted research at various IITs. Several alumni have gained international recognition for their distinguished research and excellence in teaching. Others have managed various administrative responsibilities and earned reputation.

Other Departments at Raja Bazar Science College

Raja Bazar Science College of the University of Calcutta housed several departments. Just inside the main gate of the Science College is the office of the Science College Secretary, followed by other administrative offices. The 'Centre of Advanced Studies in Applied Mathematics.' was located further inside and occasionally hosted research conferences that provided students the opportunity to engage with academics from across India. The Biochemistry Department, though relatively small was also situated there.

The campus included departments of Applied Physics, Applied Chemistry, and Radio Physics and Electronics. All of these were engineering focused. Each of these departments had a separate large building allocated to it. Students who graduated from these departments received BTech/MTech degrees. Students who passed B.Sc. with honours in Physics were eligible to study BTech at the Institute of Radio Physics and Electronics as well as the Department of Applied

Physics. The BTech programme took three years, followed by additional two years for MTech.

Similarly, students with good results in Chemistry Honours could pursue BTech in the Department of Applied Chemistry, followed by a two-year MTech course. Depending on specialization, degrees from the Department of Applied Physics were awarded in Electrical Engineering or Instrumentation Engineering. In the Department of Applied Chemistry, students could pursue BTech/MTech in Chemical Engineering, Polymer Science and Technology, or Chemical Technology. Over time, these departments experienced significant transformations.

The Saha Institute of Nuclear Physics offered post-M.Sc. diploma courses. All the aforementioned departments also had doctoral programmes. As previously mentioned, the Applied Mathematics Department was located on the second floor of the main building. The Pure Physics Department was located on the first floor and a portion of the ground floor, while a large portion of the ground floor housed the Pure Chemistry Department. Later, several new departments were opened at Raja Bazar Science College, including Biophysics, Molecular Biology & Bioinformatics, Electronic Science, and Computer Science & Engineering. Many professors from various departments at Raja Bazar Science College gained national recognition. Some even achieved international acclaim for their distinguished research, even while working under various constraints.

At the Vidyarthi Ashrama

When the author was pursuing his M.Sc. programme during 1964–66, he had the privilege of being a resident at the Ramakrishna Mission Vidyarthi Ashram in Belgharia. The founder of the Vidyarthi Ashram was Swami Nirvedananda. At that time, normally it was uncommon for M.A./M.Sc. students to stay at the Vidyarthi Ashrama. However, since the author was a student of the Vidyamandira and carried with him a recommendation letter from the Principal, Swami Tejasananda, he did not face much difficulty in securing a place there. Here he found some of his former classmates from Vidyamandira—Biswanath Das, Nityaranjan Kundu, Jyoti Prakash Ghosh, and Nishikanta Jana—who were already residing at the Vidyarthi Ashrama and doing two-year BA Hons.

The author was impressed by the large campus, which had two playgrounds, a large pond, a smaller pond, gardens with fruits and flowers, and a bakery. Additionally, there was ample land for cultivation. The bakery produced bread

Ramakrishna Mission Calcutta, Students Home

for the students. The cowshed housed many cows, providing sufficient milk for the students, with the surplus being sold. Paddy and wheat were cultivated on the land. Students performed *bhajans* and prayers in the temple early in the morning and in the evening. There were four single-storey and two double- storey buildings for the students' accommodation, capable of housing around one hundred students. There was a hall primarily used as a library. However, a room adjacent to the library served as the office of the Vidyarthi Ashrama Secretary Maharaj, and another room housed two monks (Swami Amalananda and Swami Skandananda). Additionally, there was a separate building for the kitchen and a large dining hall. Other buildings housed monks and brahmacharis who oversaw all activities of the Vidyarthi Ashrama. There was also a healthcare building for sick students. The polytechnic, named Ramakrishna Mission Shilpapeeth, was on the campus, but there was no accommodation for its students.

During the author's stay at the Vidyarthi Ashrama (1964–66), the Ashrama Secretary was Swami Santoshananda (Asesh Maharaj). He had a stern demeanor. Affectionately he used to address the author as 'Vashishtadev.' Other monks included Swami Vishokananda (Priti Maharaj), Swami Viswashrayananda (Nandi Maharaj), Swami Dhyanatmananda (Nripen Maharaj), Swami Satyaghanananda (Priyalal Maharaj), Swami Amalananda (Siddheshwar

Maharaj), Swami Skandananda (Shibdas Maharaj), and Swami Abhyasananda (Shiben Maharaj). Each of them handled their respective responsibilities with great dedication. It truly seemed like 'Shiva Jnane Jiva Seva' (serving humanity with a spirit of worshiping Shiva). They had renounced their families and were tirelessly working to fulfil their selfless objectives of creating excellent human beings for the betterment of the society. Swami Santoshananda and Swami Vishokananda were disciples of Sri Sri Ma Sarada Devi. Swami Viswashrayananda was a disciple of Swami Vijnanananda, one of the direct disciples of Sri Ramakrishna. Later, Swami Viswashrayananda took on the editorial responsibilities of the popular Bengali magazine 'Udbodhan,' published from the 'Mother's House' in Bagbazar. Swami Dhyanatmananda was an excellent orator with an exceptional memory. He could recite large poems (in Sanskrit, Bengali, and English) fluently from memory. At one time, he taught at the Vidyamandira. For many years, he played the role of Tantradharak during Durga Puja at Belur Math and Jagaddhatri Puja at Saradapith. Swami Satyaghanananda assisted Swami Santoshananda in making correspondences with different offices/people and also in carrying out various responsibilities of Secretary of the Vidyarthi Ashrama. Later, he became the manager of Belur Math (headquarters) for a long time.

Swami Viswashrayananda and Swami Amalananda authored several valuable books. Swami Viswashrayananda's works include 'Shishuder Ramakrishna,' 'Shishuder Ma Sarada Devi,' and 'Shishuder Vivekananda,' which were immensely popular. Swami Amalananda's books, 'The Story of the Ramayana' and 'The Story of the Mahabharata,' were suitable for rapid reading in Bengali at the secondary level. Additionally, Swami Amalananda handled administrative responsibilities of Shilpapeeth. Swami Skandananda efficiently oversaw the preparation, cooking, and serving of food for the residents of Vidyarthi Ashrama. Swami Abhyasananda was responsible for taking care of the sick students, initially treating them with homeopathic medicine.

If necessary, more severe cases were moved to the healthcare facility for specialist treatment. Besides caring for the sick students, Swami Abhyasananda managed the cultivation of rice, wheat, various vegetables, and fruits on the Ashrama's farmland. He also took care of the cows in the cowshed and was responsible for the bakery. It is quite apparent that the self-sufficiency of the Vidyarthi Ashrama increased due to these activities, reducing dependence on the market.

Serving Man with a Spirit of Worshipping God

Monks in various hospitals of the Ramakrishna Mission serve patients with their own hands, often putting their own lives at risk. Although the author did not have the opportunity to witness this, he had some personal experience during his stay at Vidyarthi Ashrama. Once, he contracted chickenpox, on being infected with the *varicellazoster* virus. According to protocol, he had to be isolated at the Ashrama's healthcare facility. No one else was allowed to visit him due to the contagious nature of the disease. Only revered Shiben Maharaj (Swami Abhyasananda) personally attended to all his needs until he fully recovered and resumed attending his classes in the Science College of the University of Calcutta. The quality of service was really 'outstanding'. The intensity of chickenpox was quite severe, taking longer to heal completely. However, the author never noticed any lack of dedication from Shiben Maharaj. He would prepare suitable food, cover it with a piece of cloth and bring it to the patient with a smiling face everytime. Sometimes, he would make jokes to cheer the patient up. The author will never forget those moments. The parents were informed about the illness only after complete recovery. This monk was also adept at singing. He played a leading role during prayers in the temple and at various events, often playing the harmonium. According to the traditions of the Vidyarthi Ashrama, students had to do their own work. Sundays involved some extra tasks. They had to clean their rooms, the temple, and even the toilets in their buildings.

Many a time, the author had the fortune of performing the evening *aratrikam* in the temple. During his stay at Vidyarthi Ashrama, he had another responsibility for a year, which brought him great joy and satisfaction. The Mission ran an evening school for school dropouts, and the author was entrusted with the responsibility of being the Headmaster of the evening school. The task was quite challenging because most of the students were locals whose parents had emigrated from Bangladesh and were financially struggling. They lacked a proper study environment at home and sometimes did not even get enough food to eat. At that time, there were no structured assistance programs like the Mission's 'Gadadhar Project'. Due to various reasons, the students were not very focused on their studies and often skipped the school. Even when they attended, they were mischievous. On the other hand, the teachers at the evening school were college students from the Ashrama who were often tired after returning from college in the evening. Despite this, the author managed to improve the quality of education at the night school in various ways. The school operated on the ground floor of the polytechnic college, Shilpapeeth, at the Vidyarthi Ashrama. The author often took classes himself. By the end of his tenure as the Headmaster, he was delighted to see significant improvements in the night school. Later, he occasionally met some of those students and noticed their expressions of gratitude.

Performing Saraswati Puja as Priest

Swami Dhyanatmananda

Throughout the year, several grand events are held at the Vidyarthi Ashrama, one of which is Saraswati Puja. Every year, one student is chosen to perform the puja. Generally, this responsibility is given to a Brahmin boy. During those days Swami Dhyanatmananda (Nripen Maharaj) would nominate a student to perform Saraswati Puja. In this way, he once nominated the author as the priest for Saraswati Puja during his stay at the Vidyarthi Ashrama. The Ramakrishna Mission emphasizes conducting everything according to the proper rites. Therefore, Nripen Maharaj gave him special training for about 15 days on how to perform the Saraswati Puja, ensuring that he memorized the various mantras and practiced their correct pronunciation and the different gestures (*mudras*) required for the puja. His keen attention ensured that the mantras were recited correctly. The day after the puja, a cultural event is held in the evening. Nowadays, many devotees bring their children to the Vidyarthi Ashrama on Saraswati Puja day for their initiation into learning *(haatekhori*). The current secretary of the Vidyarthi Ashrama, Swami Ekabratananda performs *haatekhori* for the small children.

Bhratri Baran (Freshers' Welcome)

Every year, after the new students arrive, there is a welcoming ceremony in the temple on a holiday. In this ceremony, the old students welcome the new ones, followed by special worship of Thakur, Ma, and Swamiji, and then the 'Vidyarthi Homa' ceremony. Details of this ceremony has been depicted elsewhere. Getting up early, attending 'Mangalarati' and taking five vows mark the day so special to the new students (freshers). The lunch prasada is also very special with sumptuous dishes. A friendly football match between the freshmen vs the rest is held in the afternoon on this special day. It is amusing to the author that he had occasions of being welcomed thrice at three different ceremonies for Bhratri Baran/Freshers' Welcome—first time, as a first year student of I.Sc., second time as a first year student of B.Sc. (Hons) (both during his total stay of five years at the R.K. Mission Vidyamandir) and third time as a new 'Vidyarthi' at the R.K. Mission Vidyarthi Ashrama, Belgharia.

Worship of Goddess Kali

Every year, Kali Puja is celebrated with great grandeur at Vidyarthi Ashrama. The program continues all night with Shyama Sangeet, accompanied by the spirited dance of the residents. Of course, nothing inappropriate occurs. Many former students join this event, making it a mini-reunion. Many alumni come with their families. During Kali Puja night, arrangements are made for female devotees to stay within the campus of the Vidyarthi Ashrama. This is the only night in the entire year, when women devotees are allowed to stay in the night, inside the Ashrama premises.

Other Annual Festivals

On Shivaratri, besides the four-phase worship of Lord Shiva, there are dances and songs throughout the night. Bengali New Year's Day is also marked by special worship and offerings to Thakur, Ma, and Swamiji. The celebration of *Holi* with songs of Radha and Krishna is very enjoyable at the Ashram. Annapurna Puja was celebrated with much pomp for several years. Many alumni also participated. But it was discontinued, later.

Every year on December 24, 'Brahmananda Day' is celebrated through various events. On this date in 1920, Swami Brahmananda, the spiritual son of Lord Sri Ramakrishna, visited the Vidyarthi Ashrama. The Ashrama was blessed by his invaluable blessings. After returning to Belur Math, he remarked, "I have seen a sage's Ashrama." Since then, this day has been being celebrated every year on 24th December with great grandeur.

Later, the Vidyarthi Ashrama was blessed by the visits of several great personalities like Swami Shivananda (the second president of Belur Math), Swami Abhedananda, and others. On the day Swami Brahmananda visited, he suggested in a childlike manner the menu for the midday meal—*karai dal, lau-chingri, koi fulkopi, bandhakopi*, mutton, *payesh*, etc. Even today, during the celebration of 'Brahmananda Day' on December 24, these items are offered to Mahadev, Ganapati, Thakur, Ma, Swami Vivekananda, and Swami

Temple and Prayer Hall at R.K.M. Belgharia

Brahmananda in the temple, followed by *prasad* distribution to everyone present. Due to the excessive rise in prices, reduction in expenditure has become inevitable, so only the essential traditions are maintained.

Previously, the Vidyarthi Ashrama was located elsewhere. Due to various reasons, it was relocated several times before having its present location at Belgharia. After moving to Belgharia, Srimat Swami Shankaranandaji did the inauguration of the Vidyarthi Ashrama temple in 1954. At that time, he was the President of the Ramakrishna Math and Mission.

Much like life at the Vidyamandira, the lives of the students at Vidyarthi Ashrama were regulated by a bell system. There was a bell for waking up in the morning, for temple prayers, breakfast, bathing, midday meals, afternoon snacks, and dinner, all according to a set schedule.

In those days, most of the residents studied in different colleges of Kolkata. After the establishment of Ramakrishna Mission Vivekananda Centenary College in Rahara, some residents of the Vidyarthi Ashrama studied there. It took about 10–12 minutes to walk from the Vidyarthi Ashrama to Belgharia Railway station. From there, the students took a train to Sealdah station, then a bus or walked down to their respective colleges. In the evening, after college, all students returned to the Vidyarthi Ashrama.

Gathering

After dinner, there was an evening assembly of the residents in the library hall, known as the 'Gathering.' This was conducted by the Ashram Secretary, Swami Santoshananda, along with one or two other monks. One of the main purposes of this gathering was to ensure that all residents had safely returned to the Ashrama. Therefore, attendance was taken by calling out the students' names. However, these assemblies evolved into vibrant events brimming with enthusiasm. They offered students a platform to exhibit their talents beyond the academic realm. Some narrated captivating stories, others delivered humorous performances with expressive gestures, and many showcased their musical prowess through songs or poetry recitations. Occasionally, the revered Maharajas would contribute by sharing amusing anecdotes, infusing the gatherings with joyous laughter.

Reflecting on my two-year Master of Science tenure, I find that the spiritual ambiance of the Vidyarthi Ashrama rendered my experience profoundly fulfilling. Upon completing my M.Sc. in 1966, I departed from the Vidyarthi Ashrama to embark on the subsequent phase of my journey. Nevertheless, my spiritual bond with this exceptional institution remains unbroken. Reunions are convened at the Vidyarthi Ashrama triennially. Life's myriad responsibilities and demands have, at times, precluded my participation in many of these reunions. Yet, whenever circumstances permitted I made it a point to visit the Vidyarthi Ashrama outside of these scheduled gatherings. For this continued connection, I am indebted to the administration and staff of the Vidyarthi Ashrama for their warm hospitality for ever.

The current Secretary, Swami Ekabratananda (Badal Maharaj), assistant Secretary Suprakash Maharaj (Swami Bhadraatmananda), and other monks have been successfully carrying forward the ideals of the founder, Swami Nirvedananda. This tradition continues to this day and for this the present monks deserve special applause. Swami Nirvedananda would tell the residents, "Vidyarthi Ashram is your second home." The sincerity, affection, and pleasant demeanor of the present monks continue to impress me. Swami Ekabratananda, is endowed with many qualities. He is an excellent speaker, soft-spoken, a good singer of devotional songs, and very prudent. He approaches any situation and resolves issues effortlessly. He attends the last rites of any alumni (from nearby places) who pass away, if possible. The monks deal with the alumni with due respect. It seems, they have inherited these qualities from revered Swami Dhyanatmananda (Nripen Maharaj). Under the visionary leadership of Swami Dhyeyananda, the Polytechnic College of the Ramakrishna Mission

Shilpapeetha, has reached a very high standard. Day and night, his focus is on Shilpapeeth. Swami Baladevananda diligently works on the Gadadhar Project.

Founded by Swami Nirvedananda, the Vidyarthi Ashrama was conceived as a sanctuary for students hindered in their educational pursuits by financial constraints. What began as a modest hostel accommodating a handful of students has flourished into a vibrant community, where over a hundred students currently reside and study. Approximately two-thirds of these students are provided with complete financial support, while the remaining third contribute partially or fully to their expenses. For those receiving full support, the institution generously covers costs including transportation to college, clothing, personal hygiene products, academic materials, and other essentials. Even services such as haircuts are financed by the Ashrama.

Since its inception in 1916, numerous students have thrived, ascending to responsible positions in the society, serving the country and receiving national and international recognition, thanks to the support of the Vidyarthi Ashrama. Their honesty and dedication have earned praise. All these have been possible due to the education, values, and spiritual awareness provided by the Vidyarthi Ashrama. The students and alumni are subconsciously influenced by Swami Vivekananda's philosophy—"Be and Make." As a result, most of the substantial expenses of the Ashram come from the voluntary contributions of its alumni.

In 2016, the author was fortunate to participate in the centenary celebrations of the Vidyarthi Ashrama. It was a grand four-day festival, meticulously planned, along with a reunion of alumni. The author resided at the Ashrama throughout the festivities. A notable feature this time was the invitation of alumni with their families. The author's wife also joined. However, arrangements for women's accommodation were made outside the Ashrama, thanks to the generosity of the alumni and their family, who are living at Belgharia. At the request of the current Secretary, the author wrote an English article for the centenary souvenir—'Our Vidyarthi Ashrama, Our Second Home.' Swami Bagishananda, one of the Vice-Presidents of the Ramakrishna Math and Mission, delivered his speech at the inauguration of this festival. He was also an alumnus of this Ashrama. Renowned poet Shankha Ghosh was the Chief Guest of this session. Sadly, both of them passed away recently. Following the desire of the Organizing Committee, the author also had an opportunity to give a brief speech at that session.

Eminent personalities such as the distinguished scientist Dr. Meghnad Saha, national professor Satyendra Nath Bose, eminent scientist and Vice-Chancellor of the University of Calcutta, Dr. Jnan Chandra Ghosh (subsequently the first Director of IIT Kharagpur), and others have visited Ramakrishna Mission Calcutta Vidyarthi Ashrama on different occasions and expressed their views on this great institution. Dr. Meghnad Saha wrote, "... At the Ramakrishna Mission Students Hostel, boys are taught the dignity of labour, they are learning self-reliance, and their studies are not confined within the four walls of textbooks". Dr. Jnan Chandra Ghosh's opinion about Vidyarthi Ashrama was—"Here, along with studies, special attention is given to the health, discipline, self-reliance, and moral character of the students. The efforts of the self-sacrificing monks for the welfare of humanity are ideals of Karma Yoga" (Ref. Ramakrishna Mission Calcutta Students' Home Diamond Jubilee Souvenir, 1976).

As an alumnus of such an institution, the author feels that he is really blessed. He further feels he received abundant resources for his future life from this institution.

By the grace of Lord Sri Ramakrishna and Ma Sarada, whatever small achievements he could make in life is undoubtedly due to the direct and indirect influence of the selfless monks of the Ramakrishna Mission.

CHAPTER 6

Initiation into Research and Teaching

In those days, scholarships for research were scarce, and their monetary value was quite low. Therefore, most people who wanted to do research, would first look for the position of a lecturer, then would do research simultaneously under the supervision of some research guide. The author was no exception. After being appointed as a lecturer in Uluberia College, he discussed the possibility of doing research with any of the professors in the Applied Mathematics Department at the University of Calcutta, who taught them during M.Sc., particularly with any of the two professors who taught the special paper on the Mathematical Theory of Elasticity and Plasticity. Professors Jnan Gopal Chakrabarti and Prafulla Prasun Chatterjee were very affectionate towards the author. However, neither of them agreed to be his research guide. They informed him that Professor Bibhuti Bhushan Sen (then head of the Mathematics Department at Visva Bharati University) and Professor Sushil Chandra Dasgupta (head of the Mathematics Department at BE College) were conducting good research in elasticity.

Meeting Prof. Bibhuti Bhusan Sen

The author first met Professor Sen in his residence at 64 Jodhpur Park, Kolkata. He expressed his intention and requested him earnestly to kindly guide him for doing research. However, Prof. Sen informed that due to various health issues—diabetes, high blood pressure, etc., and his advanced age, he had decided not to take on any new students after those, who were working under him at that time. Despite the author's persistent requests, he did not agree.

Encounter with Prof. Sushil Dasgupta

Determined not to give up, he then went to the Mathematics Department at BE College in Shibpur the next day and met Prof. Sushil Dasgupta, expressing his intention. The following conversation (which took place in Bengali) is still vivid in the author's memory, and it makes him smile whenever the conversation comes to his mind, because it was quite amusing.

Prof. Dasgupta: Where is your home?
Me: Midnapore.

Prof. Dasgupta: Oh! Medinipur. Where in Medinipur?
Me: Contai.

Prof. Dasgupta: Oh! Kanthi.

(*Note:* In Bengali, Midnapore is *Medinipur* and Contai is *Kanthi.*)

He then mentioned that he already had many students doing research under him and that he did not want to take any more. Despite repeated requests, he did not change his decision. However, the author did not find anything unpleasant in his demeanor. Prof. Dasgupta refused in a very polite and convincing manner. He was a Doctor of Science (D.Sc.), yet very humble. The author noticed the qualities of a true scholar in him.

Seeking Guidance of Prof. A.K. Gayen (February 1919 – February 1978)

A few days later, the author went to IIT Kharagpur to inquire about research opportunities. At that time, the head of the Mathematics Department was Prof. Anil Kumar Gayen, who had earned his Ph.D. from Cambridge University. He was a Fellow of the Statistical Society of London and had great national and international acclaim in the field of Mathematics and Statistics. He was later instrumental to establishing Vidyasagar University in Midnapore. Although the author was initially nervous about meeting such a distinguished academician, his kind and soft-spoken nature put him at ease. He informed the author that IIT Kharagpur would soon advertise in leading English newspapers for research scholar positions and advised him to apply that time. During conversation, when he mentioned that he had been selected for a lecturer position at a degree college, Prof. Gayen advised him to join the lecturer position and pursue part-time research. This was because, at that time, a full-time research scholar received only 250 rupees a month (currently, at least Rs. 31,000). He also mentioned that there were five IITs in India then, so getting a lecturer position in one of them after completing Ph.D. should not be very difficult. To-date there are 23 Indian Institutes of Technology (IIT) and 31 National Institutes of Technology (NIT)!

The Influence of Prof. B. Sen (1897–1976): A Small Tribute

Prof. Bibhuti Bhusan Sen

Following this conversation, I approached Prof. Jnan Gopal Chakrabarti again, and sought further guidance from him. He strongly advised me to revisit Bibhuti Bhusan Sen and attempt one more time to persuade him. Regarding Prof. Sen, he said that it would be best if he agreed, as he was a "teacher of teachers". Many students conducted research under him simultaneously, and each one obtained Ph.D. Many of these scholars later became faculty members in Mathematics Departments of various colleges/ universities in West Bengal.

Prof. B. Sen was born on March 1, 1897, in the Chittagong district of present-day Bangladesh. He studied at a school in Chittagong, famous for the Chittagong Armoury Raid led by Masterda Surya Sen. After passing the matriculation examination from a school in Chittagong in 1913, he completed his I.Sc. from Presidency College under Calcutta University in 1915. He did B.Sc. (Honours) in 1917 also from Presidency College. During this time, he was a student of the renowned scientist Acharya Prafulla Chandra Ray. He then completed his M.Sc. from the Mixed Mathematics (now Applied Mathematics) Department of Calcutta University. He secured first place in both his B.Sc. (Honours) and M.Sc. examinations at Calcutta University.

During his M.Sc. programme, Prof. Satyendra Nath Bose taught them the special paper on Elasticity. Professor Sen used to tell his students stories about how Prof. Satyendra Nath Bose would stimulate curiosity among students in various ways. Prof. Bose would advise students to read the research papers cited in the footnotes of good textbooks. This would enhance their ability to conduct research in Elasticity in the future.

In 1919, Prof. Sen topped the Imperial Forest Service (IFS) examination. The British government of India wanted to send him to England for higher training. However, just before his departure, he had to return to Kolkata from Bombay at his father's instruction, as his father was unwilling to send his son to England across the "black waters" (*Kala Pani*). Consequently, he could not take the M.Sc. exam at that time. This incident highlights Prof. Sen's deep filial devotion to his parents. Sri Ramakrishna said that not even a leaf moves without God's will. We believe that whatever God does is for our well being.

Had he gone to England for training and become an IFS officer, so many researchers and professors would not have had the rare opportunity to be his students.

After the aforementioned incident, he completed his M.Sc. examination and received the gold medal from Calcutta University in 1921. It is instructive for present and future generations to know that the subsequent life of even such a person who secured first place in so many examinations was not smooth. After passing his M.Sc., he joined the Gun and Shell Factory in Ichhapur as an instructor. But this job was not to his liking at all, as he was looking for a job where he could have the opportunity to do research and teach in the field of mathematics. Therefore, after sometime, he resigned from that job and accepted a position in the Mathematics Department at Bagerhat College (now in Bangladesh). After some time, he joined Ramjas College in Agra, Uttar Pradesh. He stayed there for about a year. During this time, Sir Ashutosh Mukherjee was the Vice-Chancellor of Calcutta University. In early 1924, he invited Prof. Sen to join Calcutta University as a full-time lecturer in mathematics. Unfortunately, Sir Ashutosh passed away before this invitation could be realized. Subsequently, Prof. Sen joined the Bengal Government Educational Service, which gave him the opportunity to work in several government colleges in Bengal. Initially, he became a lecturer in the Mathematics Department of Chittagong Government College. From there, he was transferred to the Mathematics Department of Krishnanagar Government College. His research in mathematics mainly began there. However, at that time, Krishnanagar College did not have the necessary books or journals in its library for his research. So he often went to Kolkata to read various books and research papers on Elasticity. Later, he was transferred to Islamia College in Kolkata (now known as Maulana Azad College). Compared to before, his opportunities for research increased significantly. But the materials and environment necessary for research became even more favourable when he was transferred to Bengal Engineering College in Shibpur or Presidency College in Kolkata. In these colleges, he had many more opportunities to conduct research.

Important Aspects of Prof. B. Sen's Life

Although Prof. Sen used to spend a lot of time on research, he never neglected his teaching duties. One of the hallmarks of his teaching was that he used to make jokes and quote various sayings of Rabindranath Tagore during lecture in order to break the monotony of the classroom. His books on Special

Functions, Laplace Transform and Numerical Analysis became very popular among students. Teachers also used these books to teach these subjects in the classroom. Even researchers sometimes used these books, while carrying out their research. He also achieved success in academic administration. He handled the responsibilities of the head of the Mathematics Department at Presidency College quite well. Later, he became the Principal of Hooghly Government College. He held this position until his retirement from the West Bengal Educational Service in 1953. But despite his administrative duties, he never slackened in research and teaching. His research was published in renowned international journals, such as Proceedings of the Royal Society of London, Quarterly of Applied Mathematics and Philosophical Magazine. His numerous research papers were cited in various textbooks. For his significant contribution to directly deriving Elastic Stress from Stress Equations in Mathematical Elasticity, he was awarded the Doctor of Science (D.Sc.) degree.

After retiring from government service in 1953, he served as a research Professor at Birla College of Engineering (now Birla Institute of Technology and Science, B.I.T.S.) in Pilani, Rajasthan for about two years (1954–1956). At the invitation of Rector (Vice-Chancellor) Triguna Sen, he joined as the Professor and Head of the Mathematics Department at Jadavpur University. He was also the Dean of the Science Faculty at Jadavpur University until 1963. At the age of 65, he retired from Jadavpur University. Shortly afterwards, he joined Visva-Bharati University as the Head of the Mathematics Department and the Principal of Vidya Bhavan (the postgraduate college for arts and sciences). He was invited to these positions by the then Vice-Chancellor of Visva-Bharati, Sudhiranjan Das (former Chief Justice of India), with special approval from the then Chancellor of Visva-Bharati, Prime Minister Jawaharlal Nehru. Prof. Sen significantly improved Vidya Bhavan and strengthened the Mathematics Department. After working at Visva-Bharati for a few years, he rejoined Jadavpur University as an Hon. Emeritus Professor until the end of his life (December 13, 1976). Under his guidance, 54 students earned their Ph.D. degrees. It is particularly noteworthy that he was a Fellow of The National Institute of Sciences (F.N.I.) of India (now F.N.A., Fellow of the Indian National Science Academy). In 1952, he was elected President of the Mathematics Section of the Indian Science Congress. He was also elected President of the Calcutta Mathematical Society in 1968.

The purpose of narrating the story of such a great researcher and teacher in some detail is to let the younger generation of students and researchers know how difficult was the life of such a great academician! The story may serve as an inspiration for them. Prof. Sen moved forward patiently on the path of life, and thus he was able to reach the pinnacle of success in later life. I never noticed any expression of frustration on Prof. Sen's face. He had no hatred, malice, or selfishness in his character. When students and friends visited his house, he always offered hospitality.

Second Attempt to Secure Prof. Sen's Mentorship

Following Prof. Jnan Gopal Chakraborty's suggestion, I went to Prof. Sen's house in Jodhpur Park (Kolkata) again. He was then working at Visva-Bharati. He used to come to his house in Kolkata one day a week (only Wednesdays). On seeing me, he said, "I told you that day, I will not take any more students. I have become old, and I have various types of illness. Look for a younger guide." Saying this, he rejected all my requests again. What to do! I left his house in utter disappointment. I used to live at Uluberia those days. I returned home. Almost two months after this incident, I went to the Applied Mathematics Department to meet my teachers. That day, Prof. Sen also came for a meeting of the Calcutta Mathematical Society. On seeing me from a distance, he asked me to come close to him. He enquired if I could find any research guide in the meantime. Knowing that I hadn't, Prof. Sen said, "Then you can do research under me." At that moment, my feeling was as if the moon had fallen into my hands! Then he advised me when to meet him, what to read before starting research, etc.

Beginning of Teaching: Pania-Sardabard High School

My teaching career began in 1964, shortly after completing my B.Sc. (Hons.) examination. Since my M.Sc. admission was still a month and a half away, I decided to teach at the nearby Pania-Sardabarh High School. They gladly welcomed me to teach at their school. I taught there for about a month and a half without any remuneration (voluntary service). I enjoyed teaching various subjects in different classes, including mathematics in class seven/eight. I enjoyed the experience immensely even though it meant walking three kilometers each day to and from the school.

Teaching at Naipur Santisudha Institution

Our M.Sc. examination was postponed due to the general elections in the country in 1966. At that time, the M.Sc. exams were usually held in November-December. But for that batch the M.Sc. examination took place in January-February, 1967. The results were published by the end of May. While waiting for the results, last week of February 1967, I returned to my native village, Bagmari. From March to May 1967, I taught at Naipur Shantisudha Institution, a higher secondary school about 10 kilometers from my home. At that time, the headmaster of this institution was Sri Radhanath Das Adhikari (former MLA). He warmly welcomed me. I stayed in the school's hostel. Several other teachers also lived in the hostel—mathematics teacher Ashok Roy, life science teacher Kanan Pramanik, commerce teacher Anant Kumar Laya, among others. Four teachers stayed in each room. Although I was the youngest among the teachers in that school, I could quickly develop friendship with everyone.

A Humorous Incident

One day, an amusing incident happened at the nearby post office when I went to buy postal stamps. The postmaster, Sri Atul Kulavi, asked, "Which class are you in?" Surprised, I responded, "I am a teacher here. I joined a few days ago." This kind of mistake happened frequently even after joining Uluberia College as a lecturer. Even today when I travel to Germany, people often underestimate my age by at least ten years.

Thus began my journey in research and teaching, setting the foundation for an academic career filled with learning, perseverance, and the guidance of remarkable mentors.

Further Details of Naipur Santisudha Institution

Both Sri Radhagobinda Das Adhikari and his younger brother Haripada Babu were teachers at that school. Although Haripada Babu was much older than me, he stayed in the same room as me in the hostel. Soon I developed good friendship with him. Teacher Kanailal Nayak used to commute from his home by riding bicycle. He also became a close friend of mine. After some time, when he got married, I had the opportunity to attend his wedding ceremony. In September 2020, the author was invited from the IIT campus to the bicentennial birth anniversary celebration of Iswar Chandra Vidyasagar, held at that school. Despite being ill, Kanai Babu came to meet me. I noticed that his affection and warmth had not faded even a bit, although I had been his colleague for only three months before joining Uluberia College, that too more than 50 years ago. Near the school, another teacher named Bimal Das used to run a mess for dining. Occasionally I used to eat in that mess.

One particular incident from this period, remains vivid in my memory. One day while returning from Giridih, due to a delay in getting the bus, it got very late at night. So I decided to get off from the bus at my maternal uncle's house in Sauri. The plan was to stay there overnight and go to Naipur School early in the morning to take the class. When I arrived at my uncle's house at 11 p.m., I found out that everyone had already gone to bed, having closed the doors and windows, and switched off the lights. Not wanting to disturb anyone, I lay down and slept on a cot outside. It is against my nature to cause any inconvenience to others. Early in the morning, my maternal elder uncle and aunt were very angry to see me sleeping outside the house. Eventually, they scolded me a lot that day out of affection.

All is Your Will, O Mother!

The results of the M.Sc. exam were published in the last week of May, 1967. I was elated to secure a first class. This raised my hopes of obtaining a lecturer position in a college. Around this time, Swami Satyagahananda from Ramakrishna Mission in Belgharia sent me a letter, informing that Ramakrishna Mission Vidyapith in Purulia needed an M.Sc. in mathematics. He also wrote that according to their system, they could offer a salary of over 400 rupees per month, which was higher than what other school teachers received at that time. He suggested that if I wished, I should send my application directly to them. I first felt very excited after receiving this letter, thinking that I would be able to continue to live in the divine atmosphere of the Ramakrishna Mission.

But I found myself grappling with a crucial decision—should I apply?

I reasoned that if I applied and was selected, I would have no choice but to join. Moreover, I realized that if I join Purulia Ramakrishna Mission Vidyapith, conducting research would be nearly impossible. This, in turn, would mean that I would have never become a professor at IIT, nor would I have had the opportunity to mentor students pursuing their doctorates, significantly shaping their careers.

Ultimately, an unseen force seemed to guide me away from applying. Reflecting on this, I often find myself thinking—"Mother! All is your will; You alone fulfill desires."

Initiation into Teaching: Uluberia College

At that time, there was no College Service Commission (C.S.C.). Each college formed its own selection committee (of course, following government rules and regulations) to fill various subject vacancies in the college. Government-

Uluberia College, Howrah

nominated members and distinguished academicians were also part of the selection committee. The college principal, members of the managing committee, the college secretary or his representative, and external subject experts were also in the selection committee.

Almost immediately after the M.Sc. results were published, several colleges advertised for mathematics lecturer positions. I sent applications to almost all the places that came to my attention. I recall that a college in Assam and Kailashahar College in Tripura selected me solely based on my application and bio-data and sent appointment letters without an interview. I was also called for an interview before the selection committees for appointment of lecturers at Uluberia College (Howrah), Midnapore College (West Midnapore), and Katwa College (Burdwan). I received appointment letters from all these three colleges. Katwa College was very keen that I join their college.

Midnapore College, being a bigger institution, closer to my home, and government-sponsored was an attractive choice. At that time, considering job security, people preferred government-sponsored colleges to private institutions like Uluberia College. Considering these three points, I felt inclined to join Midnapore College. Uluberia College was entirely private. Its only advantage was its proximity to Kolkata. It usually took 45 minutes to travel from Uluberia to Howrah station by local electric trains. Also, being close to Kolkata would greatly facilitate my research. At the time, I had already started research work with Prof. B. Sen. When I mentioned about Midnapore College to him, he made it clear that I wouldn't be able to carry out research under his guidance had I joined there, the reason being that Midnapore is far away from Kolkata.

He made it clear that to continue my research with him, I must continue in Uluberia. With my aspirations firmly set on completing Ph.D. as soon as possible, I took the final decision to continue in Uluberia College without any further thinking.

Affection: An Act of Deep Emotion

There is a saying, 'Affection teaches us first to notice, then to endure, then to smile at, then to enjoy'... Here is an illustration of this assertion. Mr. Subodh Kumar Jasu was a respected gentleman in Uluberia and adjoining areas. He was very affectionate towards me. Even when I moved from Uluberia to IIT Kharagpur in 1971, his affection for me did not fade, although we completely lost contact after that. Many years later, in 2004, when the author was awarded the 'Rammohan Prize' for his outstanding contributions to the field of mathematics, the news was published prominently in various English, Bengali, and Hindi newspapers. Subodh Babu then an octogenarian, wrote me a heartfelt postcard, stating:

> *"There was once a mathematics professor at Uluberia College, named Jagadis Chandra Misra. If you are the same Jagadis, I would be greatly obliged if you could meet me one day while travelling to/from Kolkata. ..."*

The day after receiving his letter, I travelled to Uluberia to see him. After searching I found his house near a crematorium. He had become a spiritual recluse, living in a small, electricity-less dwelling. At dusk, I finally saw a frail, long-beared man unclosing the door. It took me a moment to recognize him, as decades had passed since our last meeting.

He looked at me affectionately for a while and then said, "You have to travel a long way back to Kharagpur, so don't delay any longer." I bid him farewell with a respectful bow. I understood that he was not in a condition to talk much. Besides asking about my well-being, he had nothing much to say either. So, I proceeded to catch the train at the Uluberia Railway Station. As I walked away, I reflected—affection is indeed a very complex emotion!

Living in a Favourable Environment at Uluberia

After joining Uluberia College as a lecturer in Mathematics on July 23, 1967, the first person I became close to was Prof. Ajay Banerjee (Jhintu Da), the head of the Bengali department. He was the middle brother of the college principal, Prof. Jayanta Banerjee (Pintu Da). Shortly after joining the college, I was fortunate to find a beautiful house. It was a one-storey house with just one bed room, a bathroom, and a kitchen. The rent was 30 Rupees. The owner, Mr. Ashwini Kumar Das, was a renowned lawyer at the Uluberia Court. He had built the house for a bachelor gentleman, but after living there for only a few months, the gentleman left. Ashwini Babu was a devotee of the Ramakrishna Math and Mission and had taken initiation from the second President, Srimat Swami Shivananda. On the first day, he told me, "You will stay here as one of my sons." Indeed, I lived there for about four years. He would personally take care of all my needs and I never had any inconvenience, during my stay there.

Prof. Ajay Bandopadhyay

Lakshmi Came Home!

In 1969, when my marriage was settled, and the house-owner came to know this, he decided to construct an upper floor on the house. The first floor had two small rooms but no bathroom or kitchen. Still, it was suitable for a small family of two persons. The rent then was raised to Rs. 60. When my newly-wedded wife came to Uluberia after marriage, the house-owner's wife would often visit us, bringing home-cooked meals as if welcoming a new 'Grihalakshmi' (goddess of the household) into their family. Ashwini Babu arranged for their servant Haru to do our market shopping and clean our utensils, which was very convenient since my wife Shorasi had just enrolled in the B.Ed programme at Uluberia College. My father, who was taking my middle brother Dines to see a doctor in Kolkata, had planned to stay with us for a couple of days on the way, but since the upper floor was not yet built, the house-owner arranged for them to stay in his living room.

Neighbours

Ashwini Babu had three sons—Chittaranjan, Pritiranjan, and Vivekranjan. The eldest, Chittaranjan, was somewhat reserved, while Pritiranjan was more talkative, and Vivekranjan was always cheerful and witty. He remained unmarried all his life. The principal, Jayanta Banerjee, and his brother Ajay Banerjee lived very close to us in a rented house. Jayanta Banerjee's wife Mrs. Meena Banerjee was an economics faculty at Howrah Girls' College, and Ajay Banerjee's wife Mrs. Sunipa Banerjee was a school teacher. Being close, I often visited their house to chat with Jhintu Da (Prof. Ajay Banerjee), whenever both of us had free time. Within a few days, I had developed a friendly relationship with everyone in their family. I would often be offered tea and snacks there and couldn't refuse due to their heartfelt hospitality.

I was fortunate to have very good neighbours: our landlord Ashwini Babu, the Principal Jayanta Banerjee, and Bijay Das. There was a pond nearby our residence, where Mr. Jayanta Banerjee and Mr. Ajay Banerjee would bathe at different times. They would greet me as 'Master' when passing by our gate and chat for a while. Mr. Jayanta Banerjee, although a bit reserved, would talk to me on his way to bathe. Mr. Bijay Das's family, who lived closest to us, was very respectful towards me. Bijay Babu was a widower with three sons and four daughters. His eldest son, Satyen (a schoolteacher), and his middle son, Soumen (a veterinary doctor), lived at different locations with their families. The eldest daughter was married, and the youngest son, Shambhu, was pursuing B.Sc. at Uluberia College, while the daughters Putul, Guli, and Tuli were studying for their B.A. They all treated me with great respect, and their father, Bijay Babu, was very courteous. Their household included an elderly widowed maid, Ranidi, who would often help my wife Shorasi.

Faculty Colleagues

It used to take me only five minutes to walk to the college from the residence. Those days, like some other faculty members, I used to wear a dhoti. There weren't many faculty members then, and the relationship among colleagues was very cordial. Many faculty members commuted from Kolkata by local train, and there were lively discussions in the common room when there were no classes. Some of the colleagues included Sunil Babu and Mr. Subinay Dhar from the English department; Ajay Banerjee, Deepak Dey, Alok Banerjee, Swapna Majumdar, from the Bengali Department; Prabir Banerjee, Kanai Chattopadhyay, Shibnath Banerjee, Jahanara Begum from the history department; Manoranjan Maity, Shankar Panigrahi, Alok Sarkar, Dr. Sen from the Chemistry department; Nirmal Chatterjee, Gourishankar Maity from the physics department; Alok Sanyal from the Biology department; Dr. Majed Molla, Prafulla Bag, Prantikumar Pal, Pratul Das from the Mathematics department; Sri Shambhu Ghosh from the philosophy department; Sri Nirmal Bose from the Political Science department, and Librarian Saroj Ghosal (Chhonada). I fondly remember Balai Ghosal, the office superintendent, head clerk Gopal Dutta, Nishith Ghosal, and Kashem Ali who had a friendly relationship with the faculty members. Whenever anyone faced any difficulty, everyone, regardless of their position, would extend a helping hand.

I still remember the amazing tea made by Ashru Da (with condensed milk). Saroj Ghosal's father, the venerable Professor Haripada Ghosal, was the founder Principal of Uluberia College. Profs. Shambhu Ghosh and Nirmal Bose were actively involved in politics (both affiliated to Forward Bloc Party). At that time, Nirmal Bose was an MLC (Member of Legislative Council), and Shambhu Ghosh was an MLA (Member of Legislative Assembly). In the first United Front government, Shambhu Ghosh was the Minister of Small and Cottage Industries, while during the second United Front government, he was the Minister of Higher Education. He was extremely courteous and kind-hearted. I recall when I was teaching at IIT Kharagpur, Prof. Shambhu Ghosh, spotting me from a distance, called me over warmly during one of his visits for a meeting at IIT Kharagpur. He was truly humble and unassuming. Unfortunately, he passed away prematurely due to cancer.

Relation between Faculty and Staff Members

Relationship among all the faculty and staff members was very cordial at Uluberia College. Everything was conducted in a homely atmosphere. Those who commuted by train from Kolkata would engage in lively conversations, making the monotony of daily commuting enjoyable. Whenever a new faculty joined the college, the head clerk Sri Gopal Datta would invariably approach him for doing life insurance, to which no one could say 'no' due to his warm behavior. He also used to play another role that everyone in the college enjoyed. Whenever someone got married, Gopal Datta would arrange a feast at the college, featuring various dishes of 'Hilsa' fish from the Ganges, among other items. He would oversee the cooking and other arrangements. The newlyweds only had to discuss with him and hand over the requisite amount of expenditure. However, Gopal Da always ensured that the expenses were not excessive, being conscious that the newlyweds needed to set up a new household.

In the Role of a Priest

During the four-year stay in Uluberia, I also had to perform a little priestly duties. Once, during Saraswati Puja, Prof. Ajay Banerjee's wife wanted me to perform the '*Hatekhari*' (the ritual of initiating a child into reading and writing) for their daughter Rili. Once she had the idea, there was no turning back. As soon as I came to their house, both Prof. Banerjee (Jhintu Da) and his wife insisted, "Master, you have to perform Rili's 'Initiation to Studies' (*Hatekhari*) on Saraswati Puja day" (In familiar circles at Uluberia, people used to fondly call me as 'Mastermoshai'). Despite my refusal for not knowing the rituals and mantras, they wouldn't listen. Mrs. Banerjee continued, "If you perform her *Hatekhari*, my daughter will excel in studies." Finally, I had to agree. Such is the strength of affectionate bonds! On the day of Saraswati Puja, wearing a dhoti and shawl, I performed the first *Hatekhari* ceremony as a Brahmin soul! Suddenly, I saw Uluberia's photojournalist Mr. Swadeshranjan Das taking photos of the ceremony. The news, along with a large photo, was published in the local newspaper. Prof. Banerjee and his wife proudly showed it to me, and they had framed the photo in their house, giving me a copy as well. Next year, Gopal Da insisted that I should perform his son's *Hatekhari*. I had to oblige him as well. That was not the end of the story! Many years later, Prof. Hemendra Nath Dutta of the Mining Engineering Department at IIT Kharagpur also asked me to perform the *Hatekhari* for his grandson. Both he and his wife were also the disciples of Srimat Swami Shankarananda. Long after that, the office superintendent at IIT Kharagpur, Sri Chiraranjan Das, insisted that I recite the Gita for his father's Adya Shraddha (first death anniversary). Despite my limited expertise in this matter, I had to agree due to my familiarity with his father. I performed the complete Gita recital on that occasion. I also voluntarily recited the complete Gita on the occasion of the Adya Shraddha of my daughter Sumita's both parents-in-law, my father-in-law and brother-in-law, Deepak.

'Mastermoshai'—A Very Sweet Address

Soon, the author developed a harmonious and cordial relationship with many locals in Uluberia. While walking down the street, people of various ages would address him as 'Mastermoshai' and engage in conversations, exchanging pleasantries for a minute. Although Uluberia was a sub-divisional town, to the author, it appeared like a big village those days. Perhaps that's why the warmth and intimacy were so palpable. After college hours, he used to go for a walk by the Ganges river every evening. Even then, people would call out 'Mastermoshai' from both sides of the street.

Initially, Jhintu Da accompanied me during evening walk, followed by Sri Dipak De from the Bengali department and then Sri Alok Sanyal (Biology). However, on Wednesdays and occasionally on some other days, I had to go to Kolkata for research work. So others would not go for evening or afternoon walks on those days. The usual evening walk route was from my house, passing by the college, Uluberia Court, then along the road in front of Uluberia Kalibari, passing Dhara's sweet shop, and then walking along the Ganges river bank for quite a distance (about 2 km). On the way back, all of us would stop at Dhara's shop for samosa and sweets. The shop was famous for these two items. Dhara's shop had a great location; it was on the river, offering a beautiful view of the Ganges. Unfortunately, it was heard that the shop later collapsed into the river and had to be relocated.

Temple of Goddess Kali in Uluberia is also very beautiful. Next to the temple of Goddess Kali, there is a temple of Lord Shiva. The view of the Ganges from Kalibari premises is very picturesque. Many people come here to perform various rituals and pujas.

Birth of the Eldest Son, Subhas

Despite being pregnant, Shorasi remained dedicated to her studies and successfully completed her B.Ed. course while residing in Uluberia. Naturally, she experienced discomfort at times but her determination and enthusiasm never wavered. The affection and support of her friends provided immense comfort and her elderly classmates played a crucial role in offering mental and emotional support. On certain days, they even cooked for her. One day Alok Da (Sanyal)'s mother invited us for lunch. The cooking taste of each item was superb, all the items were highly delicious! Their ancestral home was in Bangladesh, and it is well-known that the cooking skills of Bangladeshi mothers are exceptional. That day we got to experience it firsthand. The preparation of every dish, including fried Hilsa fish, steamed and boiled chicken, and some vegetarian dishes, along with *payesh* (a sweet rice pudding), was outstanding! Words failed to capture how exquisite the meal was!

Jolly Di (Prof. Swapna Majumdar) from the Bengali department lived with her family (father, mother, elder brother, and sister) in Uluberia at that time. She wasn't married then. They invited us for meals several times. Later, she married Prof. Alok Banerjee from the Bengali department, while her younger sister Poly married Prof. Alok Sanyal from Biology department.

For Shorasi's prenatal check-up, we used to take her to the Chief Medical Officer of Uluberia Hospital, a skilled Gynaecologist. I accompanied her for regular check-ups, reassured by his expertise. Our eldest child Subhas was born just seven days after Shorasi's B.Ed examinations ended. Subhas was born early in the morning. As that time we didn't have a telephone, the hospital contacted Prof. Jayanta Banerjee's house to convey the news. Principal Pintu Da himself came over to our house and said, "Jagadis, you are now the father of a son."

Shortly after, I went to the hospital with my mother in a rickshaw to see the mother and the newborn. To ensure Shorasi had no trouble, our loving mother came from Bagmari to stay with us in Uluberia well in advance. She cooked tasty meals for Shorasi and her presence was also very helpful. A few days later, my mother returned to Bagmari with her daughter-in-law and grandson.

A Beloved Student Goes Missing

Shortly after I joined the Uluberia College as a lecturer, one evening Jolly Di (Prof. Swapna Majumdar) came to my residence with a boy named Dipendu Ghosh. I recognized the boy as a first-year honours student in Mathematics. After some conversation, she said that they lived next door and that Dipendu was very eager to take private tuition from me. I tried to dissuade them, saying I needed a lot of time for research. However, Jolly Di was insistent, emphasizing Dipendu's strong desire to learn from me. She said, the boy would come to my residence three evenings a week. When she asked about the fees, I said it was not necessary.

Eventually, I agreed, thinking it would reduce my feeling of loneliness to some extent. However, at the end of the month, Dipendu's father came and paid 75 Rupees, which he continued to pay at the end of every month. Dipendu was a very polite, gentle, soft-spoken, calm, and intelligent boy.

However, about a year later, I was devastated to hear that Dipendu had gone missing. Years passed, yet no information surfaced regarding his whereabouts. I remained deeply saddened by this incident and continued to inquire about him even after leaving Uluberia. To this day, the thought of him fills me with sorrow.

A Distinguished Colleague and Friend: Prof. Pranati Kumar Pal

Prof. P.K. Pal

About four months after I joined the Uluberia College, another faculty, Sri Pranati Kumar Pal, joined the Mathematics department. We quickly formed a close bond. Initially, he commuted from Kolkata for a few years, but we had many friendly conversations whenever there were no classes. He was originally from Khejuri in East Medinipur.

When I left Uluberia for joining IIT Kharagpur, I arranged for him the house where we lived on rent. After living there for a few years, he built a three-storeyed house in Fuleshwar and lived there. I visited and stayed at that house several times. Prof. P.K. Pal and his wife were very hospitable. He possessed many qualities—he was a dedicated teacher, a true seeker of knowledge, honest, and principled. Such a person is rare to find. He completed his Ph.D. a bit later, but he had no aspiration to become a university professor. He was a student of pure mathematics. He had also been a resident at Belgharia Ramakrishna Mission Vidyarthi Ashram during his B.Sc. (Hons.) programme.

After the house in Fuleshwar was constructed, his sister-in-law, her husband Sri Bimal Kuilya, and their son lived with them. Bimal had once been Prof. P.K. Pal's student at Uluberia College. Bimal is very polite, humble, and helpful, worked in a bank and now retired. Sadly, Prof. Pal recently passed away suddenly leaving a void in our hearts. I pray for his soul's peace.

Progress of My Research Work

Under the mentorship of Professor B. Sen, I delved into my research with great enthusiasm. He guided me, teaching me the principles of scientific inquiry. As I made progress, he once remarked, "A Ph.D. is training in research." I didn't fully understand what he meant by this at that time. Despite having several research papers published in esteemed journals, I wondered why he made that statement. Years later, after guiding several of my Ph.D. students at IIT, I could understand depth of his insight.

Another senior professor at IIT once said, "Research and teaching should go hand in hand." That is, research and teaching are complementary to each other. It took me quite some time to truly internalize this principle. Once I did, I made sure to impact this wisdom to all my doctoral students.

The Journey to Ph.D. Registration

Once I made considerable progress in my research, Sir instructed me to collect a Ph.D. registration form from the Ph.D. Section of Jadavpur University. At that time, I had no idea what Ph.D. registration entailed or why it was necessary. Coming from my background such a lack of awareness is understandable. However, after having a look to the form, I realized I had to fill out most of it myself.

After getting Sir's signature, I submitted the form at the University Office, where I was assured that everything else would be handled administratively. Soon, I received official confirmation of my Ph.D. registration.

Colleagues' Reactions to My Kolkata Visits

During a conversation in the faculty common room of Uluberia College, once I mentioned that I travelled to Kolkata every Wednesday, my off-day, to have academic discussions with my research guide. Many senior colleagues and Vice Principal Professor Arun Dasgupta were present. Some asked, "When and what do you eat during these trips?" I replied, "When I go out, I never eat rice at a hotel. Instead, after meeting Sir, I have bread, two rosogollas, two bananas, and one hundred grams of yogurt. After that, I go to various places for research-related work. I eat rice at home at night." I also explained that my research was theoretical and it was required to visit various libraries, such as the Central Library of Jadavpur University, the National Library, the British Council Library, the Library of Rajabazar Science College, and sometimes the BE College (currently IIEST), library at Shibpur. Travelling by bus was very challenging. I had to study in the libraries, and write down notes in some long bound exercise books.

When they heard that the author didn't eat at hotels, various colleagues gave him different suggestions. But Vice Principal, Prof. Arun Dasgupta reacted strongly, "What, Jagadis! You are now too young. This stubbornness is not good for you. After completion of your Ph.D., you will have to go to various universities abroad to deliver lectures, attend conferences, etc." To be honest, back then I didn't have any such aspirations—I was simply focused on earning my Ph.D. However, Prof. Dasgupta's words eventually came true when I later travelled to Germany.

Thesis Preparation

One day, Sir instructed me to compile my thesis using the manuscripts of different research papers that were submitted for publication in different scientific journals. Although six of my research papers had already been published in various journals by then, and several others were pending publication, I had no idea if that was enough for a Ph.D. degree. Following Sir's instructions, I gathered all my published papers, structured them as per his guidance and prepared a preface. Since those days mathematical symbols weren't available on typewriters, I had to write them by hand on all the five copies of the thesis.

For diagrams, a student from a local polytechnic helped by preparing about 15 original drawings and five copies (blueprints) of each. Despite the meticulous process, Sir was pleased with my work. I submitted my thesis in August 1970, and my Ph.D. viva voce was scheduled for February 1971.

Due to the prevailing Naxalite disturbances those days, the external examiner expressed reluctance to enter Jadavpur University premises. As a result, the university arranged for my viva voce at an alternative location. Despite the challenges, the examination processes ended smoothly.

After the Ph.D. degree was awarded to me, the faculty members and students of Uluberia College organized a felicitation for me. The Principal, Vice Principal, many colleagues, and students attended. The felicitation ceremony was held in the hall (Room No. 7) on the other side of the pond in the college premises.

Felicitation to the Author at Uluberia College after the Award of Ph.D. Degree,
Left to Right: Vice Principal, Author, Principal

One of my students, Sushil Mandal, was doing B.Sc. at the time. As his brother had a photo studio, he had some expertise in photography. He took some good photographs of the reception ceremony, which he later gifted me in beautifully framed prints—a cherished memory of my academic journey.

Gratitude

I feel highly grateful to Uluberia College, where my journey as a college lecturer began and where my research work took its first steps. The college played a pivotal role in shaping my academic and professional life. One of the most memorable aspects of my time at Uluberia College was teaching in its large hall (Room No. 7). The Mathematics class for the first year B.Sc. pass course was held in that hall. The number of students was 170–180. In those days, there was no arrangement for audio-visual teaching methods in the classroom, not even a microphone. Teaching in such a large class required a strong voice and effective engagement with students—skills that later proved invaluable to me. When I, moved to IIT Kharagpur, I encountered similar class room dynamics. At IIT, there was a subject called 'Advanced Engineering Mathematics' (Subject No. MA 614). All first-year M.Tech students across all engineering disciplines had to study this subject (compulsory). Therefore, the number of students in that class was sometimes 170–180 in just one section. The classes were held in the Raman Auditorium or Bhatnagar Auditorium of IIT. When I used to teach that subject, there was no audio-visual system or microphone in the classroom. So the experience of handling large classes at Uluberia College proved very useful to me. Four years at Uluberia College passed quickly. After I received my doctoral degree, there was an advertisement from IIT Kharagpur. I submitted my application for the position of lecturer in Mathematics and subsequently I received an interview call. Fortunately, I was able to answer almost all the questions fairly well during the interview, and IIT Kharagpur sent me an appointment letter in due course.

Initially, I considered taking a one-year leave from Uluberia College. But my well-wishers strongly advised me to resign from Uluberia College without any hesitation. They said there would be many more opportunities for career advancement at IIT. Trusting their guidance, I made the difficult decision to resign there. However, I never regretted it. On the contrary, I firmly believe it was the right decision for both my professional advancement and the college itself, as my departure allowed the institution to promptly appoint a new faculty member.

Even today, memories of Uluberia fill my heart with joy—not just mine, but also my wife Shorasi's. She had even more reasons to cherish our time there. In just one year, she received her B.Ed. degree, our eldest son and some more friends and well-wishers.

My mother, though she stayed in Uluberia for only about three months, also had fond memories. During my research trips to Kolkata, I would bring fresh Hilsa fish from Uluberia Station, knowing how much she loved it. Her joy was evident, as she would personally clean, cook and serve the fish with utmost care, especially, to her daughter-in-law.

So many cherished moments and so many heartfelt recollections crowd in my mind when I think of Uluberia. But perhaps it is time to conclude this reminiscence here.

CHAPTER 7 Teaching and Research

IIT Kharagpur

In August 1970, after submitting my Ph.D. thesis to Jadavpur University, as mentioned earlier. I came across a newspaper advertisement for a lecturer position in the Mathematics Department at IIT Kharagpur. Excited by the opportunity, I promptly sent my application via registered post. Never had I imagined that I would be associated with such a prestigious institution.

Following my Ph.D. viva voce, I sent an attested copy of my provisional Ph.D. certificate from Jadavpur University to IIT—one copy to Registrar's office and another to the Head of Mathematics Department. A few days later, I received an invitation for attending an interview before the Selection Committee.

The Interview Experience

On the day of interview, I took a local train from Uluberia to my younger great uncle's (mother's uncle) house in Kausalya, Kharagpur. My great uncle, delighted by my visit, welcomed me warmly to his newly built home 'Milan Kutir'. I vividly remember watching him catch fish from a small pond using a net, while my grandmother and aunt lovingly prepared a meal for me. My uncle, Debabrata was so enthusiastic that he even ironed my clothes to ensure I looked smart for the interview. Before leaving, they made me promise to visit them again after the interview was over.

The Selection Committee was chaired by IIT's Director Brigadier S.K. Bose, and included the Head of the Department Prof. A.K. Gayen, senior Mathematics Professor D.N. Mitra, and external experts such as Prof. Saxena from Ranchi University and Prof. P.K. Ghosh from Calcutta University. Brig. Bose was a civil engineer. After retirement from defence service, he was appointed by the Govt. of India as the Director of IIT Kharagpur. As the Chairman of the Selection Committee, he first introduced each candidate before the Selection Committee and immediately after that he started the interview process by posing some general questions of fundamental nature.

I handed over my Ph.D. thesis and reprints of some research publications to him. When the director noticed that my research was concerned with thermal stresses, he inquired about its definition and applications. Since these topics aligned with my thesis, I could confidently answer his questions, citing turbine blades as an example. He advised me to collaborate with researchers from Mechanical, Civil, or Applied Mechanics Departments, a piece of advice that remains etched in my memory.

After reviewing my thesis, the director passed it to the experts. The external experts, Prof. Saxena and Prof. Ghosh asked further questions which I could answer with satisfaction. Reflecting on the experience, I believe my satisfactory performance at the interview was due to having the experience of both teaching and research activities simultaneously. Two or three months later, I received my offer letter from IIT Kharagpur.

August 9, 1971, marked a significant milestone in the life of the author, when he joined IIT Kharagpur as a Lecturer in the Mathematics Department on this date. He considers this day as the second turning point in life (the first turning point in life being the date on which he joined Ramakrishna Mission Vidyamandira, Belur Math as an I.Sc. student).

IIT Kharagpur Main Building

Pay Structure of IIT Faculty Members in Those Days

It is worth mentioning that the salaries of faculty members at IITs were not very attractive back then. The pay scales for various levels of faculty were as follows:

- Lecturer : Rs. 400-40-800-50-950
- Assistant Professor : Rs. 700-50-1250
- Professor : Rs. 1100-1600

Today, IIT teachers are categorized as Assistant Professors, Associate Professors, and Professors, with significantly improved salaries and higher standard of living compared to the past.

Early Days of Teaching

On my first day at IIT Kharagpur, I completed recruitment formalities at the Establishment Section in the morning and started taking M.Sc. classes in the afternoon. The next morning, I had a B.Tech class. Back then, many senior professors in the science departments used to feel reluctant to take B.Tech classes due to the large number of students. Thus, mostly newly appointed young teachers were assigned B.Tech classes. The author taught B.Tech classes in both semesters year after year. Though demanding, I enjoyed teaching, as it clarified my own understanding of various concepts. The following verse from the Mahabharata is very relevant in this context:

> *"By applying one's mind, one acquires a fourth part of the desired knowledge, by listening to the teacher one acquires another fourth part, by discussing with others one acquires a third fourth part, and by meditating on what one has learnt, one acquires the remaining fourth part."*

Shortage of Accommodation

Those days, there was an acute scarcity of residential quarters at IIT Kharagpur. A newly joined faculty had to stay in the Gokhale Hall of Residence for at least a few months. However, when I joined, there were no vacant rooms in that hostel. I approached Prof. Birendra Nath Niyogi, the warden of the B.C. Roy Hall of Residence, which was meant exclusively for research scholars. Though it was unconventional for faculty to stay in the students' hostels, realizing the situation, Prof. Neogi allowed me to stay in the guest room of B.C. Roy Hall for two months. That room was on the first floor of B.C. Roy Hall. Since I was quite young then (only 27 years old), I had no problem mingling with some of the research scholars like friends. At that time some of the residents, like S.S. Alam, A.R. Roy, Anjan Sarkar, and Dilip Dutta were research scholars in the Mathematics Department. Later, S.S. Alam, Akhil Roy, and Anjan Sarkar joined as lecturers in the Mathematics Department after receiving their doctorates. A physics research scholar, Devadidev Mahanti, who also stayed in B.C. Roy Hall those days was a very cheerful person. He became very friendly with me.

Celebration of Teacher's Day

A few days after I joined, it was Dr. Sarvepalli Radhakrishnan's birthday (September 5), celebrated as Teacher's Day in educational institutions throughout India. Like other educational institutions in India, IIT Kharagpur students celebrated it with various events, honouring their teachers in different ways. In the evening, students of Radhakrishnan Hall of Residence organized a programme for all faculty members from IIT Kharagpur. One significant item of that programme was the 'Best Teacher Award'. That year, the award was given to Professor N. Keshavamurthy from the Electrical Engineering Department. He was known to be an excellent teacher, dedicated to improving his lectures by recording and reviewing them several times. He loved teaching deeply. Although he did not have a formal doctorate of his own, many scholars obtained their doctorates under his guidance.

A Missed Opportunity

About a month after I joined, I saw an advertisement for a three-month lecture series programme in Trieste, Italy. I took a copy of the advertisement to Director Brigadier S.K. Bose to request him for granting leave. At that time, Prof. A.K. Gayen, the head of the Mathematics department, was also present in the office of the Director. He also requested the director to grant me three months' leave. However, the director said that leave for going abroad could not be granted until three years of service had been completed.

The Mathematics Department at IIT Kharagpur

Prof. A.K Gayen

When the author joined as a lecturer in the Mathematics Department, as already mentioned the internationally renowned mathematician and statistician, Prof. Anil Kumar Gayen, was the head of the department. Despite being born into poverty and losing his father at a young age, his brilliance and perseverance led him to great heights. He had obtained his Ph.D. from Cambridge University and was a fellow of the Statistical Society of London. He was elected a Fellow of the Indian National Academy (INSA), New Delhi in 1966 and was well-known for his research findings on the effect of non-normality on standard tests of significance, linear statistical inference and applications and the distribution of product-moment correlation coefficient. He also contributed significantly to the measurement of discriminating powers in psychometric and educational measurement problems. He was elected President of the Statistics Section of the Indian Science Congress in 1971. His encouragement and guidance significantly shaped the author's academic career.

At that time, Prof. Anadi Shankar Gupta and Prof. Devendra Nath Mitra held D.Sc. degrees in Mathematics at IIT Kharagpur. Later, the author also earned a D.Sc. in applied mathematics from Calcutta University. Prof. Sudarshan Nanda received his D.Sc. from Berhampur University, Odisha. Although Prof. Guruprasanna Bhattacharya had his Ph.D. in Statistics, he was the first to start research in Computer Science at IIT Kharagpur. He, along with Prof. Nanigopal Dutta, Prof. C.N. Kaul, and later Profs. D.K. Gupta, A. Goswami, S. Sundar, P. Niyogi, R. Biswas as well as Pawan Kumar handled research supervision and teaching of various computer science subjects at the Department of Mathematics, along with various mathematical research fields. All these faculty members were instrumental in running the five-year integrated M.Sc. programme in Mathematics and Computing and two-year M.Tech. programme in Computer Science and Data Processing. Subsequently both these courses gained popularity for their demand in the job market.

Among others, Profs. R. Biswas, Somesh Kumar, Ashok Nanda, P.V.S.N. Murthy, Adrijit Goswami, Debjani Chakrabarti, Pratima Panigrahi, Pawan Kumar, and Saurav Mukhopadhyay played pivotal roles in the growth of the department at a later stage. Prof. M.L. Venkatanna gained popularity among first and second year B.Tech students for teaching engineering mathematics in earlier days.

Some of the faculty members at the Mathematics Department, Prof. D.N. Mitra and Prof. U.K. Sen used to wear dhotis. Prof. U.K. Sen and Dr. A.K. Rao initiated the teaching of 'Operations Research' (O.R.) in the Mathematics Department. Later on Dr. A.K. Rao migrated to Australia. Prof. J.R. Rao and Prof. S.B. Sinha started guiding research scholars in Operations Research. Professor R.N. Tiwari shifted his research focus from Relativity to Operations Research.

Those days, Prof. Gagan Bandopadhyay was a well-known name at IIT Campus Kharagpur. However, sometimes people used to find him absent minded. The author saw him as a professor of Physics Department, but he was previously a faculty of the Mathematics Department. He guided several research scholars in the Mathematics Department, including Prof. A.S. Gupta and Prof. J.R. Rao. Prof. Ajit Bhattacharya and Prof. Guruprasanna Bhattacharjee did their Ph.D under the supervision of Prof. A.K. Gayen. Most of the remaining teachers earned their Ph.D. under the guidance of the founder head of the Mathematics Department, Prof. B.R. Seth. At that time, in the professor cadre besides Prof. A.K. Gayen, Prof. D.N. Mitra and Prof. A.S. Gupta, there was another, Prof. Sahib Ram Mandan. His health was not very good, so he used to come to the department only in the afternoon. I would occasionally visit his office and engage in pleasant conversations. A few years later, he retired at the age of 60.

He informed me that his forefathers had settled in Delhi after migrating from West Punjab (Pakistan). His research area was geometry. He taught one or two geometry subjects in the Architecture & Regional Planning Department. Prof. Arun Sanyal was his Ph.D. student. Prof. S.R. Mandan had a blackboard in his office. A few months before his superannuation, he wrote on that board: 'I am retired but not tired!'

Next to the four above-mentioned professors, there were four assistant professors. Sometime after I joined, they all were promoted as professors. Among them, Prof. R.S. Nanda already became a Professor and head of the Applied Mathematics Department at BHU's Institute of Technology. However, after getting the professor position at IIT Kharagpur, he returned to his old institution. Prof. M. Maity was a student of pure mathematics during his M.Sc. at Calcutta University. He later obtained his Ph.D. in Elasticity from England and joined IIT Kharagpur as an assistant professor. Prof. G. Ramanaiah started taking interest in Boolean Algebra in the department of Mathematics. Occasionally he used to deliver seminars on this topic and later supervised Ph.D. students in this area. However, he left IIT after a couple of years to join an institution in Andhra Pradesh.

Other faculty members at Mathematics Department included Profs. K.S. Sastri, V.U.K. Sastri, and M.L. Venkatanna from Andhra Pradesh. V.U.K. Sastri was an associate lecturer. When I was appointed as a Lecturer, he was promoted to the lecturer position. Later, we became friends, and our closeness lasted until his retirement. We walked together almost every evening and visited each other's homes freely. Dr. Arabinda Biswas also joined as a lecturer along with me. He had done his doctorate on Elasticity under Prof. S.B. Sinha.

Some Senior Faculty Members at Other Departments Prior to 2000 AD

From various other departments, some of the senior faculty members with whom I had come in contact on different occasions include:

Electrical Engineering

Dr. K.B. Menon, Dr. N. Keshava Murthy, Dr. P.K. Rajagopalan, Dr. D.V.S. Murty, Dr. T.N. Saha, Dr. A.K. Chattopadhyaya, Dr. M.K. Ghosh, Dr. S.K. Basu, Dr. S.B. Sinha, Dr. K.B. Mishra, Dr. S. Maka.

Electronics and Communications Engineering

Profs G.S. Sanyal, J. Das. M.N. Faruqui, B.N. Das, R.C. Ganguli, M.C. Mallick, B.K. Saraf, B. Chatterjee, T.S. Lamba, S.L. Maskara.

Computer Science and Engineering
Profs. P. Pal Chaudhuri, A.K. Majumdar, Ajit Pal.

Metallurgical Engineering
Profs. U.K. Chaterjee, Bimalendu Sasmal.

Mechanical Engineering
Prof. K.G. Chandiramani, Prof. K.C. Sahu, R. Mishra, B.G. Ghosh, A.K. Mahanti.

Civil Engineering
Profs. S.K. Mallick, B.N. Neogi, S.K. Neogi, Nirjhar Dhang, S.K. Barai, S.K. Kar.

Aerospace Engineering
Profs. C.N. Laxminarayana, S. Basu, Ranajit Karmakar.

Chemical Engineering
Profs. N.C. Roy, N.K. Roy, D.K. Acharjee.

Material Science
Profs. D.N. Bose, Sukumar Maiti, Amal Pal, Haradas Banerji.

Mining Engineering
Profs. M.A. Ramlu, H.N. Datta, S. Sen, G.B. Misra.

Geology and Geophysics
Prof. T.C. Bagchi, Ashoke Mukherjee, A. Chakraborty.

Humanities and Social Sciences
Profs. D. Sen, B.P. Sandilya, P.S. Das, B.S. Das.

Physics and Meteorology
Prof. H.N. Bose, S. Datta Majumdar, G.B. Mitra.

Chemistry
Profs. D. Nasipuri, D. Sen, A.B. Sannigrahi, K.B. De.

Economics faculty Purnendu Sekhar Das, from Humanities and Social Sciences Department, was a close family friend. His wife, Sutapa Devi, was very close to my wife, Shorasi. History faculty of Humanities Department Prof. Binod Shankar Das was also a family friend of ours. There was mutual respect and love among us. Prof. Subhash Chandra Mahapatra, who belonged to the Rural Development Department, significantly contributed to the development of that department. His expertise in various subjects was commendable. Being a relative (brother-in-law), I had the opportunity to observe him closely. His family could be seen as a model of a happy family. His wife, Namita, had an M.D. in homeopathy, and her excellent medical expertise always kept us worry-free. Prof. Ramchand Bhuniya from the Physics Department and his family were very close to us. We frequently visited each other's residences. Late Pramathanath Bhattacharya, a mathematics teacher at Hijli High School, and Late Kanan Bihari De, a chemistry Professor of IIT, were both alumni of the Ramakrishna Mission Vidyarthi Ashrama, which fostered a cordial relationship among our families.

Life on the Residential Campus of IIT Kharagpur

Two months later, we were allotted Bachelor's Flat No. 1/11 (Apartment Bldg. No. 1, Flat No. 11). These houses were quite good for small families. There was one bedroom, one drawing room, one bathroom, and a kitchen. For convenience on the campus, at least one bicycle was essential, so we bought one. From then on, Shorasi lived at IIT with our eldest son Subhas (Babu) and daughter Sumita (Mamani). Occasionally, my mother would also come to stay in the IIT quarters. From the balcony of our flat which was on the second floor of the apartment, we had a good view of the campus roads. Babu and Mamani enjoyed watching the scooters and other vehicles running on those roads from the balcony of BF 1/11.

My younger brother Dines (Mantu) stayed with us and studied at Kharagpur Homeopathy Medical College. In the flat in front of ours (1/12), Prof. S.C. Panigrahi from the Metallurgical Engineering Department lived. He was from Odisha. While living in this flat, Shorasi took Babu and Mamani to a nearby park every afternoon, introducing them to other children of their age.

One day, Prof. D.N. Mitra called me and mentioned that the daughter of a gentleman he knew was studying B.Sc. at Medinipur Women's College. They lived in a one-storey B-type quarters near the market. At his request, I tutored her for four months.

Radhamadhab Goswami, and my Early Teaching Experience

Radhamadhab Goswami, the son of a kind lady living in Hijli Co-operative Society, was pursuing B.Sc. at Kharagpur College. At her request I tutored him in mathematics for about four-five months before his examinations. Over time, he became my friend. He used to come to our house, and after studying, would help me practise cycling for a few days. I still remember a sentence that he once told me: "Sir, do not try to overtake anyone while cycling; that way, you will avoid accidents." The advice remained etched in my memory. I followed this advice for a long time and realized its wider significance—whether in accumulating wealth or seeking job promotions, trying to overtake others often leads to mental unrest.

Connections Developed at IIT Kharagpur

Upon joining IIT, I was surprised to learn that Prof. Hemendranath Dutta (H.N. Dutta) from the Mining Engineering Department and his wife had both received spiritual initiation (Mantra Diksha) from Swami Shankaranandaji. That way they were my spiritual brother and sister. They lived in a one-storey B-type quarters near the IIT market. Both of them loved Shorasi and me very dearly, and this affection lasted throughout their lives. Their son, Soumendranath (Partha), worked at IIT Kharagpur and is now retired.

After sometime, we moved to quarters No. C-89. This house had three rooms. During our stay here, younger brother Dines lived with us while studying at Kharagpur Homeopathy Medical College. Cousin brother Shaktipada (Madal) also stayed with us while studying for his B.A. at Medinipur College. Unfortunately, Partha's mother (our spiritual sister) passed away prematurely due to incurable cancer. As long as she was healthy, she treated my wife Shorasi as her own sister and gave her necessary advice and guidance for her future well-being. Prof. H.N. Datta (Partha's father) lived a long life, passing away at the age of 93. Another spiritual brother, Sri Phani Sarkar, was a teacher at Hijli High School and lived in the Prembazar Hijli Housing Cooperative Society.

Friendship with Non-teaching Staff of IIT

Over the years, we developed a cordial relationship with several non-teaching staff and their families, such as Anil Mahapatra, Naba Kumar Shi, Ashutosh Bera, Khudiram Panda, and Kshitish Maiti. They respected and loved my parents and eventually became our friends. However, our close family friend and benefactor was Mr. Ramachandra Acharya, who worked at the IIT electricity complaint office. He lived in H-1 type quarters with his mother and sister before moving to his own two-storey house that he constructed in the Hijli Cooperative Society. He was very popular as an astrologer and for his priestly duties. He deeply respected and loved our parents and treated me like a younger brother. His family also loved my wife Shorasi. His wife was an excellent cook, and we often enjoyed meals prepared by her at their house. Ram Chandra Babu performed rituals for us, considering us as his family friends.

Vivekananda Study Circle

As alumni of the Ramakrishna Mission Kolkata Vidyarthi Ashrama, we formed a study group, called 'Vivekananda Study Circle.' We used to meet once every month at one of our houses with our families, reading books on Sri Ramakrishna, Sri Sarada Devi, and Swami Vivekananda. After the reading of the religious books, we used to have some refreshments as prasada. Members included Prof. Kanan Dey, Sri Pramatha Nath Bhattacharya, Prof. Ramchand Bhuniya, Prof. Basudeb Adhikari, and others. Subsequently it was decided that any alumni of any educational institution run by any centre of the Ramakrishna Mission could join the Study Circle. A research student named Dulal also participated so long as he was in Kharagpur. Late Umashankar Mitra (a teacher at the IIT Central School) was also a member.

Weekly Movies at IIT

Every Saturday and Sunday, the Technology Film Society (T.F.S.) screened a movie at the Netaji Auditorium at IIT—typically one Bengali film, two Hindi films, and one English film each month. My father regularly took my mother to watch Bengali films.

Life in Bungalow House & Kitchen Garden

After my father's retirement from Tikrapara High School, my parents settled in our IIT quarters, and enjoyed good health. My father often remarked that moving from our native village Bagmari to the campus of IIT Kharagpur had prolonged his life. The three-room C-type bungalow house was more convenient, with Dines staying in the middle room. We maintained a kitchen garden in the compound of our small bungalow, growing various vegetables like cauliflowers, cabbages, carrots, beans, and potatoes, and even planted a few banana trees. We worked hard to cultivate these. The soil being quite fertile, yield was very good. This brought immense joy to our family.

Purchasing a Plot for Housing in Hijli

My father discovered a plot for sale for housing in the Hijli Cooperative Housing Society, very close to the Shiva-Kali Temple. He purchased this plot, measuring six katha (about 10 decimals), for me, with the hope that I would build a house there. Later, he also provided some money to my brother, Parames for purchasing another plot, in the same housing society.

Various Courses in the Mathematics Department

In those days, Higher Secondary education lasted 11 years, followed by a five-year of B.Tech program. Students from all departments had to study mathematics in the first two years of B.Tech. programme. Some departments had mathematics in the first semester of the third year and the fifth semester as well. M.Tech students had mathematics in the first semester. The Mathematics Department also offered a three-year B.Sc. (Honours), a two-year M.Sc., a one-year postgraduate diploma course called DIIT programme, and a Ph.D. programmes. B.Sc. (Honours) students in Physics and Chemistry had a Mathematics course (Maths-V) in the first semester of the third year (fifth semester). The author taught this course for several years.

Memorable Interactions with Senior Faculty from Sister Science Departments

Professor Harshanath Bose (H.N. Bose), who had an excellent reputation in teaching, was the head of the Physics Department. When the author went to take Maths-V classes in that department, he would sometimes call him to chat. One day he said, "Give quizzes to students occasionally." Similarly Prof. D. Sen, Head of Chemistry Department occasionally called him for a chat. I vividly recall his words: "If you walk early in the morning, you will see nature at its most beautiful around 5 A.M. Many flowers remain unbloomed then, but within half an hour, they all blossom. This beauty is unmatched at any other time of the day."

Teaching Specialized Mathematics Courses

In the fifth year of B.Tech (ninth semester), there was an elective subject titled 'Thermal Stresses', usually taken by students from the Civil and Mechanical Engineering departments. I thoroughly enjoyed teaching this subject as it aligned with my Ph.D. thesis. Another significant course for M.Tech students was 'Advanced Engineering Mathematics' (MA614). Many colleagues were reluctant to teach this subject because it had around 170–180 students in one section, and there were no audio-visual aids. I taught this subject for many years. At that time, being the youngest faculty member in the Mathematics department, I never expressed reluctance to teaching any assigned course, feeling it gave me the opportunity to learn many new subjects properly. I remember I used to feel elated whenever a class lecture went well.

There was a subject in the M.Sc. programme called 'Theory of Potential,' which I was not very familiar with. The head of the department then was Prof. A.S. Gupta. No one was willing to teach this subject in one particular year, so he requested me to teach it. I accepted the challenge, eager to expand my knowledge and contribute to the Department.

Research Guidance

About 2 months after I joined the Mathematics Department, a research scholar, named Sri Radhamadhab Achari joined the Mathematics Department under the Quality Improvement Programme (QIP). The programme was meant for engineering college teachers to do their Ph.D. I was given the responsibility of guiding Sri Achari, who was older than me. He was an assistant Professor at B.I.T. Sindri. He became my first research scholar, and we shared a respectful and friendly relationship.

Three to four months later, another scholar, Sri Sachindra Nath Maiti joined me for doing research, becoming my second research scholar. Sri Achari's research focused on studying the effects of heat on various elastic and viscoelastic bodies under different conditions, the solid bodies having varied geometrical configurations, while Sri Maiti's research involved analytical studies on the highly intensified stress around cracks (discontinuities) in elastic bodies due to thermal flow.

Both of them worked very diligently, successfully completing their research and submitting their theses within three years. Their work was published in prestigious international journals. For both of them, the thesis reports arrived on time and were unanimously favourable, allowing for the prompt scheduling of their viva voce examinations to be held on the same day. They received their provisional Ph.D. certificates shortly after the viva voce examinations.

Dr. Radhamadhab Achari returned to his college with a doctorate degree, while Dr. Maiti was selected as a lecturer in the West Bengal Educational Service. He was engaged in teaching in various government colleges of West Bengal. Both of them are now retired. I recall that during viva voce of both these scholars, I was in Germany as a fellow of the Alexander von Humboldt Foundation, doing post doctoral research at the Institute of Mechanics, Hannover Technical

University. However, their doctoral degrees were not delayed due to my taking all necessary actions in time.

Open-Air Theatre

Director Bose being a civil Engineer and a visionary felt the necessity of an Open-Air Theatre for a vast institution, like IIT Kharagpur. He has been instrumental in the construction of some important structures, like the 'Open-Air Theatre' (O.A.T.). These constructions had faced much criticism and opposition at the initial phase from some senior professors of the Institute that time. However, its necessity became evident later. It can accommodate about 10,000 people and serves as a vital venue for events such as IIT Spring Fest and large meetings. It was later renamed as 'Tagore Open Air Theatre' (TOAT).

Various Departments and Administrative Offices

When I joined IIT, the director's office was situated on the first floor of the main building. The main building also housed the Physics, Chemistry, Mathematics, Geology and Geophysics, Humanities and Social Sciences, and Electrical Engineering departments.

Prof. T.C. Bagchi, a Geology professor, was the deputy director then, and his office was also in the first floor of the main building. The deputy director generally oversaw the administration of non-teaching staff with the registrar's assistance. The registrar's office has been on the second floor of the main building since then.

As administrative work increased, several professors were appointed as deans to assist the director in Institute administration. Initially, there were three deans one each for undergraduate studies, postgraduate studies, and faculty and planning. With increasing administrative demands, the number of deans was increased.

In the 1970s, sponsored research at IIT was minimal. Government agencies like CSIR and DST sponsored some research projects, with the Accounts Section managing the finances. As the number of sponsored research projects increased, all of IIT Kharagpur's sponsored research and industrial consultancy (S.R.I.C.) came under the supervision of a dean. Professor Amal Pal from the Materials Science Department once served as Dean (S.R.I.C.). The offices for different deans and a common office for all the deans were located on the first floor. Currently, the S.R.I.C. office and Dean (S.R.I.C.)'s chamber have moved to the Nalanda Complex. Other administrative offices remain on the second floor of the main building, with some in the old building, now named 'Shahid Bhavan' in honor of freedom fighters. This building was once the Hijli Jail, where two freedom fighters were shot dead by the British police.

Nehru Museum

In 1990, the Nehru Museum of Science and Technology was established on the ground floor of Shahid Bhavan. The museum houses a diverse collection of exhibits collected from institutions across India and even some from abroad. It showcases numerous technical models and features an outdoor exhibit area, which includes a Hunter plane and a steam engine. Additionally, one room is dedicated to the artefacts related to the history of IIT Kharagpur and the undivided Medinipur district, making it a significant attraction, especially for school children.

Nehru Museum/ Old Building of IIT Kharagpur

Opportunities for Pursuing Advanced Research Abroad

In 1974, I noticed an advertisement for a DAAD (Deutsche Akademische Austauschdienst/German Academic Exchange Service) scholarship on the department's notice board. Then, I filled out the application, got the department head's signature, and sent it to the establishment section. As per IIT's procedure, the establishment section sent the file to the registrar, who, after verifying everything, sent it to the director for approval. At that time, the position of Dean (Faculty) had not yet been introduced. Nowadays, the establishment section sends the file to the Dean (Faculty), who forwards it to the director with his observations. The director's approval is crucial. The IIT administration then sends the application as per the advertisement's instructions. Back then, for DAAD fellowship the UGC in New Delhi handled selections for science disciplines, while AICTE managed engineering disciplines.

After a long wait, I received a letter from the UGC inviting me for an interview at New Delhi. With only three or four days to prepare, I travelled to Delhi in the general-class without a reservation. Those days air journey used to be very expensive and air fare was not reimbursed by government offices. Around the same time, I also applied for the Humboldt Fellowship (Alexander von Humboldt Fellowship). The application for this fellowship had to be sent directly to the Humboldt Foundation's office in Germany. The foundation reviewed applications globally and selected candidates, sending official letters to the successful applicants.

Humboldt Fellowship: A Significant Turning Point

Fortunately, the author received selection letters for both the DAAD and Humboldt Fellowships. As it was not possible to avail both fellowships simultaneously, he chose the prestigious Humboldt Fellowship, renowned for its rigorous selection process, comparing applicants from various scientific fields worldwide in terms of research quality. The offer letter for the Humboldt Fellowship was signed by the distinguished German scientist Prof. Werner Heisenberg, who was the President of the Humboldt Foundation at that time. Heisenberg internationally acclaimed for his Principle of Uncertainty and other fundamental discoveries, won the Nobel Prize in Physics in 1932.

Receiving the Humboldt Fellowship was the third significant turning point in the author's life.

First Foreign Trip and Air Travel

For carrying out advanced research in Germany, IIT Kharagpur granted me two years of paid study leave. The leave approval letter included several pieces of advice that were crucial at the time. Since there was no internet, having knowledge about the country, its history, geography, and social structure was important. So, IIT advised me to collect relevant books from IIT Central Library to become well-informed about Germany before the trip. This would help avoid many initial difficulties in a foreign country.

The second piece of advice was to be well-versed with the history, geographical position, ancient heritage, and culture of India. This would enable us to act as an 'ambassador' representing India abroad. International travel was rare then, and it was essential to create a positive impression among foreign academics and researchers.

On the Eve of the First Trip to Germany. The Author Sitting on the First Row (Second from Right), among the DAAD and Humboldt Fellows, New Delhi (9 June, 1975)

On 9th June 1975, the long-awaited day arrived. On that day, I flew from Kolkata to New Delhi on an Indian Airlines flight—my first experience of air travel. From New Delhi, I boarded on a Lufthansa flight to Frankfurt, Germany. The in-flight experience, with air hostess serving snacks and meals and periodic pilot announcements about our location was fascinating. The nonstop flight from Delhi to Frankfurt took 9 hours and 10 minutes, followed by a 50-minute local Lufthansa flight to Hamburg. From there, I travelled by train to a small town, Lüneburg.

At that time, DAAD and Humboldt Fellows were required to undergo German language training, completing Basic Courses I and II (Grundstufe I and II), each lasting two months. Some did only one course before starting research at the university. However, doing both courses ensured a better grasp of the German language. I learned German at the Goethe Institute in Lüneburg, taught by a Brazilian lady named Miss Richter. She employed innovative teaching techniques, using tape recorders and headphones to develop accurate pronunciation for the trainees. She conducted classes exclusively in German, ensuring effective language immersion.

I learnt German in 1975, and due to their unique methods of teaching even after 50 years, I can still manage conversations in German language during my trips to Germany. Lüneburg, a small, yet picturesque town, became my home for four months. I resided in a modest room in a German couple's house as a paying guest, sharing a bathroom with other tenants. The house-owner couple lived on the ground floor, with four tenants upstairs. Today, many Germans know reasonably good English, as it is taught in German schools. However, in the 1970s and even in 1980s, very few Germans spoke English, even among university professors, and so language proficiency was very essential for daily interactions and survival.

First Day in Germany

I vividly remember my first day in the rented house in Lüneburg. Fortunately, my accommodation was pre- arranged, allowing me to go directly from the Railway station to my new home. It should be kept in mind that the provision of online booking did not exist in those days. Upon arrival, the landlady welcomed me, showed me my room, and provided essential instructions about the electric switches, bathroom, windows, and doors.

In European countries, where snow fall occurs, roofs are often slanted to help melted snow drain away. My room had a window in the slanted roof, and the landlady advised keeping it closed when I went out to avoid rain soaking the bed. Since they knew no English and I didn't know German, communication was challenging for the first two weeks, relying mostly on gestures. Despite the language barrier, they would occasionally give me a pear, an apple, or some cherries from their orchard.

Experience at the Goethe Institute

Learning German at the Goethe Institute in Lüneburg was a delightful experience. Every morning, we had breakfast at the institute before starting our lessons. Our class consisted of about 60 students from diverse countries—China, Japan, India, Ecuador, Brazil, Argentina, Chile, Iran, Iraq, Pakistan, Bangladesh, Thailand, Sri Lanka, and several African and European countries.

Our German teacher, Miss Richter, was very popular, always maintaining a cheerful demeanor. Another Bengali student in our section was Dr. Amal Mukhopadhyay, a physics faculty at Banaras Hindu University. He had a French-cut beard and was a cheerful person. We became good friends quickly.

Among the classmates, Miss Fung from China had joined the course to prepare herself for further studies in Germany. Another student Mr. Chikaya from Ecuador (a country in the northwestern South America) was a cheerful young man who played the violin whenever he had time. For lunch we often visited the Lüneburg marketplace, where our usual meal consisted of half a roasted chicken and a plate of French fries, costing 3.50 Deutsche Marks (DM). (One DM was equivalent to 16 Indian Rupees at that time). Later, German currency transitioned to the Euro. Some of the first German words I learned for survival were:

Pomme Frites (French fries)
Ein Halbes Hähnchen (half a chicken)
Wasser (water)

From May to August, Lüneburg's natural beauty is usually at its peak, attracting numerous tourists on weekends and holidays. However, eating the same food daily became monotonous as there were no cooking facilities at the residence. There was a Chinese restaurant in town where we occasionally went for dinner, spending around 9 DM for a moderately decent meal.

Each German language course lasted two months, culminating in a final exam with two class tests in between. I recall scoring the highest marks in one of the class tests. After four months of learning German, I could converse reasonably well. Germans often complimented me, saying, *"Sie sprechen aber gut Deutsch!"* ("You speak good German!"). They always appreciated foreigners making an effort to learn their language.

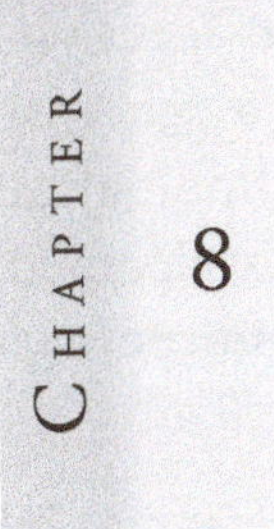

Research and Seminar Lectures at Several Foreign Universities

Hannover Technical University

After completing language training, the author moved from Lüneburg to Hannover Technical University in the last week of September 1975. At that time, Hannover was a city of West Germany (now Germany). His host Professor was Prof. Oskar Mahrenholtz, the director of the Institute of Mechanics at that university. Upon arrival at Hannover, the author visited the Institute of Mechanics on Apfel Strasse and met with Prof. Mahrenholtz. They had a brief discussion about the research, and it was decided that the author would work in the field of biomechanics during his stay in Germany as a Humboldt Fellow.

Technical University of Hannover, Germany

Prior to this, while in Lüneburg, Prof. Mahrenholtz had sent the author some of his lecture notes on various branches of biomechanics. After reviewing them, the author expressed interest for carrying out research in biomechanics, to which Prof. Mahrenholtz readily agreed. During their first meeting, Prof. Mahrenholtz suggested including Dr. Christoph Hartung, a scientist from the Department of Biomedical Engineering and Hospital Technology at Medical University in Hannover, in the research team. The author welcomed this suggestion, recognizing the potential for enhanced collaboration and outcomes.

The author was thrilled to have the opportunity to conduct research in biomedical science and engineering an emerging and promising field, which filled the author with excitement. He acknowledges that his contribution to biomechanics, biomedical mathematics and physiological fluid dynamics have played a significant role in his recognition as a researcher.

At that time, Professor Mahrenholtz was a well-known figure across Europe. The advantage with him was that he could speak good English, having spent a year as a visiting professor at a Canadian university and travelled to various other English-speaking countries. Compared to other Germans, he was more open-minded. The author learned that two Indians had previously carried out research with him: Dr. Ramamurthy from IIT Madras, who went to Germany on a DAAD fellowship, and Dr. Lalwani, who was a Humboldt Fellow.

Prof. Oskar Mahrenholtz (2nd from right, 1st row)

Professor Mahrenholtz had two secretaries: Miss Simon, a full-time secretary who worked both mornings and afternoons, and Mrs. Poock, a part-time secretary who worked only in the afternoons. In Hannover, the author stayed at the guest house of Hannover Technical University on Dorotheenstrasse. The rent was 300 DM per month for a bedroom with a shared kitchen (for four people) and a shared bathroom, but he never faced any issues. Next to the author's room lived Dr. R.S. Sachan, an Indian, and in the following room, Dr. Celebi from Turkey. They were both DAAD fellows. Dr. Sachan was an assistant professor at Pantnagar Agricultural University and was in Hannover for a year for doing advanced research in agricultural sciences.

International Students in Technical University of Hannover

Learning Hindi in Germany

Until then, the author was not very proficient in speaking Hindi. The IIT environment did not require fluent Hindi, but having Dr. Sachan as a neighbour, the author felt inclined to improve his Hindi. He asked Dr. Sachan to always converse with him in Hindi. They spent a lot of time together at the guest house, preparing meals, having tiffin and dinner, and shopping—splitting expenses equally at the end of each month. Their walks and outings further strengthened their bond and enhanced the author's proficiency in Hindi. It was an amusing irony that his stay in Germany led to an improvement in his Hindi alongside his German.

Harsh German Winter

The author moved from Lüneburg to Hannover in the last week of September, 1975 just as winter was setting in. Winter in Germany lasts from mid-September to mid-April, with rain occurring anytime but rarely heavy. The author bought a winter-appropriate overcoat (Mantel in German) and some additional clothes from a large clothing store named C&A. The overcoat served well for both rain and cold.

Indian Community in Hannover

Apart from Dr. Sachan, several other Indians lived in Hannover around the same time, some affiliated with the university and engaged in different professions. Among the Humboldt fellows was Dr. Ashok Chattopadhyay, a professor from the Chemical Engineering Department at IIT Bombay. He was there with his wife and two daughters, staying at another guest house of the university in Im Moore, Hannover.

Dr. Trilok Raj Sharma from Rajasthan, associated with the Faculty of Agricultural Sciences, was a cheerful person. There were also two veterinary scientists, Dr. De and Dr. Montu Ghosh, who were not affiliated with the university but were in business. Both were unmarried at the time. Every Friday or Saturday, they would gather to cook and eat together. Dr. Sharma was enthusiastic and made excellent potato parathas.

At the Hannover Technical University library, the author met Mr. Arun Ghosh, who had completed his M.Sc. in Pure Mathematics from Calcutta University and was looking for a job in Germany. His wife, Shubhra Bhattacharya, worked as a teacher in Hannover. They occasionally visited the guest house, and the author also visited their home sometimes.

Outside the university circle, the author and his Indian acquaintances used to meet at a coffee shop near the Railway Station of Hannover. On several occasions, they visited each other's houses. Most of them were either Punjabis or Bengalees. There was a Kundu family from Howrah district. Mrs. Kundu was a medical doctor. She was employed in a hospital. Her husband, Mr. Kundu was very hospitable, frequently inviting the author to have dinner in their house. In Hannover, there lived another Bengalee from Uluberia (known to our friend, Prof. Ajay Banerjee). His wife was a German lady, named Ms. Karin. She was working as a secretary in some office. The friendliness of these individuals made the author's two-year stay in a non-English-speaking country enjoyable.

Passing away of Middle Brother Dines

Professor Ajay Banerjee (Jhintu Da) from Uluberia College had a brother, Amitava Banerjee (Andu da), who built a house in Uelzen, near Hannover, after graduating in engineering from Germany. His wife, Irene, was German. The author's beloved middle brother, Dines, lived with the parents in the village, Bagmari, while the author was staying in Hannover. The author regularly sent medicines from Germany to help manage his brother's health, which remained stable for the initial months. However, Dines eventually passed away, finding place at the feet of the Lord.

Understanding the emotional impact this news would have on the author, his father requested Amitava Banerjee (Andu Da) and his wife, Irene to console him. This kind-hearted couple extended their support by taking the author to their home in another town Uelzen. Andu Da worked in a factory, while Irene was a nurse. On one occasion, Irene took the author to her father's house, where he experienced the joy of picking fresh cherries from a tree.

Prof. Mahrenholtz's Research Team

Between 1975 and 1977, Prof. Mahrenholtz, supervised 12–14 doctoral students (Dr. Ing) including: Lothar Gaul (1946–2018), later a professor of Mechanics at the University of Stuttgart; Hans Josef Rath (1947–2012), who became a professor of applied mechanics and microgravity at the University of Bremen; Horst Irretier (1949–2016), who later became a professor of machine dynamics at the University of Kassel; Mr. Grawosky and Mr. Boehm: Doctoral students under Prof. Mahrenholtz; Mr. Pitsch: a draftsman assisting Prof. Mahrenholtz.

Prof. Lothar Gaul,
University of Stuttgart, Germany

Mr. Boehm's room was of bigger size, and the author was given his office in that room. Mr. Boehm spoke reasonably good English, which was helpful for the author to gather a variety of information about Germany and its customs. Perhaps this was why Prof. Mahrenholtz arranged for the author to have his office in Mr. Boehm's room. Mr. Boehm would occasionally share various stories with the author.

First Research Meeting

One day, Dr. Christoph Hartung visited the Institute of Mechanics at Hannover Technical University for a meeting arranged by Prof. Mahrenholtz. After discussing several potential research topics in the field of Biomechanics, the author chose to work on the impact response of the skull and brain (grey matter) using mathematical modelling and simulation techniques. The topic greatly intrigued him.

Medical University of Hannover, Germany

Research at Hannover Medical University

The author visited Hannover Medical University twice a week to discuss research progress with Dr. Hartung. Dr. Hartung was a professor in the Department of Biomedical Engineering and Hospital Technology at the Medical University. He introduced the author to the head of this department, Dr. Otto Anna. One day, Dr. Anna introduced him to Mr. Wittenburg, a laboratory assistant, who later assisted the author in generating graphs using a computer, significantly aiding his theoretical research.

University Canteen (Mensa)

Dr. Sachan and I together prepared breakfast and dinner at the kitchen of the guest house, while we used to have lunch at the university canteen, known as Mensa in Germany. Generally, there used to be three choices for meals daily. Initially, the author would ask the canteen staff, which material was included in each menu. Sometimes they would explain, but other times they would say, *Ich weiss nicht* (I don't know). Over time he stopped asking and selected his meal from the available options.

Saturday Market

On Saturdays, Sundays, and holidays, the author, along with Dr. Sachan would cook their meals at the guest house kitchen. A few months later, they discovered a market that used to operate every Saturday morning. To facilitate travel, they purchased monthly tickets for trams (Strassenbahn) and buses, which allowed unlimited travel within the zone. They often bought fresh vegetables from the Saturday market, where the farmers sold their produce directly. They also bought a fish similar to *Catla*, which the shopkeepers used to clean and cut into pieces. Like *Catla*, or south Asian Carp, the fish was a fresh water fish. It was native to rivers and lakes. Like *Catla*/Carp, it was a fish with large and broad head, a large protruding lower jaw, and an upturned mouth. It had large, greyish scales on its dorsal side with a whitish belly. Its average weight used to be around 2 kgs. The market offered fresh and reasonably priced vegetables and fish making it a preferred shopping destination.

Party at Professor Mahrenholtz's House

Prof. Mahrenholtz built his house at a place outside the city of Hannover and drove himself. Being a warm and sociable individual, he often hosted parties at his home. He invited the author to every party while he was in Hannover. Prof. Mahrenholtz's wife was also very kind and had a charitable nature. She often engaged the author in long conversations, enquiring about life in India, marriage customs, and other topics. She also shared their customs with the author. On one occasion, she informed the author that arranged marriage was once common in Germany.

Prof. Mahrenholtz personally drove the author to his house for these gatherings and ensured his return. The author fondly remembers staying overnight at his house once, and he took him back to the guest house the next day in the morning. Prof. Stein from Hannover University, a professor of Statics, was a friend of Prof. Mahrenholtz and attended one of these parties. He had also visited India and humorously mentioned that housewives in India spent a lot of time in the kitchen, enjoying cooking various dishes.

During that time, slide shows with projectors were a popular medium for sharing travel experiences. At one party, Prof. Mahrenholtz showed numerous slides from his trips to India, explaining each image. One particular set of pictures showing traditional laundry areas amused the guests, as washing machines were already widely used in Germany.

Prof. Mahrenholtz had three children: Thomas, Martina, and Martius. He also had a company named Mahrenholtz + Partner. Later he transitioned from Hannover Technical University to Hamburg Technical University as the Director of the Institute of Mechanics and Ocean Engineering. That time his son Thomas bought his house and company in Hannover. Professor Mahrenholtz then built a new house in Hamburg. His daughter, Martina, became a school principal.

An avid traveller, Prof. Mahrenholtz visited several countries, including multiple trips to India, more to IIT Chennai. A few years after the author returned to India, he came to IIT Delhi for a conference. Learning about his visit, the author travelled to IIT Delhi to meet him, a gesture that was greatly appreciated by Prof. Mahrenholtz. He fondly recalled this meeting in every subsequent encounter. Due to limited transportation options at the time, the author travelled in the general class on the train for this visit.

In 1999, when the author organized an international conference ICOMMONS at IIT Kharagpur, he invited Prof. Mahrenholtz as the Chief Guest for the inaugural ceremony. Prof. Mahrenholtz graciously accepted the invitation and delivered a keynote address. He stayed only for one day, and the author went to meet him at the guest house with his wife.

Doctoral Hat (Doktorhut) Ceremony

In 1976, the author had the opportunity to witness a grand celebration of the doctoral degree award ceremony at the Institute of Mechanics in Hannover. Several doctoral students of Prof. Mahrenholtz, including Lothar Gaul, Hans Rath, and Horst Irretier, received their doctoral degrees that year. Each recipient wore a specially designed hat adorned with a physical model representing their thesis topic. Prof. Mahrenholtz personally placed the hats on the heads of the new doctoral degree recipients. In Germany, the doctoral supervisor is traditionally called the "Doctoral Vater", meaning "Doctoral Father"; the German word for hat is 'Hut'.

Prof. Horst Irritier,
University of Kassel, Germany

The celebration included a variety of food and drinks, and the expenses were borne by the doctoral graduates. Dr.-Ing. Lothar Gaul later became a professor at Stuttgart University, while Dr. Horst Irretier became a professor at Kassel University.

Research and Seminar Lectures at Multiple German Universities

Thanks to the support of the Humboldt Foundation, the author had opportunities to conduct research with different professors at multiple universities in Germany. These visits typically lasted for three months. During these stays, the author also had the opportunity to deliver invited lectures at various universities, sometimes receiving honorariums. In this way he delivered seminar lectures at Stuttgart University, Kassel University, Hannover University, Hamburg Technological University and Berlin Technical University etc. These experiences will be discussed in more detail later.

In June 1976, during the author's tenure at Hannover Technical University, he had the opportunity to participate in an educational tour organized by the Humboldt Foundation. The 14-day tour covered all major cities of West Germany, visiting prestigious universities including Göttingen, Stuttgart, Karlsruhe, Bremen, Heidelberg, Berlin, Munich, Aachen, Hamburg, Bonn, Cologne, and Kiel. The temporary capital of West Germany at the time was Bonn, where the author had the chance to meet and shake hands with the then President of West Germany, Mr. Walter Scheel, as part of a tradition for Humboldt Fellows.

The Fall of the Berlin Wall and Reunification of Germany

During the Humboldt tour, the author had an opportunity to visit the famous Berlin Wall that separated East Germany from West Germany. For many years, it acted as a physical barrier symbolizing the political divisions of the time. The 155 km long barrier cut through the middle of the city center, surrounded West Berlin from August 13, 1961 to November 9, 1989. The wall was designed to prevent people from escaping from East Berlin to the West.

In 1990, the fall of the Berlin Wall led to the reunification of East and West Germany, and the capital was relocated to Berlin. From May to July 2016, while the author was a visiting scientist (Humboldt) at Hamburg Technical University, he had the opportunity to attend a session organized by the Humboldt Foundation in Berlin in the month of June. There he had the opportunity to meet and shake hands with the then German President, Mr. Joachim Gauck.

Participation in International Conferences

During his stay in Hannover from 1975 to 1977, the author had the chance to attend several international conferences held in different European countries.

The first conference he attended was the Niedersachsen Mechanics Conference. 'Niedersachsen 'is a German word meaning Lower Saxony, which is the second-largest region in northwestern Germany, encompassing cities like Hannover, Hamburg, and Bremen. Prof. Mahrenholtz was supposed to deliver a lecture at this conference. He invited the author to accompany him. They returned together as well. Although the author didn't understand much German at that time, he found listening to lectures in German language quite enjoyable. However, he could understand a bit more, when the lectures were related to mathematical modelling.

About a month later, there was the annual session of GAMM in Amsterdam, the Netherlands. GAMM stands for Gesellschaft für Angewandte Mathematik und Mechanik (Society for Applied Mathematics and Mechanics). In 1977, the author became a member of this prestigious organization. Ludwig Prandtl and Richard von Mises founded this organization in 1922 to promote the advancement of applied mathematics and mechanics. Although some lectures at this conference were in German, most were in English. Prof. Mahrenholtz drove to Amsterdam with the author, engaging in discussion about Dutch land reclamation efforts during the journey.

Later, the author attended the EUROMECH Colloquium at Graz University of Technology in Austria. He received some funding from the Humboldt Foundation for this purpose. This university is the oldest in Austria, where technical education and research began. It is located in a very serene environment. The language of Austria is also German. From Graz, the author travelled to Austrian capital, Vienna (Wien in German), both cities being nestled within the picturesque Alps.

Ecole Polytechnique, France

In 1976, the author had the opportunity to participate in a scientific session at Ecole Polytechnique in France. This institution is one of the most prestigious educational institutions in Europe. He vividly recalls seeing the names of former researchers and professors of the institution inscribed on a wooden board. He was very surprised to see that many famous mathematicians and physicists of ancient times had been associated with this institution, either as faculty members or researchers. Most of them were Nobel Prize winners.

During his visit an amusing incident occurred. At that time, there were no mobile phones or the internet. Seeking directions, the author approached a local gentleman and asked, "Do you speak English?" He replied, "I know English, but I hate speaking that language." Later, the author heard from friends that the French were quite protective of their language. He was also informed that the Germans too had a similar attitude in the past, translating good English books on science and technology into German. However, with time, Germany has adopted a more open approach. English is now taught widely in German schools, and many researchers and professors at German universities are fluent in English. Even in public places, these days it is not difficult to find people who speak English.

14th International Congress on Theoretical and Applied Mechanics (ICTAM), Delft, the Netherlands (August 30 – September 4, 1976)

From August 30 to September 4, 1976, the 14th International Congress on Theoretical and Applied Mechanics was held at Delft University of Technology in the Netherlands. This esteemed conference attracted senior researchers from various countries, with renowned experts presenting their research findings in different branches of mechanics. For young researchers, participating in such scientific conferences is an invaluable opportunity. It not only allows them to listen to the lectures but also facilitate interactions with leading researchers, allowing attendees to gain insights and seek guidance. Of course, these days establishing and maintaining professional connections has become much easier in the digital age through email and the internet.

When this conference was held, the author was in Germany, making it an excellent opportunity for him to participate in this prestigious Conference. For this participation, he also received partial financial support from the Humboldt Foundation. The registration fees for these international conferences are usually quite high. Sometimes, Professor Mahrenholtz arranged for the author's registration fees from his research fund. He is grateful to him because, without his support and encouragement, it would have been impossible for him to attend so many international conferences at that stage in his career.

By then, the author had developed expertise in the research fields of thermoelasticity and fracture mechanics. He had already supervised two research students for their doctorates in these areas. During his time in Germany, he had also explored aspects of biomechanics further broadening his knowledge. Therefore, he was able to enrich himself by listening to various lectures in these three research areas of mechanics. Here, in the ICTAM Conference, he got the opportunity to meet the renowned thermoelasticity expert Witold Nowacki from Poland. He was a very kind gentleman. During his Ph.D., the author had read his book, "Theory of Thermoelasticity." Engaging with such a respected scholar was an enlightening experience.

"I Don't Know!"

One of the highlights of the conference was attending a special lecture by J.D. Achenbach from the USA, a prominent figure in fracture mechanics of that time. He had read some of his research papers on thermoelastic crack propagation, making this lecture particularly enriching.

An incident during the lecture left a lasting impression on the author. At the end of his lecture, during the question-and-answer session, someone from the audience stood up and asked a question that was relevant to the contents of the lecture. Although the author is not able to recollect the exact question, he bears the impression that the question was under the purview of the lecture material. Achenbach's immediate response was: "I don't know." Despite being a prominent figure in that research field, he did not attempt to fabricate an answer. This moment underscored an important lesson for young researchers: even experts do not have answers to every question. It is far better to acknowledge uncertainty than to provide misleading or confusing responses.

J.H. Argyris, FRS (Germany/UK), delivered another keynote lecture on "Computers and Mechanics," which was very engaging.

Meeting Two Applied Mathematics Stalwarts from India

The author fondly recalls his meeting with Prof. P.L. Bhatnagar and Prof. B.R. Seth at that conference in the Netherlands. Although Prof. B.R. Seth was the founder head of the Mathematics Department at IIT Kharagpur, he had become the Director of BIT Mesra before the author joined IIT Kharagpur. Prof. P.L. Bhatnagar was the head of the Department of Applied Mathematics at the Indian Institute of Science, Bangalore. After retirement, he founded the Mehta Research Institute (MRI) in Allahabad. Though they had never met the author before, it seems, they were aware of the author's modest research contributions. Despite their seniority and stature, they conversed with the author with warmth and encouragement. Prof. Bhatnagar mentioned that he was the founding Director of the Mehta Research Institute (MRI) in Allahabad. He also said that he had arranged for Prof. Phoolan Prasad to work at MRI for two years after consulting with the director of IISc. Prof. Bhatnagar informed that he had planned to involve the author at MRI upon his return from Germany, but sadly, he passed away before that could materialize. The Mehta Research Institute (MRI) was later renamed the Harish Chandra Research Institute (HRI).

First Visit to the United Kingdom

During his stay in Hannover, Germany, the author had the opportunity to travel across the United Kingdom and visit renowned universities, such as the University of Cambridge, the University of Oxford, the University of Birmingham, the University of Liverpool, Imperial College London, and several universities in Scotland.

Short Visits to Historic Universities: Oxford

The author walked through the campuses of the historic universities, visiting places like Trinity College, Lincoln College, and Jesus College. Sometimes, he sat by the River Thames and enjoyed the natural beauty. Every year, 400 of the most talented students from around the world are selected for the Rhodes Scholarship. The head office of the Rhodes Foundation, 'Rhodes House,' is located here. He also had the opportunity to visit several other famous colleges, including Magdalen College, and Queen's College. The famous statue of the 'Virgin and Child' was truly captivating. At Oxford, he met several renowned researchers in applied mathematics, biomechanics, and elasticity.

During his visit to Scottish universities, he had the opportunity to meet a renowned applied mathematician, Ian N. Sneddon, FRS, FIMA. His books, such as 'Fourier Transforms' and 'Partial Differential Equations', are very popular among students and teachers. These books are still used as authoritative textbooks in mathematics. The author found him to be a very humble, polite, and calm person during conversation. His book, 'Mixed Boundary Value Problems in Potential Theory', was very helpful to the author during his research in Fracture Mechanics.

While the author appreciated the academic excellence at Oxford, he observed that not all academics shared Sneddon's humility. In one incident, he asked someone whether two specific Oxford scientists held the title of Professor. The response was dismissive: "No, they are not professors; they are readers. But they are better than American professors." This remark led the author to reflect that an academic's reputation should be judged by the quality of their teaching and research rather than their official designation. Through these experiences, the author gained invaluable exposure, formed meaningful connection, and witnessed the cultural richness of different countries—lessons that continue to shape the author's academic journey.

In addition to visiting various British universities, he also travelled to many remote places in Great Britain. He visited the city of Aberdeen, located in the far north of Scotland. Even in June, it felt very cold there. There was an Indian restaurant in that remote area, owned by a Punjabi proprietor. Following a friend's advice, he had purchased a *'BritRail Pass'* from Hannover which was valid for ten days. This ticket must be purchased outside Great Britain, allowing unlimited travel on British trains. During this trip, the author enjoyed the hospitality of his friend from Vidyamandira (who lived in Hijli), Subhendu Mitra, and his wife, Susma. He occasionally visited their home in London during those ten days. Susma prepared delicious meals with great warmth, and Subhendu's hospitality left a lasting impression.

The author also visited the Imperial College and met two distinguished scientists, who were working in the fields of interest to him. During this trip, he took a tourist bus for a day for sightseeing in London. They showed various tourist places around London from morning to evening. The next day, the author spent more time to visit several selected places. His sightseeing in London included iconic landmarks such as Buckingham Palace, where he witnessed the 'Change of the Guards' ceremony, Wellington Arch, Westminster Bridge, Big Ben, Westminster Abbey, Tower Bridge and the Tower of London. Unfortunately his visit had to be cut short due to bad weather.

Returning to India

After conducting research on 'Physiological Problems of Brain Injury' for 1 year and 8 months at Hannover Technical University in collaboration with Hannover Medical University, the author returned to India and joined IIT Kharagpur on May 18, 1977.

Within three months of his return, Ms. Kasturi Roychowdhury, Santabrata Chakraborty, V.V.T.N. Murthy, and Minati Mishra joined as research scholars under his supervision. Before this, they had all completed the required coursework in the Plasticity and Rheology group in the DIIT (Postgraduate Diploma) course in the Mathematics Department and had done DIIT (Diploma of IIT). They all wrote their DIIT projects under the supervision of the author on different areas of biomechanics, as mentioned below.

Kasturi Roychowdhury : Mathematical modelling and simulation of blood flow;
Santabrata Chakraborty : Head impact modelling;
V.V.T.N. Murthy : Biomechanics of bones;
Minati Mishra : Bone fracture mechanics

After completing DIIT, all the four received research scholarships and started their Ph.D. programme under the author's supervision. Previously R.M. Achari, had already obtained his Ph.D. under his guidance. He was from Tamil Nadu but was settled in Purulia district of West Bengal. The author's second Ph.D. student, Dr. S.N. Maity was from West Bengal. Among the four who were with the author simultaneously, Santabrata Chakraborty and Kasturi Roy Chowdhury (Sen) were from West Bengal, V.V.T.N. Murthy was from Andhra Pradesh, and Minati Mishra (Samantaray) was from Odisha. A few months later, Salam Ibosana Singh from Manipur, joined as a Ph.D. scholar under his supervision focusing on the cardiovascular system dynamics.

Research Challenges and Achievements

During that time, research facilities were not as advanced as they are today. IIT Kharagpur did not have high-speed computer facilities those days. So research students had to go to the Regional Computer Centre in Jadavpur for their computational work. Usually they would get allotted time there late at night and return to their hostel at IIT by the last train. Since there was no internet then, we had to rely primarily on the central library at IIT for reference purpose. Finding the necessary research papers from old bound volumes of various journals was very time-consuming and required a lot of patience and hard work. The author remembers working late into the night at the central library after classes. Our research group's scholars worked very hard. We were fortunate that our research findings were published in various renowned international journals, such as 'Journal of Biomechanics', 'International Journal of Engineering Science', 'Journal of Mathematical Biology', 'Bulletin of Mathematical Biology', 'Biorheology', 'Rheologica Acta', and 'Journal of Thermal Stresses' etc. Only research papers of the highest quality were accepted for publication in these prestigious journals.

Multidisciplinary Research

Fields like biomechanics, biomathematics, and biorheology are multidisciplinary in nature, requiring knowledge in various subjects such as mathematics, mechanics, anatomy, physiology, and physics during research. To strengthen the research environment the author invited experts in these fields to give some lectures and organize discussion sessions. These small sessions were usually held in the author's office or an adjacent classroom. Over time, the research group included students from different backgrounds, not just mathematics. For example, Subhas Samanta, a professor of physics at Medinipur College, did his Ph.D. under the author's supervision in thermoelasticity. Beyond his doctoral research, he made significant contributions to bone biomechanics. He helped explain physical concepts to some of our research group members and sought mathematical solutions for his work.

First Promotion (1979)

In early 1979, the author was promoted from lecturer position to the position of an assistant professor at IIT Kharagpur. During the interview, the then-director, Prof. Sankar Lal, highly impressed by his multiple research publications in different prestigious international journals, remarked, "I find you are a very strenuous writer!" An external expert later conveyed to some faculty friends that the author's research contributions were highly appreciated by the selection committee.

'Round-The-World' Trip (1981)

In 1981, the author had the opportunity to attend the Fourth International Congress of Biorheology in Japan. This conference was held at Tokyo Medical University from July 27 to August 1. The author had submitted a research paper for presentation at this conference, based on his research on "Deformation and Stresses in the Arterial Wall." After about three months, he received a letter confirming the acceptance of his paper for presentation at the congress. The next challenge was to procure funding—how to raise enough money for airfare, other expenses, and conference registration fees. At that time, IIT provided very limited funding for conference participation. So he sought additional funding from organizations like the Indian National Science Academy and the UGC.

Securing a Round-The-World (RTW) Ticket

While purchasing his flight ticket from Everest Travel Service in Dharamtala, Kolkata he discovered that for a slightly higher price than a round-trip ticket to Tokyo, he could get a Round-the-World (RTW) ticket, allowing visits to multiple cities world wide, before returning to Kolkata. Remaining aware that this was a bold decision, he opted for the RTW scheme, relying on his ability to arrange delayed payment through funds received from various Indian organizations after returning.

Arrangements of Seminar Lectures at Overseas Universities

Since there was no internet at the time, the author wrote to professors of various universities/research institutes located at different cities in various countries he planned to visit, expressing his interest in delivering seminar lectures and requesting hospitality arrangements. Communication took three to four weeks, but most professors responded positively, offering:

(i) *Airport pickup and accommodation;*
(ii) *Opportunities to deliver seminar lectures;* and
(iii) *Honorarium for seminar presentations.*

Japan Visit

Departure for Tokyo

On the morning of his departure, the author's wife Shorasi, feeling excited, personally went to the market, bought good vegetables and varieties of fish and cooked palatable dishes, all by herself. After lunch, the author went to his department, meeting each research scholar individually, discussing their work and offering guidance before heading to Kolkata Airport via train.

Arrival in Tokyo

Upon arrival, Dr. Manoranjan Santra, a postdoctoral researcher in Chemistry at the University of Tokyo received him at Tokyo airport and warmly hosted him for 2–3 days. Manoranjan did his Ph.D. from the Chemistry Department of IIT Kharapur. He was from Hijli Housing Cooperative Society. He prepared Bengali meals and took the author on a sightseeing tour of Tokyo.

Kobe University Visit

From Tokyo, the author took a train from Tokyo to Kobe on the pre-scheduled day. There were some difficulties during this journey. When he arrived at the designated platform at Tokyo Railway Station, he found a train with all its doors closed, even though it was not time for departure. The author tried to ask some local people on the platform why all the doors were closed, but he didn't know Japanese, and they didn't know English. So, he tried to communicate with gestures, but it wasn't easy. There were announcements in Japanese over the loudspeakers, which he couldn't understand. After a while, the author saw a Japanese woman and asked her if she spoke English. She replied, "a little." She explained that the railway was announcing that a part of the track between Tokyo and Kobe was submerged due to heavy rain, causing a delay. The train would depart once the water receded. Recollection of that frightening situation still sends chills down the author's spine.

Kobe University, Japan

When the author arrived at Kobe Station, he found the host Prof. Y. Seguchi waiting for him on the platform to receive him. Prof. Seguchi told, he was aware of the train delay. He then drove the author to the hotel. Prof. Seguchi had taken responsibility for hosting the author during his stay in Kobe. He stayed there for three days and delivered two seminar lectures on bone biomechanics, one of the fields of his research interest. Prof. Seguchi conducted experimental research on bone mechanics and so he was interested in the lectures. One day, Prof. Seguchi invited the author to his home for dinner. Mrs. Seguchi had prepared various Japanese dishes. She was taller than most Japanese women. Prof. Seguchi's mother lived with him, much like in Indian families. Many

Japanese families have similar living arrangements for the old parents. The Japanese are known for their hospitality. While in Kobe, Professor Seguchi took the author to various places of tourist interest. One day we went to the seaside and bought watermelon, which we enjoyed while having long interactions.

National Cardiovascular Center, Osaka

National Cardiovascular Center, Osaka, Japan

From Kobe, the author travelled to Osaka. The main purpose was to visit the National Cardiovascular Center in Osaka and meet its Director, Prof. Syoten Oka. The author had previously read some of Prof. Oka's seminal research papers on cardiovascular fluid mechanics. Since the author had done some theoretical research on blood flow in arteries, he was eager to discuss some specific matters on his research topics with him. Their discussions were insightful, and Prof. Oka personally guided him through the institution.

Fourth International Congress on Biorheology, Tokyo

After visiting Kobe and Osaka, the author returned to Tokyo on July 26, 1981, the day before the Fourth International Congress on Biorheology began at Tokyo Medical University. The congress started as per schedule on July 27. The author felt privileged to interact with several stalwarts there, including Prof. Y.C. Fung (University of California, San Diego), who gave a special lecture at the congress. Prof. Fung's presentations were characterized by clear and simple communication. The author also met Prof. A.L. Copley, a distinguished researcher and professor of biorheology and fluid mechanics at the City University of New York. During the conference dinner, the author had the opportunity to interact with Prof. R.N. Vaishnav from Catholic University in the USA. The author had read some of his research papers on the nonlinear rheological behavior of vascular tissues, which had been useful in the author's research. As scheduled, the author presented his research paper on the designated day at the Congress.

Los Angeles, USA

After the conference, the author visited the University of California, Los Angeles (UCLA). His former student from IIT, Sajal Kanti Kar, was doing postdoctoral research there. He welcomed the author to stay with him for 3–4 days. Sajal introduced him to the Mathematics Department at UCLA and took him on a tour of the city.

This marked an incredible academic journey, filled with valuable experiences, networking and research collaborations across continents.

University of California, San Diego, USA

Prof. Y.C. Fung was a distinguished professor at this university. Much like the author, initially he was a faculty of applied mathematics and his research focused on solid and fluid mechanics. He had written books on these subjects. However, he gained widespread recognition for his pioneering research in biomechanics, producing numerous publications in this field. He had written several books on various branches of biomechanics. The author had already established contact with him, so Prof. Fung picked him up at the airport and invited him to stay at his home, rather than in a hotel. During their conversation, he gave some useful suggestions to the author on conducting research in biomechanics. He mentioned that doctors in many countries are not much interested in research, as they are always busy treating patients. He recommended building personal friendships with doctors and to encourage them to get involved in research. Additionally, he advised taking a short nap after lunch to sustain productivity throughout the day. He informed

Prof. Y.C Fung, University of California, San Diego, USA

that he did not take tea/coffee and remarked, "Why to excite the system?" He also shared that he was born in China and moved to the USA after World War II. The following day, they travelled together to the University of Southern California in his car, where he was collaborating with a researcher of experimental biomechanics.

Visit to Vedanta Society & Ramakrishna-Vivekananda Center, New York

Swami Tathagatananda, Minister-in-charge, Vedanta Society of New York

The author had informed Swami Tathagatananda (Lakshinarayan Maharaj) about his visit to New York. Those days, he was the head of the Vedanta Society at 34 West 71st Street in New York, founded by Swami Vivekananda in 1894. It is managed by the Ramakrishna Mission. As mentioned elsewhere, there is another center called the Ramakrishna-Vivekananda Center of New York at 179th Street, established by Swami Nikhilananda in 1933. In 1981, Swami Adishwarananda was the head of this center. When the author was studying at Vidyamandira near Belur Math, Swami Tathagatananda was the warden of the South Hostel and was very affectionate towards the author. Maharaj graciously arranged for his stay at the Vedanta Society of New York for 4–5 days, ensuring a smooth arrival by sending two people to pick him up from the airport.

Seminar Lecture at Courant Institute of Mathematical Sciences, New York

Courant Institute of Mathematical Sciences, New York, USA

While in New York, the author had the opportunity to visit the prestigious Courant Institute of Mathematical Sciences, where he was invited by Prof. Charles S. Peskin of the Courant Institute to deliver a seminar lecture. The lecture topic "Mathematical Modelling of Blood Flow in Arteries" was of particular interest to Prof. Peskin who was known for his work on mathematical modelling of blood flow in the heart and heart valves. As a recognition of his contribution, the author was paid some honorarium.

Prof. Charles Peskin

The next day, the author had an invitation to deliver a seminar lecture at Cornell Medical Center, a constituent of New York Hospital. The lecture was on "Mathematical Modelling of Brain Injury Due to Head Impact." The author remembers talking to a professor at Cornell Medical Center who asked the author about his first impression on his visit to USA. The professor humorously remarked, "Americans speak very fast, don't they?"

Cornell Medical Centre, New York Hospital, USA

Swami Tathagatananda ensured the author had the opportunity to explore New York and arranged for a companion to accompany him on sightseeing trips. To integrate into the Center's daily activities, Maharaj advised the author to assist with dishwashing, aligning with the Western practice of self-sufficiency. The Center held a weekly service in the hall every Sunday, led by the minister-in-charge. Maharaj had informed the author about this in advance. At 11 am, Maharaj stood at a designated spot in the hall wearing a suit. The service began with a Sanskrit invocation, followed by Maharaj translating the verses into English. Then there was a guided meditation for about ten minutes, followed by Maharaj's lecture in English. It was a beautiful lecture, and the entire programme lasted for about an hour. At the end, according to custom, a plate was passed around for a 'service' offering. Each person contributed according to their ability and willingness. The attendees included locals and some Indians/Bengalees.

When Maharaj was at the Center, he always wore saffron robes. Whenever he had time, he talked to the author about India and Indians. Despite living in far away New York, Maharaj kept himself updated on everything related to India and recent events. The author noticed that the emotional nature he observed in Maharaj while he was at the Vidyamandira had not waned over the years. The author remembers him visiting Belur Math once, joining a study circle on the IIT campus, and giving lectures on various religious texts. The next morning, he visited the author's quarters (C1-63). When he learned that the author's wife, Shorasi, knew a bit of Sanskrit, he asked her to recite a few Sanskrit verses. Shorasi recited the first three verses of Kalidasa's "Meghaduta," which pleased Maharaj greatly. He also enjoyed engaging with the author's children.

Academic Visits and Research Collaborations

The author then travelled to Calgary, Canada by Greyhound bus to visit the University of Calgary, where he worked with Prof. Samir Majumdar, an alumnus of the Ramakrishna Mission Calcutta Students' Home. During his two-and-a half-month stay, he tried to make some contribution to Prof. Majumdar's research project. Additionally he engaged in discussions with Prof. Ranjit S. Dhaliwal, an expert in thermoelasticity in the same Department.

Calgary University Mathematical Sciences Dept., Canada

Prof. Majumdar and his wife hosted the author several dinners and invited him to a Bengali Community event featuring *Satyanarayan Puja*, attended by local Indian families. At these gatherings, the author felt happy to meet some of the alumni of IIT Kharagpur.

During the author's stay in Calgary, Prof. Samir Majumdar took him to several places of tourist attraction, such as the Calgary Tower and the Rocky Mountains. The Calgary Tower, located in the city's center, is 62 feet tall. From this tower, one can see the entire city of Calgary and the Rocky Mountains. The tower is a popular attraction for visitors. It was previously known as the Husky Tower. It is the tallest tower in Calgary and the second tallest in Canada, after the Toronto Tower. The tower has two elevators, and its rotating restaurant, which completes a 360-degree rotation every hour, is very popular.

University of Alberta, Edmonton, Canada (Author's lecture, 1981)

During his return journey from Canada to India, the author visited several cities and universities in Europe as per the previous plan. After landing at Heathrow Airport in London, the author stayed there for a few days, took a guided tour, and revisited some attractions, including the 'Changing of the Guards at Buckingham Palace', Tower Bridge, and Westminster Abbey. He also visited Rome, the capital of Italy, before returning to India.

Visiting Fellow, Hannover Technical University, Germany (1982)

In May 1982, during the summer break, the author went to Hannover Technical University as a Humboldt Fellow, with Prof. Oskar Mahrenholtz as his scientific host. This visit focused on research into the Mechanics of Bones, a shift from his previous work on mathematical modelling and simulation of brain injury (1975–77).

Visiting Professor, IIT Kanpur, 1983

In 1983, when the author was an Assistant Professor at IIT Kharagpur, he was selected as a Visiting Professor at IIT Kanpur for a year. However, he served IIT Kanpur as a Visiting Professor only during the summer break, May-June 1983. The reason was that during that time many research scholars were doing Ph.D. under his supervision at IIT Kharagpur and he thought, his absence for a long time would disturb their research progress.

Doctor of Science (D.Sc.), 1984

In 1983, the author submitted his thesis to the Department of Applied Mathematics for the Doctor of Science (D.Sc.) degree at the University of Calcutta. The D.Sc. is considered the highest doctoral degree awarded by the university. The title of the thesis was "Mathematical Modelling in the Realm of Biomechanics and Structural Mechanics." Three eminent professors from countries like UK, USA, Germany, and France evaluated the thesis, as per Calcutta University tradition. All the three examiners highly praised the thesis. Based on their unanimous approval, the University of Calcutta awarded the author the degree of Doctor of Science in Applied Mathematics during the 1984 convocation, when Prof. Santosh Bhattacharyya was the Vice-Chancellor of the University and Shri A.P. Sharma was the Governor of West Bengal. As a recognition of this prestigious achievement, the Board of Governors of IIT Kharagpur granted him an additional monthly increment.

Promotion to Professor Cadre at IIT Kharagpur on the Consideration of Merit (1985)

At IIT Kharagpur, faculty promotions followed a structured process. In 1985, the Board of Governors, introduced an exceptional provision allowing eligible Assistant Professors and Senior faculty members to apply for promotion. The selection committee comprising external experts and a representative appointed by the President of India, evaluated candidates. The author was promoted to Professor cadre based on merit, a distinction granted under the third eligibility criterion recognizing distinguished academic contributions.

Over the years, IIT's faculty promotion process has evolved, with structured career progression based on research, teaching and administrative contributions.

Visiting Researcher/Professor at Overseas Universities

As described earlier, the author first went abroad for advanced research at Hannover Technical University in Germany in 1975. He conducted research with Professor Oskar Mahrenholtz and returned in June 1977. Five years later, in 1982, he went to Germany for the second time for four months, again to Hannover. Meanwhile, in 1978, Hannover Technical University was renamed as "University of Hannover." However, there were no significant changes in the system of education. Later, the university's name was changed again. In 2006, the university's Senate decided to rename it as "Leibniz University Hannover" after the name of the renowned German scientist Gottfried Wilhelm Leibniz, who was a distinguished mathematician, physicist, and philosopher. The university library, "German National Library of Science and Technology," is the largest library in the world for science and technology. Several professors from this university had earlier won Nobel Prizes. Established on May 2, 1831, this university is one of Germany's oldest and largest universities. After 1982, the author continued research work at several other universities abroad as a visiting professor.

Hong Kong (2002)

In 2002, the author had the opportunity to work as a visiting professor at the Hong Kong University of Science and Technology for a few days. The city's

Hong Kong University of Science and Technology, Hong Kong

culture is a unique blend of Eastern and Western influences. As Hong Kong was under British rule for almost a century, many people here speak English. The accommodation was arranged in the university's guest house, and since many locals spoke English, the author faced no problem in communicating with others. The university provided the author with a separate office, where the department displayed the author's name in front of his office.

Bremen University, Germany (2005–2006)

ZARM, Bremen University, Germany

Prof. Hans Rath, Bremen, Germany

In May-June 2005 and May-June 2006, the author spent a total of four months at the Center for Applied Space Technology and Microgravity (ZARM) at Bremen University, Germany. There he collaborated with Prof. Hans Rath for research related to cardiovascular fluid dynamics. Notably, the author had first met Rath at Hannover Technical University, where Rath was pursuing his doctorate under Prof. Mahrenholtz. At Bremen University, Hans Rath had established a Drop Tower, where various experiments could be conducted under zero gravity conditions. Researchers from various branches of science worldwide used to come here to conduct observations in a zero-gravity environment.

Prof. Rath was famous not only for establishing the Drop Tower but was also a renowned scientist with a curious mind, a good research manager, and a skilled artist. The author remembers one Saturday, Prof. Rath invited the author to his home in Bremen for dinner. He was the only guest, and both he and his wife, Britta Rath, extended warm hospitality. Hans showed the author various artworks he had created, and Britta shared her hobbies, including her love for reading various books, for which she had a small library at home. After dinner and long hours of engaging discussions and a tour of Rath's artistic creations, the author was driven back to his guest house, as Rath adhered strictly to Germany's stringent laws against drinking and driving. It is known that if the police discover that someone is driving under the influence of alcohol, they impose severe penalties, including revoking the driver's license. However, the police do not harass anyone without any valid reason. Hans mentioned that he had been married once before and had a daughter from that marriage. He explained that the divorce was due to differences in likes and dislikes. However, they still communicated when they met occasionally. Bremen University left a strong impression on the author, offering a conducive research environment with significant opportunities for interdisciplinary collaboration.

University of Malaya, Malaysia (2007)

Malay University, Kuala Lumpur, Malaysia

In 2007, the author visited the University of Malaya in Malaysia for a short academic engagement. Over a week-long stay, he delivered a total of five lectures on mathematical modelling in different areas of biomechanics at the Mathematics Department. He stayed at the guest house of the University of Malaya, and the days were quite pleasant. During his stay, he connected with Prof. Rafiqul Islam from the International Islamic University of Malaysia. Rafiqul had completed his Ph.D. from Mathematics department at IIT Kharagpur. During the author's visit, Rafiqul was very hospitable, taking the author to several tourist spots. The day before his return, he invited the author to his home, where he stayed overnight. The next morning, Rafiqul drove him to the airport.

National University of Singapore (NUS) 2007

National University, Singapore

Prof. Y.C. Tay had invited the author to deliver lectures at the National University of Singapore (NUS). Upon arrival, the author was greeted at the airport by Prof. Tay. The author had a five-day program in Singapore. He opted to stay at the Ramakrishna Mission in Singapore. At the National University of Singapore, he delivered two lectures on biomechanics over two days. Besides the NUS faculty, a few individuals from Nanyang Technological University (NTU) in Singapore also attended the lectures. During his five-day stay, the author also had the pleasure of meeting several professors at NUS, who were alumni of IIT Kharagpur, and they invited him to lunch. Exploring Singapore's attractions further enriched his experience, leaving him with fond memories of the picturesque country.

Leibniz University, Hannover (2008, 2009)

Prof. Joerg Wallaschek, Leibniz University, Hannover

In May-June 2008 and June 2009, the author collaborated with Prof. Joerg Wallaschek, Director of the Institute of Dynamics and Vibration Research at Leibniz University in Hannover, Germany. Prof. Wallaschek was highly regarded for his enthusiasm and hospitality, making the research experience exceptionally engaging.

Hamburg University of Technology (2012, 2013, 2016)

Hamburg University of Technology, Germany

Prof. Heinz Herwig

In May-June 2012 and July 2013, the author conducted research on different problems of biofluid dynamics with Prof. Heinz Herwig at the Institute of Thermofluid Dynamics at Hamburg University of Technology. Based on this work, the author published a joint research paper in 2015 in 'Journal of Hydrodynamics'. The title of the paper was "Estimates of Blood Flow in Bio-fluidic Devices."

In 2016, the author worked for three months (May-July) at the Institute of Mechanics and Ocean Engineering at Hamburg University of Technology with Professor Robert Seifried. Incidentally, Prof. Mahrenholtz, after leaving Hannover, became the founding director of this institute. It is interesting that the author's seating arrangement here was in the same room where Prof. Mahrenholtz used to sit, when he was the Director of this Institute. During author's stay at the University, Prof. Mahrenholtz once came down from his house in Hamburg to meet the author, but he seemed very depressed, as his third wife (a Canadian woman) had passed away sometime ago. He had carried this grief for many years and told the author that he had to live alone in his Hamburg home. Of course, he informed that his children visited him occasionally. Germans are generally individualistic by nature, but the author's closeness with Prof. Mahrenholtz remained intact from 1975 until he passed away. On a previous occasion, when the author had gone to deliver a lecture at the Technical University of Hamburg-Harburg, Prof. Mahrenholtz had already retired, and his third wife was still alive. At that time, he had taken the author to his Hamburg home. He mentioned it was Valentine's Day, so the author presented a bouquet of flowers to his wife. We all had cake and coffee, and then Prof. Mahrenholtz drove the author to the nearby Harburg railway station. In Germany, train schedules are printed on the timetable, and they usually do not change under any circumstances. Prof. Mahrenholtz stood on the platform until the train left, observed the author.

Prof. Robert

Berlin Technical University (Author's Lecture, 1982)

Humboldt Fellows Reception (2016)

Every year around June 22–23, the German President hosts a reception in Berlin for Humboldt Fellows. The Humboldt Foundation usually invites former Humboldt Fellows who are in Germany that time to attend this reception. In 2016, the author had the opportunity to attend this reception hosted by the then German President, Mr. Joachim Gauck, who shook hands with each Humboldt Fellow present. There was also a lunch provided by the German President. Since Sudip became a Humboldt Fellow, we usually try to visit the same university together.

In 2016, Sudip went to Hamburg University, and the author went to Hamburg University of Technology. We stayed at a guesthouse of a church in Hamburg. The younger daughter-in-law Satamita, grandson Devadeep (Gopal), and grand daughter Devadrita (Chandramukhi) also accompanied us. Shorasi could not join us as she stayed back at the IIT residence to care of my mother. We visited several tourist attractions every weekend (Saturday/Sunday) under Sudip's appropriate planning.

Mother's Demise (December 2016)

We returned from Germany in July 2016. However, a few days before our return, my mother fell ill. She was first admitted to the IIT hospital and later transferred to KPC Medical College and Hospital in Kolkata. Author's daughter Sumita came to Kharagpur and took her to Kolkata. After recovering at the hospital, Sumita kept her at her in-laws' house for a few days. We brought my mother to our flat in Santoshpur when we returned from Germany at the end of July. The author along with Shorasi stayed with her, and arrangement was made that two attendants cared for her in shifts. During this time, the author's sister also stayed with the mother in Santoshpur for about 15–20 days. In early December, when the author's mother's health deteriorated, she was readmitted to KPC Hospital, Kolkata. Author's younger brother Parames came from Canada and met the mother. However, within a couple of days, our mother passed away. Upon receiving the news, Sudip immediately came to the hospital by taxi from Kharagpur and joined us. According to mother's wishes, her last rites were performed near the Ganges at the Boral crematorium in Garia. Her ashes were immersed in Ganga River at Babughat. Cousin Tarapada, brothers-in-law Nantu and Poltu, son-in-law Achintya, Namita and Subhash, Haru and Papu, and a few other relatives were present during the last rites. The author along with Parames performed mother's funeral rites together, before Parames returned to Canada.

Friedrich-Alexander University (FAU) Erlangen-Nuremberg, Germany (2019)

In 2019, the author visited Friedrich-Alexander University (FAU) Erlangen-Nuremberg, where he worked as a guest scientist. Sudip worked with Professor Robert Schober at the Institute for Digital Communications (IDC), while the author worked at the Institute of Applied Mechanics with Professor Paul Steinmann. We stayed there for three months, from May to July. This visit was particularly enjoyable for all of us because Shorasi accompanied us. Satamita, Devadeep, and Devadrita, who had gone with us on previous trips, also came along. With Sudip's enthusiasm and proper planning, we could explore several other European countries (Italy, France, and the Czech Republic) apart from Germany.

Prof. Paul Steinmann, Friedrich Alexender University, Nuremberg-Erlangen, Germany

On May 3, 2019, we flew from Kolkata airport to Indira Gandhi International Airport in Delhi on an Air India flight. From there, we arrived at Frankfurt Airport in Germany the following evening. From Frankfurt, we took a train to Nuremberg, arriving at around 12:30 AM. We took a taxi to our apartment, which Sudip had booked online in advance. When we arrived, it was almost 2 AM (local time). We had a light meal with the food we had with us and then went to bed. The next day, the author and Sudip both went to FAU in Erlangen. The author was warmly received by Prof. Paul Steinmann, who scheduled their discussions. Sudip met his host Prof. Robert Schober at the Institute for Digital Communication of the same university.

A few days later, on a Saturday, we took a tram to the Documentation Centre in Nuremberg. The museum houses many documents, photographs, and exhibits related to Germany's dictatorial ruler Hitler and his Nazi Party. There are many poignant accounts of the era, including stories of atrocities, displayed on several boards. There is a nearby lake by the side of which many prisoners used to sit. From there, we took a bus to see the Central Market and the nearby Frauenkirche (Church of the ladies). The church's architecture is stunning. On another day, we visited the Imperial Castle in Nuremberg, situated on a small hill. Nowadays, Nuremberg and Erlangen are considered as twin cities. Our university, Friedrich-Alexander University, is located in these twin cities. The university has a large botanical garden, which we have visited several times. We saw various plants, including many medicinal ones. There are also several small water bodies with different aquatic plants and fish. The garden has several large glasshouses (greenhouses), where we saw various plants from different climates worldwide. Some greenhouses contain different types of cacti, while another houses plants from tropical rainforests, with a humid climate maintained inside to suit these plants.

Prague Trip

On Saturday, June 10, 2019, we visited Prague, the capital of the Czech Republic. This city has historical significance and is a political, cultural, and economic center in Central Europe. While, many European countries have been affected by the refugee crisis, the Czech Republic, along with Denmark, Austria, Portugal, Switzerland, and Slovenia, has largely remained unaffected. We travelled from Nuremberg to Prague, by Deutsche Bahn (DB) bus, enjoying picturesque views along the way. It took 3 hours and 30 minutes to reach the Prague bus station. From there, we bought public transport tickets and travelled to our apartment, in about 45 minutes. In the evening, we visited Prague Castle, admiring its exquisite architectural details. We also visited the Charles Bridge. The next morning, we toured another beautiful castle. The weather was quite hot during those days. The following day, we returned to Nuremberg, again by DB bus.

Garmisch Trip

On June 15, 2019, we travelled to Garmisch, a popular vacation destination located in southern Germany (Bavaria). Known for its skiing, ice skating and hiking opportunities, the town offers a picturesque retreat. We took a train from Nuremberg to Munich in the morning and then a smaller train to Garmisch. From the Garmisch train station, we boarded a narrow gauge train to a place called Eibsee. From there, we took a cable car to Zugspitze, the highest peak in the German Alps. The cable car ride was a thrilling experience for everyone. From Zugspitze, we took another cable car to view the glacier. We returned to Nuremberg the same day, arriving at around 11:30 PM.

Italy Trip

On June 25, 2019, we embarked on a trip to Italy, visiting three iconic cities: Venice, Pisa, and Rome. Our journey began with an ICE train from Nuremberg to Frankfurt Airport, followed by a flight with Ryanair to Venice. We arrived at Venice-Treviso Airport after a flight of one hour and 20 minutes. Our taxi and apartment were pre-booked, and we stayed in an apartment in Mestre. We arrived there at around 8:30 PM.

Venice

The next morning, we purchased public transport tickets and first went to the city center of Venice via tram. We noticed that all the trams there looked much different than those in Germany. From there, we took a boat ride on the Grand Canal and disembarked at St. Mark's Square. We explored the nearby areas on foot, then took another boat to the Murano Islands, famous for their glass factories. We toured one of the factories, where we saw beautiful items being made from melted glass into various shapes and colors. They also provided a demonstration and explanation for the visitors. Each factory had a shop. From Murano Island, we took another boat to the Burano Islands, known for their stitching items. From there, we returned to St. Mark's Square and walked around to see St. Mark's Basilica, Doge's Palace, and the Rialto Bridge.

St. Mark's Basilica is famous for its famous stunning Byzantine architecture, intricate mosaics, and its status as the final resting place of Saint Mark relics. It stands as a symbol of Venetian history, culture and religious devotion, attracting visitors from different corners of the globe to admire its grandeur and beauty. Doge's palace in Venice is famous for being a masterpiece of Venetian Gothic architecture. This magnificent palace is visited by over 2 million tourists in a year. In Venice St. Mark's basilica is the largest point of attraction, Doge's palace being the second largest. Rialto Bridge is the oldest bridge across the Grand Canal in Venice. It is famous for its unique architecture and marvelous engineering. This unique bridge was designed following a design competition in Venice. The design and construction was made by Antonio da Ponte and his nephew Antonio Contanio.

Pisa

From Venice, we travelled by train to Pisa, passing through Florence. Although Florence has some notable sights, we went straight to Pisa, located in the

Tuscany region of Italy. The Leaning Tower of Pisa, is an architectural marvel. The eight-storied tower stands approximately 56 meters tall and weighs around 14, 500 tons. It currently leans at an angle of about 3.99 degrees and has 294 steps. The construction of the tower began in 1173 and was completed in 1372. Initially, the tower did not lean; it began to tilt after the third floor was built in 1178. The soft ground and shallow foundation of only three meters are considered the main reasons for the tower's leaning, along with its design. The tower was originally intended as a bell tower. The intricate carvings of the nearby cathedral are exceptionally beautiful. In 1987, the Leaning Tower and the adjacent cathedral, baptistery, and cemetery were designated as UNESCO World Heritage Sites. Despite the hot weather, we enjoyed meeting visitors from various countries, including South Korea and India.

Rome

On June 28, we travelled by train from Pisa Central Station to Rome, the capital of Italy. After checking into our apartment, we first visited the Colosseum, a large elliptical amphitheatre that can accommodate 50,000 spectators at a time.

Vatican City

The following day, we visited Vatican City, an independent state located within Rome, Italy. It is the smallest state in the world, covering an area of 110 acres. The Pope serves as the head of state. Vatican City is the headquarters of the Roman Catholic Church and is situated in a triangular area on Vatican Hill in northwestern Rome. It houses the main church of the Roman Catholics, St. Peter's Basilica. The Vatican city also has an astronomical research center, the Vatican Observatory. The weather in Rome was very hot during our stay, so after visiting the basilica, we returned to our apartment. After spending five days in Italy, we flew back to Nuremberg Airport in Germany on June 30 from Rome's Ciampino Airport via Ryanair. The flight took one hour and 45 minutes.

(Ryanair is a low-cost airline having its headquarters in Dublin, Ireland. It offers airline services to 28 countries in Europe and also in Morocco. The low-cost strategy adopted by Ryanair is founded on extreme operating efficiency.)

Paris Trip

On July 7, 2019, we travelled from Nuremberg Central Station to Stuttgart by Intercity (I.C.) Express train, a journey of 2 hours and 30 minutes duration.

From Stuttgart, we took a T.G.V. train to Paris, the capital of France. The train journey was very enjoyable, with the T.G.V. train reaching speeds of up to 230 km/h. The journey from Stuttgart Station in Germany to Paris Gare de l'Est took about 4 hours and 30 minutes. We arrived at the station at around 10:30 PM. Paris is a very large city, and its metro service is excellent. We had booked a flat near the Paris airport a few days earlier. The flat was on the sixth floor, making access slightly challenging as there was no elevator in the building.

Eiffel Tower

The next morning, we visited the famous Eiffel Tower, a 320-meter (about 1,050-foot) tall structure designed by Gustave Eiffel and completed on March 15, 1889. It was the tallest structure in the world until 1929 when the Chrysler Building in New York surpassed it. The tower has three levels and seven elevators. We bought tickets for ascending to the second floor, enjoying breathtaking views of Paris. After visiting the Eiffel Tower, we went to see the Seine River, which flows into the English Channel. The Seine River is 777 km long and has an average depth of 9.5 meters. It is the second-longest river in France.

Arc de Triomphe and Louvre Museum

The Arc de Triomphe stands 51 meters tall and 45 meters wide, with one side featuring the Louvre Museum and the other side housing financial institutions. The construction of this monument took almost 30 years (1806–1836). On July 9, we toured the Louvre Museum, one of the world's largest and most important museums. The museum is located in the Louvre Palace, built by King Philip II of France between the 12th and 13th centuries as a fortress. The remains of this fortress can still be seen in the museum's basement. Over time, it evolved into the primary residence of French royalty. The building underwent several expansions over the years, giving it its current form. The museum is home to the world-famous Mona Lisa. From there, we went to see the famous Tuileries Garden, a large garden covering 22.4 hectares. After the French Revolution, it was turned into a public park. We then visited the famous Alexander Bridge, built in 1896 and designated a special landmark in 1975. The bridge spans the Seine River in Paris and is 160 meters long and 40 meters wide. Next, we went to see the famous Palais Garnier, a renowned opera house in Paris. The opera house can accommodate 1,979 spectators and was recognized as a historic monument in France in 1923.

The Paris Opera Library-Museum is also located inside the opera house. Like the Eiffel Tower and the Louvre Museum, the opera house is also a symbol of Paris. We also visited the Shopping Mall and Galleries Lafayette, one of Paris's famous landmarks. Although the shopping mall is very popular and attracts visitors, the prices of goods are generally affordable. The mall offers products suitable for men, women, and children.

After spending four days in Paris, we returned to Nuremberg via T.G.V. train to Stuttgart and then via I.C. train on July 10.

Bamberg, Bavaria, Germany

Bamberg is a small town located in the Bavarian region of Germany. Despite its small size compared to other cities, Bamberg boasts of its beautiful natural scenery. It is home to Bamberg Otto Friedrich University, which has around 13, 000 students studying subjects such as Social Science, Humanities, and Business Studies. Another institution in the city is the Bamberg University of Applied Sciences, which offers higher education in various aspects of Public Health.

On July 21, we visited Bamberg. Our journey started from Nuremberg in the morning and we returned at night. The city is situated on seven hills at the confluence of the Regnitz and Main rivers. Many old buildings from the 11th to the 19th centuries are well-preserved here, including the famous Altes Rathaus (Old Town Hall). The walls of these buildings feature various paintings and carvings. The city's numerous bridges are also ornate. The main cathedral, with its Romanesque architecture and artistic style, draws particular attention. This cathedral features four towers and is a UNESCO-protected site.

Bamberg's island city is known for its historical district of fishermen and is often referred to as "Little Venice." The medieval half-timbered houses along the small rivers add to the picturesque view, reminiscent of Venice, Italy. The charming sight of boats floating between the rows of houses enhances the area's appeal.

In the last week of July 2019, we returned to Kharagpur. We travelled by train from Nuremberg to Frankfurt. Our friends—Saroj Nayak and Sardarji, along with their families—came to Nuremberg station to bid us farewell. They brought for us homemade food for our journey. Their warmth and hospitality were very touching.

Lectures at Other Foreign Countries

The author has also been invited to deliver lectures on biofluid dynamics at Edmonton University in Canada and as a keynote speaker at conferences at the University of Dhaka, Shahjalal University of Science and Technology in Sylhet, and Nepal College of Information Technology in Nepal in different years. The author continues to engage in research to the best of his ability. In recognition of his work, he received an invitation to conduct research at the University of Erlangen-Nuremberg in Germany from May to July 2022. However, due to the severe COVID-19 outbreak in that region, the visit could not materialize.

CHAPTER 9

Distinguished Research

A Summary

The author's initial training in applied mathematics has enabled him to explore various branches of science and engineering by developing mathematical models and employing extensive computational analysis. Below is a summary of his significant research contributions. In the past, mathematics and physiology/medicine were considered to be mutually exclusive branches of science. However, with emergence of interdisciplinary domains such as biomathematics, biomedical mathematics, biomechanics and physiological fluid dynamics, scientific perspectives have shifted. These fields leverage mathematical modelling and simulation to explore a variety of novel information in various branches of biology and medicine. Through his dedicated efforts, the author along with his research group made humble attempt to contribute significantly to the following research areas:

1. Cardiovascular Dynamics
2. Mechanics of the Physiological Problem of Brain Injury
3. Fracture and Remodelling Mechanics of Bones
4. Peristaltic and Electroosmotic Flows of Physiological Fluids
5. Modelling of Drug Delivery using Nanofluid Flow
6. Biomathematics: Modelling of instabilities of host parasite system, gene identification, DNA knots and links and tumor cell aggregation
7. Mechanics of Fluids and Solids

The Role of Mathematical Modelling in Human Physiology

Scientific consensus dictates that experimental observations should align with theoretical prediction. However, for living human body, it is not possible to perform any harmful experiment. Instead, research relies on sub-human primates (rats, monkeys, dogs, etc.), or on use of human cadavers. Unfortunately, physiological responses in these models often fail to accurately reflect those in living humans. There is another type of difficulty. Mechanical properties of different constituents/organs like arteries and vascular tissue properties and age-related physiological differences further complicate experimental research. Data for infants/children can be much different from those of adults. Various physiological data for a normal human body are different from those in pathological states.

All this indicates that mathematical modelling together with the use of the method of variation of parameters by using experimental data can play a vital role in exploring a variety of information for living human beings. A well-constructed mathematical model incorporates realistic assumptions that reflect actual biological conditions as closely as possible.

Recognition through Research Contributions

The author's research has garnered national and international acclaim, while addressing issues, such as the pressure on the heart valves, blood flow in arteries, mechanics of brain injury, the mechanics of bone fracture and remodelling, as well as nano-fluid flows in physiological systems. His extensive body of work with nearly 250 research papers published in various international journals and 13 advanced level books, has earned him a place among the world's top 2% scientists during the last 6 consecutive years (2020–2025) as per the list published by a group of researchers from Stanford University, USA led by Prof. P.A. Ioannidis. This achievement is partially attributed to the collaboration of his research students.

Cardiovascular Dynamics

The author's research on cardiovascular dynamics encompasses heart muscle mechanics and blood flow dynamics under various conditions. A key focus has been the left ventricle, the thick-walled chamber responsible for pumping oxygenated blood throughout the body. During the contraction of the heart, blood enters the left ventricle. Thus, the health of the left ventricle is closely linked to the overall health of the human body. The left ventricle can suffer from various pathological conditions, one of which is aneurysm, that is an abnormal outward bulging of the heart or arterial walls, which may lead to a clot formation and rupture, causing severe complication. This can be hereditary or can result from acquired diseases. An aneurysm can also be formed in the heart wall after a heart attack. Cerebral aneurysms, if they create pressure on the brain's structure, can lead to various symptoms. Symptoms may include fatigue, loss of balance, loss of perception, and double vision. In the event of rupture of an aneurysm, severe headaches, neck pain, or stiffness may occur. Angiography is used to determine the location of an aneurysm. Former U.S. President Joe Biden experienced two aneurysms in his brain, from which he recovered through surgery in 1988.

The author proposed a mathematical model for early-stage myocardial infarction in the left ventricle. Myocardial infarction, commonly known as a heart attack, occurs when the blood supply to the heart muscle is blocked, leading to potentially fatal consequences. By mathematically analyzing the model and using diastolic pressure-volume data available for an infarcted heart, the model predicts potential heart muscle rupture. This research has applications in heart surgery and treatment. The findings of the author were published in the American journal 'Computers and Mathematics with Applications' in 1988 under the title "Study on the Mechanics of Aneurysms in the Left Ventricle of the Heart." Further, the author developed a model to measure stress-distribution in the ventricular wall. The detailed analysis was published in 1985 in another American journal 'Bulletin of Mathematical Biology' under the title "Distribution of Stresses in the Left Ventricular Wall of the Intact Heart."

In 2021, his team published the details of another study on left ventricular mechanics in the 'Journal of Mechanics in Medicine and Biology', a journal published from Singapore. The study, titled "Stress Distribution in the Left Ventricular Wall during Cardiac Contraction: A Mathematical Model," concluded that increased diastolic filling can enhance ventricular contraction of the left ventricle, improving blood ejection efficiency.

Mathematical Modelling of Blood Flow

Numerous factors can influence the efficiency of blood flow in the human body. The cardiovascular system adopts to ensure sufficient oxygen delivery. However, under certain conditions, blood flow in the circulatory system to different organs may be impaired.

Blood flow in the human body is a highly complex process, and blood is a complex fluid and no single model can fully capture its behaviour. Thus, different mathematical models are designed to focus on specific physiological aspects.

Blood Flow in Normal Physiological States

Over the past four decades, the author together with his research students have published extensively, reporting a variety of important information on blood flow mechanics. Along with blood flow, the deformation and stress distribution of the arterial wall were also investigated by them. Experimental research on animals indicate that arterial wall vibrations influence blood flow, and vice versa. Despite this, many researchers have modelled arterial walls as rigid structures, leading to inaccuracies.

To address this limitation, the author's research group developed a mathematical model, by taking into account the nonlinearly viscoelastic orthotropic material behavior of arterial walls, as revealed by experimental observations. However, when these realistic material properties are taken into consideration, the mathematical analysis becomes too much complicated and hence it becomes quite difficult to obtain the theoretical solution of the complex non-linear problem, requiring computational solutions. The numerical estimates reported by the author's research team obtained by using computational techniques provided various physiological/pathological conditions.

One of the author's pioneering studies on nonlinear stress fields in blood vessels, published in Blood Vessels (1982), confirmed the relevance of his research in physiology and medicine. In another study, published in Journal of Mathematical Biology (1983), the author investigated the role of initial stress on wave propagation in arteries. His subsequent model simulated pulse wave velocity in the aorta; the results appeared in the Bulletin of Mathematical Biology (1984).

A significant breakthrough was the author's study of the compressibility effects and anisotropic properties in the study of blood flow models. His research findings on stress distribution in arterial walls were published in Rheologica Acta (1980) and Journal of Biomechanics (1982). Previous researchers had treated arterial walls as rigid or linearly elastic, but experimental findings reported by Prof. Y.C. Fung (University of California, San Diego) and Prof. K.R. Rajagopal (Texus A&M University) later validated the author's approach.

The author along with one of his associates conducted another theoretical research in which they considered the above-mentioned properties of vascular tissues. This model simulated the pressure exerted by blood on the endothelium (inner wall) of the vascular medium and the pressure exerted by the surrounding connective tissues on the adventitia (outermost layer). The model is highly realistic, as the computed values matched quite well with the experimental observations of Prof. Y.C. Fung, mentioned above. This study emphasized the importance of considering the pressure exerted by surrounding connective tissues in simulating the stress field in the arterial wall. The detailed findings of the author appeared in the Journal of Biomechanics (1982) with the title "Dynamic response of Arterial walls in vivo."

Blood Flow in Pathological States

The author developed several mathematical models also for blood flow under diseased conditions. One of the significant arterial diseases is atherosclerosis or arteriosclerosis, a condition in which fatty deposits accumulate inside arteries, restricting blood flow. Sometimes, this condition is referred to simply as sclerosis. This sticky substance hardens the affected artery over time, narrowing the blood flow pathway.

The terms arteriosclerosis and atherosclerosis are often used interchangeably, though they can refer to slightly different phenomena. Atherosclerosis develops slowly over many years, often without symptoms. It can start in childhood, but symptoms may not appear for many years. If plaque forms in a major artery, it can grow quickly, causing various problems. This disease can reduce blood flow and oxygen supply to vital organs and limbs. Reduced blood supply to the heart can lead to a heart attack. If muscles of the heart cannot pump blood efficiently, heart failure may occur. Blockages in the coronary arteries (supplying blood to the heart) can cause heart failure, and plaque formation in the carotid arteries (that supply blood to the brain) can lead to a stroke. Risk factors for atherosclerosis include smoking, high blood pressure, high cholesterol and triglyceride levels, a diet high in saturated fats, type 1 diabetes, lack of physical activity, and obesity.

1. *Mathematical Modelling of Flow in Atherosclerotic (Stenosed) Arteries*

Together with his research students, the author has conducted studies on blood flow in stenosed arteries. Their work has been extensively published in various distinguished journals. His first research paper on this topic appeared in 1986 in the research quarterly 'Journal of Biomechanics', published from USA titled "Flow in Arteries in the Presence of Stenosis." The paper was reviewed by three referees who praised the development and analysis of the mathematical model and the simulation study. The paper was noted also for its high-quality presentation and language, making a remark that English was the author's native language. The Referees (anonymous) made an observation that this research paper is useful for the measurement of viscosity variation of blood in stenosed arteries. Thus it bears the potential of important medical applications. The referees' favourable comments led to the acceptance of the manuscript for its publication after three or four rounds of revision, as suggested by them.

Despite the effectiveness of the findings, the study assumed blood as a Newtonian fluid (with constant viscosity). However, experimental studies on blood have shown that blood behaves as a non-Newtonian fluid, with viscosity varying during flow. Recognizing this, the author conducted further research using a non- Newtonian model for blood flow in stenosed arteries. This work was also published in the 'Journal of Biomechanics' in 1993 under the title "A Non-Newtonian Fluid Model for Blood Flow Through Arteries Under Stenotic Conditions." This improved model provided more accurate representations of real-life conditions compared to the earlier Newtonian approach.

In these studies, a semi-analytical approach was used, combining analytical and numerical methods (finite difference). Additionally, a fully analytical method, the momentum integral method, was also employed by the author to study blood flow in stenosed vessels. Due to the novelty of the method, the paper "Momentum Integral Method for Studying Flow Characteristics of Blood Through a Stenosed Vessel" was published in 1989 in the prestigious British journal 'Biorheology'.

Different mathematical models have been used to account for the variation in the non-Newtonian nature of blood flow. But the Herschel-Bulkley model is considered to be more suitable. This non-Newtonian model was used by the author in another theoretical research, which revealed that resistance to blood flow increases with the height of the plaque in an atherosclerotic artery. The findings of this investigation were published in the 'International Journal of Engineering Science' in 2006 under the title "Blood Flow Through Arteries in a Pathological State."

In cases where lifestyle changes or medications like anticoagulants and anti-platelets are insufficient, surgery may be required for treatment of atherosclerosis. Procedures like coronary angioplasty, where a balloon is inflated at the site of blockage, or stent placement to keep the artery open, are common treatment.

The author and his research students, developed a mathematical model for non-Newtonian blood flow in a catheterized, bifurcated stenosed artery, using the Herschel-Bulkley fluid model. The study reveals important information useful for predicting the onset of some arterial diseases and for treating some circulatory disorders of the cardiovascular system, particularly for a situation when atherosclerotic plaques form at the bifurcation of an artery.

Further research by the author explored the flow of blood from a feeding artery into a branch capillary, focusing on the concentration of erythrocytes in the core region. Variation of the hematocrit reduction for this study was published in Mathematical and Computer Modelling, Vol. 15, 1991 (pages 9-19).

He was a co-author of another paper on the effect of blood flow and dual-phase lag on tissue temperature during tumor treatment by magnetic hyperthermia. This computational modelling study was published in 2021 in the American journal 'Mathematics and Computers in Simulation'. This paper, titled "Computational Modelling of the Effect of Blood Flow and Dual Phase Lag on Tissue Temperature during Tumor Treatment by Magnetic Hyperthermia", contributed to the advancement in hyperthermia-based cancer treatments.

In 2019, the author along with others published another significant paper, "Pulsatile Flow and Heat Transfer of Blood in an Overlapping Vibrating Atherosclerotic Artery: A Numerical Study," which examined the effects of an externally applied magnetic field and vibration on blood flow. The numerical model also considered the rotation of blood micro-particles to enhance modelling accuracy. The paper was published in the Journal "Mathematics and Computers in Simulation," Vol. 166 (2019).

In the course of daily activities of life, human body is exposed to vibration environments in various ways. While riding in vehicles or while flying in aircraft or spacecraft, human body is often subjected to unintentional body acceleration. In vibration physiology, studies related to the effects of vibration on blood flow are of great concern. Keeping this in view, the author investigated the influence of whole body accelerations on blood flow in single arteries. He conducted a theoretical research to investigate the fully developed flow of blood in a vibrating artery, by considering the effect of micro-rotation of blood cells. Results of the study were published in 1990 in the Journal 'Mathematical and Computer Modelling' (Vol. 13, pages 7-17). His later study on couple stress effects in a vibrating artery, which demonstrated enhanced blood velocity and reduced arterial wall stress, was published in the Journal of Mechanics in Medicine and Biology (Vol. 18, 2018).

Most recently, the author along with his co-investigators published a paper entitled "Haemodynamic characteristics of blood flow in an inclined overlapped stenosed arterial section" (Partial Differential Equations in Applied Mathematics 11(2)100829, 2024), which explored the behaviour of blood flow in an angled arterial segment with an atherosclerotic plaque.

The above-mentioned papers, particularly those on blood viscosity measurement and flow obstruction detection in healthy and diseased arteries, are of great practical importance, particularly in the pathogenesis of arterial diseases. They are useful in explaining the mechanism by which an arterial disease develops and progresses. Comparison of the changes in blood viscosity and flow resistance in diseased arteries with those in healthy arteries can help predict the onset of arterial diseases. The author extends his gratitude to all the co- investigators.

2. *Biomechanics of Brain Injury*

As mentioned earlier, the author received his Ph.D. in 1971 and pursued post-doctoral research at Hannover Technical University, where he worked with Prof. Oskar Mahrenholtz in collaboration with Prof. Christoph Hartung from the Biomedical Engineering Department of Hannover Medical University. In Hannover, his research focused on the biomechanics of brain injury, leading to several important research publications.

His first research paper in this field, titled "Axisymmetric Vibration of Human Skull-Brain System," was published in the German journal 'IngenieurArchiv' in 1978. Two other collaborative papers with Prof. Mahrenholtz and Dr. Hartung were published: "Effect of Pulse Loading on Brain Injury" in 'Mechanics Research Communications' (1977) and "Stresses in a Human Skull Due to Pulse Loading" in 'IngenieurArchiv' (1978). All these theoretical studies accounted for the viscoelastic properties of the skull and the brain and took into account the eccentricity of the skull-brain structure under the purview of a single mathematical model. This model was quite close to the realistic situation.

The importance of research on brain injury mechanics is evident from the observation that about 75% of the fatalities resulting from accidents involve head injury, with brain trauma being particularly critical. Although head injury may mean injury to any part of the head, brain damage being the most serious problem is of greatest concern from the phenomenological, pathogenic and corrective view points. But the difficulty lies in the fact that it is often not possible to detect damage to the brain macroscopically. Therefore its presence needs to be detected from physiological or neurological dysfunction. There exist several postulates on the mechanics of the production of this trauma. They are: (i) cavitation hypothesis and (ii) rotation hypothesis. Experimental observations on rhesus monkey exhibit the material damping (viscoelastic) properties of skull and brain tissues.

After his return from Germany, the author continued to conduct further research on the fascinating topic of the physiological problem of brain injury. Together with a doctoral research student, he further carried out a series of theoretical investigations using the improved model he proposed during his stay at the Technical University of Hannover (Germany) by accounting for the material damping of skull and brain, under the purview of the hypothesis mentioned above. One of the research papers was published with the title, 'A free vibration analysis of the human cranial system'. This investigation was carried out by taking into account also the mechanical influence of the scalp. Analysis of the model used in this study reveals that material damping of the skull can significantly affect the frequency spectrum of the skull-brain system. Another investigation entitled 'A study on rotational brain injury' was carried out by the author for exploring brain injury mechanism when the human head is subject to an input angular acceleration. On the basis of this research study, the author and his co-worker conjectured that eccentricity of the skull has a significant role in causing brain injury. The results of both these investigations were published in 'Journal of Biomechanics' in 1982 and 1984 respectively.

He along with his research student further developed a poroelastic model to analyze stress distribution in the skull and brain under impact loads, published in Journal of Mathematical Analysis and Applications (Vol. 103, 1984). Another theoretical study, "Dynamic Response of a Head-Neck System", developed with the doctoral student, modelled the head-neck system as a fluid-filled prolate spheroidal shell under impulsive loading. The results, validated against experimental findings, were published in Mathematical Modelling (Vol. 6, 1985).

Peristaltic Flows in the Human Body

Peristalsis, the rhythmic contraction and relaxation of tubular structures, facilitates fluid transport in the human body, including blood circulation, food movement and urine flow. The author and his research students developed mathematical models to study peristaltic mechanism in various physiological and industrial contexts. Interestingly, leeches, among other creatures, suck blood from a host and circulate it through their bodies using a peristaltic pumping pattern. For this reason, leeches are sometimes used in the treatment of tumors, mental disorders, and skin diseases to remove blood from the affected area.

Peristaltic processes are also applied in industries, such as the transport of sanitary fluids and toxic liquids in nuclear production. Medical devices like heart-lung machines and blood pumps widely use peristalsis. The author in collaboration with his research students, has conducted research on various fluid circulation processes in the human body through peristaltic mechanisms using the mathematical models he developed.

His first research on peristalsis analyzed urine transport in the ureter and was published in 'Computers and Mathematics with Applications' (1994). In 2002, he extended this research to investigate "Peristaltic Transport of Blood in Small Vessels", identifying the role of peripheral layer viscosity in blood transport. The study revealed that the higher the viscosity of the peripheral layer, the greater is the rate of blood transport via peristaltic processes. Moreover, as the peripheral layer thickness decreases, the rate of blood transport increases.

Further contributions include models for esophageal swallowing (Mathematical and Modelling, 2001), bile flow in pathological conditions (International Journal of Engineering Science, 2011), and peristaltic blood pumping in small arteries (ASME Journal of Applied Mechanics, 2012). His most advanced swallowing model, incorporating non-Newtonian effects, was published in Applied Mathematics and Mechanics (2012). These studies enhance our understanding of physiological fluid dynamics and contribute to exploring a variety of medical and industrial applications.

Emerging Topics in Modern Fluid Mechanics Research

In the second decade of the 21st century, the author concentrated on addressing some critical questions in contemporary fluid mechanics. His research spanned multiple areas, including human microcirculation, bio-microfluidics, electrokinetic and electroosmotic blood flows, and nano-fluid dynamics. These studies were made possible through a research grant approved by the Science and Engineering Research Board (SERB) of the Department of Science and Technology, Govt. of India. During this period, the author collaborated with a research student. This collaboration enabled him to explore cutting-edge topics and contribute to significant scientific advancements.

Electrokinetic and Electroosmotic Flow

Electroosmotic flow is a unique type of fluid motion driven by a Coulomb force acting on net mobile electric charges in a solution under the influence of an electric field. This phenomenon has gained interest recently due to its widespread application in various biomedical lab-on-a-chip devices for fluid transport, such as sample injection, chemical reactions, drug delivery, DNA analysis, and detection of biological/chemical agents.

The author, in collaboration with his research students, studied the electroosmotic flow of micropolar fluids. They developed a mathematical model and conducted a theoretical analysis using advanced mathematical methods. Their numerical analysis revealed that the microrotation of red blood cells significantly alters the electroosmotic flow of blood in microfluidic devices. The details of this research were published in 2014 in the American journal *Applied Mathematics and Mechanics* under the title "Electroosmotic Oscillatory Flow of a Micropolar Fluid in Microchannels: Application to Dynamics of Blood Flow in Microfluidic Devices."

In a prior study on the electroosmotic flow of viscoelastic fluids, the author explored viscoelastic behaviour of blood, providing deeper insights into its electroosmotic transport properties. This work was published in 2011 in *Applied Mathematics and Computation* under the title "Electro-osmotic Flow of a Viscoelastic Fluid in a Channel: Applications to Physiological Fluid Mechanics."

Another significant research effort in 2014 analyzed the electroosmotic flow of micropolar physiological fluids under the influence of an external AC electric field. This study, published in the 'Central European Journal of Physics', bearing the title "Electroosmotically Actuated Oscillatory Flow of a Physiological Fluid in a Porous Micro-Channel Subject to an External AC Electric Field Having Dissimilar Frequencies," provided a crucial mathematical analysis in order to validate experimental and numerical models in microfluidic devices.

Further research in this area explored the combined effects of external electric and magnetic fields on electroosmotic transport of non-Newtonian fluids, including heat transfer effects. The findings published in 2018 in *The European Physical Journal Plus* under the title "Impact of Cattaneo-Christov Heat Flux on Electro-osmotic Transport of Third-order Fluids in a Magnetic Environment", demonstrated that an increase in magnetic field strength brings about a reduction of blood flow in micro-arteries while entropy generation near arterial walls increases.

As mentioned earlier, in 2019, the author worked as a Humboldt Scientist for three months at Friedrich Alexander University in Erlangen-Nuremberg, Germany. His host Professor, this time, was Dr. Paul Steinmann. During this tenure, the author investigated electrokinetic flow, temperature distribution, and entropy generation in a microfluidic tube under the influence of electrothermal heat flow. The research, completed upon his return to India, was published in 2020 in *Meccanica,* with the title as "Temperature Distribution and Entropy Generation During Darcy-Forchheimer-Brinkman Electrokinetic Flow in a Microfluidic Tube Subject to a Prescribed Heat Flux."

Bio-Nanofluid Simulation

Nanofluids—colloidal suspensions of nanoparticles are increasingly utilized for enhancing thermal conductivity and convective heat transfer. These engineered fluids, with nanoparticles made of metals, oxides or carbides find applications in transportation cooling, industrial cooling and biomedical treatments, such as drug transport and antimicrobial therapies. The heat transfer capacity of biofluids like blood can be significantly enhanced by incorporating magnetic nanoparticles—a principle fundamental to hyperthermia treatments and various biomedical applications.

In 2010, the author published a study in *Applied Mathematics and Mechanics* titled "Flow of a Biomagnetic Viscoelastic Fluid: Application to Estimation of Blood Flow in Arteries During Electromagnetic Hyperthermia, a Therapeutic Procedure for Cancer Treatment". This research explored the potential of magnetic nanoparticles in cancer therapy.

In 2022, the author, along with a research student, discussed the combined effects of nonlinear thermal radiation, viscous dissipation, and Joule heating on entropy generation during nanofluid flow in a hydrophobic cylindrical microtube. This research paper, titled "Interplay of Steric Factor and High Zeta Potential on Entropy Generation during Nanofluid Slip Flow in a Microfluidic Tube," was published in 'The European Physical Journal Plus'. The study demonstrated that nonlinear thermal radiation reduces overall system entropy, thereby improving efficiency. Another piece of research conducted in 2019 and published in *Engineering Science and Technology, an International Journal* as "Peristaltic Flow of Eyring-Powell Nanofluid Under the Action of an Electromagnetic field", revealed that increasing nanoparticle concentration enhances nanofluid momentum transport, with significant variations when gold nanoparticles are used.

In 2011, the author along with his collaborators published a research paper in the *International Journal of Applied Mechanics and Engineering,* titled "Effects of Stenosis and Dilatation on Flow of Blood Mixed with Suspended Nanoparticles: A Study Using Homotopy Technique" in which they demonstrated how resistance and impedance peak at the dilatation neck while minimizing at the stenosis neck.

In 2018, important information emerged from their research on entropy generation and heat transfer during the electrokinetic flow of nanofluids. Observations revealed that the combined effect of a magnetic field and an induced electric field during MRI tests significantly reduces the rate of blood flow if the magnetic field is sufficiently strong. The study shows that increasing the amount of nanoparticles mixed with blood raises the temperature of the nanofluid (blood mixed with nanoparticles). Due to the Hall effect, the system's cooling increases. The study further indicated that entropy generation near the arterial wall is much higher than in the central region of the artery. The detailed report of this key study was published in 2019 in the journal '*Applied Mathematics and Mechanics* (English Edition)' under the title "Influence of Hall Current and Joule Heating on Entropy Generation During Electrokinetically Induced Thermoradiative Transport of Nanofluids in a Porous Microchannel." The study has significant applications in magnetic resonance angiography (MRA) as both strong magnetic field and the Hall current influence the human body during MRA tests. The study also has implications for chemotherapy, as controlled nanoparticle infusion can aid in drug delivering and cancer treatment.

In 2023, a comprehensive study on irreversibility in electrothermal transport of micropolar fluids was conducted, that bears the promise of important applications in the design of advanced medical devices. The findings were published in *the Journal of Thermal Analysis and Calorimetry*, Vol. 28.

Biomechanics of Bones

The author together with a couple of research students extensively studied various problems of bone biomechanics, offering valuable insights into bone-related disease analysis, diagnosis, and treatment. Their research can be categorized into three main areas:

1. Vibration and Wave Propagation in Bones;

2. Mechanics of Bone Fracture and Remodelling;
3. Effect of Heat on Bones.

The skeletal structure of humans and all vertebrates is primarily composed of bones, with calcium being the main constituent. Bones are similar to inorganic hard substances, such as metals or non-metals, in terms of hardness, although quantitatively less so. Therefore, bones exhibit properties similar to those of inorganic solids, though they differ in some fundamental ways. For example, the physical properties of bones change over time—children's bones are flexible and less likely to break, while older adults' bones become brittle. Additionally, the physical, chemical, and biological properties of bones vary with age.

Like hollow metal pipes, bones can produce resonant sounds when struck, which can be used to measure properties such as Young's modulus, density, and other elastic constants. Bones are not only elastic materials but also exhibit viscous and electromagnetic properties. When mechanical stress is applied, an electric field is induced in bones. Thus, mechanical waves propagating through bones can induce electric and magnetic waves, which can mobilize calcium ions in the bone, aiding in the healing process of diseased bones.

Bones are heterogeneous, meaning their density varies across different regions. For example, measuring the density of different parts of a bone specimen reveals different values, indicating non-uniform physical properties. Consequently, Young's modulus differs when measured along the bone's length compared to a cross-sectional cut. This heterogeneity and anisotropy are further compounded by the fact that bones expand with heat and generate electricity under pressure, exhibiting piezoelectric properties similar to certain crystalline solids. Additionally, when waves propagate through bones, they gradually attenuate, resulting in energy dissipation, a common property in many inorganic solids.

Given these complex characteristics, it is challenging to develop a comprehensive mathematical model that accurately represents bone behaviour in real-life scenarios. The author's research in this domain provides critical insights into bone mechanics and aids in understanding the mechanical behaviour of bones under various physiological conditions.

1. *Research on Vibration and Wave Propagation in Bones*

The author has extensively studied the propagation of mechanical waves and vibrations through bones, specifically focusing on long, cylindrical, piezoelectric, anisotropic, elastic, and heterogeneous properties of bones. His research explored the effects of wave propagation on pressure variations and the induced electric and magnetic fields due to the piezoelectric nature of bones. By analyzing these electromagnetic signals, it is possible to determine whether bones are healthy or diseased. This is almost similar to MRI technology. In this study they considered significantly lower magnetic field strength and frequencies higher than sound waves. The study was published in 1988 in *Journal of Mathematical Biology* under the title "Induced Electric and Magnetic Fields Due to Wave Propagation in a Tubular Bone."

It is known that the human spine comprises 23 small circular discs, of which six are located in the cervical region (neck), twelve in the middle back (thoracic region) and five in the middle back (lumbar region). Changes in the spacing between these discs can lead to various issues, including back pain and even brain damage. Experimental data indicate that the bones forming these discs are heterogeneous, anisotropic, and piezoelectric.

Moreover, vibrations or waves propagating through these bones rapidly dissipate energy. To understand the mechanics of vertebral discs, the author together with an associate conducted a theoretical study using the technique of mathematical analysis, taking into account these properties. The findings, which highlight how even minor vibrations can have severe consequences, were published in 1988 in '*Computers and Mathematics with Applications*' under the title "A Mathematical Model for the Biomechanics of the Body of a Vertebra."

Bones share similarities to common solid materials but differ in that they are anisotropic and possess multiple elastic constants due to their heterogeneous nature. Additionally, bones are dissipative materials, as their energy diminishes when waves propagate or vibrations occur. In one study, the author together with a research student mathematically analyzed the vibrations of a tubular bone, accounting for these properties, and calculated the vibration spectrum using experimental data. This research was published in 1986 in the British journal *Mathematical Modelling* under the title "Vibration of a Tubular Bone in Axial Planes."

Another study analyzed torsional waves propagating along the axis of a tubular bone. The bone was assumed to be crystalline, piezoelectric, heterogeneous, and dissipative. The resulting differential equation and the corresponding boundary conditions were derived. Using experimental data, the phase velocity and damping coefficient of the waves were determined, along with the influence of bone heterogeneity. The findings were extended to PMMA (polymethyl methacrylate), a material used as bone cement. This mathematical research was published in 1983 in the *Journal of Mathematical Analysis and Applications* under the title "Propagation of Torsional Waves in Tubular Bones." The study revealed that dissipative material behaviour and material nonhomogeneity are more prominent for PMMA material than for bone tissues. It also shows that for PMMA, dispersion waves is significantly prominent at higher modes and lower frequencies.

Further investigation focused on the propagation of acoustic waves along the axis of a cylindrical composite bone. The theoretical study provided a general dispersion relation, although extracting some practical information required ignoring the bone's piezoelectric properties. This study revealed the extent to which material damping of bone tissues affects wave propagation. The detailed report was published in 1984 in the *International Journal of Solids and Structures* under the title "Wave Propagation in Tubular Bones."

The effects of external forces and moments on bones were also examined, considering forces acting along or perpendicular to the axis of the bone. The analysis yielded solutions for both long-term and transient forces. This theoretical study was based on an appropriate mathematical model, detailed in the *Journal of Mathematical Analysis and Applications* in 1991 in a research article entitled "A Mathematical Study of the Stress Field in a Long Bone."

2. *Fracture and Remodelling of Bones*

While the studies described above focus on the mechanical properties of bones, living bones undergo constant remodelling. Bones are flexible and soft at birth, gain strength in midlife, and become brittle with age. This dynamic nature distinguishes living bones from common materials like iron or copper, whose atomic structures remain unchanged over time. Bone remodelling involves continuous changes in bone structure, influenced by age and other physical properties.

Remodelling can occur naturally or can be induced artificially by orthopaedic surgeons to treat bone diseases. When remodelling occurs within the confines of the outer bone surface, it is called internal remodelling, affecting bone density. In contrast, surface remodelling (also called external remodelling) involves changes in the inner and outer surfaces of the bone, potentially influenced by the piezoelectric properties of bones.

The author together with his research students conducted several intriguing theoretical studies on the factors influencing bone remodelling. One study demonstrated that the intrinsic dissipative properties of bones affect both internal and surface remodelling processes. Published in 1987, in the *Journal of Biomechanics* under the title "Effect of Material Damping on Bone Remodelling", the study aligned with scientific views emphasizing the role of bone piezoelectric properties in surface remodelling.

Another study considered a realistic model of a long, anisotropic bone with a non-uniform cross-section, showing how these realistic assumptions can significantly alter bone remodelling dynamics. This research, published in 1989 in *Mathematical Modelling* under the title "Influence of Non-isotropy of Osseous Tissues and Cross-Sectional Non-uniformity of a Long Bone on the Internal Remodelling Dynamics of Osseous Tissues", provided critical insights.

Earlier in 1983, the author along with a research student published a research paper on internal bone remodelling, offering a comprehensive discussion on the subject. This study, published in the *Bulletin of Technical University of Istanbul (Turkey)* under the title "A Mathematical Model for Studying the Physiological Process of Internal Remodelling", was complemented by, another study on surface remodelling, induced by intramedullary nailing, published in the journal *Rheologica Acta*, also in 1983.

Like other materials, bones can develop fractures, which concentrate stress fields at the crack tips. Measuring these stress fields is crucial for determining fracture strength of bones. The author conducted multiple studies on stress fields at crack tips in various types of bones, in varied situations, the details of these studies have been published in leading international journals.

One such study, "An Estimate of the Stress-Field in an Osseous Medium Having a No-slip Interface Crack," was published in 1983 in *Engineering Fracture Mechanics*. Another study on patella fractures appeared in 'Aeronautical Quarterly' of the Royal Aeronautical Society of London. A couple of other communications on exterior cracks in bones were published in *Engineering Fracture Mechanics* in 1984 and 1985, respectively. These studies, conducted using the Airy stress function and Mellin transforms, analyzed stress fields around cracks, demonstrating how bone anisotropy intensifies stress fields.

In 1986, the author independently analyzed stress distribution in bones with exterior cracks, considering the bones as a transversely isotropic media. He used experimental data to measure stress values. The details of the study were published in 1986 in *Rheologica Acta* under the title "Distribution of Stresses in a Pre-cracked Bone Specimen." A 1989 study, published in *'Computers and Mathematics with Applications'*, further examined stress distribution under varied situations using the principles of theoretical mechanics.

3. *Research on the Effects of Heat on Bones*

Environmental heat, such as prolonged exposure to the Sun, can significantly impact bones. The author hypothesized that heat transport inside the head depends on the radical and angular distances from the skull. Using the technique of mathematical modelling, he calculated stress values at different points in the head, with significant implications for medical science. His findings were published in 1986 *in Rheologica Acta* under the title "Stresses in the Human Head Due to Thermogenesis." This research work was also carried out independently by the author.

These theoretical investigations in the field of the biomechanics of bones conducted by the research group of the author more than four decades ago, remain relevant even today. Recent experimental investigations carried out at the Indian Institute of Science in Bangalore (as reported by the *Times of India* on January 6, 2023, Bengaluru) validate the author's pioneering research.

Theoretical Solid Mechanics

Among the author's publications in theoretical solid mechanics, a few stand out for their depth and originality:

1. *Thermal Shock in a Viscoelastic Half-Space (Journal of Thermal Stresses, 1982)*

This paper investigates the effects of thermal shock caused by the sudden heating of the boundary of a viscoelastic solid. The study reveals that both stress and temperature fields in this scenario result from the superposition of two shock waves—one originating from mechanical factors and the other from thermal relaxation.

2. *Thermoelastic Waves in an Infinite Aeolotropic Body with a Cylindrical Cavity (Computers and Structures, 1974).*

This research explores thermoelastic wave behavior in an aeolotropic (direction-dependent) material with a cylindrical cavity. Using integral transform techniques, the study provides insights into stress and displacement distribution around the cavity surface, more particularly into the effects of relaxation time and viscosity.

3. *Torsional Wave Propagation in a Heterogeneous Aeolotropic Stratum (International Journal of Theoretical Geomechanics, 2018).*

In collaboration with other researchers, the author examined a unique class of viscoelastic media (aeolotropic and non-homogeneous) subject to initial stress conditions. The study focused on torsional wave propagation, offering significant implications for geodynamics, earthquakes, and underground explosions.

It may be noted that the author's research in elasticity spans several key areas, including thermoelasticity, fracture mechanics, and wave propagation in solid media.

4. *Stress Concentration in the Vicinity of Cracks in a Sandwiched Medium* (International Journal of Fracture, 1984).

This fracture mechanics study analyzes stress concentration around penny-shaped cracks in a cylindrical solid embedded within a different material. The findings have important implications for material strength analysis in composite structures.

5. *Interaction of Magnetic, Thermal, and Elastic Fields*

The author also explored the complex interplay between magnetic, thermal, and elastic fields, which has direct applications in technologies like fusion plasma systems, magnetic refrigeration, and controlled fusion reactors. One notable study involved analyzing a large, non-isotropic viscoelastic solid with a cylindrical cavity exposed to a uniform temperature field and axial magnetic field. Numerical simulations were conducted to assess the impact of these fields under specific conditions.

Through his multi-disciplinary expertise, the author made significant theoretical advancements in solid mechanics, many of which have practical implications in engineering, geophysics, and biomechanics.

Theoretical Fluid Mechanics

The research findings of the author and his research group in theoretical fluid mechanics are of significant importance, with potential applications across various engineering and medical fields. Several of these studies have been published in prestigious journals, contributing valuable insights into fluid dynamics under different physical influences.

Key Research Contributions in Fluid Mechanics:

1. *Biomagnetic Viscoelastic Fluid Flow in a Channel*

Published in the *Journal of Applied Mechanics* (ASME, 2009), this study examines the flow of a viscoelastic fluid within a channel subject to an externally applied magnetic field generated by a magnetic dipole. A mathematical model was developed and computational methods were employed to investigate the fluid velocity and pressure. The application of the model to blood flow demonstrated that an external magnetic field can reduce blood velocity, similar to the case of biomagnetic fluids, offering potential benefits in controlling blood flow during surgeries and in cancer treatments such as magnetic drug targeting and hyperthermia.

2. *Magnetohydrodynamic (MHD) Stagnation Point Flow and Heat Transfer*

A 2014 study, published in the *ASME* Journal of Heat Transfer, explored the steady MHD stagnation point flow of an electrically conducting viscous fluid over a stretching sheet. The research, titled "Effect of Induced Magnetic Field on MHD Stagnation Point Flow and Heat Transfer on a Stretching Sheet," addressed the nonlinear problem of MHD stagnation point flow. It revealed that the magnetic parameter considerably influences both the surface velocity gradients and heat transfer, reducing surface velocity and heat dissipation.

3. *MHD Effects on the Circulatory System*

As an extension of the study of MHD flow, the author in 2017 published a paper in Physica A: Statistical Mechanics and Its Applications, in which he examined stagnation point flow over a thin porous sheet. The study applied boundary layer theory and similarity transformations to explore aspects of the microcirculatory system, concluding that stronger magnetic field induction decreases fluid velocity while increasing temperature.

4. *Hydromagnetic Flow of a Non-Newtonian Fluid in a Channel*

In 1998, a study co-authored by the author and published *in Mathematical Models and Methods in Applied Sciences* investigated the hydromagnetic flow of a second-grade, electrically conducting fluid under the influence of a transverse magnetic field. An asymptotic series solution demonstrated that increasing the magnetic parameter enhances wall shear stress, with applications in modelling blood flow in the microcirculatory system, where blood behaves as a non-Newtonian fluid.

5. *Flow in an Ekman Layer on an Oscillating Porous Plate*

A theoretical study on fluid motion in a semi-infinite viscous incompressible fluid bounded by an infinite porous plate was published in *Acta Mechanica* (2003). The study analyzed the formation of an oscillating Ekman layer and its implications in geophysical fluid dynamics, particularly concerning riverbed flows during earthquakes and industrial-scale paper manufacturing, where shaking tables are used.

6. *Oscillatory Entry Flow in a Plane Channel*

A collaborative study published in International Journal of Non-linear Mechanics (2001) examined the unsteady flow of a viscous fluid at the entrance of a parallel-walled channel. The research revealed the existence of reverse flow and investigated the effect of phase differences in wall oscillations on fluid entropy flux and shear stress. These findings offer insights into arterial blood flow dynamics.

Supervision and Collaborations in Biomathematics

The author has also mentored several students in interdisciplinary research in the field of biomathematics:

B. Dravid (B.Tech, Computer Science & Engineering) collaborated on a study involving gene transcription factor binding sites, resulting in the paper entitled "A Mathematical Model in the Study of Genes for Identifying Transcription Factor Binding Sites" (Computers and Mathematics with Applications, 2006). Dravid later secured a scholarship for higher studies in the U.S.

Shubhabrata Mukherjee (M.Sc. Mathematics) co-authored "A Mathematical Model for Enzymatic Action on DNA Knots and Links" (Mathematical and Computer Modelling, 2004). Mukherjee is now a Research Associate Professor at the University of Washington, specializing in Alzheimer's disease research, with multiple NIH/NIA grants.

Apratim Mitra (M.Sc. Mathematics) collaborated on two research papers: "Instabilities in Single-Species and Host-Parasite Systems: Period-Doubling Bifurcations and Chaos" (2006) and "Synchronization among Tumor-like Cell Aggregations Coupled by Quorum Sensing: A Theoretical Study" (2008), both published in Computers and Mathematics with Applications. Mitra later joined the National Institute of Health (NIH) in USA as a scientist.

Thus the author's contributions to theoretical fluid mechanics and biomathematics have significantly impacted both fundamental research and applied sciences. His studies have enhanced the understanding of fluid behaviour under magnetic fields and contributed to biomedical applications, offering promising avenues for future research in medical physics and engineering.

CHAPTER 10

Recognition

At Home and Abroad

DAAD, Germany, 1975

In 1975, the author was selected for the scholarship of DAAD, Germany (Deutscher Akademischer Austauschdienst/German Academic Exchange Service). This scholarship programme aims at fostering strong, internationally oriented higher education systems in developing countries that are considered capable for contributing to sustainable development.

DAAD scholarship consists of a monthly scholarship payment (currently 934 for students and 1300 for Ph.D. students) and a flat travel allowance. Those days for Indian candidates from science disciplines the selection for DAAD scholarship used to be made by the University Grants Commission (UGC), New Delhi and for engineering subjects by AICTE.

The author successfully cleared the rigorous selection interview conducted by UGC and was awarded the scholarship.

Humboldt Research Fellowship, Germany, 1975

Almost concurrently, the author also sent his application for a Humboldt Research Fellowship directly to the office of the Alexander von Humboldt Foundation in Bonn, Germany. Shortly after receiving the selection letter for DAAD scholarship from UGC he was informed of his selection for the Humboldt Fellowship also. The letter was personally signed by the Foundation's the then President, Nobel laureate Prof. Werner Karl Heisenberg, renowned for his Uncertainty Principle.

The Humboldt Research Fellowship is highly competitive. As already mentioned, its selection process is overseen by a committee of 60–70 distinguished experts from various research fields. Candidates are evaluated through a rigorous peer-review process, focusing on the originality and innovativeness of their research publications. A unique aspect of this fellowship is that the Foundation maintains a lifelong connection with its alumni, fostering ongoing professional relationship and collaborations.

At just 31 years of age, this fellowship marked the author's first major international recognition, highlighting his research excellence on a global stage.

Silver Jubilee Research Award, 1984

In 1983, the Board of Governors of IIT Kharagpur introduced the 'IIT Kharagpur Silver Jubilee Research Award' to encourage faculty members to engage in high-quality research.

All the academic departments were categorized into five groups. Group I included Mathematics, Physics, Chemistry and Applied Geology & Exploration Geophysics. The Engineering Departments came under Group II to Group V. Each year a national-level selection committee, consisting of experts from premier institutions like IITs and IISc Bangalore, reviewed applicants based on the merit of their submitted research publications.

In 1984, the author emerged as the only recipient from IIT Kharagpur deemed worthy of the award, with experts unanimously recognizing his outstanding contributions to biomechanics. The Board of Governors approved the decision, and the author was honoured with the 'IIT Kharagpur Silver Jubilee Research Award'. Over the subsequent years, faculty members from other groups also received this prestigious recognition.

Doctor of Science Degree (D.Sc., 1984)

After receiving Ph.D. degree in Applied Mathematics from Jadavpur University, the author kept on doing high quality research without any interruption, expanding into new interdisciplinary domains. During his academic journey, he became aware that the University of Calcutta conferred the Doctor of Science (D.Sc.) degree upon scholars with substantial original research contributions.

The aspiration to achieve a D.Sc. degree was planted in his mind during his M.Sc. studies at Calcutta University, where he noted that in the Department of Applied Mathematics, only one or two professors held this distinguished degree. In 1983, he meticulously prepared his thesis, titled "Mathematical Modelling in the Realm of Biomechanics and Structural Mechanics" and submitted to Calcutta University for possible award of D.Sc. degree.

A year later, the University of Calcutta received reports from three globally distinguished adjudicators: Prof. Y.C. Fung (University of California, San Diego, USA); Dr. Christoph Hartung (Medical University of Hannover, Germany); Prof. Richard B. Hetnarski (Rochester Institute of Technology, USA).

All the three experts unanimously endorsed his work, with Prof. Y.C. Fung commending his research as "valuable contributions to permanent literature". The author was awarded the D.Sc. degree at the 1984 Annual Convocation of Calcutta University—fulfilling a long-cherished academic aspiration. Recognizing this achievement, the Board of Governors at IIT Kharagpur granted him an additional salary increment, further motivating his research and teaching efforts.

Merit-based Promotion to Professor Cadre (1985)

Despite no formal vacancies at the professor level, the author's exceptional research and his academic recognition at national and international levels in the form of various awards earned him an invitation for an interview before the Selection Committee constituted for selection of professors. Based on the recommendation of the Selection Committee, the Board of Governors at IIT Kharagpur, approved his promotion to the post of Professor in 1985 in recognition of his academic excellence.

Awards and Recognition

Fellow, The National Academy of Sciences, India (NASI) (1987)

The author was elected a Fellow of the National Academy of Science, India in recognition of his distinguished contributions in the fields of Biomechanics, Mathematical Modelling and Continuum Mechanics. His induction was personally approved by the Academy's President, M.G.K. Menon, FRS.

Fellow, Institute of Mathematics and its Applications (IMA), U.K. (1988)

The author was elected a Fellow of the Institute of Mathematics and its Applications in the Council meeting of the Institute held on 29th March, 1988. The Council Meeting was presided over by the famous mathematician Douglas Samuel Jones in the presence of the distinguished applied Mathematician Sir James Lighthill, FRS (Council Member). The IMA is a professional society of U.K. and was established in Essex in the year 1964. It promotes mathematical knowledge and culture, and supports the advancement of its practical applications.

Fellow, Royal Society of Medicine, London 1989

In recognition of his pioneering applications of mathematics in medicine—an uncommon feat among mathematicians—the author was elected a Fellow of the Royal Society of Medicine of London in the year 1989. The commendation was formally signed by Dr. Robert N. Thomson, the then Executive Director of the Royal Society of Medicine.

Fellow, Institute of Theoretical Physics, Calcutta (1989)

In the year 1989, the author was designated as a Fellow of the Institute of Theoretical Physics, Calcutta for his outstanding contributions to theoretical research. Prof. A.P. Mitra, a distinguished physicist and the then Director General of CSIR, New Delhi personally felicitated the author on this prestigious achievement.

Fellow, Indian National Academy of Engineering (INAE), New Delhi (1999)

The author was elected a Fellow of the Indian National Academy of Engineering (INAE) on 24th October 1999 for his valuable research contributions in Bioengineering and Structural Engineering. The commendation was presented to him by the then - President of INAE, who was also the Chairman of the Atomic Energy Commission of India.

Rammohan Puraskar, 2004

In 2004, the author was honoured with the prestigious Rammohan Puraskar, which carried a cash prize of Rupees Five Lakhs in recognition of his 'outstanding contributions to the field of Mathematics.' That same year astrophysicist Padma Bhushan J.B. Narlikar was also awarded the Rammohan Puraskar for his remarkable contributions to Physics, while celebrated cricketer Sourav Ganguly was honoured with the same Award for his achievements in the field of sports.

During the award ceremony the author was accompanied by his wife Shorasi, daughter Sumita, son-in-law Achintya and his mother. The award has a legacy of recognizing exceptional individuals, including space scientist Padma

Vibhushan Dr. K. Kasturirangan in 2003, Padma Vibhushan Dr. M.S. Swaminathan in 2006 for pioneering role in India's Green Revolution.

Rashtriya Gaurav Award, 2004

On October 12, 2004 the author was awarded the Certificate of Excellence for the Rashtriya Gaurav Award in recognition of his meritorious service, outstanding performance and remarkable contributions. In the same year Padma Shri Dr. Bikash Sinha, Director of the Saha Institute of Nuclear Physics was also a recipient of this distinguished award.

Mr. Sanjiv Goenka, Chairman of the Board of Governors at IIT Kharagpur personally congratulated the author. In a letter dated October 25, 2004 he wrote:

> *"What an achievement! What an outstanding contribution to science and technology! Absolutely brilliant. My congratulations to you on your receiving this prestigious Rashtriya Gaurav Award."*

Platinum Jubilee Lecture at Indian Science Congress 2005

The author was invited to deliver the esteemed Platinum Jubilee Lecture at the Indian Science Congress in 2005, held in Nirma University at Ahmedabad, highlighting his significant contributions to mathematical sciences.

President, Mathematical Sciences Section (including Statistics), 2007

The 94th session of the Indian Science Congress was held at Annamalai University, Tamil Nadu, where the author was elected as the President of the Mathematical Sciences Section (including Statistics). The election took place through postal ballots conducted in advance, with votes counted during the 93rd Science Congress in January 2006. As the elected President, he presided over the Mathematical Sciences (including statistics) Section at the 94th Session in January 2007.

It is noteworthy that, in earlier years, Mathematics and Statistics had separate Sections, each electing its own President. In the past, distinguished statistician, Prof. A.K. Gayen, once held the Presidency of the Statistics Section.

Fellow, West Bengal Academy of Science and Technology, 2025

The author was elected a Fellow of the West Bengal Academy of Science and Technology (WAST). The announcement was made after the Council Meeting of the Academy held on December 17, 2024. However, it has been effective from 1st January 2025. He was the only person elected this time for the prestigious Fellowship under Mathematical Sciences Section.

Election to the Membership of Professional Bodies and Learned Societies Overseas

- In 1982, the author was elected a Member of the European Society of Applied Mathematics (Gesellschaft fuer Angewandte Mathematik und Mechanik), usually abbreviated as GAMM. This prestigious society was founded in 1922 by the famous mathematician Richard von Mises and Physicist Ludwig Prandtl.
- He became a Member of the International Society of Biorheology, New York in 1981 and the American Society of Biomechanical Engineering in 1989.
- In 1996, he was selected as an 'Active Member' of the New York Academy of Sciences.

Notable Recognition

The author's research publications have been extensively cited in different reputed international journals and also books published by renowned authors internationally. His contributions to Human Biodynamics were highlighted in the book *Natural Biodynamics*, published by World Scientific, Singapore London. Authored by Vladimir G. Ivancevic and Tijana T. Ivancevic of the University of Adelaide, Australia, the book describes the author as "*a true pioneer in human biodynamics.*"

Throughout his research career, the author has been invited to evaluate numerous manuscripts, submitted to reputed national and international journals. His recognition as a distinguished young researcher has also led to invitations for academic engagements, including:

- Delivering lectures at national conferences, such as the one held at the Centre for Cellular and Molecular Biology (CCMB), Hyderabad, even when he was quite young.

- Evaluating a Ph.D. thesis submitted to Bangalore University, Bhadravati River Project Campus, based on a nomination from the Indian Institute of Science, Bangalore at a very early stage of his career.

Contributions at the International Level

The author has been invited to serve as an expert for several prestigious international organizations, including the National Science Foundation (USA), Imperial Press (London) and World Scientific (UK). His significant contributions to biomechanics research have earned widespread recognition, with his work being extensively cited in international journals and books published worldwide.

Contributions at the National Level

At the national level, the author has been appointed as an expert member in various committees under the Council of Scientific and Industrial Research (CSIR) and the Union Public Service Commission (UPSC), New Delhi. His responsibilities have included:

- Selecting Senior Research Fellows,
- Evaluating Research Proposals,
- Designing examination question papers,
- Reviewing answer sheets, and
- Participating in the final selection of IAS candidates.

He has played a key role in faculty recruitment for various Indian Institutes of Technology (IITs), central and state universities. His expertise has been sought by institutions such as:

- Calcutta University
- Jadavpur University
- Himachal Pradesh University (Shimla),
- Utkal University and Sambalpur University (Odisha),
- Devi Ahilya University (Indore),
- Lucknow University (Uttar Pradesh),
- Anna University (Tamil Nadu), and
- Visva-Bharati University (West Bengal)

He has also participated in faculty selection for IIT Kanpur, IIT Guwahati, IIT Dhanbad, IIT Kharagpur, NIT Warangal, and NIT Rourkela, as well as serving as an external member of different committees for the Mathematics Departments of Burdwan, Kalyani, and North Bengal Universities.

Furthermore, he has been a Chancellor-nominated expert for the selection of mathematics lecturers under the West Bengal College Service Commission and for professor selection at Utkal University and Sambalpur University (Odisha). His long-term involvement includes serving on the Technical Advisory Committee and Professor Selection Committee at the Indian Statistical Institute (Kolkata).

In recognition of his expertise, the Indian School of Mines (now IIT-ISM, Dhanbad) appointed him as an advisor to aid in the development of its Applied Mathematics Department.

Additionally he was part of a three-member expert committee formed by the Government of India to evaluate the activities of the Mathematics Department at IIT Delhi, along with two senior professors from TIFR (Bombay).

Breaking His Own Bone While Researching on Mechanics of Bone Fracture

In 2001, while visiting Himachal Pradesh University (Shimla) as an external expert, the author encountered an unexpected accident. Upon arriving in Shimla, he was walking towards the university guest house with a local professor when they suddenly saw students running and throwing stones.

Seeking shelter in a small vegetable shop, they learned that a violent clash had erupted between two groups of students in the previous night, and tensions broke out again at that time.

Initially unaware of his injury, the author later noticed pain in his right hand, where he had been struck by a stone. A doctor at the university medical center suspected a fracture and recommended an X-ray at a bigger hospital.

At Indira Gandhi Hospital of Shimla, Dr. Thakur, head of the Orthopaedics Department, confirmed the presence of a serious fracture after examining the X-ray plate. The author was given the option of undergoing surgery in Shimla or Kharagpur, but he chose immediate surgery in Shimla.

During the procedure, the surgeon inquired whether he preferred the Intramedullary Nailing Method or the Plate and Screw Method. Given his background in fracture mechanics of bones, the author left the decision to the surgeon, who opted for the Plate and Screw Method.

The author requested for applying local anaesthesia, allowing him to remain conscious and observe the procedure without discomfort. Following a successful operation, his hand was placed in a sling, and he flew back to Kolkata, where his research scholar, Motahar Reza, received him and accompanied him to his residence at Kharagpur.

P.L. Bhatnagar Memorial Lecture (2001)

Despite his fractured hand, the author honoured his commitment to deliver the P.L. Bhatnagar Memorial Lecture at the 46th Annual Session of the Indian Society of Theoretical and Applied Mechanics (ISTAM), held in December 2001 at the National Institute of Technology, Hamirpur (Himachal Pradesh).

During his stay at the institute's guest house, an attendant assisted him with dressing and daily activities. The attendant, astonished by his perseverance, remarked: "Sir, you travelled all this way with a broken hand! Was it really necessary?"

This heart-felt remark remains a cherished memory for the author.

National Award (2013)

In 1999, the author was elected a Fellow of the Indian National Academy of Engineering (INAE) in recognition of his outstanding research in Bioengineering and Structural Engineering.

In 2013, INAE introduced the Outstanding Teachers Award, an honour presented annually to two distinguished educators in Engineering Education. The award includes:

- A cash prize of Rs. 1,00,000 (one lakh),
- A one-time Book Grant of Rs. 25,000, and
- A Scroll of Honour.

This prestigious award recognizes 'educators who have made exceptional contributions to engineering education and have inspired students to pursue careers in Engineering and Technology.' The author was one of the two inaugural recipients of this National Award.

Recent Recognition from IIT Kharagpur (2025)

The inauguration of the two-year long Platinum Jubilee Celebrations was held on 18th August 2025 (foundation day of IIT Kharagpur) in the morning. As a part of the Platinum Jubilee Inaugural, the Institute invited nomination of two eminent retired faculty members in order to felicitate them on this occasion. The author was selected as one of those few retired faculty who were felicitated on the day of inauguration. The Institute made arrangements to receive the invitees from Kolkata Airport, or Railway Station and to provide local hospitality to them at the Technology Guest House. In order to be able to interact better with other guests, the author opted to stay at the Guest House during the period August 17–19, 2025.

During the felicitation ceremony of previous directors, 'eminent retired faculty' and a few distinguished alumni of IIT Kharagpur, it was a matter of pleasant surprise that the veteran anchor Ms. Madhubanti Maitra first announced the name of the author and invited him to come to the dais for felicitation in the Netaji Auditorium. The felicitation ceremony was followed by the session of presentation of foundation day awards and recognitions to faculty and staff of IIT Kharagpur. It was a matter of great rejoice for the author that by the Grace of the Holy Mother, Dr. Sudip Misra, Professor of Computer Science and Engineering at IIT Kharagpur was awarded The Institute Chair Professor Award 2025 for "Outstanding Contributions towards Teaching, Research and Institutional Development", given under the seal of the Institute on the Seventy-fifth Foundation Day, the Eighteenth August, 2025.

United States Consul in Kolkata, Ms. Kathy Giles-Diaz was present as a Distinguished Guest. She handed over the "Hall of Fame Award" to the Eminent Engineering Personality, Mr. Arjun Malhotra, who graduated from the Electronics and Communication Engineering Department of IIT Kharagpur and was the recipient of Dr. B.C. Roy Gold Medal, 1970. He is a Co-founder of HCL Technologies Limited and is currently serving as an Advisor of NextGen eSolutions Private Limited.

Under the dynamic leadership of the present Director, Prof. Suman Chakraborty who has earned international recognition as an innovator and a distinguished scientist at a young age, laying of foundation stones of various new initiatives and inauguration of Manekshaw Centre of Excellence were performed on the special occasion of the 75th anniversary of IIT Kharagpur.

On seeing the photographs/video clips of the felicitation ceremony, all our friends and relatives expressed their joy and happiness.

Celebration by Sixty Plus Golden Life Association, Santoshpur, Kolkata-700075

Friends of the Golden Life Association felt very happy for the honour extended to the author by IIT Kharagpur. They celebrated the occasion by arranging a modest programme where they also felicitated the author. A cultural programme was also arranged by them to mark the occasion, which included recitation, music, etc.

The author recalls, during the Silver Jubilee of IIT Kharagpur in 1975–76, he was a lecturer, but being away to Germany on study leave for two years he could not participate in the Silver Jubilee celebrations. But he was the first recipient of IIT Kharagpur Silver Jubilee Research Award. During Golden Jubilee of IIT Kharagpur he was the Head of Mathematics Department (1998–2001) and tried his best to enhance the image of the department to the outside world by organizing several national and international events. To commemorate the Golden Jubilee, he also published a series of edited books, covering different areas of mathematical sciences as well as a book bearing the title "Mathematics and Mathematicians at IIT Kharagpur." These books were published by reputed national/international publishing houses, like World Scientific, Singapore/London, Narosa and Allied Publishers, Noida. During the Diamond Jubilee, he left the Institute after retirement, but had the chance to participate in some of the celebrations.

Message from Srimat Swami Suparnananda Maharaj, Secretary, R.K. Mission Institute of Culture, Golpark, Kolkata

Revered Jagadish da,

What a coincidence! Today is the Teachers' Day. Your letter conveying the great news of both the father and the son. It is a rare phenomenon, indeed. I congratulate Sudip Bhai and you as well on receiving accolades on the same day by the IIT on its ceremony of the Platinum Jubilee.

My regards and best wishes to both of you.

Yours affectionately,

Suparnananda

Examiner for Ph.D. Theses at Foreign Universities

The author has served as a Ph.D. thesis examiner for about a hundred theses from different Indian universities, IITs, NITs, and IISc, Bangalore. His expertise has also been sought internationally, by different institutions abroad, including the University of Adelaide, Australia.

In early 2022, he examined the doctoral thesis of Jannatun Nayeem, a scholar from Dhaka University, Bangladesh. Her thesis, titled "Mathematical Analysis of Hepatitis B Virus Dynamics", was in the field of Mathematical Biology.

For the viva voce (oral defense), the author travelled to Dhaka University on April 24, 2022. He was warmly received at the airport by two university students and stayed at the Ramakrishna Mission Guest House in Dhaka, where he enjoyed three to four days of spiritual companionship.

Before returning to India, he visited the home of Professor Chandranath Poddar, the thesis supervisor. The warm hospitality extended by Professor Poddar and his wife remains a treasured memory for the author.

CHAPTER 11 Academic Administration

Appointment of Department Heads at IIT

At IIT, the tenure of the Head of different departments is set for a period of three years. It may be noted that in IIT, the headship is not by rotation according to seniority. In the past, there were cases in which an assistant professor was chosen as the head, bypassing senior professors. In the United States, of course, this practice used to be very common. A few days before the tenure of a Head comes to an end, the Institute's Director, consults with the faculty members of the department. He takes the opinion of each faculty member confidentially.

Appointment of the Mathematics Department Head in 1998

Prof. G.P. Bhattacharjee was the head of Mathematics Department for 3 years until the middle of 1998. About 15 days before his term was supposed to come to an end, the Director Prof. Amitabha Ghosh visited the Department and held confidential discussions with each faculty member one by one regarding the next Head of Department (HoD). The incumbent HoD was not present during these deliberations. When consulted, the author expressed his preference for extending Prof. G.P. Bhattacharjee's tenure, citing his commendable leadership. However, the director at once contradicted saying, 'Should I believe that in such a large department there is no other faculty member suitable for the position!' Then the author suggested the names of several senior professors. But according to the director, none was deemed appropriate for the role. After giving his opinion, the author left.

When consultation with all faculty members was over, Director reconvened with the author and informed him that, based on faculty input, he had been chosen as the next Head of the Mathematics Department. Initially reluctant to accept this significant responsibility, the author felt that some senior colleague could be better suited for the position. However, the Director assured him that his name had received widespread support. Approximately a week later, IIT issued an official notification instructing the author to assume the role within a week.

Handover/Takeover Process

Before formally taking over as the Head of the Department, the author visited his mother to seek her blessings. She remarked, "Had your father been alive, he would have been extremely happy today!" The author deeply felt the absence of his father, who played a crucial role in shaping his academic journey. Despite his busy schedule, his father, who was also his teacher, ensured that he received the best possible education.

The author experienced a mix of excitement and apprehension as he prepared to take on the leadership role at IIT Kharagpur, a globally renowned institution. His father had not only laid the foundation for his mathematical education but had also emphasized proficiency in English, which greatly aided him in professional interactions with colleagues from India and abroad. Throughout his tenure as HOD, he often reflected on his father's guidance, which had been instrumental in shaping his career.

ICOMMONS 99

During his tenure as the head of the department, the author successfully organized several national and international conferences at the Mathematics Department. He received full co-operation from the faculty colleagues and the staff members in organizing the events. The first major event was International Conference on Mathematical Modelling of Nonlinear Systems (ICOMMONS 99) held during December 9–11, 1999. The conference was attended by 110 scientists from various universities and research institutions across India and 15 distinguished professors and scientists from countries such as the USA, Germany, the UK, and France, who presented their research findings at different sessions of the international conference. The author was the convenor and co-chairman of the organizing committee for the three-day conference, with Professor S.B. Sinha as the secretary. The event was inaugurated by Professor Oscar Mahrenholtz of the Technical University of Hamburg, with whom the author had collaborated during his Humboldt Fellowship from 1975 to 1977 and again in the summer of 1982 when Mahrenholtz was a professor at the Technical University of Hannover. Meeting him after so many years was a moment of great joy to both of them. A cultural program was organized one evening to honour of the conference delegates. Two delegates from the USA and Japan played musical instruments they had brought, making the evening memorable.

Reports on the conference appeared in major newspapers including *The Statesman* under the headline "Maths Meet" on December 20, 1999. Another detailed report appeared in *The Telegraph* (December 20, 1999), titled "Patterns Amid Chaos", highlighting the role of mathematical modelling in solving real-world problems.

UNESCO-Sponsored Training Programme

In 1999, we received a letter from UNESCO requesting to organize a training programme in our department on the "Application of Computers in Mathematics Teaching." After discussing it in the Mathematics Department faculty meeting, we agreed to host the programme and informed UNESCO of our consent. The author served as the coordinator, with Dr. A. Goswami as the assistant coordinator.

According to UNESCO's guidelines, the programme included mathematics faculty members from colleges and universities across SAARC countries. We selected teachers from all regions of India as well as from Nepal, Maldives, Bangladesh, and Sri Lanka, ensuring a diverse participation of 40 delegates as stipulated by UNESCO. The programme was held in January, 2000.

The use of computers was already becoming widespread in daily life and was increasingly integrated into teaching various subjects, including mathematics. Hence, the programme, sponsored by UNESCO, was very timely at the beginning of the new millennium. The training combined theoretical instruction with hands-on laboratory session. *The Telegraph* published a detailed report on this programme on February 14, 2000, titled "Byteful of Numbers".

Mathworx-2K: Engaging School Students with Mathematics

Recognizing the importance of engaging young students with mathematics, the Mathematics Department organized a workshop in July 2000 named Mathworx-2K. In the meantime, the International Mathematical Union had declared the year 2000 as the "World Mathematical Year," making this an opportune moment for such an initiative. The author served as the Convenor and Chairman of the organizing committee, with Prof. Somesh Kumar as the coordinator, who excellently planned and conducted the entire event. Other colleagues, including Prof. S. Sundar, Prof. A. Goswami, and Prof. Ashok Nanda, along with other members of the Mathematics Department, provided enthusiastic support.

Objectives and Structure

- The workshop was attended by 250 students from 35 schools across urban and rural areas, including participants from outside West Bengal.
- Participants from each school were accompanied by a teacher to enhance the learning experience.
- The event aimed at eliminating the fear of mathematics and making learning enjoyable through activities such as quizzes (Oracle), problem-solving contests (Headache), poster presentations (Postfix), and geometric model competitions (Tetrahedron).

Inauguration and Cultural Programme

Swami Atmaprabhananda, the Principal of Ramakrishna Mission Vidya-bhavana, Midnapore, inaugurated the event, inspiring students with his address. The workshop also featured a captivating cultural programme by the students of Pratapdighi Ramakrishna-Sarada Siksha Sadan (Nursery School) at the Netaji Auditorium of IIT. The children were thrilled to perform at the auditorium of IIT and their joy was shared by their head teacher, Shri Shaktipada Giri, and other teachers of the school who organized the event. The joy on the children's faces brought deep satisfaction to the author. The whole programme created an enriching experience for all the participants.

The enthusiastic participation of both English and Bengali medium schools, including prestigious institutions like Don Bosco and Frank Anthony Public Schools, was particularly encouraging.

Reflection on Father's Advice

The author was remembering a comment his late father made around 1968, when the author was teaching at Uluberia College and doing research at Jadavpur University under Professor B. Sen's supervision. He said, "Remember, people from villages around our native place expect something from you." This advice has always stayed with the author. Whenever an opportunity arose to assist various educational or religious institutions, he stepped forward. Whenever the author's presence was requested at various events, he tried to fulfill their wishes.

Mathematical Workshops Organized in 2001–2002

We also organized similar workshops for school children in 2001 and 2002, named Mathworx-2K+1 and Mathworx-2K+2, respectively. Swami Sukdevananda (Principal, Ramakrishna Mission Vivekananda Centenary College, Rahara) graced as the chief guest at the inaugural session of Mathwork-2K+1, while Father Malay (Principal, Sacred Heart English Medium High School, Kharagpur) presided over the Valedictory session of this workshop. As Convenor, the author delivered the welcome address. In addition to the workshops, we planned several events to celebrate IIT Kharagpur's golden jubilee and the World Mathematics Year. These events were detailed in an article titled "Campus Notes" in 'The Asian Age' on April 7, 2000. The events planned included an essay competition for students on the topic "Mathematics—A Key for Development."

World Mathematical Year, 2000

On May 6, 1992, the International Mathematical Union declared the year 2000 as the "World Mathematical Year" at its Brazil session. To commemorate World Mathematical Year, the Mathematics Department organized the following two major international events held concurrently:

(i) International Conference on "Recent Advances in Mathematical Sciences" (ICRAMS 2000).

(ii) International Symposium on "Challenges on Mathematical Sciences for the New Millennium," (December 20–22, 2000).

The author served as the convenor and co-chairman of both the events, with Professor S.B. Sinha as the Secretary. The support of all colleagues from the Mathematics Department and several professors from other of IIT departments was invaluable. The symposium dedicated to the memory of Srinivasa Ramanujan, witnessed the participation of 160 delegates from 15 countries. It was a matter of great delight that 30 esteemed mathematicians from various universities in the United States, Canada, the United Kingdom, Italy, Israel, Spain, Poland, Slovenia, Australia, Japan, China, Singapore, the Philippines, Nepal, and Iran participated in these international events. Special arrangements were made to facilitate the travel and accommodation of international guests, given Kharagpur's distance.

The 'Anandabazar Patrika' reported on December 22, 2000, in an article titled "Discussion on Mathematics at IIT," stating, "The conference was inaugurated by Prof. W. Schneider from the University of Vienna, Austria. The guest of honour was the distinguished mathematician A.M. Hinz from the University of Munich, Germany." A.M. Hinz discussed several unsolved mathematical problems and spoke about the growing opportunities in applied mathematics responsibilities of mathematics faculties to appraise their students of the opportunities. He mentioned that with the advent of high-speed computers, a new branch of mathematics called "Experimental Mathematics" had emerged. He explained that the application of mathematics is not limited to physics, chemistry, engineering, life sciences, and medicine, but is also widely used in solving various industrial problems. He cited several challenges as examples.

A report on this three-day international convention appeared in the journal *Current Science* (Vol. 81, 149–150, 2001), published by the Indian Academy of Sciences, Bangalore. The said report featured an academic review of the symposium.

Other reports about the international conference and symposium were published in various Bengali, Hindi and English newspapers. 'Bartaman' published a report titled "Symposium on Mathematical Sciences at IIT Kharagpur" on December 23, 2000; 'Aajkaal' published "Mathematics Conference at IIT" on December 28, 2000; and 'Sangbad Pratidin' published "International Conference" on December 30, 2000. National-level English newspapers provided more detailed reports. 'The Times of India' reported on December 21, 2000, under the headline "Mathematics Seminar at IIT," and 'The Statesman' published a report titled "IIT Meet on Mathematics" on December 22, 2000. The Chennai-based newspaper 'The Hindu' wrote an extensive report titled "Seminar on Mathematics" on December 23, 2000, stating:

> *"The International Symposium on 'Challenges on Mathematical Sciences for the New Millennium' dedicated to Srinivasa Ramanujan was inaugurated on Wednesday at the Department of Mathematics, IIT Kharagpur by Prof. W. Schneider of the Technical University of Vienna, Austria. Prof. Andreas M. Hinz, an applied Mathematician from the University of Munich, was the guest of honour. ... The Co-Chairman and the Convenor of both the international events, Prof. J.C. Misra, also the Head of the Department of Mathematics, introduced the delegates to the themes of the conference and the symposium. He also mentioned that the Department has already introduced, looking into the needs of the society, an integrated five-year M.Sc. program on Mathematics and Computing..."*

'The Hindustan Times', in its report titled "IIT Courses to Meet Society's Needs," published on December 28, 2000, stated, "Lectures pertaining to the challenges mathematicians may face in the present century were delivered by Prof. Enrique G. Reyes of Yale University USA, Prof. Andrea De Gaetano of the Italian Research Foundation, Prof. Thony Ton-That of The University of Iowa (USA), and other prominent mathematicians." 'The Asian Age' published various news items about the conference/symposium in its report titled "International Maths Meet held at IIT" on January 21, 2001. 'The Telegraph' published an excellent report, with a title "Weight of Numbers" on February 26, 2001, regarding the scientific discussions held at this international convention. Interestingly, the report began with the statement, "Mathematics is treading softly in the realm of life sciences," and the Reporter informed, "... The conference sought to highlight biomathematics as one of the emerging fields of research and development. It deals with the physics of breathing, the genetic coding problem, neurophysiology, and population biology. Some of the noteworthy lectures included the one by Prof. Andrea de Gaetano from the Biomathematics Laboratory of the Italian Research Council in Rome. While speaking on 'The perspectives and challenges of biomathematics,' he explained to the audience how the field of biomathematics is developing fast." The detailed report concluded with, "... The conference provided invaluable exposure for young researchers and students and helped them gain insights into the existing and future challenges that mathematics faces."

IIT Kharagpur Mathematicians' Convention (March 24–25, 2001)

Recognizing the significance of alumni and former faculty members in upholding an institution's tradition, the Mathematics Department at IIT Kharagpur organized a **special alumni event** on the eve of its Golden Jubilee. This was the first such event in the history of IIT, and it was attended by both alumni and former faculty members. Special honour was bestowed upon those who had taught in the department for over 25 years. The event also served as a forum for discussions on **teaching methodologies and research in mathematics.** The Director of IIT Kharagpur suggested that other departments should also organize such events. Besides being a reunion, the event included discussions on the teaching methods and research work in mathematics. The event was named "IIT Kharagpur Mathematicians' Convention and Workshop on Applicable Mathematics." The author was the convenor of the event, and he received full support from all his colleagues in the Department.

Several newspapers covered the event. The newspaper, *Bartaman* reported "Mathematics Workshop at IIT Kharagpur" on March 27, 2001, stating, "The two-day 'Mathematicians' Convention and Workshop on 'Applicable Mathematics: Past and Present' concluded on Sunday at IIT Kharagpur's Mathematics Department. The event was inaugurated on Saturday at the institution's S.N. Bose Auditorium by former Professor of the Department of Mathematics and former Vice-Chancellor of Rewa University in Madhya Pradesh, Prof. M.K. Jain. In his welcome address, Prof. J.C. Misra, the convenor and head of the Mathematics Department emphasized the growing importance of mathematical modelling in solving real-life problems."

Reports on the event were also published in the '*Anandabazar Patrika*' (March 26, 2001) under the title "Workshop on Applied Mathematics," in '*Aajkaal*' (March 26, 2001) under the title "Postgraduate Education in Medicine and Technology at IIT," and in '*Sangbad Pratidin*' under the title "Math Seminar."

'*The Hindu*' (March 25, 2001), a distinguished English newspaper published from Chennai, reported "Maths Convention," as "The Indian Institute of Technology at Kharagpur, started in 1951, is celebrating the 50th year of its existence with a two-day Mathematicians' convention and a workshop on 'Applicable Mathematics: Past and Present.'... In his welcome address, Prof. J.C. Misra, convenor of the convention and the workshop, reiterated the increasing role of mathematical models in solving various real-life problems."

'*The Times of India*' (March 27, 2001) wrote under the headline 'IIT-K Celebrates 50 Years of Excellence,' "...The two-day programme started on Saturday at the S.N. Bose Auditorium. Among those present were Mathematician M.K. Jain and Guest of Honour D.N. Mitra, (both former professors of the Department). Prof. Amitabha Ghosh, Director of IIT, presided over the inaugural session attended by more than 200 delegates.

J.C. Misra, convenor, mentioned that the department is now taking an active interest in interdisciplinary research in areas like biomathematics. Alumni of the department occupy important positions at distinguished educational institutes and software organizations worldwide. The department is taking special interest in improving the mathematical aptitude of school children and young mathematicians by organizing workshops every year and the response has been overwhelming."

Reporting on the same event '*The Hindustan Times*' (March 27, 2001) wrote under the title "Medical Science Course in IIT," announcing the launch of a new Master's Programme in Medical Science and Technology (MMST). Prof. Misra, highlighted the role of mathematical modelling and computer graphics simulation in DNA analysis.

'*The Statesman*' in its report, titled "Maths Workshop," dated 30 April 2001, highlighted the active interest of the Mathematics Department in interdisciplinary research..."

'*The Telegraph* ' (April 16, 2001), the National English Daily published from Kolkata, wrote an elaborate report titled "Reins on Chaos" focusing on the contributions of mathematics to various disciplines. The article reported on IIT Kharagpur's transition to a more flexible system promptly capability-based learning with a broader range of academic. .... 'The valedictory session was presided over by Prof. Misra. He concluded with the hope that, just as the department has had a glorious past and a promising present, the future would also be bright.'

Reflections and Personal Accounts

News of these events sparked enthusiasm among students, teachers and well-wishers of the author. Shri Pramatha Nath Bose, the former headmaster of Tikrapara H.S. School, who was then retired and living in his home at his native place in Bhagabanpur, expressed his happiness and excitement in a letter to the author. He wrote, "Had your father been alive today, he would have been extremely happy with your recent achievements." As mentioned already, at Tikrapara High School, the author's father was a respected colleague of Pramatha Nath who loved and respected him deeply. Another teacher, Shri Lakshmikanta Mishra (an elder relative and former teacher of the author), expressed his deep joy in a letter, saying, "Had *Kaka-babu* (uncle) been alive today, he would have been the happiest!"

Indeed, when the author had the opportunity to go to Germany for advanced research in 1975, his father, despite his conservative Brahmin background, highly encouraged him to avail the opportunity. His mother also supported this decision, even though she was deeply religious. Upon returning from Germany in 1977, the author witnessed the joy and relief of his family, including his youngest brother, relatives and school mentors.

The community celebrated his achievements, and Tikrapara Higher Secondary School honoured him with a special event, during which he delivered a lecture on his experiences abroad.

Roles Played in the School of Medical Science and Technology (SMST)

Since its inception in 2001, the author played a crucial role in faculty recruitment, research scholar selection and administrative work for the school of Medical Science and Technology (SMST). Though he was considered for the role of Head of SMST, he declined due to his pre-existing responsibilities as Head of the Mathematics Department, and Prof. R.C. Arora (Mechanical Engineering Department) was appointed instead. However, the author remained actively involved in major decision-making process for SMST.

The School started its journey with a three-year (six-semester) Master's degree course called the Master in Medical Science and Technology (MMST), which admitted only MBBS graduates. The goal was to provide MBBS graduates with appropriate training in pure sciences and technology, so that the medical graduates will be well versed with medical technologies also. The first three semesters were dedicated to coursework, while the remaining time of the MMST programme was allocated for project work. This project work could be undertaken in any suitable laboratory in India or abroad. Gradually, the MMST course gained international popularity. For the first five years, the author taught the subject 'Biomedical Mathematics' to MMST students. As mentioned earlier, teaching mathematics topics to MBBS graduates was a challenging task, but the author used his innovative teaching methods to make the topics interesting for the students. He became a popular teacher among the students of MMST, who often visited the author's residence for academic as well as personal discussions.

Later, besides MMST, the School also introduced two more M.Tech courses—one in 'Medical Imaging and Informatics' and the other in 'Biomedical Engineering.' After Prof. Arora's prolonged illness and eventual passing, the author took over as Acting Head of SMST for an extended period.

Reflecting on his career, the author takes pride in his impartial leadership and adherence to ethical principles, as guided by the *Bhagavad Gita*. His contributions in research and teaching earned him reemployment at IIT Kharagpur until April 30, 2009, after which he received an offer to serve as Pro-Vice Chancellor of SOA University in Bhubaneswar.

Joining as a Pro-Vice Chancellor

After dedicating 42 years to teaching mathematics without any career breaks, the author formally retired. His journey in academia began on July 23, 1967 at Uluberia College, where he taught until August 8, 1971. The following day, August 9, 1971 he joined the Mathematics Department at IIT Kharagpur in the morning and without delay conducted an M.Sc. class that very afternoon. He continued serving at IIT Kharagpur until April 30, 2009. That night he travelled to Bubaneswar and joined SOA University as Pro-Vice Chancellor on May 1, 2009. Thus, instead of taking a break after retirement, he transitioned seamlessly into an administrative role in academia.

A car was sent to Bhubaneswar railway station to receive him and take him to his office at the administration building of the university. On the way, he first visited the Ramakrishna Math and Mission in Bhubaneswar to seek the blessings of Sri Ramakrishna, Sri Sarada Devi, and Swami Vivekananda at the temple. His office in the university's administrative building was already prepared. It was on the ground floor. First he met the Vice-Chancellor Prof. M.P. Jain. Another Pro-Vice Chancellor, H.K. Sahu, had an office adjacent to the author's. A friendly relationship soon developed between them. Dr. Sahu had retired from the Orissa Government Medical Service as the Principal of a Medical College and was responsible for the administration and development of SOA University's medical college and hospital. The author was entrusted with the responsibilities of academic administration across all university departments.

SOA University, Bhubaneswar

Thus, after retiring from IIT Kharagpur, the author embraced the new challenge of administrative work at SOA University in Bhubaneswar. He did not take a break even for a day and served the institution for five and a half years (until October 31, 2014). For about three months after joining the university, the author stayed in the university's guest house (on the second floor of the SUM Medical College and Hospital). He often met young doctors during breakfast, lunch, and dinner at the hospital canteen and discussed various topics with them. Some of the doctors stayed at the guest house. The university arranged transportation for him to commute to and from his office at the administrative building of the University.

SOA University encompassed multiple constituent units, including the Institute of Technical Education and Research, which was the oldest and largest unit. It offered programmes in Computer Science and Engineering, Electronics and Communication Engineering, Mechanical Engineering, Electrical Engineering, and Civil Engineering, among others. Each department offered B.Tech, M.Tech, and Ph.D. programmes. Besides engineering, the university had the Institute of Medical Sciences and SUM Hospital, the Institute of Dental Sciences, the School of Nursing, the Institute of Business Studies, the School of Pharmaceutical Sciences, the School of Hotel Management, and the Institute of Law. SOA University was one of the two largest deemed universities in Bhubaneswar. The founder and president of the university was Dr. Manojranjan Nayak, whose achievement in developing such a vast institution single-handedly was commendable.

Ramakrishna Math and Ramakrishna Mission, Bhubaneswar

After nearly three months of residing in the university's guest house, the author and his wife moved into a flat on Vivekananda Marg, near the Ramakrishna Math and Mission. Both he and his wife desired to live close to the Math, founded by Swami Brahmananda, the spiritual son of Sri Ramakrishna. As indicated earlier, during the construction of this Ashram, the author's Guru, Srimat Swami Shankarananda, a disciple of Swami Brahmananda, had played an instrumental role, further strengthening the author's attachment to this particular branch centre of the Ramakrishna Math and Mission. Swami Brahmananda referred to Bhubaneswar as *"Guptakashi"*, emphasizing the city's spiritual energy. He believed that one repetition of a *mantra* in Bhubaneswar is equivalent to 500 repetitions elsewhere. Swami Shankarananda had also expressed that his profound spiritual realizations were rooted in Bhubaneswar, making it a significant place in the author's spiritual journey.

Ramakrishna Math & Mission, Bhubaneswar

Swami Shiveshwarananda served as the Secretary of the Mission for a long time, and he was still present when the author joined SOA University. Later, he fell ill for an extended period, and Swami Priyarupananda (Sudarsan Maharaj) took over as the secretary for about two years until he passed away from a heart attack. Following this, Ramakrishna Mission Head Quarters at Belur Math appointed Swami Atmaprabananda (Shubhankar Maharaj) as the Secretary of Ramakrishna Math and Mission at Bhubaneswar. The author had known him for a long time. As mentioned earlier, during his time at IIT Kharagpur, the author had invited Swami Atmaprabananda as the Chief Guest for an event organized for school students. That time he invited him to their residence for breakfast. So he was known to the author's family members as well. For this reason, both he and his wife were delighted to see him at Bhubaneswar Math after a long time.

Since, the author was living those days near the Ramakrishna Mission, he liked to visit the temple frequently for morning prayers, meditation, and sometimes for reciting the Chandi or Gita. During evening prayer and aratrikam also, he and his wife used to go to the temple there regularly. The Lingaraj Temple, about 2 kms away from his residence on Vivekananda Marg, was also a place he visited occasionally, either by walking or taking an auto-rickshaw. On holidays, they would sometimes take a taxi to Puri to visit the Lord Jagannath Temple.

Bhubaneswar Ramakrishna Math and Mission is of special significance to the monks of the Ramakrishna Order, since it was established by no other than Raja Maharaj (Swami Brahmananda). For this reason, it has been attracting monks from different centers across India and abroad. Many of them were previously acquainted with the author, providing opportunities for meaningful interactions.

Meeting with Swami Smarananananda

The author fondly recalls a memorable meeting with *Swami Smarananananda*, the then Vice President of the Ramakrishna Math and Mission (later the President), during his visit to Bhubaneswar Math. Swami Smarananananda and the author both were initiated disciples of the same Guru, *Swami Shankarananda*. So the author being a spiritual brother of Swami Smarananananda, one day on prior appointment, they had an enriching discussion lasting for about 45–50 minutes, primarily on spiritual matters. At the end of the discourse, Swami Smarananandaji graciously accompanied the author upto the door of the room, an act that remains etched in his memory. The author fondly remembers, during the discourse, the Swami asked the author to sit on a chair beside him, but out of respect the author preferred to sit on the floor in front of the Swami. That time Swami Smarananda said to him, "*Gurubat Guruputreshu.*"

Swami Suhitananda

Swami Suhitananda, (one of the present Vice-Presidents) of the Ramakrishna Math and Mission, visited Bhubaneswar Math on various occasions, because that time he was the General Secretary of the Ramakrishna Math and Mission. Known as 'Sanatanda' to the author, they shared many joyful reminiscences of the past, when *Sanatanda* was the 'Sevak' of revered *Srimat Swami Premeshanandaji Maharaj* (a very senior highly respected monk of the Ramakrishna Mission), who was staying at R.K. Mission, Sargachhi (Murshidabad). Swami Premeshananda (Indradayal Bhattacharya in his premonastic life) was known to be an affectionate *sannyasi*. The author heard that being inspired by him quite many young men joined the Ramakrishna Mission, even much before he formally joined the Ramakrishna Mission. Due to this reason he used to be (humorously) called as 'kidnapper' (*chhele dhara*). Swami Premeshananda published two small Bengali booklets, called *Atmabikash* vol. I and *Atmabikash* vol. II. These two booklets used to be very useful for children for the purpose of 'character building' and so they became very popular. This is why these booklets were reprinted by the Ramakrishna Mission several times.

During his stay at Bhubaneswar, the author once met Swami Subiranananda, who is currently the General Secretary of the Ramakrishna Mission. During his first meeting with him, he was Asst. Secretary. The author also met Swami Prabhananda (one of the former Vice-Presidents), who was also a spiritual brother (*gurubhai*) of the author.

Meeting with Swami Divyananda

Swami Divyananda (currently one of the Vice-Presidents of the Ramakrishna Mission) performed Kali Puja (as *Pujak*) at Bhubaneswar Math for several consecutive years during the author's stay at Bhubaneswar. Since in the Vidyamandira family, the author was senior, Swami Divyananda affectionately addresses him as 'Jagadis Da'. When Swami Divyananda used to visit the Ramakrishna Mission, Bhubaneswar on the occasion of Kalipuja, every year he used to stay there for a couple of days.This gave the author an opportunity to have long conversations with him. While discussing various matters, once the author asked, "In earlier days, we used to hear, those who used to join the Ramakrishna Mission as a sadhu, they used have intense feeling of renunciation. Is this assertion valid even these days?" Swami Divyananda instantly replied, "Jagadis Da, I think for those who are now joining the Mission to become a *sadhu*, the intensity of renunciation in their case is much stronger." He continued further, "Because in the present society there are too many elements of distraction and too many ways to get material pleasures and get misled. So by overcoming all these and taking up a life of renunciation is more difficult in comparison to earlier days." The author agreed, reflecting that total faith in renunciation as expressed in Adi Shankaracharya's words, "*Koupinavantah Khalu Bhagyavantah*," requires highly intensified feeling of renunciation. The conversations between Swami Divyananda and the author were always very enriching and enjoyable. He used to have a feeling of satisfying 'Sadhusanga' (divine company of a monk).

Swami Bhaktirupananda (Saroj Maharaj), a fellow student from the author's time at Belur College, would reminisce about shared memories whenever they met, at Ramakrishna Math, Bhubaneswar, or elsewhere.

Academic Contributions and Teaching Legacy

As Pro-Vice Chancellor, the author had the responsibility of overseeing the academic activities of each department within SOA university. He was invited to various departmental events and interacted with faculty members to understand their needs and challenges, striving to address them. One of his significant roles was to encourage faculty members to engage in research, apart from teaching. To this end, he arranged lectures by several renowned professors from various departments at IIT Kharagpur, known for their research expertise. He collaborated with some of them to motivate faculty members in SOA University's various science and engineering departments to pursue Ph.D. degrees. As Pro Vice-Chancellor, The author tried to take utmost care to see that some faculty members of SOA University do Ph.D. under the guidance and supervision of appropriate faculty members of IIT Kharagpur.

The author himself also made personal efforts to publish high-quality research papers, with his affiliation of SOA University, Bhubaneswar. Overall, the author achieved considerable success in improving the research environment at the university. A group of researchers from Stanford University in the USA compiled a list of the top 2% of scientists worldwide based on research from 2019. The author's name was included in this list, with his affiliation listed as SOA University. The university authorities expressed their satisfaction and sent him a message of congratulations. The author's name also appeared in the Top 2% Scientists list published in five consecutive years from 2020 to 2024.

Apart from his administrative responsibilities the author continued to teach Mathematics at the Engineering Faculty (ITER). He monitored class conduction and contributed to modernizing the curriculum and syllabi at the SOA University. He also put forward recommendations for infrastructural improvements, including faculty rooms and research cubicles, some of which were later implemented by the university authorities. His extensive experience at IIT Kharagpur played a crucial role in bringing out these improvements.

The author also cherished moments when his former students and professors recognized his teaching contributions. A former student from IIT Kharagpur once approached him at Howrah station and expressed appreciation of his teaching methodology, emphasizing how its moderate pace and depth had made learning enjoyable to the students. This reaffirmed the author's belief in maintaining a balanced teaching approach, as advised by Gautam Buddha's "middle path".

On 18th August 2025, the author met Mr. Rajiv Agarwal at the Netaji Auditorium of IIT. He received the Young Alumni Achiever Award from IIT Kharagpur on the occasion of the Foundation Day of the Institute in recognition of his distinguished contributions to the Society. He runs the

EduVerse Group of companies focused on innovative products and services for students, teachers and leaders in education.

At the end of the ceremony, on seeing the author from a distance he came nearer, bowed down and informed, "Sir, I did my B.Tech. (Metallurgical and Materials Engineering) from IIT Kharagpur in 2008 and stayed in RK Hall. You taught us Mathematics." He continued further saying, "We liked your teaching very much. What most memorable about your teaching was your caring and understanding demeanor that created a learning environment where everyone felt comfortable to ask questions. You taught most complex concepts in a simple and lucid manner and made the subject interesting in a unique manner."

This was towards the end of my tenure at IIT Kharagpur, because I left the Institute on 30th April, 2009 to take up a job elsewhere on 1st May, 2009.

In 2013, the Indian National Academy of Engineering (INEA), New Delhi honoured the author with the 'Outstanding Teacher Award' at its annual convention. Coincidentally, that year the annual convention was scheduled to be held at SOA University, Bhubaneswar. The award session was attended by many dignitaries. The author's wife Shorasi, daughter Sumita (IIEST Shibpur) and son Sudip (IIT Kharagpur) also were present during the said award ceremony. This recognition is a testament to the author's lifelong dedication to teaching and research.

Through his dual role as an academician and an administrator, the author left a lasting impact on SOA University, Bhubaneswar, further enriching its educational and research landscape.

From the Perspective of One of His Professors

Many of the author's teachers and professors have passed away. Dr. Sachindra Kumar Baksi, former Head of the Mathematics Department at Belur College, once told the author over the phone, "I have been in touch with a few of your M.Sc. students from IIT. They speak highly of your teaching. I have as well seen from them your lecture notes on Partial Differential Equations and liked them very much." In an article about the author's teaching, he wrote, "... As a teacher, he (the author) is highly successful. Students not only learned academics from him but also learned how to become good human beings." (cf. '*Nana Chokhe Ek Barenya Ganit-Sadhok*', Kabitika Prakashani, Kolkata, 2023; Editors: Haripada Maity, Manmathanath Das, and Balailal Das).

An Example of God's Protection

During the time of residing at Vivekananda Marg in Bhubaneswar, the author encountered a significant crisis. His wife was in Kharagpur at the time, and he was alone in Bhubaneswar. One morning, before heading to the office, he stepped into the bathroom to take a shower. The bathroom door had a known faulty mechanism, so as a precaution, they usually avoided locking it. However, in a moment of haste, he inadvertently locked the door.

The bathroom was of modern type and airtight, effectively preventing any sound from escaping, making it nearly impossible for neighbours to hear any calls for help. By sheer fortune, Mrs. Rath, a lecturer in Economics at KIIT University and a neighbour, was at home that day—despite it being a working day. Hearing the author's distressed cries, she quickly grasped the gravity of the situation. Acting swiftly, she sought assistance from other neighbours and contacted the police and fire brigade.

Since the main entrance to the apartment was also locked, the rescuers had to break a window to gain access to the house and unlock the bathroom door. Everyone anxiously awaited the outcome, concerned about the author's condition. To their immense relief, he was unharmed. Undeterred by the incident, he proceeded to his office as usual.

At Indian Institute of Engineering Science & Technology (IIEST), Shibpur (Howrah)

After serving the SOA University in Bhubaneswar until October 31, 2014, the author joined the Indian Institute of Engineering Science and Technology, Shibpur (IIEST) on January 2, 2015, as an Adjunct Professor at the Center for Healthcare Science and Technology. He remained associated with the institution for nearly five years. IIEST, located in Shibpur, Howrah district, West Bengal, is one of the oldest and leading engineering institutions in India. It is recognized as an outstanding institution in India and abroad for education and research in various branches of engineering and applied sciences. Previously, the Institute was known as Bengal Engineering College/Bengal Engineering and Science University.

One notable figure in the institution's history was Prof. S.R. Sengupta, a former Principal of Bengal Engineering College, who went on to become the second Director of IIT Kharagpur. He was widely known as an exceptional administrator. The Mathematics Department at BE College once boasted professors known for their research and teaching, including Prof. Bibhutibhushan Sen, D.Sc., FNA, Prof. Sushil Chandra Dasgupta, D.Sc., Prof. Subodh Kumar Chakrabarti, and Prof. S. Ganguli. Some of these professors taught as part-time teachers at the Applied Mathematics Department at the University of Calcutta. When the author was pursuing his M.Sc., Prof. S. Ganguli taught Electricity and Magnetism, and Prof. Subodh Kumar Chakrabarti later became the Head of the Applied Mathematics Department at the University of Calcutta, where he taught the author's batch, Hydrodynamics.

When the author joined IIEST as an Adjunct Professor, Prof. Ajay Ray, a former professor of the Electronics and Communication Engineering Department at IIT Kharagpur, was the Director of IIEST. He always held the author in high esteem. During his tenure at IIEST, the author was the Principal Investigator of a research project funded by the Department of Science and Technology (SERB) of the Government of India, titled 'Problems of Heat and Mass Transfer in Physiological Fluid Dynamics.' The tenure of the project was from 2015 to 2018, with Biswajit Mallik serving as the research scholar. The project was successfully completed in 2018, resulting in the publication of eight research papers in reputed international journals.

IIEST Shibpur (formerly BE College Shibpur)

The author received substantial support and assistance from various faculty members and several officers at IIEST. In particular, the cooperation of Prof. Amit Ray Choudhury, the then Head of the Centre for Healthcare Science and Technology, was instrumental in the execution of the sponsored research project. Biswajit, the project scholar, registered for his Ph.D. at IIEST. For the convenience of the research scholar, Biswajit the author meticulously reviewed and corrected the entire thesis at Belgharia Ramakrishna Mission, working with Biswajit for nearly ten days, on each day from morning till evening. At the time, Biswajit was teaching at Kalyani University. Following the successful completion of his Ph.D., Biswajit joined the Mathematics Department at VIT Chennai as an Assistant Professor. He currently holds the position of an Assistant Professor at the Mathematics Department in the Central University of Allahabad.

CHAPTER 12 The *Grihastha* Phase

Author's Parents

The first two chapters have provided a detailed account of the author's formative years, highlighting the profound influence of his parents, uncle, aunt, siblings, and other close relations in the joint family. Their love and care played a crucial role in shaping his life. These chapters also vividly describe how his parents laid the moral and educational foundations that guided him throughout his journey.

The present chapter focuses on the second phase of the author's life—the *Grihastha* stage, marked by marriage and family responsibilities.

Marriage

In earlier times, particularly in rural India, marriages were predominantly arranged by the respective families. The institution of arranged marriage proved to be resilient and adaptable to evolving social norms. The author's marriage followed this traditional system, where it was not customary for the prospective bride and groom to meet beforehand. Typically, the groom's father, accompanied by relatives and friends, would visit the bride's home to assess various aspects, followed by a reciprocal visit by the bride's family.

However, in the author's case, since he was not keen on marriage at the time, his father was unable to proceed without his consent. Despite this, many marriage proposals were received by his father from families of eligible brides. Several eminent individuals, including Dr. Prafulla Kumar Nanda, a renowned physician from Egra, and Pandit Jyotirmoy Nanda from Mugberia, visited the author's home in his native place for their daughters to discuss potential matches. Though these discussions were ongoing, the author remained undecided.

Prof. Pulin Behari Nanda, a professor of English at Bangabasi College, Kolkata also sent a proposal for his daughter. Being an alumnus of Ramakrishna Mission Calcutta Students' Home, where the author resided during his M.Sc. studies, Prof. Nanda forwarded the proposal through Swami Dhyanatmananda (revered Nripen Maharaj). The author's father and his friends visited the proposed bride at Egra, because at that time the bride's mother was working as the Asst. Headmistress of Egra Girls' High School. However, no decision could be taken then due to the author's lack of consent.

At the time, the author was a lecturer in Mathematics at Uluberia College, Howrah. During a vacation, while he was staying in his native village, Pandit Phani Bhusan Nanda from Amarpur village, along with his father-in-law, visited the author's home with a marriage proposal for his eldest daughter, Shorasi. The author's father introduced them, and they engaged in discussions before departing.

Two of the author's former high school teachers, Shri Lakshmikanta Basu and Shri Joynarayan Acharya, were familiar with both the groom's and bride's families. They played a significant role in facilitating the match, as they were well acquainted with Shorasi through their family connections in neighboring villages. Her gentle demeanor and reputation as a dedicated teacher had endeared her to some families in the locality, further strengthening their recommendation. In no time, she could also earn the affection of the author's father, even before her marriage with the author. The author's father met her once or twice before the marriage. Hearing that occasionally she felt the problem of headache, he sent her a vial of *trigun taila* (an ayurvedic medicinal oil, which cures headache).

A brief meeting between the author and Shorasi was arranged by Shri Basu, lasting about 15 minutes. A few months later, after careful deliberation, the parents of both the author and Shorasi finalized the marriage.

Following the marriage customs meticulously, the wedding ceremony was solemnized on Wednesday, May 28, 1969 (14th *Jaistha*, 1376 in the Bengali Calendar) at the bride's parental home in Amarpur village. The ceremony was conducted according to Hindu traditions, with Vedic mantras being chanted. Both the bride and groom observed a complete fast from morning until the midnight completion of the wedding rituals. Before the wedding, well-wishers advised the author to adhere to the customs for the happiness of the elders, which he followed meticulously with patience and devotion.

Family Background of the Bride

The author's father-in-law lost his father in infancy and faced severe financial hardships. He was raised with great care by his mother and paternal aunt. Overcoming difficulties, he pursued education and became a teacher at the village primary school, gradually improving the family's financial situation. Despite hardships, they maintained honesty, truthfulness, and deep faith in God.

Author's Parents-in-law

As a devout Brahmin, he followed strict religious rituals, including daily *tarpan* (offering water to ancestors), worship before meals, and evening prayers (*sandhya*). Later in life, he adopted a simple vegetarian diet and lived to the remarkable age of 97 years (Born: 5 *Kartik*, 1329, Died: 22 *Magh*, 1426). His disciplined and principled life earned him immense respect.

The bride's family had a deep sense of aesthetics, maintaining cleanliness in their home and surroundings, reflecting their refined mentality. They were known for their hospitality and courteous nature. Despite financial constraints in the early years, they prioritized education for all their eleven children (six daughters and five sons), believing that daughters deserve the same upbringing and education as sons—a rare and progressive mindset in those times. They followed the verdict of the scriptures—"*kanyapyeva palaniya, sikshaniya prayatnatata.*"

The father-in-law was well-versed in Sanskrit literature and ancient scriptures but was neither superstitious nor dogmatic. His broad-mindedness and wisdom were widely respected, even among highly educated individuals of the society. He encouraged his daughters' training also in classical dance and music, fostering a well-rounded upbringing.

One of his notable qualities was his adherence to the principle: "*Satyam bruyat, priyam bruyat, ma bruyat satyamapriyam*"—'Speak the truth, but in a pleasant manner; avoid speaking unpleasant truth.' He was known for his ability to uplift others through kind words of encouragement. Additionally, he was deeply devoted to his mother, setting an exemplary standard of filial respect.

The Author's Relationship with His In-Laws

The author was warmly welcomed into his in-laws' family. His mother-in-law, Bejoya Devi, showered him with immense affection from the very first day of marriage. Whenever he visited their home, the household took on a festive atmosphere. She took great pleasure in cooking for him, serving dishes in a bowl made of bell metal, which she had received as a gift from her parents at her own wedding. Fresh fish from their pond was a staple item in the elaborate meals, and she took great joy in ensuring the author was well-fed.

His father-in-law and father shared a friendly relationship built on mutual respect. Similarly, the author's mother and mother-in-law had a harmonious bond, often advising their daughter, Shorasi, to take care of her in-laws and husband with dedication.

Life after Marriage

Shorasi pursued B.A. (Hons.) from R.N.L. Khan Women's College (*Gope College*), Midnapore, affiliated to the University of Calcutta. Later, she completed B.Ed. from Uluberia College (Calcutta University). After obtaining her Hons. Degree, she served a girls'school as a teacher for a few months with proficiency. Despite her potential as a teacher, she chose to be a homemaker, prioritizing the upbringing of the children and managing the household with dedication. Her upbringing had instilled in her a deep sense of piety and duty, which she carried forward in her marital life.

During the author's two-year stay in Germany, she efficiently managed the extended family at Bagmari. At the IIT campus, she continued her role with grace, ensuring a spiritual and harmonious home environment. Following her parental training, she remained deeply committed to religious practices and family traditions.

After finishing religious rituals, she would first bow down to the superiors (parents-in-law and husband) and then enter the kitchen. If the author was unable to go to the market, she would herself walk down to the IIT market to buy fresh vegetables and other food items. Then she would come back on foot and immediately enter the kitchen. With all enthusiasm, she would try to prepare several items to satisfy the taste of all members of the family. The author's mother tried to help gladly in the kitchen to the best of her ability. The father also shared the household activities and tried his utmost to guide the entire family in the right direction.

Her former high school teacher, Shri Haripada Das Adhikary, had once remarked that Shorasi would be a caring and devoted wife. The author often marvelled at how such an accurate prediction could be made by a teacher about a young student.

In the IIT Quarters, the author and his family of seven members enjoyed cherished moments together. They travelled across India using Leave Travel Concession (LTC), visiting Jammu & Kashmir, North India, Gujarat, South India, and other regions several times by reserved luxury bus. These trips, though sometimes strenuous, were immensely joyful, especially for the children, who relished the close company of their grandparents during the journey.

Throughout their journey, Shorasi maintained a loving relationship with her mother-in-law, who regarded her as her own daughter. The Grihastha phase of the author's life thus unfolded as a period of deep familial bonds, shared responsibilities, and enduring love.

Deep-Rooted Family Values

The author fondly recalls the deep-rooted family values and experiences that shaped his life. During their stay at the IIT Campus, the author's parents had a tradition of attending weekend movie screenings at the Netaji Auditorium of IIT, particularly when Bengali films were shown. His father, who was highly interested in gardening, took keen interest in maintaining their kitchen garden and also the flower garden. When the author watered the plants, his father often supervised, instructing which plants needed more attention. His mother, on the other hand, occasionally plucked fresh vegetables from the garden. A particularly memorable instance was when the garden flourished with numerous *tulsi* (Holy Basil) plants. The author's father-in-law, upon seeing them, was elated and remarked, "This is like Vrindavan! Lord Krishna resides in *tulsi* plants, and the air that flows through them is beneficial to health."

The author always felt a strong bond of affection from his in-laws. They confided in him whenever they faced any difficulties, and he always extended his support to the best of his ability. A few months before his father-in-law passed away, the author along with his wife went to visit him. During one of their heartfelt conversations, his father-in-law suddenly expressed, "I am fortunate to have you as my son-in-law." Touched by his words, the author immediately stood up, bowed, and responded with deep sincerity, "Father, I am rather fortunate to have you as my father-in-law and mother as my mother-in-law." These words came from the depth of his heart, evoking a flood of cherished memories. He prays that the blessings of his departed in-laws continue to be bestowed upon him and his family.

The author's wife, Shorasi, comes from a well-respected family. She has five sisters and five brothers. Like her, all her sisters are deeply devoted to their respective husbands and possess gentle, respectful, and caring natures. They seem to have inherited these virtues from their mother, who epitomized the qualities of a traditional Hindu woman—a '*sati patibrata nari*.' Each of the sisters received higher education and is well-established in life.

Among her five brothers, two hold Ph.D. degrees—one in Mathematics and the other in Education. They are esteemed faculty members at colleges and universities. Another brother serves as the headmaster of a higher secondary school, while the remaining two are dedicated school teachers.

The author's father-in-law had five daughters-in-law, each from a diverse background. Yet, remarkably, they all shared a composed temperament, diligent habits, and numerous admirable qualities. Similar to his daughters, each daughter-in-law had pursued higher education. The family's future generations also thrived, with all the grandchildren being well-settled and of good nature. The father-in-law took pride in overseeing the construction of his two-storied home.

Both the parents-in-law exhibited immense curiosity about the world. Whenever the author returned from his travels across India/abroad, they eagerly sought details about the places he had visited, keen to share his experiences. His father-in-law's journey from a humble beginning to a life of great accomplishments was remarkable. On every special occasion, the parents-in-law invited the author's parents with warmth and sincerity as they extended to their own children. The author firmly believes that his father-in-law's success was primarily due to his unwavering faith in God, self-confidence, integrity, discipline, and honesty—an observation based on years of close association.

Life after Retirement

After retirement, the author and his wife, Shorasi, have spent the greater part of their time at the IIT Kharagpur campus, under the loving care of their youngest son, Sudip, and his wife, Satamita. The presence of their affectionate grandchildren, Devadeep and Devadrita, adds to their joy. Sudip's devotion to his parents is akin to the care he provides for his own children. Additionally, he takes care of his brother and sister's families whenever needed, a trait he might have inherited from his grandfather (author's father).

Satamita, the wife of Sudip, is a cheerful and sociable person with many friends, who are mostly mothers of her children's classmates. Despite holding an M.Sc. degree, she chose not to pursue a job and instead devote herself to her children's education with great diligence.

The author's daughter, Sumita, is a faculty member at IIEST Shibpur, which requires her to undertake a long daily commute from Santoshpur (near Jadavpur). Despite her demanding schedule, she manages her household entirely on her own, without any external help. Furthermore, she remains dedicated to her parents and siblings. While her efforts are commendable, the author worries that such an intense routine may take a toll on her health.

Sumita, has played a significant role in ensuring medical care not just for her in-laws' family but also for her parents, siblings and their families. She has been assisted in this by her husband, Achintya, and their daughter, Supurna.

On the eve of going to Patiala (Punjab) for their daughter Supurna's admission in Thapar Institute of Science and Technology, they planned to go on a trip to Bak Khali and Frazerganj. On their insistence the author accompanied them, during the trip. Their company was highly enjoyable to the author.

Life at IIT Kanpur Campus

The author and his wife also visited their eldest son, Subhas, and his family at the IIT Kanpur campus—a familiar place for the author, as he had served as a visiting professor there in the early 1980s. Though his initial visits were short, typically staying in the guest house, the family now stays there twice a year for extended periods. In August 2022, what was planned as a five-week visit turned into an extended stay of over a year due to multiple reasons.

This prolonged visit allowed them to fully enjoy campus life, facilitated by the utmost care shown by Subhas and his family. The delicious meals prepared lovingly by the elder daughter-in-law, Sulagna, further enriched their experience. Sulagna takes immense pleasure in cooking and personally serving the food, never relying on external help. Her warm and affectionate nature makes everyone feel comfortable. During a visit to her parental home in Nabadweep and some relatives in Burdwan, she even insisted the author to join them, a gesture that remains a cherished memory. The company of the grandchildren, Devarati and Devapratim, adds to their joy, both during travels and at Kanpur. Even during the journey to Chennai on the occasion of Devarati's admission to SRM University (Main Campus) Chennai on the insistence of his elder daughter-in-law Sulagna, the author went all the way from Kharagpur to Kanpur in order to accompany them to Chennai. Sulagna fondly added, if you accompany us, we shall have the feeling of having 'an umbrella over our head'. The childlike simplicity and caring nature of Subhas, Sulagna, Devarati, and Devapratim make their presence even more enjoyable to the author and his wife. Apart from managing the household, Sulagna also oversees the children's education meticulously. She holds an M.A. degree.

Life at IIT Kanpur has been quite pleasant. The well-maintained campus, covering 1,100 acres, is half the size of IIT Kharagpur Campus but equally pristine, with clean roads and lush greenery. Peacocks roam freely in the IIT Kanpur Campus, adding to the scenic beauty, much like the deer in IIT Madras Campus. The efficient work culture at IIT Kanpur ensures that complaints are promptly addressed, and staff members are notably courteous.

One of the most scenic spots, Park-67, was donated by the 1967 alumni batch of IIT Kanpur. It serves as an ideal location for morning walks, where the author formed many acquaintances. An incident, somewhat strange to the author, occurred when a fellow walker inquired about his shoe size. Days later, the same person gifted him an expensive pair of shoes, insisting on his acceptance.

Despite repeated attempts to dissuade the person by suggesting the shoes may better be presented to someone in need, the person insisted, saying, "Please accept it; I bought them only for you. You are like my father. Your blessing will bring great fortune to my life." Upon asking about the identity, the person said, "I am a professor at IIT Kanpur." The author later discovered that this generous person was a renowned Bhatnagar Award-winning professor, making the gesture even more intriguing.

IIT Kanpur's campus offers high-quality, reasonably priced meals in student hostels, open to all residents and guests. Many people here are religious minded, frequently visiting the Shiva temples scattered across the campus. A unique incident occurred when news spread of a leopard sighting, creating panic among residents. Security personnel made numerous unsuccessful attempts to capture the animal, but eventually, the sightings stopped, easing the tension.

The author holds deep appreciation for his time spent within these esteemed institutions, cherishing the bonds of family, friendships, and the wisdom gained over the years. He remains grateful for the love and care he continues to receive from all his children and their families.

CHAPTER 13 Descendants

As previously mentioned, the author is blessed with three children: eldest son Subhas, daughter Sumita, and youngest son Sudip. By the grace of the Almighty, all the three have pursued higher education and are actively engaged in teaching and research at esteemed educational institutions in India. As a father, the author finds immense satisfaction in the fact that none of them was drawn to the allure of foreign lands. Instead, they chose to serve their motherland. They are all humble, unassuming, and compassionate individuals, embodying admirable qualities such as honesty and sensitivity. A detailed account of their academic journeys and achievements follows.

Eldest Child: Subhas

Prof. Subhas Chandra Misra

Subhas received his education in English medium from the sixth to tenth grades at Hijli Higher Secondary School within the IIT Kharagpur campus. After completing his secondary education, he pursued higher secondary studies at the Kendriya Vidyalaya of IIT Kharagpur. Excelling in his twelfth-grade examinations, he took the Engineering and Medical Common Entrance Test (EAMCET) in Andhra Pradesh, where he secured a good rank.

Subhas went on to complete his B.E. in Electronics and

Communication Engineering from Andhra University College of Engineering, Visakhapatnam, one of the most prestigious government engineering institutions in Andhra Pradesh. Adjusting to a new environment, language, and cuisine was initially challenging, but he adapted well, even acquiring a reasonable proficiency in Telugu.

Following his undergraduate studies, he pursued an *M.Tech. in Computer Science and Data Processing* from IIT Kharagpur. Shortly thereafter, he began his professional career as an Assistant Executive Engineer at Indian Telephone Industries (ITI) in Mankapur, Uttar Pradesh, where he worked for a year and a half. However, his passion for higher education remained unwavering. Receiving profuse encouragements from his siblings, Sumita and Sudip, as well as his parents to pursue higher studies, he applied to multiple Canadian universities. He earned his *Master of Computer Science with a scholarship from the University of New Brunswick, Fredericton, Canada*, and subsequently completed a Ph.D. in *Information Systems Management* from the Sprott School of Business at *Carleton University in Ottawa*, an institution ranked among the best in Canada.

After obtaining his Ph.D., Subhas continued his academic pursuits as a *Postdoctoral Fellow at Harvard University, USA*, under the prestigious *NSERC Fellowship programme*. At that time, Harvard was ranked the number one university globally, according to the U.S. News and World Report (October 25, 2022). Despite opportunities abroad, Subhas made the decision to return to India permanently, aspiring to teach and conduct research at some esteemed institution, preferably an IIT. He applied for the post of Assistant Professor in the Industrial Management Engineering (IME) Department at IIT Kanpur. His seminar and interview were conducted virtually due to his stay abroad at that time. The selection process involved rigorous scrutiny by the Director of IIT Kanpur, the Head of the IME Department, and eminent external experts from leading business schools. Additionally, IIT Kanpur sought evaluations of his research publications from several experts worldwide before finalizing the selection.

In early 2008, while still at Harvard, Subhas was offered the position at IIT Kanpur. He was granted a few months for transition and finally joined as an Assistant Professor. His teaching methods quickly gained recognition, earning him popularity among students. After a few years, he was promoted to Associate Professor following another round of assessment by distinguished academicians.

Beyond teaching and research, Subhas has actively contributed to administrative responsibilities at IIT Kanpur. He served as a hostel warden for a few years. Moreover, he travelled to Ethiopia to teach a management course and successfully managed multiple research projects as Principal Investigator/Co-Principal Investigator. He also participated in an Indo-French collaborative research initiative, which led to his academic visit to France. His contributions have been acknowledged both nationally and internationally.

Subhas was elected a Fellow of several prestigious institutions, including:

- Institution of Engineering and Technology (UK),
- British Computer Society (London),
- Royal Society of Arts, Manufacture and Commerce (London),
- Institution of Engineers (India),
- Institution of Electronics and Telecommunication Engineers (New Delhi),
- Royal Society of Public Health (RSPH) in London for his significant research contributions in Personalized Healthcare Management.

In 2023, he along with others developed an innovative technology for continuous lung health monitoring.

His research interests span over multiple areas, including Project Management, Business Process Management, Change and Risk Management, Analytics, Supply Chain, IT Management, and Artificial Intelligence applications to Machine Learning, Deep Learning, and the Internet of Things. He has published 5 books and approximately 180 research papers in reputed international journals. Under his guidance, 15 research scholars have earned Ph.D. degrees. Most of them have secured faculty positions at IITs and other prestigious institutions. Additionally, around 30 students have completed their M.Tech. theses under his mentorship. He has also served as Managing Editor and Associate Editor for various international journals.

Considering all his strong credentials, a few years ago Subhas was promoted to the position of Professor at IIT Kanpur. His teaching excellence is evident from the positive student feedback he consistently receives, often earning him the Senate Citation (signed by the Director/Senate Chairman). On a Teachers' Day (September 5, 2022), he was honoured with the "Excellence-in-Teaching Award" by IIT Kanpur. In 2019, he was ranked among the world's top 2% of scientists by a Stanford University research group.

Subhas married *Sulagna*, daughter of Dr. Sachin Chatterji from Nabadweep. Sulagna holds a Master's degree and efficiently manages household responsibilities. After their marriage, she quickly became fluent in Hindi while residing on the IIT Kanpur campus. They have two children: *Devarati*, a first-year B.Tech. student at the Department of Computer Science and Engineering, SRM Institute of Science and Technology, Kattankulathur, Chennai and *Devapratim*, a ninth-grade student at Kendriya Vidyalaya, IIT Kanpur. Both have received many national and international accolades.

Devarati has been awarded the Manak Inspire Award of Rs. 10,000/- from the Department of Science and Technology, Government of India (2020–21), and secured third place in the Hindi Olympiad conducted by the Ministry of Electronics and Information Technology (2020–21). She also achieved second place nationally in the CSC Olympiad for Physics, Chemistry, and Mathematics in 2023.

Devapratim has won multiple awards, including second place in the National Science Olympiad (2019–20) and National English Olympiad (2021–22), receiving valuable prizes from the Government of India. Additionally, in the 2019–20 academic year, he secured first place internationally in the Science Olympiad Foundation (SOF) competition, earning a cash prize of Rs. 50,000 and a gold medal. In 2023, he attained an All India Rank of 6th in the Narayana Scholastic Aptitude Test (NSAT).

Alongside academics, Devarati learns Bengali and Hindi devotional songs, while Devapratim trains in Taekwondo, badminton, and violin. He was also selected to play basketball at the national level for the Lucknow region KVS team in 2024.

The journey of Subhas to success has been fraught with challenges. He has silently persevered, demonstrating immense patience and resilience. By the grace of the Almighty, he has attained commendable achievements. His humility, honesty and benevolent nature have earned him great admiration within his academic and social circles. His unwavering positivity continues to endear him to his peers and students alike.

Second Child: Sumita

Sumita is a faculty and a researcher at the School of Advanced Materials, Green Energy, and Sensor Systems at the Indian Institute of Engineering Science and Technology (IIEST) Shibpur (formerly, the famous Bengal Engineering

College). After earning her B.Sc. (Physics Hons) with Distinction and M.Sc. in Physics, she pursued her M.Tech in Material Science from the Indian Institute of Technology Kharagpur.

Prof. (Ms.) Sumita Mukhopadhyay (Misra)

Following this, she obtained her Ph.D. from the Energy Research Unit of the Indian Association for the Cultivation of Science Kolkata, conducting research on solar cells. She has been actively involved in research at this globally renowned Institution for many years and is considered *a pioneer in solar energy research within the country.*

Since the establishment of the Centre of Excellence in Unconventional Energy at IIEST Shibpur, Sumita has been actively engaged in research along with teaching in the Centre. Over the past decade, in addition to supervising research for five Ph.D. students and many M.Tech students, she played a key role in launching the postgraduate curriculum on Renewable Energy at IIEST. Her research, funded by various central research organizations, is regularly published in leading international research journals. She has to her credit 66 research papers published in International Journals, 65 international conference papers and 3 book chapters.

In collaboration with other researchers, Sumita developed an innovative technique titled *"Surface Texturization of Glass to Improve Light Management in Superstrate Type Thin Film Solar Cells"*, and *"Textured glass substrate for thin solar cell"*. These two innovations were granted patent by the Government of India in 2023, with sponsorship from the National Institute of Solar Energy.

She has presented research papers at prominent scientific conferences across India and Internationally, including countries like Italy and France. In recognition of her continuous success in the field of education, Sumita has been honoured with various national and international awards. Notably, she holds honourary fellowships from prestigious organizations such as:

- *The Institute of Engineering and Technology (IET, UK)*
- *Royal Society of Arts, Manufacture and Commerce (RSA, UK)*
- *The Institute of Electronics and Telecommunications Engineering (IETE, India)*

Despite her busy professional life, Sumita is also highly attentive and responsible towards her family.

Her husband, Dr. Achintya Mukhopadhyay, is a professor in the Mechanical Engineering Department at Jadavpur University. In addition to his work at Jadavpur University, Achintya has taught and conducted research at institutions like IIT Madras, the University of Illinois at Chicago (USA), and the Technical University of Munich (Germany). His teaching and research focus mainly on Thermal Science and Combustion Science and Technology, earning him prestigious honours such as the *Humboldt Fellowship (Germany), the INSA Teacher Award from the Indian National Science Academy, the Fellowship of the National Academy of Sciences, India, and an Honorary Fellowship from the West Bengal Academy of Science and Technology.*

Their only daughter, *Supurna* has passed her Class 12 examination from CISCE Board with 93% marks from Garden High School, Kolkata securing an all India position of within top 30. Earlier she had passed ICSE (Class 10 examination of CISCE Board) in 2022 securing 97.2% marks and had achieved an all India rank of 14. She is currently a first year B.Tech. Student at the Department of Mechanical Engineering, Thapar Institute of Engineering and Technology, Punjab. In addition to her academic success, she has demonstrated exceptional talent in literature, dance, music, recitation, painting and sports. Her performances in dance, music, recitation and painting at various events, both at her school and public functions have won her many awards and accolades. She also has a passion for writing and has got several of her works published.

For her skills in fine arts, she has regularly won distinction and medals from the Calcutta Talent Search School. She was awarded First position in the art competition organized by the Calcutta Talent Search. Her painting was featured in TeleKIDS, the children's newspaper by the Telegraph Group, at the tender age of five. She also received the best of training in Indian Classical Music (for 10 years) and Indian Classical Dance (for 12 years) from celebrated teachers of leading institutions like Dakshinee (which has remained a centre of excellence in Rabindra sangeet for over 50 years), Udayan (headed by celebrated artist, Mamata Shankar) and Kalamandalam (headed by veteran exponent of dance, Thankamani Kutty). She has excelled in a number of National and International Olympiads winning several Gold, Silver and Bronze medals and securing top ranks at both national and international levels. She has also been selected as an Asset Talent Search Scholar due to her extraordinary performance in the ASSET evaluation, held in schools all over the world. Supurna won the second prize in an inter school science event competing against students from reputed schools from all over West Bengal, which tested her scientific, oratory and artistic skills.

Supurna is also an accomplished sportsperson, having won gold medals in athletic events at Annual Sports in her school and has played a stellar role in making her team the Kho Kho champion. She has also excelled in inter-club swimming competitions, competing against renowned swimming training clubs from Kolkata.

Adventure-loving Supurna had participated in numerous nature study and rock climbing camps, receiving training in these activities before she was even 10 years old.

Creative Supurna always spends her leisure time experimenting with various handcrafts to create home decor and ornamental items. She enjoys cooking and loves experimenting with making innovative dishes. For her all-round abilities and excellent leadership qualities, she was first appointed a Prefect and then elevated to the post of a Senior Prefect in her school.

Worth mentioning, Supurna possesses a charming personality and is adored by everyone for her sweet and humble nature.

Youngest Child: Sudip

Prof. Sudip Misra

Sudip commenced his education at St. Agnes Primary School on the IIT Kharagpur campus until the fourth grade and subsequently continued his secondary and higher secondary studies at Kendriya Vidyalaya, IIT Kharagpur. After completing his undergraduate studies in Applied Geology at IIT Kharagpur, he pursued a Master's degree in Computer Science at the University of New Brunswick, Fredericton, Canada. He then did his *Ph.D. in Computer Science from Carleton University*, Ottawa, Canada, in 2006. *His doctoral thesis was recognized as the best across all departments at Carleton University*, earning him the *University Outstanding Graduate Student Award (Doctoral Level)* and the prestigious *Governor General's Academic Gold Medal* in the same year.

Following his doctorate, Sudip engaged in postdoctoral research as an *NSERC Fellow at Cornell University and Yale University in the United States*. Between 2005 and 2007, he also served as an *Adjunct Professor* in the Computer Science Department at Ryerson University, Toronto. During his time in Canada, he accumulated substantial *industrial experience* by working in various software industries alongside his academic pursuits.

Despite achieving success in North America, Sudip chose to return to India for two key reasons: his feeling of discomfort with Western society and culture and his deep-seated desire to serve his motherland. With a strong connection to his homeland and family, he applied for teaching positions at several IITs and NITs. During a brief visit to India, he was invited to deliver seminar lectures at a few IITs, including IIT Kharagpur. Subsequently, he was interviewed virtually via Skype and was offered Assistant Professor positions at IIT Kharagpur, IIT Guwahati, and IIT Roorkee. Some of these institutions even proposed higher pay, and NIT Calicut considered offering him a full professorship based on his impressive research credentials. Ultimately, Sudip chose to join IIT Kharagpur as an Assistant Professor in 2007, after completing his postdoctoral research programme at Yale University, USA.

From the outset of his tenure at IIT Kharagpur, Sudip engaged in teaching, research, and administrative responsibilities. His primary research areas include *Wireless Sensor Networks and the Internet of Things (IoT).* He is the *Director and Co-Founder of the IoT startup Sensor Drops Networks Private Limited.* To date, he has published over *500* research papers in prestigious international journals. Additionally, he co-authored a *white paper* in collaboration with his Indian and Chinese colleagues. The title of the white paper is "AIoT Healthcare: A cooperative Blueprint in China and India" and it was published by the China Branch of BRICS Institute for Future Networks. He has been mentoring research scholars since the beginning of his academic career and has earned many national and international awards within a short period.

Sudip was promoted to Associate Professor in February 2013 and to Professor in February 2018 at IIT Kharagpur. Mother Jagadamba had prepared him for these positions, and by Her grace, he secured these positions without much difficulty. Swami Vivekananda often encouraged the youth to have faith in themselves and in God. Sudip seems to have followed this invaluable advice. Through tireless efforts and Mother's blessings, he has received several awards and recognitions from various academic and professional bodies in India and abroad. A brief summary of these honours is provided below, as they may act as a source of inspiration for future generations directly/indirectly.

- At the 2012 GLOBECOM conference held in California, USA, Sudip received the "IEEE Comsoc Asia Pacific Outstanding Young Researcher Award" from the Institute of Electrical and Electronics Engineers (IEEE). He has also received the 'Young Scientist Award' from the National Academy of Sciences (NASI), the 'Young Systems Scientist Award' from the Systems Society of India, and the 'Young Engineer Award' from the Institution of Engineers, India. In 2008, Sudip was awarded the "Swarna Jayanti Puraskar" (Golden Jubilee Award) by the National Academy of Sciences, India (NASI) and the 'Biman Bihari Sen Memorial Award' by the Institution of Electronics and Communication Engineers (India), New Delhi for his pioneering contributions to Emerging Communication Technology. The same year, he received the "Samsung Innovation Award."
- In 2018, the then Minister of Human Resource Development (MHRD), Shri Prakash Javadekar, presented Sudip with the 'Careers 360 Outstanding Faculty Award' in Computer Science. In 2018, under Sudip's guidance, his students developed a battery-less IoT sensing node to aid farmers in agriculture. In recognition of this innovative research, the President of

India awarded them the Technological Innovation Award named after Mahatma Gandhi. For his 'significant contributions to research and his leadership role in advancing the engineering profession in India', Sudip received the '*Abdul Kalam Technology Innovation National Fellowship*', from the Indian National Academy of Engineering (INAE, New Delhi) in 2019.

- An article in The Hindu, a national daily, reported on March 5, 2017, about the low-cost unmanned aerial drone developed by Sudip and his research team, which can be used in natural disasters and military operations. The 'AmbuSens System' developed by Sudip and his research students was broadcasted on the ETV Bangla television channel and in various national newspapers (includingTimes of India, Hindustan Times, Deccan Herald, Indian Express, Economic Times, Enadu, and Business Standard) on June 2–3, 2017.
- Sudip was elected a Fellow of the National Academy of Sciences, India (NASI) in 2017, a Fellow of the Indian National Academy of Engineering, New Delhi in 2020, a Fellow of the Institution of Electronics and Telecommunication Engineers (IETE), New Delhi in 2018 and a Fellow of the West Bengal Academy of Science and Technology (WAST) in 2023.
- Among international professional organizations, he was elected a Fellow of the Institution of Engineering and Technology (UK) in 2018, the British Computer Society (BCS) and the Royal Society of Public Health (RSPH) in 2019. *Sudip was elected an IEEE Fellow in 2021.*
- In 2012, at a prestigious event called The Court, the Director of IIT Kharagpur specially congratulated Sudip for his excellence in research. In 2021, Sudip was elected a *Distinguished Member of the the Association for Computing Machinery (ACM),* a renowned international scientific and industrial computer society based in New York. For the academic year 2020–2021, he was selected as an IEEE Communications Society (ComSoc) *Distinguished Lecturer.* Sudip has been invited to deliver lectures at international conferences and universities worldwide, on several occasions, as the Chief Guest. He serves as an editor/associate editor for several prestigious international journals, including those published by IEEE. He held the positions of Vice Chair (Awards) of IEEE India Council and Council Member of ACM India.

He has also been *recognized with the ACM India Outstanding Contributions to Computing Education (OCCE) Award in 2023*. The selection committee, comprising international experts, recognized Sudip for his significant contributions to computing education. The ACM India OCCE Award recognizes individuals who have made fundamental, innovative and impactful contributions to computing education in India. The award carries a prize of Rs. 7 lakhs, sponsored by *Microsoft Research India.* Sudip was recognized "*For impactful contributions to IoT and Networks education through online courses, textbooks, short term courses, research and laboratory development*" (https://www.acm.org/articles/acm-india-bulletins/2023/occe-2023-misra).

- Sudip has also received many awards and recognition from IIT Kharagpur, including the '*Faculty Excellence Award*' at the Associate Professor level in 2017 and the Professor level in 2022. He received a series of Best Paper Awards at various International Conferences including the Best Paper Award, IEEE GLOBECOM 2023, SAC Tracks, Kuala Lumpur, 2023. In the same year, he also *received the MS Ramanujan Lecture Award,* Institution of Engineers India, at the Annual Convention of Computer Engineers, Salem, 2023. In 2025, Sudip has been selected as a *Chair Professor of the Indian National Academy Engineering (INAE), New Delhi* for a period of three years.
- In December 2024, he has *earned the international recognition of being elected to highly prestigious honourary Fellowship of ACM, New York, USA (Association for Computing Machinary).* The Fellows induction ceremony was held on June 14, 2025 in *San Franscisco, California, USA at the ACM Awards Banquet. Sudip had been invited to participate in the said induction ceremony. But he had to cancel his journey at the last moment and the documents have been sent to him by postal service.*

Sudip has authored *seven textbooks/reference books* on IoT and related topics in Networks, published by Cambridge University Press, Wiley, CRC Press, and Springer. He has also edited multiple books in these areas. These books are widely used not only in India but abroad.

Sudip is the only academic from India among the 55 fellows selected this year for his significant contribution to intelligent service-centric sensing and sustainable data processing in large scale IoT networks.

The faculty and alumni of the Institute are very joyous at this astounding achievement of Sudip particularly because he is the first to bring this accolade to IIT Kharagpur. On this occasion, IIT Kharagpur made an official announcement stating:

> *"IIT Kharagpur is proud to share that Prof. Sudip Misra from Department of Computer Science and Engineering has been elected as a Fellow of the prestigious Association for Computing Machinery (ACM), the prime Computing Association in the World."*

Most of the National newspapers of India published the news prominently in February 2025. The caption of the news in The Times of India dated 11th February was "IIT-Kgp Prof. now fellow of global computing body", while the news came in The Statesman as "IIT Kharagpur Professor elected ACM Fellow for 2024."

About Sudip's achievement and prestigious recognition, on February 13, 2025, The Economic Times wrote "A senior IIT-Kharagpur professor has been selected as a Fellow of the Association for Computing Machinery (ACM), becoming the only one to be Indian out of 55 fellows this year."

The National Daily, 'Hindustan Samachar' on 12th February 2025, wrote, "In a remarkable achievement for Indian academia, Professor Sudip Misra from IIT-Kharagpur has been named a Fellow of the Association for Computing Machinery (ACM). Out of the 55 distinguished fellows selected globally in 2025, he is the only one from India, the Institute announced in a statement."

In an email dated March 10, 2025, Shrimat Swami Gautamananda, President, Ramakrishna Math & Ramakrishna Mission wrote to the author, "I am glad at the great achievements achieved by your dear son, Sudip Misra. I convey my congratulations and blessings to him. My blessings to you and all others in your family. My prayers to Sri Ramakrishna to shower his blessings on him for onward and upward progress in the years to come...."

Sudip is always ready to help his students. He is a very compassionate person. If a family member is sick, he prioritizes their treatment and care.

In August 2025, Sudip was appointed Associate Dean, Infrastructure—Electrical, Electronics & Computing, IIT Kharagpur for a period of three years. On 18th August 2025 at the Inaugural Session of the Platinum Jubilee celebrations of IIT Kharagpur Sudip received the Institute Chair Professor Award 2025 for "Outstanding Contributions towards Teaching, Research and Institutional Development".

Sudip's wife, Satamita, holds an M.Sc. degree in Botany. They have one son and one daughter. Their son, Devadeep, is currently a twelfth-grade student at DAV Model School on the IIT Campus in Kharagpur. He is also *very interested in sports, showing enthusiasm for various outdoor games, including football and cricket.* In the 'IIT KGP Children Sports Meet 2023' organized by IIT Kharagpur, Devadeep won the first prize in the football competition and third prize in the Discus Throw competition. Although he is a student of English medium, he can recite Bengali poems. He also can sing and play music. He is a cheerful boy with a keen interest in academics. In the academic year 2020–21, he *secured first place at the national level (AIR-1) in the Mathematics Olympiad conducted by the Ministry of Electronics and Information Technology Common Services Centre (C.S.C.)* and received an electric bicycle as a prize. In the academic year 2019–20, he *secured third place at the national level (AIR-3) in the English Olympiad organized by C.S.C.* Additionally, he achieved a zonal rank of 2 in the International Social Studies Olympiad conducted by SOF in 2020–21 and *qualified for the Second Level of the INSPIRE Mayank Awards by the Department of Science and Technology, Government of India,* in the academic year 2019–20. In 2022–23, *Devadeep won the first runner-up (second prize) trophy and a cheque for Rs. 30,000 in the Young Scientist India (YSI) Challenge competition organized by Space Kidz India. The competition consisted of three stages, with the final round held at the Russian Cultural Centre in Chennai* on May 3–4, 2023. Participants were required to demonstrate and explain their innovative projects to the judges and give a brief extempore speech on the subject of their invention. The primary objective of this competition was to foster innovative research attitudes among school students in various scientific and technological fields. *Devadeep invented a "Shock Alarm Band" as part of his innovative project, designed to alert users to potential electrical hazards and prevent electric shock.*

Sudip's daughter, *Devadrita, is in the sixth grade* at DAV Model School on the IIT Campus. She is skilled in *dance and music.*

CHAPTER 14

The Extended Family

For a teacher, family extends far beyond just parents, spouse, and children. In the author's view, his family comprises countless students accumulated over nearly six decades of teaching. Although it is difficult to quantify exactly how many students he has taught, many have gone on to become directors, vice-chancellors, deans, and heads of departments at various IITs/Universities and other institutions. Several of his students have also received various prestigious awards and have been elected fellows of national and international Academic/Professional Bodies. The author has supervised 30 Ph.D. students, as listed below. Any omissions are inadvertent, and he extends his apologies for any oversights.

List of Doctoral Students Supervised by the Author

1. Dr. Radhamadhav Achari, Ph.D., Professor, Bihar Educational Service (Former faculty at various state government colleges in Bihar).
2. Dr. Sachindranath Maiti, Ph.D., Associate Professor, Jhargram Raj College, Jhargram/Barasat Government College, Kolkata.
3. Dr. Santabrata Chakrabarti, Ph.D., Professor, Department of Mathematics, Visva-Bharati University, Santiniketan.
4. Dr. Kasturi Ray Chowdhury (Sen), Ph.D., New Jersey, USA.
5. Dr. V.V.T.N. Murthy, Ph.D., USA.
6. Dr. Minati Mishra (Samanta Ray), Ph.D., Associate Professor, Odisha Educational Service.
7. Dr. Subhas Samanta, Ph.D., Associate Professor, Midnapore College.
8. Dr. Salam Ibosana Singh, Ph.D., Former Associate Professor, Manipur University, Imphal, Manipur.
9. Dr. Sukhendu Bikas Kar, Ph.D., Headmaster, Tikrapara Higher Secondary School.

10. Dr. Saktipada Nanda, Ph.D., Associate Professor, Sree Chaitanya College, Habra, West Bengal.
11. Dr. Gopal Chandra Bera, Ph.D., Principal, Midnapore College (Autonomous).
12. Dr. B.K. Sahu, Ph.D., Faculty, Gandhi Mahavidyalaya, Rourkela, Odisha.
13. Dr. Bidyut Kanti Kar, Ph.D.
14. Dr. Sudhanshu Ray, Ph.D., IIT Kharagpur.
15. Dr. Mrityunjay Kumar Patra, Ph.D., Associate Professor, Pingla Thana Mahavidyalaya, West Midnapore.
16. Dr. Sukumar Chandra, Ph.D., Principal, Pingla Thana Mahavidyalaya, West Midnapore.
17. Dr. Sanjay Kumar Pandey, Ph.D., Professor and Head, Department of Mathematical Sciences, IIT (BHU), Varanasi, Uttar Pradesh.
18. Dr. Gopal Chandra Sheet, Ph.D., Professor, Department of Mathematics, Jadavpur University, Kolkata.
19. Dr. Sushil Kumar Ghosh, Ph.D., Associate Professor, Garhbeta College, West Midnapore.
20. Dr. Aniruddha Sinha, Ph.D., Associate Professor, Palpara Yogoda Satsang Mahavidyalaya, East Midnapore.
21. Dr. Somnath Maiti, Ph.D., Assistant Professor, LNM Institute of Information Technology, Jaipur, Rajasthan.
22. Dr. S. Mahapatra, Ph.D.
23. Dr. A. Bhattacharya, Ph.D.
24. Dr. S.D. Adhikari, Ph.D., Former Assistant Professor, SOA University.
25. Dr. Biswajit Mallik, Ph.D., Assistant Professor, Department of Mathematics, Allahabad University (Central University), Uttar Pradesh.
26. Dr. S. Dandapat, Ph.D., Kolkata.
27. Dr. Motahar Reza, Ph.D., Associate Professor & Head, Department of Mathematics, GITAM University, Hyderabad, Telangana.
28. Dr. Biswajit Pal, Ph.D.
29. Dr. Narayan Chandra Chattopadhyay, Ph.D., Associate Professor, Seva Bharati Mahavidyalaya, West Bengal.
30. Dr. Pratima Panigrahi, Ph.D., Professor, Department of Mathematics, IIT Kharagpur (Postdoctoral Fellow).

Among these individuals, Dr. Kasturi Ray Chowdhury and Dr. V.V.T.N. Murthy have established themselves in various organizations in U.S.A. Their children also studied in the United States and are now well-established there.

Legacy

Many of the author's students have advanced to leadership roles in diverse industries. Internationally, former students have assumed senior positions in prominent institutions. In India and abroad, the relationship between Ph.D. supervisors and their students often mirrors that of a parent and child. For example, in Germany, supervisors are called "Doktorvater" (Doctor Father), underscoring a paternal bond. In India, the relationship is sometimes described as that of a "Friend-Philosopher-Guide." Supervisors frequently provide support beyond academics, assisting with personal challenges, health issues, or financial needs, thereby forging lifelong bonds.

During the early years of his teaching career, the minimal age gap between the author and his postgraduate students fostered close friendships. Several of his M.Sc. and Ph.D. students were either older or contemporaries, leading to enduring personal relationships. Despite geographic distances, many students have maintained contact with the author via email, bringing him immense joy.

Dr. Sanjay Kumar Pandey and His Contributions in Biofluid Dynamics

Dr. Sanjay Kumar Pandey, a Professor and Head of the Department of Mathematical Sciences at IIT (BHU), conducted research on "Peristaltic Flows of Physiological Fluids" for his Ph.D. from IIT Kharagpur under the supervision of the author. Under Dr. Pandey's supervision, nine students have earned their Ph.Ds, and another has done post-doctoral work. One of his former students, Dr. Dharmendra Tripathi, is now an Associate Professor and Dean (Research and Consultancy) at NIT, Uttarakhand, having completed his Ph.D. under Dr. Pandey. Additionally, six students pursued Ph.Ds in Biofluid Dynamics under Dr. Tripathi's guidance. Dr. Pandey himself was a Ph.D. student under the author, who had begun his research in this captivating field while he was a Humboldt Fellow at the Technical University of Hannover, working with Prof. Oskar Mahrenholtz. A significant part of the author's D.Sc. thesis involved mathematical modelling and analysis of various biomechanics problems, continuing his academic legacy.

Dr. Santabrata Chakrabarti and the Biomechanics Legacy

The author's third Ph.D. student, Dr. Santabrata Chakrabarti, conducted his doctoral research on the "Biomechanics of Head Injury." After submitting his thesis, he continued to explore various problems on "Blood Flow in Atherosclerotic Arteries" with the author's guidance, facilitated by a CSIR research associateship. Later, as he began supervising Ph.D. students at Visva-Bharati University, he directed research towards blood flow mechanics and introduced an elective course in biomathematics for M.Sc. students, for which the author served as an external examiner for many years. Under Dr. Chakrabarti's mentorship, ten students completed their Ph.Ds in biomechanics/biomathematics. Prashanta Kumar Mandal, who initially sought the author's supervision for a Ph.D. in biomechanics at IIT Kharagpur, at the advice of the author, finally did his degree under Dr. Chakrabarti at Visva-Bharati University and went on to become a professor and head of the mathematics department in Viswabharati. Lakshmi Narayan Guin did Ph.D. under the supervision of Dr. Mandal and is currently a faculty at the Department of Mathematics at Viswabharati. This multi-generational legacy—author, Santabrata, Prashanta, and Lakshmi Narayan Guin—was highlighted by the then Head of Mathematics Department in the same University. Prof. Prashanta Chatterjee, himself was also a student of the author during his M.Sc. at IIT Kharagpur.

Dr. Gopal Chandra Shit's Journey in Physiological Fluid Dynamics

Another student, Dr. Gopal Chandra Shit, worked for his Ph.D. in physiological fluid dynamics under the supervision of the author and received the degree in 2008. He is now a professor in the Department of Mathematics at Jadavpur University. Known for his dynamic personality and adept teaching, Dr. Shit received an award in 2009 for the best research paper presentation in the Mathematical Science Section at the Indian Science Congress Association (ISCA). He was also honoured as a BOYSCAST Fellow by the Indian government (DST), enabling him to conduct advanced research at Paris XII University during the 2010–11 academic year. Dr. Shit has visited several European universities, published over 100 research papers, and supervised ten Ph.D. students, many of whom now teach in and around Kolkata. One of his students is currently engaged in postdoctoral research at the University of Colorado, Boulder, USA. Additionally, he has served as a postdoctoral fellow at the Indian Institute of Science, Bangalore, and a visiting associate at the

Institute of Mathematical Sciences, Chennai, while completing seven research projects sponsored by DST and UGC. Thus, Professor Gopal Chandra Shit continues the author's legacy.

Dr. Salam Ibosana Singh: A Tale of Excellence and Tragedy

Dr. Salam Ibosana Singh, a native of Manipur, who was a doctoral student of the author excelled in both mathematics and the physiological sciences related to cardiovascular dynamics through persistent efforts and dedication. His high-quality research, published in esteemed international journals, earned him recognition early in his career. After receiving his Ph.D., Ibosana joined the Department of Mathematics at Manipur University as an Assistant Professor. Tragically, his promising career was cut short by a neurological disease, despite receiving treatment at premier institutions like the National Institute of Mental Health and Neurosciences (NIMHANS) in Bangalore and the All India Institute of Medical Sciences (AIIMS) in New Delhi. The author recalls with deep emotion Ibosana's profound respect and affection—he often referred to the author as "Guru." One memorable instance was when Ibosana personally prepared a meal of fish curry and Bengali dishes for the author during a seminar visit to Manipur University. Although Dr. Singh worked at the university for only four years, during which he guided two Ph.D. students, his untimely death left an indelible impact on all who knew him.

Other Notable Contributions and Relationships

The author's most other Ph.D. students now serve as educators in government institutions. For instance, Dr. Radhamadhav Achari retired from the Bihar Educational Service after a distinguished career of teaching in various engineering institutions, while Dr. Sachindranath Maiti, another early Ph.D. student in Mathematical Thermoelasticity, retired from the West Bengal Educational Service after teaching at different colleges such as Jhargram Raj College and Barasat Government College. Dr. Minati Mishra (Samanta Ray) served in Odisha's government colleges and is now retired. Her husband, Dr. Samanta Ray, is a practicing physician. Minati visited the author several times in Bhubaneswar and Kharagpur, even after she left Kharagpur on completion of her Ph.D.

Shri Gopal Chandra Bera, who completed an M.Sc. in Physics and a Ph.D. in Applied Mathematics on "Fracture and Remodelling of Bones" under the author, recently retired from the position of Principal of Midnapore

College (Autonomous). Known for his administrative acumen, he has built a strong reputation in teaching. Similarly, Dr. Sukumar Chandra, who earned his Ph.D. on "Electro-osmotic Flow" under the author, is currently the Principal of Pingla Thana Mahavidyalaya in West Midnapore, after teaching Physics at Sabang College for a number of years.

Professor Subhas Samanta, another former student who completed his Ph.D. in Applied Mathematics under the author, has maintained a close relationship with the author. Subhas has supervised several students to their Ph.D. completion, and many of the author's other research students have continued to publish influential research. Notable among them are Dr. Sushil Kumar Ghosh, Dr. Aniruddha Sinha, Dr. Somnath Maiti, Dr. Biswajit Mallik (Assistant Professor at Allahabad University), Dr. Motahar Reza (Professor at GITAM University, Hyderabad), Dr. Saktipada Nanda, Dr. Sukhendu Bikas Kar, and Dr. S.D. Adhikari.

Among the many student-friends who have maintained enduring relationships with the author are Professors Subhash Samanta, Narayan Chattopadhyay, Santabrata Chakrabarti, Sanjay Kumar Pandey, Gopal Chandra Sheet, Aniruddha Sinha, Motahar Reza, and Biswajit Mallik. Particularly, Professors Subhash Samanta and Narayan Chattopadhyay share a close bond with the author's family due to their minimal age difference with the author. Many of these students continue to offer assistance whenever needed, reinforcing the lasting legacy of their mentor..

CHAPTER 15

Some Selected Works Published Previously

PROPER EDUCATION

[Transcription of the valuable speech delivered by Dr. Jagadis Chandra Misra, Professor, Department of Mathematics, IIT, Kharagpur, as the Chief Guest at the Annual Convocation (1995–96) of Shri Ramakrishna Mission Vidyabhavan, Medinipur. During his student years, this illustrious figure in the field of education resided at the Ramakrishna Mission Vidyamandira, Belur Math, and the Ramakrishna Mission Kolkata Vidyarthi Ashrama in Belgharia. Naturally, the guidance of the monks and the spiritual environment helped him advance along the path of righteousness.]

—Editor, Unmesh

Swami Vivekananda's educational philosophy offers a model not only for India but for the entire world. Education should be a process of self-discovery, where students advance through self-determination while teachers serve as facilitators rather than enforcers. Swami Vivekananda aptly compared this process to nurturing a sapling, emphasizing that education should build character above all else.

The ultimate goal of education should be to ensure that the joy of childhood does not fade into the despair of youth, and that the enthusiasm of youth does not lead to a burdensome old age. Vocational education, though essential, is merely a subset of the broader educational spectrum. While subjects such as science, literature, and philosophy contribute to intellectual growth, the true essence of education lies in cultivating humanity and moral integrity.

Moral Education: An Urgent Necessity

Although students today exhibit remarkable intellectual advancement compared to previous generations, there has been an alarming decline in moral values. Therefore, the urgent need of the hour is moral education. As a poet once remarked, "When violence departs from the world, every sword shall turn into wood." An education system that fosters selfishness, jealousy, and violence, promotes excessive patriotism at the cost of other nations, or gives rise to religious fanaticism while disregarding other faiths, is fundamentally flawed.

In ancient times, the *Gurukul* system emphasized holistic education, integrating moral and spiritual wisdom. While modern education has transitioned to institutionalized schooling, Ramakrishna Mission institutions strive to preserve the spirit of the *Gurukul* tradition by instilling cultural values and ethics alongside contemporary knowledge. This balanced approach is essential for proper education.

At the same time, physical fitness must be prioritized. Swami Vivekananda's words, often reiterated by Swami Tejasananda, Principal of Ramakrishna Mission Vidyamandira (Belur Math) at our time, emphasize the need for "muscles of iron and nerves of steel." Physical vigour complements intellectual and moral strength, making students more capable of contributing to society. Swami Tejasananda himself encouraged students to engage in sports, sometimes even participating in games like football and volleyball.

The Importance of Self-Control

In Vedic society, self-control was instilled in students from an early age. Unfortunately, modern misconceptions have led many to believe that self-discipline is required only for religious practitioners. This notion is incorrect; self-control is vital for everyone. The best way to calm the restless mind is through the proper application of vital energy. Emotional turbulence depletes this energy, making it crucial to remain calm and composed in all situations. Engaging in meaningful discussions, fostering respect for all religions, and embracing a sense of universal kinship can lead to both personal and global harmony.

Spiritual Insights on Life and Karma

The great spiritual luminaries of India have delved deeply into the nature of existence and arrived at profound truths listed below:

1. Every living being undergoes countless rebirths, assuming different physical forms after the demise of the previous one to experience the sensory pleasures of the world.

2. The experiences of past lives shape the body and mind of the next incarnation, compelling individuals to reap the consequences of their prior actions.
3. Upon death, only the gross body is destroyed, while the accumulated good and bad '*sanskaras*' remain within the subtle body-commonly referred to as 'fate' or 'destiny.'
4. Each individual is solely responsible for his/her actions and must bear the consequences of past deeds.
5. A proper understanding of the laws of karma and judicious application of these principles can help avoid sufferings and wrongdoings.

Recognizing these spiritual truths can significantly reduce mental unrest and anxiety. Across the world, conflicts arise from differences in race, caste, culture, and traditions. Unfortunately, many mistakenly associate these conflicts with religion, fostering fear and misunderstanding. However, the essence of true spirituality lies in recognizing the unity of all beings.

The Bhagavad Gita (18.61) states: *"Ishvarah sarva-bhutanam hrid-deshe Arjuna tisthati, Bhramayan sarva-bhutani yantrarudhani mayaya."*

("The Supreme Lord dwells in the hearts of all living beings, O Arjuna. According to their karmas, He directs the wanderings of souls, who are seated on a machine made of material energy.")

This universal realization must be cultivated from the student life itself, as it forms the foundation of personal, social, and national ethics—ultimately, the bedrock of civilization. To reinforce this foundation, we must internalize Swami Vivekananda's immortal words:

"You say I have done something tangible. If that is true, remember that I was once a very insignificant boy—playing on the streets of Calcutta. If I have achieved so much, think how much more you can do! Arise, awake, the world is calling you. Do not think you are poor; do not think you are friendless; who has ever made a man with money? Men have always made money. All the progress in the world has come through the power of man, the power of enthusiasm, the power of belief. What we need is faith. Unfortunately, faith has almost disappeared from India. This is our misfortune. The difference in men lies in their degree of faith, nothing else. It is this difference in faith that makes one great and another small. Let this faith enter your being. The blood of our nation is infected with a terrible disease—taking everything lightly—

The lack of seriousness. We must completely discard this fault. Be brave, have faith, and everything else will follow automatically. Do not be afraid, for the history of mankind shows that all great power has come from the common people. Do not fear anything. Then you will be able to achieve marvels. Fear is the root cause of all the miseries of the world; it is the greatest superstition. Therefore, "Uttishthata Jagrata Prapya Varan Nibodhata' (Arise, awake, and stop not until the goal is reached)."

Note: This is the English version (with minor modifications) of an article, published in the 1996 Annual Magazine of Shri Ramakrishna Mission Vidyabhavan, Medinipur, 'Unmesh', Vol. 20, pp. 34–37, 1996. This article was based on the author's address at the Annual Convocation of Ramakrishna Mission Vidyabhavan, Midnapore in 1996.

The Journey of a Village Boy through Ramakrishna Mission Institutions*

Preamble

Swami Vivekananda once said, "Education is the manifestation of the perfection already in man." For this perfection to emerge over time, individuals require additional training and guidance beyond conventional classroom learning. Such efforts should begin at an early stage of life. The integrated approach adopted by the Ramakrishna Mission educational institutions helps students develop a sound mind and a strong physique, enabling them to grow into responsible citizens and virtuous human beings.

Many individuals who have held or currently hold esteemed positions in organizations across India and abroad have received their early education from Ramakrishna Mission institutions. These institutions, founded in alignment with Swami Vivekananda's vision, serve students from diverse socio-economic backgrounds, including both rural and urban areas. One such institution, the Ramakrishna Mission Calcutta Students' Home, Belgharia, was established by Swami Nirvedananda (Anadi Maharaj) during his pre-monastic life. Its mission is to support students from underprivileged families by providing not only shelter and nutritious food but also quality educational assistance, including coaching.

This institution functions as a 'home away from home' in the truest sense. The serene environment fosters concentration, while the structured system cultivates self-reliance, confidence, and moral values such as honesty, unselfishness, mutual cooperation, and kindness. The dedicated monks at the Students' Home provide invaluable care and guidance, shaping the character of the residents. Through this holistic approach, students develop a deep sense of love and respect for their motherland. Many alumni maintain lifelong ties with the institution, exemplifying the enduring impact of its teachings.

The author of this article, Jagadis Chandra Misra, is a testament to the transformative power of the Ramakrishna Mission. Born in a remote village in West Bengal, he faced numerous challenges, including the lack of proper roads, electricity, and higher education opportunities. Despite these adversities, he benefitted immensely from the support of the Ramakrishna Mission, which

* Abridged version of the original article published in '*Achinpurer ak Pathik*', Kabitika Publishers, Kolkata, 2023, which was initially prepared at the request of the Ramakrishna Mission Calcutta Students' Home, Belgharia.

played a pivotal role in his personal and academic development. This article provides a brief account of his journey, contributions, and achievements, highlighting his deep sense of gratitude toward the Mission. It is hoped that this story will inspire future generations.

Early Life and Schooling

Jagadis Chandra Misra, known in the scientific community as J.C. Misra, was born in Bagmari, a remote village in the Midnapore district (now East Medinipur), West Bengal. As a child, he was a bit mischievous, inattentive, and indifferent to studies, presenting a significant challenge for his mother, Pramila Devi, and other family members. However, his mother, an embodiment of patience, remained hopeful that he would mature over time. His father, Ganes Chandra Misra, a dedicated teacher and social worker, took concrete steps to instil discipline and academic focus in him.

Jagadis attended Tikrapara High School, located two kilometers away from his home. With no paved roads in the area, he had to walk along muddy paths daily, a task made especially difficult during the rainy season. His father, an esteemed teacher at the same school, was proficient in Mathematics, English, and Sanskrit. He played a crucial role in laying a strong academic foundation for his son, inspiring him to pursue a teaching career. Beyond academics, his father emphasized character-building and holistic development, advocating for an education system that fosters self-reliance and moral strength.

Recognizing the value of the Ramakrishna Mission's emphasis on practical education and moral instruction, his father sought to enroll Jagadis in one of its institutions.

Higher Education at Ramakrishna Mission Vidyamandira, Belur Math

After passing the School Final Examination in 1959, Jagadis was admitted to Ramakrishna Mission Vidyamandira, Belur Math, for his Intermediate Science (I.Sc.). This marked a turning point in his life. Under the administration of Swami Tejasananda, the college provided him with an environment conducive to all-round education. As a resident of East Hostel, he received immense care and guidance from the hostel superintendent, Govinda Maharaj (later Swami Gokulananda), who influenced his spiritual journey. On April 9, 1960, he was initiated by Srimat Swami Shankarananda, the seventh President of Ramakrishna Math and Mission and a disciple of Swami Brahmananda.

Although initially selected for B.Sc. (Hons.) at Presidency College, Calcutta, his spiritual guide advised him to continue at Vidyamandira, where a three-year B.Sc. (Hons.) programme had recently been introduced. Without hesitation, Jagadis chose to stay at Vidyamandira, benefiting from the spiritual and academic guidance of several senior monks, including Swami Vishuddhananda, Swami Tejasananda, and Swami Gokulananda. During his time there, he also learned to recite passages from 'Sri Sri Chandi' and chant the 'Srimad Bhagavad Gita'. He used to chant first slokas 54–72 of the Second chapter of Gita, which depict the symptoms of a '*Sthitaprajna*', that is a man of steady wisdom. These slokas give directions for remaining calm under any circumstances.

Postgraduate Studies and Life at Ramakrishna Mission Calcutta Students' Home

After completing his B.Sc. (Hons.) in 1964, Jagadis pursued an M.Sc. in Applied Mathematics at the University College of Science, Calcutta University. He resided at the Ramakrishna Mission Calcutta Students' Home, Belgharia, for two years. This institution, founded by Swami Nirvedananda, was more than just a residence—it became his true home. Under the guidance of Swami Santoshananda, the then secretary of the students home and Swami Dhyanatmananda, the assistant secretary, he received immense support.

Swami Dhyanatmananda personally trained him in performing Saraswati Puja, demonstrating meticulous care in teaching rituals and traditions. Other monks, such as Swami Vishokananda, Swami Satyaghanananda, and Swami Abhyasananda, played vital roles in managing different aspects of the Students' Home, from administration to healthcare. Jagadis fondly recalls the unwavering care he received from Swami Abhyasananda when he fell ill with chickenpox, experiencing a level of compassion he never encountered elsewhere.

Career and Further Contributions

After completing his M.Sc. in early 1967, Jagadis briefly taught at Naipur Shantisudha Institution, a higher secondary school in East Medinipur. Later that year, he joined Uluberia College as a Lecturer in Mathematics, continuing his research as a Ph.D. candidate registered to Jadavpur University under the guidance of the eminent scholar, Prof. Bibhuti Bhusan Sen. In 1971, after earning his Ph.D., he secured a position of a Lecturer at the Indian Institute of Technology (IIT) Kharagpur, marking a significant milestone in his academic career.

Dr. Misra considers this as the second turning point in his life. He wishes to express his deep sense of gratitude to revered Swami Dhyanatmananda and Swami Satyaghanananda of the Ramakrishna Mission Calcutta Students' Home for their invaluable guidance, support, and blessings.

Upon joining IIT Kharagpur, Dr. Misra found himself under the mentorship of Prof. Anil Kumar Gayen, the then Head of the Mathematics Department and an alumnus of the Students' Home. Dr. Misra remains deeply thankful to Prof. Gayen for his guidance during the formative years of his academic career at IIT Kharagpur. Prof. Gayen, born into a humble family in the village of Henria in East Medinipur District, was able to pursue higher education as a resident of the Students' Home. His academic journey led him to the University of Cambridge, where he earned his Ph.D. degree. He later joined ISI Kolkata as a faculty member before moving to IIT Kharagpur, where he became a distinguished professor and head of the Mathematics Department. Recognized for his contributions to mathematics and statistics, he was elected a Fellow of the Indian National Science Academy (INSA), New Delhi, and the Statistical Society of London. Dr. Misra fondly recalls his association with Prof. Gayen, who was moving with his mission to establish Vidyasagar University in Midnapore.

In 1975, Dr. Misra received a memorable letter from Prof. W. Heisenberg, President of the Alexander von Humboldt Foundation, Germany, informing him that he had been selected for the Humboldt Fellowship. He felt immensely elevated, particularly because the letter bore the signature of Prof. Heisenberg, the renowned physicist famous for his Principle of Uncertainty. Dr. Misra departed for Germany on June 9, 1975, to work as a Humboldt Fellow under Prof. Oskar Mahrenholtz, Director of the Institute of Mechanics at the Technical University of Hannover, in collaboration with Prof. Christoph Hartung from the Division of Biomedical Engineering and Hospital Technology, Medical University of Hannover. It was here that he was introduced to the fascinating interdisciplinary field of Biomechanics, an emerging area of research at the time. During his stay in Hannover, his work focused on the biomechanics of brain injury, which he considers the third major turning point in his life.

After spending two years in Germany (1975–1977), Dr. Misra returned to India and resumed his duties at IIT Kharagpur on June 19, 1977. He expanded his research into interdisciplinary areas such as Biomechanics, Physiological Fluid Dynamics, Biomedical Mathematics, and Bioinformatics. By forming a dedicated research team, he successfully established a robust research school in these fields within the Department of Mathematics at IIT Kharagpur. His sincere efforts also contributed to the establishment of the School of Medical Science and Technology (SMST) at IIT Kharagpur. As a professor, he was highly regarded for his innovative teaching methods, particularly in offering the Biomedical Mathematics course for MBBS graduates enrolled in the SMST master's program.

Dr. Misra was promoted to the position of Assistant Professor in 1979, and in 1984, the University of Calcutta awarded him the prestigious Doctor of Science (D.Sc.) degree in Applied Mathematics in recognition of his contributions to mathematical modelling in the fields of Biomechanics and Structural Mechanics. Among the foreign examiners of his thesis, the eminent scientist Prof. Y.C. Fung of the University of California, San Diego, highly praised his work, stating, "Dr. Misra has written and published an excellent series of papers in Biomechanics and the Mechanics of Fluids and Solids. His standard is very high, and many of his papers contain significant results, making valuable contributions to permanent literature."

The same year, Dr. Misra became the first recipient of the "IIT Kharagpur Silver Jubilee Research Award," granted to faculty members whose 'research contributions are deemed outstanding.' Despite no available vacancy at the professorial level, he was promoted to Professor of Mathematics in 1986 in recognition of his academic excellence. He later served as Head of the Department of Mathematics during 1998–2001 and acted as the Head of SMST for a period.

Dr. Misra has nearly 250 research publications in esteemed international journals, has supervised 30 Ph.D. scholars, and has published 12 advanced-level books in mathematical sciences, including a monograph. These books are published by eminent publishing houses, such as World Scientific, Singapore, and Narosa, New Delhi, etc. His pioneering research in Cardiovascular Mechanics, Mechanics of Brain Injury, Mechanics of Bone Fracture and Remodelling, and Peristaltic Flows in Physiological Systems has earned him international acclaim. His findings on vascular tissue compressibility led to significant breakthroughs in arterial biomechanics and were later validated by Prof. Y.C. Fung experimentally. His research on cerebral concussion due to rotational head acceleration introduced new insights into neurological research and neurosurgery, helping determine the threshold of human cerebral concussion in terms of angular acceleration. Additionally, his work on osseous tissue damping effects on bone remodelling has provided critical insights into surgical procedures.

In recognition of his significant contributions to medical and physiological sciences, Dr. Misra was elected a Fellow of the Royal Society of Medicine, London, in 1989.

Throughout his career, Dr. Misra has held visiting professorships at the University of Calgary in Canada; the University of Bremen and Leibniz University Hannover in Germany, Malay University in Malaysia; and the University of Science and Technology in Hong Kong. He delivered invited lectures at renowned institutions, including the Courant Institute of Mathematical Sciences, New York; Cornell Medical Center, New York. He visited the Universities of California (Los Angeles and San Diego); Imperial College of London; the Universities of Cambridge, Oxford, Manchester, and Glasgow in the UK; and several esteemed universities across Europe and Asia.

Dr. Misra has played a pivotal role in international conferences, delivering plenary lectures and chairing sessions at the Fourth International Congress of Biorheology in Tokyo, the International Conference on Computational and Applied Mathematics in Brussels, and the Applied Mathematics and Mathematical Physics Conference in Sylhet, Bangladesh. He delivered the prestigious P.L. Bhatnagar Memorial Lecture in 2001 and the Indian Science Congress Platinum Jubilee Lecture in Mathematical Sciences in 2005. In 2006, he was elected President of the Mathematical Sciences Section (including Statistics) of the Indian Science Congress.

His expertise has been sought by various national and international organizations, including the National Science Foundation (USA), Imperial Press (London), and World Scientific (Singapore). He has served on expert committees of the Council of Scientific and Industrial Research (CSIR), the Union Public Service Commission, the Indira Gandhi National Open University (IGNOU), and the Technical Advisory Committee of the Indian Statistical Institute (ISI).

After 38 years of service at IIT Kharagpur, Dr. Misra was appointed Pro Vice-Chancellor of SOA University, Bhubaneswar, on May 1, 2009. Following his tenure there, he joined the Indian Institute of Engineering Science and Technology (IIEST), Shibpur, on January 2, 2015, as an Adjunct Professor at the Centre for Healthcare Science and Technology. He continued to contribute to research as the Principal Investigator of a project sponsored by the Science and Engineering Research Board (SERB), Department of Science and Technology (DST), Government of India, while also supervising and mentoring a full-time Ph.D. scholar.

Recognitions

The author has been the recipient of several prestigious awards and recognitions for his contributions in the fields of mathematics, biomedical engineering, and applied sciences. A list of his accolades is provided below:

Fellowships and Memberships

1. Elected Fellow of the National Academy of Sciences, India (1987).
2. Fellow of the Institute of Mathematics and its Applications, UK (1988).
3. Fellow of the Institute of Theoretical Physics, Calcutta (1988).
4. Fellow of the Royal Society of Medicine, London (1989), in recognition of his significant contributions to mathematical modelling in biomedical engineering.
5. Fellow of the Indian National Academy of Engineering (2000), acknowledging his research impact in biomedical engineering and technology.
6. Active Member of the New York Academy of Sciences (1996).
7. Member of the Biomechanical Engineering Society, USA (1989).
8. Member of the International Society of Biorheology, New York (1981).
9. Member of Society of Applied Mathematics and Mechanics (GAMM), Germany (1982).
10. Life Member of the Indian Science Congress Association.
11. Life Member of the Indian Society of Theoretical and Applied Mechanics.
12. Life Member of the Indian Society of Technical Education.
13. Elected Fellow of the Institution of Engineering and Technology, UK (2019), for his distinguished work in mathematical modeling of engineering systems.
14. Elected Fellow of the West Bengal Academy of Science and Technology (2025) for his distinguished contributions in Applied Mathematics.

Awards and Recognitions

1. *INAE Outstanding Teachers Award (2013)* – Conferred by the Indian National Academy of Engineering, New Delhi. Upon receiving this honour, Professor Misra informed the revered President Maharaj, Swami

Atmasthanandaji, who responded with heartfelt blessings and words of appreciation.

2. *Lifetime Achievement Award (2015)* – Conferred by the Venus International Foundation in Chennai for his lifetime contributions to applied mathematics.
3. *EET CRS Best Scientist Award (2014)* – Bangalore.
4. *CEGR Shiksha Gaurav Puraskar (2014)* – New Delhi.
5. *Ram Mohan Puraskar (2004)* – Awarded for outstanding contributions in the field of mathematics.
6. *IIT Kharagpur Silver Jubilee Research Award (1984)* – Conferred for his 'research publications adjudged outstanding by a national-level committee.'
7. *Rashtriya Gaurav Award (2004)* – Presented by the India International Friendship Society, New Delhi, in recognition of his meritorious services and remarkable research contributions in mathematics.
8. *Alexander von Humboldt Fellowship (1975)* – Germany.
9. *P.L. Bhatnagar Memorial Lecture (2001)* – Delivered at a prestigious scientific forum at NIT Hamirpur.
10. *Indian Science Congress Platinum Jubilee Lecture (2005)* – Delivered in the Mathematical Sciences (including Statistics) Section.
11. *Described as a "True Pioneer in Human Biodynamics"* – Recognized by authors V. Ivancevic and T. Ivancevic (University of Adelaide, Australia) in their book Natural Biodynamics (World Scientific, 2005), which extensively cites his research contributions.
12. *Appointed as an Expert Committee Member* – Selected by the National Science Foundation (USA), Imperial Press (UK), and World Scientific (Singapore).
13. *President of Mathematical Sciences Section (including Statistics), Indian Science Congress (2006).*
14. Editorial Appointments:

    Associate Editor, International Journal of Artificial Life Research (USA).

    Member, Editorial Board, International Journal of Biomathematics (World Scientific, Singapore).

    Member, Editorial Advisory Board, Journal of Mechanics in Medicine and Biology (World Scientific, Singapore).

15. *Doctor of Science (D.Sc.) Degree* – Awarded by the University of Calcutta.
16. *Special Appointment as Professor at IIT Kharagpur*—A distinguished recognition for his academic excellence.
17. *Best Poster Paper Presentation Award (2007)* – Awarded at the Indian Science Congress for the research paper on Mathematical Modelling of Biomagnetic Fluid Flow over a Stretching Sheet.

Family and Personal Life

The author's wife, Shorasi, is a devout follower of the Ramakrishna Math and Mission. Together, they have raised three children – Subhas, Sumita, and Sudip – all of whom pursued part of their education at IIT Kharagpur and both the sons went on to complete Ph.D. programmes abroad, while Sumita did her Ph.D. at IACS Kolkata.

- *Subhas Chandra Misra*—Professor, Department of Industrial Management Engineering, IIT Kanpur
- *Sumita Mukhopadhyay (Misra)*—Asst. Professor, Centre for Green Energy, Indian Institute of Engineering Science and Technology (IIEST), Shibpur.
- *Sudip Misra*—Professor, Computer Science and Engineering Department, IIT Kharagpur
- *Dr. Achintya Mukhopadhyay* (Son-in-law)—Professor of Mechanical Engineering, Jadavpur University, Kolkata.

Professor Misra finds his greatest satisfaction in seeing his children grow into responsible and religious human beings. All his children and younger daughter-in-law, Satamita, are initiated disciples of the Ramakrishna Math and Mission.

Memorable Family Moments

After his father's retirement, Professor Misra's parents moved to IIT Kharagpur, where they spent their final years with their eldest son and grandchildren. His father, a guiding figure, played an active role in his grandchildren's education, while his mother, Pramila Devi, provided love and care to the family until her passing in December 2016 at the age of 92. She remained mentally alert and provided wisdom to the family until her last day.

Connection with the Ramakrishna Mission Students' Home

Professor Misra cherishes his deep-rooted bond with the Ramakrishna Mission Students' Home, which continues to shape his life. The Home, under the able leadership of Swami Ekabratananda and supported by other dedicated monks, maintains its tradition of holistic education and spiritual guidance.

Reflecting on his journey, Professor Misra acknowledges that if his story is regarded as a "success story," it is entirely due to the grace of Sri Ramakrishna, Sri Sri Ma Sarada Devi and Swami Vivekananda. He humbly dedicates all his contributions and achievements to their divine feet.

Real Education: Some Thoughts**

Education has been defined in various ways by eminent thinkers. According to Swami Vivekananda, "Education is the manifestation of the perfection already in man". His philosophy should inspire the entire student community of India and holds global significance as well. A student must advance with mental strength and self-confidence, while a teacher's role is to provide guidance rather than to dictate. In this process, the teacher's contribution is comparable to that of a gardener nurturing the growth of a plant.

The primary objective of education should be to shape character and cultivate humanity. As Swami Vivekananda emphasized, humans are born of divine joy and possess a latent divinity. When properly nurtured, this potential ensures that the joy of childhood does not turn into sorrow in youth, nor does the happiness of youth transform into misery in later stages of life. Only this kind of education deserves to be called 'real education.'

While education aimed at earning a livelihood is essential, it is merely one aspect of the broader purpose of learning. Subjects like science, literature, and philosophy undoubtedly enhance our intellect, but the true purpose of education is to nurture human qualities that reflect the divinity within us. While intellectual capabilities have significantly advanced over the years, there has been a noticeable decline in moral and ethical standards. Therefore, a proper education that fosters ethical values and empathy is desperately needed.

An ideal society is one where violence is replaced by peace, where iron swords are transformed into wooden ones. Education that promotes selfishness, jealousy, or blind patriotism leading to hatred towards other nations is highly detrimental. Likewise, education that fosters religious intolerance under the guise of devotion is harmful.

In ancient India, the 'Gurukul' system was prevalent. Though this system has largely disappeared, institutions like those run by the Ramakrishna Mission strive to revive its essence while blending it with modern education. Besides the standard curriculum, these institutions teach subjects like Indian Heritage, Indian Culture, the Upanishads, and Moral Values. This balanced approach is ideal for imparting a comprehensive education.

**The original elaborate article was published in the book "Mathematics and Mathematicians at IIT Kharagpur" (Ed. J.C. Misra) Allied Publishers Pvt. Limited, New Delhi, 2003.

Furthermore, physical fitness and mental strength are emphasized. Students are encouraged to build "muscles of iron and nerves of steel" through active participation in games and sports.

The Vedic society taught 'self-control' from early childhood, but today, it is often considered relevant only to religious individuals. This misconception should be corrected. Everyone should learn and practice self-reverence, self-education, and self-control. Speech control, in particular, is one of the most effective ways to achieve self-discipline. Additionally, spiritual power can be a potent tool to calm the mind, provided it is used with good intentions. If we can remain calm and composed in all circumstances, we can preserve our spiritual energy and use it effectively for the betterment of ourselves and society.

Our minds should be consistently engaged in positive, humanitarian thoughts. Seeing all individuals as relatives and respecting all religions is not only beneficial for personal growth but also for global harmony.

In the Bhagavad Gita, Lord Krishna describes the qualities of a true devotee:

> *"One who is the same to friends and foes, who remains unaffected by honour and insult, heat and cold, pleasure and pain, who is free from attachments, who values praise and criticism equally, who controls speech, remains content with whatever comes unasked, has no fixed abode, and possesses a steady mind—such a person is dear to Me."*

Ancient scriptures from India often stress universal brotherhood and goodwill towards all beings. As exemplified by this verse from the Markandeya Chandi:

> *"May the Divine Mother be gracious to all who bow to her, and may She grant blessings to all beings." Another beautiful verse from the Upanishads expresses a universal wish:*
>
> *"May all be happy, may all be free from disease, may all experience goodness, and may none suffer." The Upanishads also impart messages of goodwill for humanity:*
>
> *"May Indra, the wise one, bless us; may Pusha, the all-knowing, guide us; may Tarkshyo, the remover of obstacles, protect us; may Brihaspati shower us with goodness."*

In India, people who have attained self-realization have extensively researched on life's stages with dedication. Their insights include:

1. The pursuit of worldly pleasures results in an endless cycle of rebirth.

2. Based on experiences from past lives, the body and mind are formed, and individuals reap the consequences of their actions.
3. While the physical body perishes with death, the impressions of past deeds remain within a subtle body, collectively known as "fate."
4. Everyone is responsible for their actions and must face the consequences of their deeds.
5. Understanding these truths can help avoid suffering caused by wrongful actions.

Accepting these principles and applying them can significantly reduce mental distress and anxiety. Conflict arising from differences in race, caste, and religion has long plagued humanity. Many mistakes such conflicts for true religion, forgetting that the same soul exists in all beings. Recognizing the beauty of this universal soul should begin in childhood, as it forms the foundation of an individual's, society's, and nation's principles.

Swami Vivekananda's message holds powerful relevance today—

> *If I have achieved something, it is because I once was an ordinary boy who wasted time playing in the streets of Kolkata. If I could achieve so much, you can do even more. Arise, awake, and respond to the world's call. Don't think you are poor, nor believe that you lack friends. Money doesn't create greatness; it is man who earns money. All great changes in the world have been brought about by the strength, inspiration, and confidence of individuals. What is lacking is respect and love for others. Respect has nearly vanished from India, and this is a root cause of our misery.*
>
> *The differences among individuals stem from differences in respect (shraddha). Because of this disparity, some people become great, while others remain ordinary. Respect should be embraced by all. Bravery, respect, and determination will lead you to success. Throughout history, all progress has emerged from the strength of common people. Fear is the root of all misery. Arise, awake, and stop not till the goal is reached.*

This timeless message encourages us to pursue a higher standard of education, one that cultivates character, humanity and genuine strength.

Our Vidyarthi Ashrama, Our Second Home***

The Ramakrishna Mission Calcutta Students' Home, fondly known as *'Vidyarthi Ashrama'*, is currently located at Belgharia. For years, it has been dedicated to the noble mission of "*Shiva Jnane Jiva Seva*"—serving humanity with the recognition of divinity in every being. Through 'man-making' and 'character-building' education, the institution has empowered the youth of our nation without any discrimination of caste, creed, race, or religion. The selfless efforts of the sannyasins of the Ashrama are truly commendable and deserve immense appreciation.

Inspired by the ideals of Swami Vivekananda, the Vidyarthi Ashrama was established by Sri Surendra Nath Mukherjee, later known as Br. Anadi Chaitanya after his *Brahmacharya* and Swami Nirvedananda after taking *Sannyasa*. Revered as Anadi Maharaj, he was an exceptionally brilliant student and a classmate of distinguished Indian scientists Prof. Satyendra Nath Bose, Prof. Meghnad Saha, and Dr. Jnan Chandra Ghosh at Presidency College, Calcutta. Numerous stories highlight the academic excellence of Surendra Nath, illustrating his brilliance alongside these renowned personalities.

The Students' Home had a humble beginning in 1916 in a small rented house at Bowbazar, Kolkata. Four years later, in 1920, it was officially recognized as a center of the Ramakrishna Mission. Even before its formal recognition, Swami Nirvedanandaji, in his pre-monastic life, had already initiated the institution with the noble, selfless vision of actualizing Swamiji's educational ideals: "We want that education by which character is formed, strength of mind is increased, intellect is expanded, and one can stand on one's own feet.' Although the Students' Home became a regular branch of the Mission in 1920, the official year of establishment is considered to be 1916, leading to its centenary celebration in 2016.

The Students' Home moved to Gouripur in 1932, remaining there until 1941. The subsequent years from 1941 to 1954 were challenging, with the institution undergoing numerous relocations within Kolkata. Despite facing severe difficulties, Anadi Maharaj remained unwavering in his commitment to establishing a permanent location for the Ashrama at Belgharia. His dedicated associates, revered Swamis Santoshananda (Ashes Maharaj), Vishokananda (Priti Maharaj), Dhyanatmananda (Nripen Maharaj), and others, offered

*** Abridged version of the article published earlier in '*Achinpurer ak Pathik*', Kabitika Publishers, Kolkata, 2023.

invaluable support to his mission. Their collective efforts made the acquisition of land and construction of buildings a reality.

The Students' Home is not just a hostel but a truly unique institution with distinctive characteristics. Its environment and operation, managed by the monks of the Ramakrishna Mission, bear resemblance to the ancient *Gurukula System*. This holistic approach to education helps students develop a good physique and sound mind, ultimately shaping them into responsible citizens with strong character and a deep love for the nation.

Many alumni of the Students' Home have attained esteemed positions in India and abroad, attributing their success to the values and training received here. A number of ex-students have even embraced the monastic life of the Ramakrishna Math and Mission, dedicating themselves to the welfare of humanity with the motto: '*Atmano mokshartham jagaddhitaya cha*'—seeking personal liberation and the good of the world.

The Students' Home has always aimed at assisting deserving young men from economically challenged backgrounds, providing them with not only food and shelter but also essential educational resources, including coaching and mentorship. It serves as a true 'home away from home', fostering an environment of simplicity, integrity, hard work, cooperation, and kindness.

Under the affectionate guidance of the monks, residents grow into well-rounded individuals, equipped with self-reliance, self-confidence, and a sense of service toward humanity.

The beloved traditions of the Students' Home, such as the daily 'Gathering' sessions, play a significant role in character-building. These sessions, typically held in the Library Hall, include storytelling, moral lessons, and joyful interactions that leave lasting impressions on the students.

Another cherished event is the annual *Kali Puja* celebration, where both current and former students reunite to participate in the festivities. The highlight of the occasion is the exuberant dancing and singing of *Shyama Sangeet*, bringing together generations of alumni.

Today, the Students' Home continues to thrive under the leadership of Swami Ekavratanandaji (Badal Maharaj), the current Secretary. His remarkable dedication, affectionate personality, and God-gifted voice have made him a beloved figure among students and alumni alike. The tradition of maintaining strong bonds between the alumni and the institution is still very much alive.

The author, a humble example of the *Vidyarthi Ashrama's* enduring influence, came from a remote village in West Bengal where basic amenities like electricity and proper educational facilities were non-existent. Thanks to the nurturing environment of the Ramakrishna Mission Calcutta Students' Home, he received the guidance and support necessary to pursue higher education and build a successful career.

The all-around training provided by the Students' Home has made a lasting impact on the author's life. While his own children did not receive their education from any of the Ramakrishna Mission Institutions, they have nevertheless inherited the values of humility, diligence, and compassion instilled in him during his formative years at the Ashrama.

All his three children, Subhas, Sumita and Sudip possess compassion for the underprivileged, along with genuine love, kindness, truthfulness, honesty, and integrity. Their devotion to the motherland and dedication to serving the nation are truly commendable. Moreover, all of them are initiated disciples of the Ramakrishna Math and Mission. This observation can be regarded as an indirect influence of the Mission's teachings.

It is likely that many other alumni of the *Vidyarthi Ashrama* share similar experiences. The author firmly believes that whatever humble achievements he has attained in life are solely due to the grace of Sri Ramakrishna, Sri Sri Ma Sarada Devi and Swami Vivekananda. He attributes all credit to the Ramakrishna Mission Vidyamandira, Belur Math, and Vidyarthi Ashrama, Belgharia.

Even as societal changes have led to some liberalization of traditional practices, the core principles of the *Ashrama* continue to flourish, with students adhering to the rules of the institution and valuing them voluntarily, inspired by a genuine sense of belonging. Indeed, for its residents and alumni alike, the Students' Home remains a cherished 'Second Home'.

Reminiscing the Days at the 'Home Away from Home'****

Born in a remote village in the *Medinipur* district (now *East Medinipur*), I embarked on a remarkable journey of education and spiritual growth that began in the hallowed halls of Ramakrishna Mission Vidyamandira, in 1959. I completed my I.Sc. (equivalent to today's Higher Secondary) and was selected for a B.Sc. (Honours) at Presidency College. It was during this transformation period that I first set foot in the Vidyarthi Ashram, staying briefly in its serene and disciplined environment.

However, as mentioned earlier, I was fortunate to have a momentous spiritual encounter. On April 9, 1960, I was initiated by Srimat Swami Shankaranandaji Maharaj, the seventh president of the Ramakrishna Math and Mission and a spiritual son of Swami Brahmananda. His blessings, coupled with his guidance, have remained a corner stone of my life.

When I visited Belur Math to seek Guruji's advice regarding my next part of education, he suggested I continue my studies at the Vidyamandira, which had by then introduced a three-year degree course. This would allow me to stay close to the Math and benefit from its spiritual atmosphere. I followed his advice, enrolling in B.Sc. (Mathematics Honours) at the *Vidyamandira*. In retrospect, this decision shaped my life in ways I could not have imagined.

After completing my degree in 1964, I pursued an M.Sc. in Applied Mathematics at the University of Calcutta, with *Vidyarthi Ashrama* graciously allowing me to continue as a postgraduate resident. To this day, I take immense pride in being an alumnus of the *Ashrama*—a sanctuary of discipline, learning, and spirituality.

Life at the Vidyarthi Ashrama

During my time, the *Vidyarthi Ashrama* was under the able leadership of *Swami Santoshananda (Ashesh Maharaj), a direct disciple of the Holy Mother.* His commanding yet gentle demeanor left an indelible mark on everyone. He used to fondly call me "*Vashisthadev.*" Despite his serious nature, he often shared humorous stories during evening gatherings, lightening the atmosphere for the students.

**** This is an abridged version of the author's article that appeared in the Souvenir of the Ramakrishna Mission Calcutta Students' Home, Belgharia, December 2024.

The Ashrama's daily operations were managed by a team of dedicated monks: Swami Dhyanatmananda, Swami Vishokananda, Swami Satyaghanananda, Swami Vishwashrayananda, Swami Amalananda, Swami Skandananda, and Swami Abhyasananda. Each of them, with their unique qualities, contributed to the Ashrama's nurturing environment.

Swami Dhyanatmananda (Nripen Maharaj) had a prodigious memory and a talent for reciting poetry in Bengali, Sanskrit, and English. He was the primary fundraiser for the *Ashrama*, yet he always made time to interact with students, often providing guidance and care. His devotion to rituals, coupled with his personal touch, endeared him to all.

Swami Satyaghanananda was a quiet, compassionate presence, always ready to assist students. His gentle demeanor and selfless service left a lasting impression on me.

Swami Vishwashrayananda brought cheer to our lives with his jovial nature and storytelling. His illustrated books for children on Sri Ramakrishna, Ma Sarada Devi, and Swami Vivekananda gained high popularity.

Swami Amalananda managed the *Shilpapith* (a polytechnic institution run by the Mission) with exceptional skill, while also authoring engaging Bengali books for young students.

Swami Skandananda, despite suffering from health issues, tirelessly managed the kitchen and pantry. His dedication was a lesson in resilience.

Swami Abhyasananda embodied the spirit of selfless service. Whether it was decorating the temple, caring for students' health, or maintaining the Ashrama's gardens, his every action reflected his devotion to the ideals of the Ramakrishna Mission.

Festivals and Celebrations

Life at the *Ashrama* was vibrant, punctuated by a series of festivals that enriched our spirits. Among them, *Sri Sri Kali Puja* held annually stood out as a grand celebration, bringing alumni together in a joyful reunion. Cultural programmes involving both current students and alumni added a special touch to these gatherings.

The annual *Bejoya Sammelan*, *Saraswati Puja*, and the *Ratha Yatra* were equally delightful, creating a sense of community and belonging. Even during quieter times, the *monks* ensured that we felt at home, arranging special treats like *pitha* during the winter festival of *Poush Parbon.*

Spiritual Guidance

The *Vidyarthi Ashrama* was more than an educational institution—it was a sanctuary of spiritual growth. The monks, with their profound wisdom and compassion, guided us through life's challenges. I still remember the care and attention I received when I fell ill with chickenpox. Isolated in the *Arogya Bhavan,* I was personally attended to by *Swami Abhyasananda,* whose every gesture exemplified the ideal of *serving God through serving humanity.*

As I look back, I see the *Vidyarthi Ashrama* not merely as a place of study but as a melting pot where character was forged and ideals took root. The selfless monks and the sacred atmosphere instilled in us values that have guided our lives.

The *Ashrama* has evolved over the years, with improved infrastructure and expanded services. Yet, the spirit of its founders and the legacy of *Swami Nirbedananda* remain intact. The warmth and hospitality extended to alumni by the current generation of monks are a testament to this enduring legacy.

During my time at the Bhubaneswar Math, I had the privilege of interacting with esteemed monks like Swami *Smaranananda, Swami Suhitananda* and *Swami Divyananda.* Their insights reaffirmed my belief in the timeless relevance of the ideals upheld by the Ramakrishna Mission.

The *Vidyarthi Ashrama* continues to inspire, nurturing generations of students with the same spirit of service, devotion, and learning. As an alumnus, I feel fortunate to have been a part of this remarkable institution, which remains a guiding light in my life.

APPENDIX

Curriculum Vitae

1. **Name: Dr. Jagadis Chandra Misra**
   E-mail: misrajc@gmail.com
   Mobile: +91-8373843896
   Address for Communication:
   Qrs. B-74, IIT Campus, Kharagpur-721302, West Bengal, India

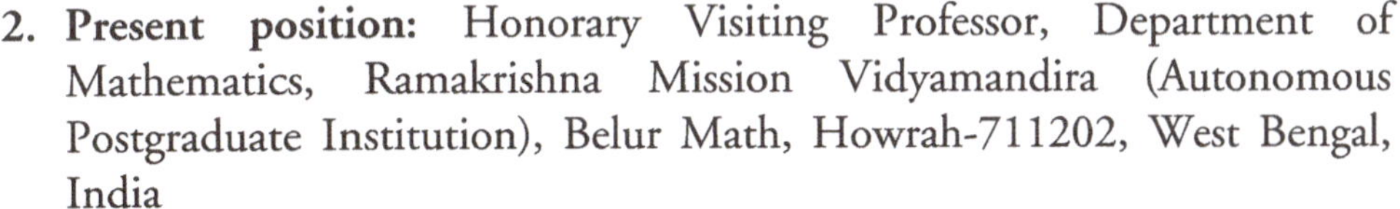

2. **Present position:** Honorary Visiting Professor, Department of Mathematics, Ramakrishna Mission Vidyamandira (Autonomous Postgraduate Institution), Belur Math, Howrah-711202, West Bengal, India

3. **Areas of Specialization:**
   Applied Mathematics, Biomathematics, Modelling and Simulation, Physiological Fluid Dynamics, Mechanics of Fluids and Solids.

4. **Fellowships of National/International Academic/Professional Bodies:**
   - Was elected a **Fellow of West Bengal Academy of Science & Technology,** 2025 (He was the only person elected in 2025 from Mathematical Sciences Section).
   - Was elected a **Fellow of the Indian National Academy of Engineering** in (INAE) 2000 in recognition of the valuable impact of his research contribution in Structural Engineering and Bio-engineering.
   - Was elected a **Fellow of the National Academy of Sciences, India (NASI)** in 1987.
   - Was elected a **Fellow of the Institute of Mathematics and its Applications** (U.K.) in 1988.
   - Was elected a **Fellow of the Institution of Engineering and Technology (IET), UK** in 2019.
   - **Fellow of the Institute of Theoretical Physics,** Calcutta.

- Was elected a Fellow of the **Royal Society of Medicine, London** in 1989 in recognition of the significant impact of his research contribution in the field of Biomedical Engineering.
- Was elected a **Fellow of the Royal Society of Public Health, London** 2019 in recognition of impact of his research contributions in Physiology and Medicine.
- Was elected a **Fellow of the Royal Society of Biology, London** 2020 in recognition of his research contributions in Physiological Fluid Dynamics.

5. **Awards, Distinctions and Recognition:**

(a) Prof. J.C. Misra figures in the **global list of Top 2% scientists**, during the last six consecutive years from 2020 to 2025 as per the study conducted by Stanford University, USA.

(b) Was among the few selected 'eminent retired faculty members' felicitated during IIT Kharagpur Platinum Jubilee Inaugural on 18th August 2025.

(c) Was one of the two recipients of '**INAE Outstanding Teachers Award-2013**', Indian National Academy of Engineering, New Delhi.

(d) Received the prestigious Award '**Ram Mohan Puraskar**' in 2004 **for 'Outstanding Contributions in the Field of Mathematics'**. The Award consisted of a cash prize of **Rs. five lakhs, a memento,** and **a citation**. Other recipients in the same year were Astrophysicist Prof. J.B. Narlikar and cricketer Sourav Ganguly.

(e) Recipient of the prestigious award, 1984 IIT Kharagpur **Silver Jubilee Research Award,** the research publications submitted by him having been adjudged by a **National Level Committee** to be **outstanding** (He was the only recipient of this award in 1984). This award consisted of a cash prize and a certificate.

(f) Recipient of **Dr. A.P.J. Abdul Kalam Award for Lifetime Contribution in Science,** Panama Labs, Chennai, 2017.

(g) Recipient of EET CRS **Award for Research Excellence**, Mumbai, 2017.

(h) Recipient of EET CRS "Best Scientist Award-2014", Bangalore.

(i) **Recipient of CEGR Shiksha Gourav Purskar-2014**, New Delhi.

(j) **Recipient of Lifetime Achievement Award-2015**, VENUS International Foundation, awarded in Chennai on 5th July 2015.

(k) Recipient of '**Rashtriya Gaurav Award**' in 2004 by India International Friendship Society, New Delhi for meritorious services and remarkable research contributions in Mathematics (along with nuclear physicist Padma Shri Dr. Bikash Sinha, Director of Saha Institute of Nuclear Physics, Calcutta).

(l) Received the coveted **Alexander von Humboldt Fellowship,** Germany in 1975.

(m) Delivered the prestigious **Indian Science Congress Platinum Jubilee Lecture** 2005 in the Section of Mathematical Sciences (including Statistics). Past lecturers include Prof. C.R. Rao, FRS, and Prof. C.S. Seshadri, FRS.

(n) Was nominated as an Active Member of the **New York Academy of Sciences** in 1996.

(o) Was elected a Member of **Biomechanical Engineering Society, USA** in 1989.

(p) Was elected a Member, **International Society of Biorheology, New York,** 1981.

(q) Was elected a Member, **Society for Applied Mathematics and Mechanics (GAMM), Germany,** 1982.

(r) Life Member, **Indian Science Congress Association.**

(s) Life Member, **Indian Society of Theoretical and Applied Mechanics.**

(t) Life Member, **Indian Society of Technical Education.**

(u) He has been described as "**a true pioneer in human biodynamics**" by the authors V. Ivancevic and T. Ivancevic (University of Adelaide, Australia) in their book entitled "Natural Biodynamics", World Scientific, 2005 (London/USA/Singapore), who have very extensively referred to Misra's research contributions in the book.

(v) He was appointed by the **National Science Foundation of USA, Imperial Press (UK) and World Scientific, Singapore** as a Member of their Expert Committees.

(w) Was elected in 2006 **President of the Mathematical Sciences Section** (including Statistics) of the **Indian Science Congress.**

(x) Was awarded the highly coveted **D.Sc.** (Doctor of Science) degree by the University of Calcutta.

(y) His appointment to the post of Professor was a special offer from IIT Kharagpur, '**in recognition of his academic excellence**'.

6. **Positions held (in chronological order)**
   (a) Lecturer, Dept. of Mathematics, Indian Institute of Technology Kharagpur: 1971–'78.
   (b) Asst. Professor, Dept. of Mathematics, Indian Institute of Technology Kharagpur: 1978–'85.
   (c) Professor, Dept. of Mathematics, Indian Institute of Technology Kharagpur: 1985–2009.
   (d) Head, Dept. of Mathematics, Indian Institute of Technology Kharagpur: 1998–2001.
   (e) Pro Vice-Chancellor, SOA University, Bhubaneswar: 2009–'14.
   (f) Adjunct Professor, Center for Healthcare Science and Technology, Indian Institute of Engineering Science and Technology, Shibpur, West Bengal: 2015–2020.
7. **Visiting Positions held**
   (a) Visiting Professor, Friedrich-Alexander University of Erlangen-Nuremberg (FAU), Germany, 2019.
   (b) Visiting Professor, Institute of Mechanics and Ocean Engineering, Technical University of Hamburg, Germany, 2016.
   (c) Visiting Professor, Institute of Thermo-fluid Dynamics, Technical University of Hamburg (Germany), 2012.
   (d) Visiting Professor, Leibniz University, Hannover (Germany), 2009.
   (e) Visiting Professor, University of Bremen, Bremen (Germany), 2006.
   (f) Visiting Scientist, University of Calgary, Calgary (Canada), 1981.
   (g) Visiting Fellow, Technical University of Hannover, Hannover (Germany), 1982.
   (h) Humboldt Fellow, Technical University of Hannover, Hannover (Germany), 1975–77.
   (i) Visiting Professor, Hong Kong University of Science & Technology, 2002.
   (j) Visiting Professor, Malay University, Kuala Lumpur, Malaysia, 2007.
8. **Short Visits Abroad**

   Prof. Misra paid short visits to many distinguished institutions/abroad, delivered seminar lectures, including:

- Universities of Oxford and Cambridge,
- University of Scotland,
- Universities of Kobe and Osaka in Japan,
- Courant Institute of Mathematical Sciences, New York,
- Cornell Medical Center of the New York Hospital,
- Universities of California, San Diego and Los Angeles in USA,
- University of Alberta, Edmonton in Canada,
- Graz University in Austria,
- Ecole Polytechnique Institute in France,
- Technical University of Berlin,
- University of Kassel,
- University of Stuttgart in Germany,
- University of Malaya, Malaysia, etc.

9. **Academic Qualifications**

    (a) S.F.: W.B. Board Sec. Edn., First Division with credit marks in Mathematics, 1959.

    (b) I.Sc.: Ramakrishna Mission Vidyamandira, Belur Math, Calcutta University, First Division with credit marks in Mathematics, 1961.

    (c) B.Sc. (Hons.): Honours in Mathematics, Ramakrishna Mission Vidyamandira, Belur Math, Calcutta University, 1964.

    (d) M.Sc. (Applied Mathematics): Calcutta University, 1st Class, 1966.

    (e) Ph.D.: Applied Mathematics, Jadavpur University, 1971

    (f) D.Sc.: Applied Mathematics, Calcutta University, 1984.

10. **A. Achievement of Former Students**

    His Undergraduate/Masters/Ph.D. students are well-placed in India and abroad. Some of them occupied responsible positions like Directors of IITs, Managers in Industries, Deans, HoDs and Professors at IITs/NITs/Universities, while several of them have turned out to be distinguished researchers.

    B. Places where work has been referred/cited in Reviews

    His work has been extensively referred/cited in Mathematical Reviews, Applied Mechanics Reviews, Citation Index and in a large number of research papers published by other researchers worldwide.

C. **Sponsored Research Projects**

(a) Principal Investigator of a Research Project on Mathematical Modelling of the effects of wall deformation on blood flow in arteries, **CSIR**, New Delhi, 1985–1988.

(b) Principal Investigator of a Major Project on the Network Environment, sponsored by **MHRD**, New Delhi, 1999–2000.

(c) Principal Investigator of a Major Project on Modelling and Computer Graphics Simulation for the Analysis of DNA, **MHRD**, New Delhi, 2000–2003.

(d) Principal Investigator, Research Project entitled "Effects of non-linearity and viscoelasticity of wall tissues and blood viscoelasticity on magnetohydrodynamic flow in arteries in normal and pathological states, **CSIR**, New Delhi, 2006–2009.

(e) Principal Investigator, Research Project entitled "Problems on Heat and Mass Transfer in Physiological Fluid Dynamics: Modelling and Simulation", **SERB**, DST, New Delhi, 2015–2018.

All these projects were already completed successfully.

11. **Some of the Invited lectures delivered in India/Abroad.**

(a) **Courant Institute of Mathematical Sciences,** June 1981 New York. Topic of Lecture: Deformation and Stresses in arterial walls under normal physiological loading.

(b) **Cornell Medical Center of the New York Hospital**, June 1981. Topic of Lecture: Fracture and remodelling of bones.

(c) **Euromech Colloquium held at Paris**, December 1976. Topic of lecture: Propagation of cracks in thermally stressed solids.

(d) **Fourth International Congress of Biorheology Tokyo (Japan)**, May 1981. He was delegated to by the Indian National Science Academy, New Delhi. Topic of lecture: Deformation and flow in arteries.

(e) Was invited to deliver a lecture and to chair a session at the **Fifth International Congress of Biorheology held in Baden Baden, Germany.**

(f) Delivered the prestigious **P.L. Bhatnagar Memorial Lecture, NIT Hamirpur, Himachal Pradesh**, 2001.

(g) Delivered an invited lecture and chaired a Plenary Session at the **International Congress on Computational and Applied Mathematics, Brussels, Belgium**, 2002.

(h) Delivered two invited lectures at the **National University of Singapore**, 2002.

(i) Delivered an invited lecture at the **Hong Kong University of Science and Technology**, 2002. Delivered a keynote address on Mathematical Modelling and chaired a Plenary Session at the International Conference of Applied Mathematics and Mathematical Physics, **SUST, Sylhet, Bangladesh**, 2003.

(j) Delivered an invited lecture in Bio-informatics at the **International Conference on Information Technology, Kathmandu**, 2003.

(k) Delivered an invited lecture on Mathematical Modelling in the Mechanics of Blood Flow at the **University of Hamburg-Harburg, Germany**, 2005.

(l) Delivered an invited lecture on Mathematical Models in Cardiovascular System Dynamics at the **University of Kassel, Germany**, 2006.

(m) Delivered an invited lecture on Blood flow in arteries in pathological states, **University of Alberta, Edmonton, Canada**, April 2006.

(n) Delivered an invited lecture on Challenges in Biofluid Dynamics, **University of Hamburg-Harburg, Germany**, 11 June 2007.

(o) Delivered an invited lecture on Mechanics and Biology: Past and Present at the Institute of Mechanics, **Technical University of Berlin, Germany**, 14 June 2007.

(p) Delivered an invited lecture on Mathematics, Mechanics and Medicine at the **Institute of Mechanics, University of Stuttgart, Germany**, 18 June 2007.

(q) Delivered an invited lecture on Biomechanics: Past and Present at the **University of Bremen, Germany**, 21 June 2007.

(r) Delivered an invited lecture on Biomedical Mathematics: Prospects and Challenges at **Leibniz University of Hanover, Germany**, 25 June 2007.

(s) Delivered an invited lecture on "Origin and current status of Biomedical Engineering" at the **University of Malay, Kuala Lumpur**, 19th September 2007.

(t) Delivered an invited lecture on "Modelling the Dynamical Behaviour of the Cardiovascular System" at the **University of Malay, Kuala Lumpur**, 20 September 2007.

(u) Computational Biology: Prospects and Challenges, National Workshop of Mathematical Modelling in Biology, **SPM University, Tirupati**, AP, February 23–27, 2008.

(v) Non-Newtonian Flow of blood Through Arteries in Normal and Pathological States, National Workshop on Mathematical Modelling in Biology, **SPM University, Tirupati**, AP, February 23–27, 2008.

(w) Mathematics in Medicine and Biology, National Conference on Advances in Mathematics, **Guwahati University**, September 4–7, 2008.

(x) Mathematics and Spirituality, Fourth All India Students' Conference on Science and Spiritual Quest, **NIT Tiruchirapalli**, December 27–29, 2008.

(y) Leonhard Euler and his contributions in Mathematics, Invited lecture at National Seminar on Emerging areas in Mathematics and Applications, **Burdwan University**, February 18–20, 2009.

(z) Non-linearities in Biology and Medicine, invited lecture delivered at National Seminar on Advances in Nonlinear Systems, **Visva-Bharati, Santiniketan**, February 21–23, 2009.

(aa) Delivered an invited lecture on "Blood flow in arteries in a vibratio n environment" at **Institute of Dynamics and Vibration, Leibniz University of Hanover, Germany**, May 28, 2010.

(ab) Delivered an invited lecture on "Flow of non-Newtonian fluids in channels: Application to blood flow in arteries" at **Institute of Thermo-fluid Dynamics, Technical University of Hamburg-Harburg (Germany)** on 23rd May 2011.

(ac) Chief Guest at National Symposium on Mathematical Sciences, National Mathematics Year 2012, held at **Calcutta Mathematical Society, Salt Lake, Kolkata,** April 21–22, 2012. Topic of the lecture: Mathematical Physiology.

(ad) Chief Guest at the National Conference on Computational Mathematics and Nonlinear Dynamics, 19–21 February 2016 held at **Visva-Bharati University, Santiniketan;** Topic of the lecture: Application of Mathematics in Life Sciences.

(ae) Keynote speech "Mathematical modelling of Physiological fluid flows" (two lectures) delivered at National Workshop on Recent Advances in Fluid Dynamics and Applications in Science and Technology, **MITS, Andhra Pradesh**, 25–26 May 2018.

(af) Keynote speech "Mathematical Modelling of Electro-osmotic Flows in Physiological Systems" delivered at International Conference on Mathematical Modelling and Scientific Computing (ICMMSC 2018), **IIT Indore,** 19–21 July 2018.

(ag) Keynote Speech "Modelling in Physiological Fluid Dynamics, October 24–26, 2019", International Conference on Applied Mathematics in Science and Technology, **SOAU, Bhubaneswar.**

(ah) Keynote Speech "Use of Mathematics in Biology", **Ramanujan Memorial Lecture, Mugberia College, Vidyasagar University, West Bengal**, 2020.

(ai) Invited Lecture "Impact of Heat Transfer on Electro-osmotic Flows in Micro-vessels: Modelling of Blood Flow in the Micro-circulatory System", 1st International Conference on Applied Analysis, Computational and Mathematical Modelling in Engineering (AACMME-2021) **National Institute of Technology Rourkela, Odisha,** February 24–26, 2021.

(aj) Was invited for delivering an Invited Lecture at the 2nd International Conference on Recent Advances in Applied Mathematics, **IIT BHU**, July 03–05, 2024.

Summary of Relevant Contributions

1. Total number of papers published (in refereed journals): 245
2. Total citation record and h-index:

   h-index: 41; i-10 index: 112

   Total citations: 5325 (Database used: Google Scholar)
3. Number of books published: 15
4. Number of completed Research Projects as Principal Investigator: 5
5. Number of research students guided and awarded doctoral degrees: 30
6. Number of invited lectures delivered in Distinguished Institutions/ Universities in India and Abroad, as well as in National/International conferences: 35

12. **Complete list of Publications in standard refereed Journals:**

(a) *Published*

1. R. Prodhan, M. Ferdows, **J.C. Misra**, E. Tzirtzilakis and M.G. Murtaza (2024). Non-Similar Analysis of Mixed Convection Biomagnetic Boundary Layer Flow Over a Vertical Plate with Magnetization and Localized Heating/Cooling, *European Journal of Computational Mechanics,* Vol. 33(2): 91–120 doi: 10.13052/ejcm2642-2085.3321.
2. M. Dhange, G. Sankad, U. Bhujakkanavar, K.K. Das and **J.C. Misra** (2024). Hemodynamic characteristics of blood flow in an inclined overlapped stenosed arterial section, *Partial Differential Equations in Applied Mathematics,* Vol. 11, 2024, 100829. https://doi.org/10.1016/j.padiff.2024.100829
3. B. Mallick, A. Choudhury and **J.C. Misra** (2023). Irreversibility analysis for ion size dependent electrothermal transport of micropolar fluid in a microtube, *Journal of Thermal Analysis and Calorimetry*; Vol. 148(21): 12017–12035, https://doi.org/10.1007/s10973-023-12538-x
4. M.G. Murtaza, **J.C. Misra,** E.E. Tzirtzilakis and M. Ferdows (2023). Numerical study of Biomagnetic Maxwell fluid past a nonlinearly stretching sheet with considering magnetization and electrical conductivity, *Journal of Mechanics in Medicine and Biology*, 23, 2350034.

5. **J.C. Misra,** S. Dandapat and B. Mallick (2023). Effect of structure and mechanics on left ventricular aneurysm: a theoretical study, *MOJ Applied Bionics and Biomechanics*, 7(1), 1–6.
6. M.R. Islam, M. Ferdows, **J.C Misra** and M.G. Murtaza, (2022). Two-Dimensional thin layer convective flow and heat transfer of a dusty fluid on a nonlinear stretching sheet, *Multiscale Science and Engineering*, 4, 111–118. 10.1007/s42493-022-00080-1
7. S. Maiti, S.K. Pandey and **J.C. Misra** (2022). Electroosmotic flow of a Rheological Fluid in Non-Uniform Micro-Vessels, *Journal of Engineering Mathematics,* 135: 8, https://doi.org/10.1007/s10665-022-10234-7, Springer. SCI, *Impact Factor*: 1.444
8. B. Mallick and **J.C. Misra** (2022), Interplay of steric factor and high zeta potential on entropy generation during nanofluid slip flow in a microfluidic tube, *The European Physical Journal Plus,* 137, 868, https://doi.org/10.1140/epjp/s13360-022-03069-9 Springer, SCI Journal, *Impact Factor: 3.758.*
9. M. Ferdows and **J.C. Misra** (2022), Heat and Mass Transfer during MHD Flow of a Nanofluid Containing Gyrotactic Microorganisms on a Stretching/Shrinking Sheet, accepted for publication in *Multiscale Science and Engineering,* 4, 55–65, https://doi.org/10.1007/s42493-022-00077-w
10. K.M. Prasad, P.R. Yasa and **J.C. Misra** (2021). Characteristics of Blood Flow Through a Porous Tapered Artery having a Mild Stenosis under the Influence of an External Magnetic Field, *Journal of Applied Science and Engineering,* 24(4), 661–671.
11. A. Bera, S. Dutta, **J.C. Misra,** G.C. Shit (2021). Computational Modelling of the Effect of Blood Flow and Dual Phase Lag on Tissue Temperature During Tumor Treatment by Magnetic Hyperthermia, *Mathematics and Computers in Simulation* (Elsevier), 188, 389–403.
12. **J.C. Misra,** S. Dandapat and S.D. Adhikary (2021). Stress distribution in the left ventricular wall during cardiac contraction: Study of a mathematical model, *Journal of Mechanics in Medicine and Biology,* 21(3), 2050056.
13. R. Tiwari, **J.C. Misra** and Rashmi Prasad (2021). Magneto-thermoelastic wave propagation in a finitely conducting medium: A comparative study for three types of thermoelasticity I, II and III, *Journal of Thermal Stresses,* (Taylor & Francis), 44(7), 785–806.

14. D. Tripathi, J. Prakash, M. Gnaneswara Reddy and **J.C. Misra** (2021). Numerical simulation of double diffusive convection and electroosmosis during peristaltic transport of a micropolar nanofluid on an asymmetric microchannel, *Journal of Thermal Analysis and Calorimetry*, 143, 2499–2514.
15. **J.C. Misra**, S. Dandapat and S.D. Adhikary (2021). Wave Propagation in the Cranium and the Cerebrospinal Fluid, *Journal of Mechanics in Medicine and Biology*, Vol. 21 (1), 2050045, 1–26.
16. T. Sudha, Umadevi, M. Dhange, S. Manna and **J.C. Misra** (2021), Effects of stenosis and dilatation on flow of blood mixed with suspended nanoparticles: A study using homotopy technique, *International Journal of Applied Mechanics and Engineering*, 26(1), 251–265.
17. M. Ferdows, G. Murtaza, **J.C. Misra**, E.E. Tzirtzilakis and A. Alsenafi (2021). Dual solutions for boundary layer flow and heat transfer of biomagnetic fluid over a stretching/shrinking sheet in presence of a magnetic dipole and a prescribed heat flux, *International Journal of Applied Electromagnetics and Mechanics,* 65(2), 235–251.
18. **J.C. Misra,** B. Mallick and P. Steinmann (2020). Temperature distribution and entropy generation during Darcy-Forchheimer-Brinkman electrokinetic flow in a microfluidic tube subject to a prescribed heat flux, *Meccanica*, 55, 1079–1098.
19. R. Tiwari and **J.C. Misra** (2020). Magneto-thermoelastic excitation induced by a thermal shock: a study under the purview of three phase lag theory, *Waves in Random and Complex Media*, 32, 797–818. doi: 10.1080/17455030.2020.1800861
20. M. Ferdows, G. Murtaza, **J.C. Misra**, E.E. Tzirtzilakis and A. Alsenafi (2020). Dual solutions in biomagnetic fluid flow and heat transfer over a nonlinear stretching/shrinking sheet: application of lie group transformation method, *Mathematical Biosciences and Engineering*, 17(5), 4852–4874.
21. J.I. Ira, M.S. Islam, **J.C. Misra** and M. Kamrujjaman (2020). Mathematical Modelling of the Dynamics of Tumor Growth and its Optimal Control, *Intl. J. Ground Sediment & Water* (USA), 11, 659–679.
22. B. Mallick, **J.C. Misra** and A. Roy Chowdhury (2019). Influence of Hall current and Joule heating on entropy generation during electrokinetically induced thermoradiative transport of nanofluids in a

porous microchannel, *Applied Mathematics and Mechanics* (Springer), 40(10), 1509–1530.

23. G.C. Shit, S. Maiti, M. Roy and **J.C. Misra** (2019). Pulsatile flow and heat transfer of blood in an overlapping vibrating atherosclerotic artery: A numerical study, *Mathematics and Computers in Simulation* (Elsevier), 166(2019), 432–450.
24. M.G. Murtaza, M. Ferdows, **J.C. Misra** and E.E. Tzirtzilakis (2019). Three-dimensional biomagnetic Maxwell fluid flow over a stretching surface in presence of heat source/sink, *International Journal of Biomathematics* (World Scientific Publishing Company), 12, No. 3 (2019) 1950036 (20 pages).
25. S. Gupta, M. Ahmed and **J.C. Misra** (2019). Effects of periodic corrugated boundary surfaces on plane SH-waves in fiber-reinforced medium over a semi-infinite micropolar solid under the action of magnetic field, *Mechanics Research Communications*, 95(2019), 35–44. DOI: 10.1016/j.mechrescom.2018.11.007
26. B. Mallick and **J.C. Misra** (2019). Peristaltic flow of Eyring-Powell nanofluid under the action of an electromagnetic field, *Engineering Science and Technology, an International Journal* 22 (2019) 266–281.
27. S. Manna, **J.C. Misra**, S. Kundu and S. Gupta (2018). Surface wave propagation in an initially stressed heterogeneous medium having a sandy layer and a point source, *Geomechanics and Engineering, An International Journal*, 16(2), 169–176. DOI: https://doi.org/10.12989/gae.2018.16.2.169
28. **J.C. Misra**, B. Mallick, A. Sinha and A. Roy Chowdhury (2018). Impact of Cattaneo- Christov heat flux on electroosmotic transport of third-order fluids in a magnetic environment, *The European Physical Journal Plus* (Springer), 133:195.
29. **J.C. Misra** and S. Chandra (2018). Effect of couple stresses on electrokinetic oscillatory flow of blood in the microcirculatory system, *J. Mech. Med. Biol.* 18(2), 1850035.
30. S. Manna, S. Kundu and **J.C. Misra** (2018). Theoretical Analysis of Torsional Wave Propagation in a Heterogeneous Aeolotropic Stratum over a Voigt-Type Viscoelastic Half-Space, *International Journal of Geomechanics*, Vol. 18(6), 04018050, DOI: 10.1061/(ASCE)GM.1943-5622.0001144

31. **J.C. Misra**, G.C. Shit and R. Pramanik (2018). Non-Newtonian flow of blood in a catheterized bifurcated stenosed artery, *Journal of Bionic Engineering*, Vol. 15(1), 173–184.
32. **J.C. Misra**, S.D. Adhikary, B. Mallick and A. Sinha (2018). Mathematical Modelling of blood flow in arteries subject to a vibrating environment, *Journal of Mechanics in Medicine and Biology (World Scientific)*, Vol. 18 (1), 1850001, DOI: 10.1142/ S0219519417500634.
33. **J.C. Misra,** B. Mallick and A. Sinha (2018). Heat and Mass Transfer in asymmetric channels during peristaltic transport of an MHD fluid having temperature-dependent properties, *Alexandria Engineering Journal* (Elsevier), 57(1), 391–406.
34. **J.C. Misra,** A. Sinha and B. Mallick (2017). Stagnation point flow and heat transfer on a thin porous sheet: Applications to flow dynamics of the circulatory system, *Physica A: Statistical Mechanics and its Applications* (Elsevier), Vol. 470, 330–344, DOI: 10.1016/j.physa/2016.10.051.
35. **J.C. Misra** and S.D. Adhikary (2017). Flow of a Bingham fluid in a porous bed under the action of a magnetic field: Application to magneto-hemorheology, *Engng. Sc.Tech-an International Journal (Elsevier)*, Vol. 20(3), 973–981.
36. S. Chandra and **J.C. Misra** (2016). Influence of Hall current and micro-rotation on the boundary layer flow of an electrically conducting fluid: Application to Haemodynamics, *Journal of Molecular Liquids (Elsevier)*, Vol. 224, Part A, 818–824.
37. **J.C. Misra** and S.D. Adhikary (2016). MHD Oscillatory channel flow, heat, and mass transfer of a physiological fluid in presence of chemical reaction, *Alexandria Engng. Journal* (Elsevier), Vol. 55, 287–297.
38. R. Saha, Sarifuddin, **J.C. Misra** and P.K. Mandal (2016). Impact of luminal flow on mass transport through coronary arteries: a study relevant to drug-eluting stent, *Intl. J. Maths. Comp.* Vol. 27, 40–58.
39. A. Sinha, **J.C. Misra** and G.C. Shit (2016). Effects of heat transfer on unsteady MHD flow of blood in a permeable vessel in the presence of non-uniform heat source, *Alexandria Engng. Journal* (Elsevier), Vol. 55 (2016) 2023–2033.
40. S.K. Ghosh and **J.C. Misra** (2016). Effects of Joule Heating and Viscous Dissipation on MHD Viscous Fluid Flow past a Porous Stretching Surface, *Intl. J. Maths. Comp*, vol. 27, 10–22.

41. **J.C. Misra**, S. Chandra, and H. Herwig (2015). Flow of a micro-polar fluid in a micro-channel under the action of an alternating electric field: Estimates of flow in bio-fluidic devices, *Journal of Hydrodynamics*, Vol. 27, 350–358 (Elsevier).
42. **J.C. Misra** and A. Sinha (2015). Electro-osmotic Flow and Heat Transfer of a Non-Newtonian Fluid in a Hydrophobic Micro-channel with Navier Slip, *Journal of Hydrodynamics*, vol. 27, 647–657 (Elsevier).
43. A. Sinha and **J.C. Misra** (2014). MHD Flow of Blood through a Dually Stenosed Artery: Effects of Viscosity Variation, Variable Hematocrit and Velocity-Slip, *The Canadian Journal of Chemical Engineering* (Wiley-Blackwell), Vol. 92(1), 23-31, DOI 10.1002/cjce.21792.
44. A. Sinha and **J.C. Misra** (2014). Effect of Induced Magnetic Field on MHD Stagnation Point Flow and Heat Transfer on a Stretching Sheet, *ASME Journal of Heat Transfer*, Vol. 136 (11) 112701.
45. A. Sinha and **J.C. Misra** (2014). Mixed Convection Hydromagnetic Flow with Heat Generation Thermophoresis and Mass Transfer over an Inclined Nonlinear Porous Shrinking Sheet: A Numerical Approach, *Journal of Mechanics* (Cambridge University Press), Vol. 30 (5), 491–503.
46. S.K. Ghosh, G.C. Shit and **J.C. Misra** (2014). Heat Transfer in Hydromagnetic Fluid Flow: Study of Temperature-Dependence of Fluid Viscosity, *Journal of Applied Fluid Mechanics*, Vol. 7 (4), 633–640.
47. **J.C. Misra**, S. Chandra, G.C. Shit and P.K. Kundu (2014). Electroosmotic Oscillatory Flow of Micropolar Fluid in Microchannels: Application to dynamics of blood flow in Microfluidic Devices, *Applied Mathematics and Mechanics* (Springer), Vol. 35 (6), 749–766.
48. **J.C. Misra,** S. Chandra (2014). Electro-osmotically Actuated Oscillatory Flow of a Physiological Fluid on a Porous Microchannel Subject to an External AC Electric Field Having Dissimilar Frequencies, *Central European Journal of Physics* (Springer), Vol. 12 (4), 274–285.
49. **J.C. Misra** and A. Sinha (2013). Effect of thermal radiation on MHD flow of blood and heat transfer in a permeable capillary in stretching motion, *Heat and Mass Transfer*, Germany (Springer), Vol. 49, 617–628, DOI 10.1007/s00231-012-1107-6.

50. S. Maiti and **J.C. Misra** (2013). Non-Newtonian characteristics of peristaltic flow of blood in micro-vessels, *Communications in Nonlinear Science and Numerical Simulation* (Elsevier), Vol. 18, 1970-1988, http://dx.doi.org/10.1016/j.cnsns.2012.12.015.

51. **J.C. Misra** and A. Sinha (2013). Effects of Hall Current and Heat Radiation on Flow of a Fluid Through a Porous Medium Subject to an External Magnetic Field, *Special Topics & Reviews in Porous Media—An International Journal* (Begell House, USA), Vol. 4 (2), 147–158.

52. S.D. Adhikary and **J.C. Misra** (2013). Pulsating Flow of a Couple Stress Fluid in a Channel with Permeable Walls, *Engineering Research/ ForschungImIngineurwesen*, Germany (Springer), Vol. 77, 49–57.

53. **J.C. Misra** and S. Chandra (2013). Electro-osmotic flow of a second-grade fluid in a porous micro-channel subject to an AC electric field, *Journal of Hydrodynamics* (Elsevier), Vol. 25, 309–316.

54. **J.C. Misra**, S. Chandra, G.C. Shit and P.K. Kundu (2013). Thermodynamic and magnetohydrodynamic analysis of blood flow considering rotation of micro-particles of blood, *Journal of Mechanics in Medicine and Biology*. World Scientific (Singapore/London /USA), Vol. 13, No. 1, 1350013(16 pages).

55. **J.C. Misra** and S. Maiti (2012). Peristaltic Pumping of Blood Through Small Vessels of Varying Cross-section, ASME *Journal of Applied Mechanics*, Vol. 79, No. 6, 061003: 1–19 (19 pages), DOI: 10.1115/1.4006635.

56. **J.C. Misra** and S. Maiti (2012). Peristaltic Transport of Rheological Fluid: Model for Movement of Food Bolus Through Esophagus, *Applied Mathematics and Mechanics*, Springer, 33(3), 315–332.

57. A. Sinha and **J.C. Misra** (2012). Numerical study of flow and heat transfer during oscillatory blood flow in diseased arteries in presence of magnetic fields, *Applied Mathematics and Mechanics* (Springer), Vol. 33, 649–662.

58. S. Maiti and **J.C. Misra** (2012). Peristaltic Transport of a Couple Stress Fluid: Some Applications to Haemodynamics, *Journal of Mechanics in Medicine and Biology* (World Scientific, London, Singapore & USA), Vol. 12, 1250048:1–21 (21 pages).

59. A. Sinha and **J.C. Misra** (2012). Influence of Slip Velocity on blood flow through an artery with Permeable Wall: A Theoretical Study,

International Journal of Biomathematics, World Scientific, Vol. 5, No. 5, 1250042: 1–20 (20 pages)

60. **J.C. Misra**, S. Dandapat and S.D. Adhikary (2011). Non-Newtonian Flows in Contracting/Expanding Blood Vessels: A Theoretical study, *International Journal of Biomathematics,* Vol. 4, Issue: 3 pp. 347–363.
61. **J.C. Misra,** A. Sinha and G.C. Shit (2011). A Numerical Model for the Magnetohydrodynamic Flow of Blood in a Porous Channel, *Journal of Mechanics and Medicine in Biology,* World Scientific, Vol. 11, No. 3, pp. 547–562, DOI: 10.1142/ S0219519410003794.
62. **J.C. Misra,** G.C. Shit, S. Chandra and P.K. Kundu (2011). Electro-osmotic flow of a viscoelastic fluid in a channel: Applications to physiological fluid mechanics, *Applied Mathematics and Computation* (Elsevier), Vol. 217, 7932–7939.
63. S. Maiti and **J.C. Misra** (2011). Peristaltic flow of a fluid in a porous channel: A study having relevance to flow of bile within ducts in a pathological state, International Journal of Engineering Science (Elsevier), Vol. 49, 950–966. *[Included in the List of TOP 25 Hottest Articles published by Science Direct.]*
64. **J.C. Misra,** A. Sinha and G.C. Shit (2011). Mathematical Modelling of Blood Flow in a Porous Vessel Having Double Stenoses in the Presence of an External Magnetic Field, *International Journal of Biomathematics* (World Scientific), Vol. 4, 207–225.
65. S.D. Adhikary and **J.C. Misra** (2011). Unsteady two-dimensional hydromagnetic flow and heat transfer of a fluid, *International Journal of Applied Mathematics and Mechanics,* Vol. 7(4), 1–20.
66. **J.C. Misra,** G.C. Shit, S. Chandra and P.K. Kundu (2011). Hydromagnetic flow and heat transfer of a second-grade viscoelastic fluid in a channel with oscillatory stretching walls: application to the dynamics of blood flow, *Journal of Engineering Mathematics* (Springer) Vol. 59, 91–100.
67. **J.C. Misra,** S. Dandapat and S.D. Adhikary (2010). A Mathematical Model for a Vibrating Human Head, *International Journal of Artificial Life Research* (USA), 1(2), 29–42.
68. **J.C. Misra,** A. Sinha and G.C. Shit (2010). Flow of a Biomagnetic Viscoelastic Fluid: Application to Estimation of Blood Flow in Arteries during Electromagnetic Hyperthermia, a Therapeutic Procedure for

Cancer Treatment, *Applied Mathematics and Mechanics* (**Springer**), Vol. 31(11), 1405–1420.

69. **J.C. Misra** and G.C. Shit (2009). Flow of a Biomagnetic Visco-elastic Fluid in a Channel with Stretching Walls, *ASME Journal of Applied Mechanics,* (**USA**), Vol. 76, No. 6, 06106:1–9
70. **J.C. Misra** and G.C. Shit (2009). Biomagnetic Viscoelastic Fluid Flow over a Stretching Sheet, *Applied Mathematics and Computation* (**Elsevier**), Vol. 210 (2), 350–361.
71. **J.C. Misra,** G.C. Shit and H.J. Rath (2008). Flow and Heat Transfer of a MHD Viscoelastic Fluid in a Channel with Stretching Walls: Some Applications to Haemodynamics, *Computers & Fluids* (Elsevier), Vol. 37, No. 1, 1–11. [*Occupies The 6th Position in the List of Top 25 Hottest Articles Published by Science Direct.]*
72. **J.C. Misra**, S. Maiti, G.C. Shit (2008). Peristaltic Transport of a Physiological Fluid in an Asymmetric Porous Channel in the Presence of an External Magnetic Field, *Journal of Mechanics in Medicine and Biology (World Scientific)*, Vol. 8, No. 4, 507–525.
73. **J.C. Misra**, S.D. Adhikary and G.C. Shit (2008). Mathematical Analysis of Blood Flow Through an Arterial Segment with Time Dependent Stenosis, *Mathematical Modelling and Analysis* (Taylor & Francis) Vol. 13, No. 3, 401–412 (Wiley).
74. **J.C. Misra,** A. Sinha and G.C. Shit (2008). Theoretical Analysis of Blood Flow Through an Arterial Segment Having Multiple Stenoses, *Journal of Mechanics in Medicine and Biology*, (*World Scientific),* Vol. 8, No. 2, 265–279.
75. **J.C. Misra** and A. Mitra (2008). Synchronization among Tumor-like Cell Aggregations Coupled by Quorum Sensing: A Theoretical Study, *Computers and Mathematics with Applications* (USA), Vol. 55, Issue 8, 1842–1853.
76. **J.C. Misra,** S.D. Adhikary and G.C. Shit (2007). Multiphase Flow of Blood Through Arteries with a Branch Capillary: A Theoretical Study, *Journal of Mechanics in Medicine and Biology*, Vol. 7, No. 4, 395–417 (World Scientific), Singapore.
77. **J.C. Misra** and G.C. Shit (2007). Effect of Magnetic Field on Blood Flow Through an Artery: A Numerical Model, *Journal of Computational Technologies* (Russia), Vol. 12, No. 4, 3–16.

78. **J.C. Misra** and M.K. Patra (2007). A Study of Solitary Waves in a Tapered Aorta by using the Theory of Solitons, Computers *and Mathematics with Applications* (USA), Vol. 54, 242–254.
79. **J.C. Misra** and G.C. Shit (2007). Role of Slip-velocity in Blood Flow Through Stenosed Arteries: A Non-Newtonian Model, *Journal of Mechanics in Medicine and Biology*, Vol. 7, No. 3, 337–353 (World Scientific).
80. **J.C. Misra** and A. Mitra (2006). Instabilities in Single-species and Host-parasite Systems: Period-doubling Bifurcations and Chaos, *Computers and Mathematics with Applications* (USA). Vol. 52, 525–538 (Elsevier).
81. **J.C. Misra** and G.C. Shit (2006). Blood Flow through Arteries in a Pathological State: A Theoretical Study, *International Journal of Engineering Science* (UK). Vol. 44, 662–671.
82. **J.C. Misra** and B. Dravid (2006). A Mathematical Model in the Study of Genes for Identifying Transcription Factor Binding Sites, *Computers and Mathematics with Applications* (USA), Vol. 51, 621–630.
83. A.S. Gupta, **J.C. Misra** and M. Reza (2005). Magnetohydrodynamic Shear Flow along a Flat Plate with Uniform Suction or Blowing, **ZAMP** (Switzerland), Vol. 56, 1030–1047.
84. **J.C. Misra**, S. Mukherjee and A.K. Das (2004). A Mathematical Model for Enzymatic Action on DNA Knots and Links, *Mathematical and Computer Modelling* (USA), Vol. 39, 1423–1430.
85. A.S. Gupta, **J.C. Misra** and M. Reza (2003). Effects of Suction or Blowing on the Velocity and Temperature Distribution in the Flow Past a Porous Flat Plate of a Power-law Fluid, *Fluid Dynamics Research*, Vol. 32, 283–294.
86. **J.C. Misra** and S.K. Ghosh (2003). Pulsatile Flow of a Viscous Fluid through a Porous Elastic Vessel of Variable Cross-section—a Mathematical Model for Haemodynamic Flows, *Computers and Mathematics with Applications* (UK), Vol. 46, 947–957.
87. A.S. Gupta, **J.C. Misra** and M. Reza (2003). Flow in the Ekman Layer on an Oscillating Porous Plate, *Acta Mechanica* (New York), Vol. 165, 1–16.
88. **J.C. Misra** and S.K. Pandey (2002). Peristaltic Transport of Blood in Small Vessels-study of a Mathematical Model, *Computers and Mathematics with Applications*, (U.K.) 43, 1183–1193.

89. **J.C. Misra** and S.K. Pandey (2001). Peristaltic Flow of a Multi-layered Power-law Fluid through a Cylindrical Tube, *International Journal of Engineering Science*, Vol. 39, 387–402.

90. **J.C. Misra** and S.K. Ghosh (2001). A Mathematical Model for the Study of Interstitial Fluid Movement Vis-a-vis the Non-Newtonian Behaviour of Blood in a Constricted Artery, *Computers and Mathematics with Applications* (U.K.), Vol. 41, 783–811.

91. **J.C. Misra**, B. Pal, A. Pal and A.S. Gupta (2001). Oscillatory Entry Flow in a Plane Channel with Pulsating Walls, *International Journal of Non-linear Mechanics* (U.K.), Vol. 36, 731–741.

92. **J.C. Misra** and S.K. Pandey (2001). A Mathematical Model for Oesophageal Swallowing of a Food-bolus, *Mathematical and Computer Modelling* (U.K.), Vol. 33, 997–1009.

93. **J.C. Misra**, N.C. Chattopadhyay and S.C. Samanta (2000). Stress Field Generated in a Visco-elastic Aeolotropic Continuum by a Distributed Heat Source, *Journal of Thermal Stresses* (USA), Vol. 23, 169–195.

94. **J.C. Misra**, N.C. Chattopadhyay and A. Chakravorty (2000). Study of Thermoelastic Wave Propagation in a Half-space Using GN Theory, *Journal of Thermal Stresses* (USA). Vol. 23, 327–351.

95. A.S. Gupta, A. Pal, **J.C. Misra**, B. Pal and H.S. Takhar (2000). Hall Effects on Magnetohydrodynamic Flow and Heat Transfer over a Stretching Surface, In: *Mathematics and Its Application to Industry and New Emerging Areas*, 49–62, Special Volume (Ed. S.K. Malik) INSA, New Delhi, 2000.

96. **J.C. Misra** and S.K. Ghosh (2000). Flow of a Casson Fluid in a Narrow Tube with a Side Branch, *International Journal of Engineering Science* (England), Vol. 38, 2045–2077.

97. **J.C. Misra** and B.Pal (1999). A Mathematical Model for the Study of Pulsating Flow of Blood under an Externally Imposed Body Acceleration, *Mathematical and Computer Modelling* (USA), Vol. 29, No. 1, 89–106.

98. **J.C. Misra** and S.K. Pandey (1999). Peristaltic Transport of a Non-Newtonian Fluid with a Peripheral Layer, *International Journal of Engineering Science* (U.K.), Vol. 37, No. 14, 1841–1858.

99. B. Pal, **J.C. Misra**, A. Pal and A.S. Gupta (1999). Hydromagnetic Flow of a Viscoelastic Fluid in a Parallel Plate Channel with Stretching

Walls, *Ind. Journal of Mathematics*, Vol. 41, No. 2, 231–247 (B.N. Prasad Birth Centenary Commemoration Volume).

100. **J.C. Misra** and S.K. Ghosh (1998). Flow of a Non-Newtonian Fluid through a Channel with a Porous Pulsating Wall—Applications to Haemodialysis/Ultrafiltration in Artificial Kidney, Modelling, *Measurement and Control* (France), Vol. 57, 47–63.

101. **J.C. Misra**, B. Pal and A.S. Gupta (1998). Hydromagnetic Flow of a Second-Grade Fluid in a Channel—Some Applications to Physiological Systems, *Mathematical Models and Methods in Applied Sciences*, (Italy), Vol. 8, No. 8, 1323–1342.

102. **J.C. Misra** and S.K. Ghosh (1998). Pulsative Flow of a Couple Stress Fluid through a Narrow Porous Tube of an Elliptic Cross-Section—a Model for Blood Flow in a Stenosed Arteriole, Engineering *Simulation* (The Netherlands), Vol. 15, 849–864.

103. **J.C. Misra** and S.K. Ghosh (1997). A Mathematical Model for the Study of Blood Flow through a Channel with Permeable Walls, *Acta Mechanica* (Wien/New York), Vol. 122, 137–153.

104. B. Pal, **J.C. Misra** and A.S. Gupta (1996). Steady Hydromagnetic Flow in a Slowly Varying Channel, *Proc. Nat. Acad. Sci. India*, Vol. 66(A), 247-262.

105. **J.C. Misra**, N.C. Chattopadhyay and S.C. Samanta (1996). Study of the Thermoelastic Interactions in an Elastic Half-space Subjected to a Ramp-type Heating—A State-space Approach, *International Journal of Engineering Science* (UK), Vol. 34, No. 5, 579–596.

106. **J.C. Misra** and S.K. Pandey (1995). Peristaltic Transport in a Tapered Tube, *Mathematical and Computer Modelling* (USA), Vol. 22, No. 8, 137–151.

107. **J.C. Misra** and S.K. Pandey (1994). Peristaltic Transport of a Particle-fluid Suspension in a Cylindrical Tube, *Computers and Mathematics with Applications* (UK), Vol. 28, No. 4, 131–145.

108. **J.C. Misra**, M.K. Patra and S.C. Misra (1994). Laminar Boundary-layer Flow of a Newtonian Fluid Through a Curved Pipe—Some Applications to Arterial Flow Dynamic s, *International Journal of Engineering Science* (UK), Vol. 32, No. 12, 1997–2010.

109. **J.C. Misra**, N.C. Chattopadhyay and S.C. Samanta (1994). Thermoviscoelastic Waves in an Infinite Aeolotropic Body with a

Cylindrical Cavity—a Study Under the Purview of Generalised Theory of Thermoelasticity, *Computers and Structures* (UK), Vol. 52, No. 4, 705–717.

110. **J.C. Misra**, N.C. Chattopadhyay and S.C. Samanta (1994). Thermoelastic Stress Waves in a Spherically Aeolotropic Medium with a Spherical Cavity Induced by a Distributed Heat Source within the Medium, *International Journal of Engineering Science* (UK), Vol. 32, 1769–1789.
111. **J.C. Misra** and M.K. Patra (1993). Biorheological Aspects of Arterial Flow Near Bifurcations, *Computers and Mathematics with Applications* (UK), Vol. 26, No. 9, 53–65.
112. **J.C. Misra** and M.K. Patra (1993). Oscillatory Flow of a Viscous Fluid Through Converging—Diverging Orthotropic Tethered Tubes, *Computers and Mathematics with Applications* (UK), Vol. 26, No. 2, 87–106.
113. **J.C. Misra** and M.K. Patra (1993). A Non-Newtonian Fluid Model for Blood Flow Through Arteries Under Stenotic Conditions, *Journal of Biomechanics* (UK), Vol. 26, 1129–1141.
114. **J.C. Misra,** and A.K. Chakrabarti (1993). Thermally Induced Vibrations in an Infinite Anisotropic Viscoelastic Solid with a Cylindrical Cavity in the Presence of a Uniform Axial Magnetic Field, *International Journal of Engineering Science* (UK), Vol. 31, No. 7, 1047–1052.
115. **J.C. Misra,** S.C. Samanta and A.K. Chakrabarti (1993). Magnetic-mechanical Interaction in an Aeolotropic Cylindrical Shell at an Elevated Temperature, *Computers and Structures (UK),* Vol. 46, No. 5, 851–857.
116. **J.C. Misra,** A.K. Chakrabarti, S.C. Samanta (1992). Influence of Thermomechanical Coupling on the Transient Thermoelastic Deformation of a Cylinder in the Presence of a Magnetic Field, *Mechanics Research Communications* (USA), Vol. 19, 415–426.
117. **J.C. Misra** and G.C. Bera (1992). Remodelling of Diaphysial Surfaces of a Long Bone Induced due to Force-fitting of a Medullary Pin, *Computers and Mathematics with Applications* (UK), Vol. 24, No. 7, 3–15.
118. **J.C. Misra** and M.K. Patra (1992). Unsteady Flow of Blood Through Narrow Blood Vessels, *Computers and Mathematics with Applications* (UK), Vol. 24, No. 10, 19–31.

119. **J.C. Misra** and A.K. Khankari (1992). Thermal Shock in a Semi-infinite Non-Homogeneous Elastic Rod, Modelling, *Simulation & Control, B,* (France), Vol. 41, No. 4. 9–21.

120. **J.C. Misra,** S.C. Samanta and A.K. Chakrabarti (1991). Magneto-thermoelastic Interaction in an Aeolotropic Solid Cylinder Subjected to Ramp-type Heating, *International Journal of Engineering Science* (UK), Vol. 29, 1065–1075.

121. **J.C. Misra,** N.C. Chattopadhyay and S.C. Samanta (1991). Thermal Stresses Generated in a Viscoelastic Inhomogeneous Anisotropic Cylindrical Shell Irradiated by Intense Electromagnetic Waves, *Modelling, Simulation and Control, B,* (France) Vol. 42, No. 2, 49–64.

122. **J.C. Misra** and B.K. Kar (1991). A Mathematical Analysis of Blood Flow from a Feeding Artery into a Branch Capillary, *Mathematical and Computer Modelling* (UK), Vol. 15, No. 6, 9–18.

123. **J.C. Misra** and G.C. Bera (1991). A Mathematical Study of the Stress Field in a Long Bone Subjected to an External Load, *Journal of Mathematical Analysis and Applications* (UK), Vol. 161, No. 1, 474–507.

124. **J.C. Misra** and S. Roy (1991). Mathematical Analysis of a Specimen of Tubular Bone Subjected to Torsional Loading, *Computers and Mathematics with Applications* (UK), Vol. 21, No. 2–3, 141–147.

125. **J.C. Misra,** S.C. Samanta, A.K. Chakrabarti, and S.C. Misra (1991). Magneto thermoelastic Interaction in an Infinite Continuum with a Cylindrical Hole Subjected to Ramp-type Heating, *International Journal of Engineering Science* (UK), Vol. 29, No. 12, 1505–1514.

126. **J.C. Misra,** S.C. Samanta and A.K. Chakraborti (1991). Magnetothermo-mechanical Interaction in an Aeolotropic Viscoelastic Cylinder Permeated by a Magnetic Field Subjected to a Periodic Loading, *International Journal of Engineering Science* (UK), Vol. 29, No. 10, 1209–1216.

127. **J.C. Misra** and B.K. Kar (1990). Unsteady Flow of Blood Through Arteries in Vibration Environments, *Mathematical and Computer Modelling* (UK), Vol. 13, 7–17.

128. **J.C. Misra** and B.K. Kar (1989). Momentum Integral Method for Studying Flow Characteristics of Blood Through a Stenosed Vessel, *Biorheology* (UK), Vol. 26, 23–35.

129. **J.C. Misra** and B.K. Sahu (1989). Forced Contraction and Expansion of a Valved Blood Vessel, *Mathematical and Computer Modelling* (UK), Vol. 12, No. 7, 761–776.

130. **J.C. Misra** and B.K. Sahu (1989). Unsteady Flow of Blood Through Vessels of Non-uniform Endothelial Cross-section, *Modelling, Simulation and Control, C* (France), Vol. 15, 31–64.

131. **J.C. Misra** and B.K. Sahu (1989). A Limit Process Asymptotic Analysis of the Convective Nonlinearities Associated with Blood Flow in Arteries, *Mathematical and Computer Modelling* (UK), Vol. 12, 319–333.

132. **J.C. Misra** and S. Roy (1989). Mechanics of Bone Remodelling Vis-à-vis Non-homogeneity of Osseous Tissues, *Modelling, Simulation and Control, C,* (France), Vol. 15, No. 4, 41–63.

133. **J.C. Misra** and B.K. Sahu (1989). Propagation of Pressure Waves Through Blood Vessels: Blood Viscoelasticity, *Mathematical and Computer Modelling* (UK), Vol. 12, 333–349.

134. **J.C. Misra,** G.C. Bera and S. Samanta (1989). Electric and Magnetic Fields Induced due to Thickness-shear Vibration of a Tubular Bone, *Modelling, Simulation and Control, C* (France), Vol. 17, 1–24.

135. **J.C. Misra,** G.C. Bera and S. Samanta (1989). Influence of Non-isotropy of Osseous Tissues and Cross-sectional Non-uniformity of a Long Bone on the Internal Remodelling Dynamics of Osseous Tissues, *Mathematical Modelling* (UK), Vol. 12, 611–624.

136. **J.C. Misra** and S. Roy (1989). Stresses in the Neighbourhood of an Exterior Crack in a Bone Specimen, *Computers and Mathematics with Applications* (UK), Vol. 17, 1493–1502.

137. **J.C. Misra** and B.K. Sahu (1988). Flow Through Blood Vessels Under the Action of a Periodic Acceleration Field, *Computers and Mathematics with Applications* (UK), (UK), Vol. 16, 993–1016.

138. **J.C. Misra,** G.C. Bera and S. Samanta (1988). Induced Electric and Magnetic Fields Due to Wave Propagation in a Tubular Bone, *Journal of Mathematical Biology* (USA), Vol. 26, 105–120.

139. **J.C. Misra** and B.K. Kar (1988). Formation of a Boundary Layer in Steady-state Blood Flow, *Journal of Biomedical Engineering* (England), Vol. 10, 220–224.

140. **J.C. Misra** and S. Samanta (1988). A Mathematical Model for the Biomechanics of the Body of a Vertebra, *Computers and Mathematics with Applications* (UK), Vol. 15, 85–96.

141. **J.C. Misra** and S.I. Singh (1988). Study on The Mechanics of Aneurysms in the left Ventricle of the Heart, *Computers and Mathematics with Applications* (UK), Vol. 15, 17–27.
142. **J.C. Misra** and S. Roy (1988). Free and Forced Vibrations of the Cranial Vault, *Computers and Mathematics with Applications* (UK), Vol. 16, 247–266.
143. **J.C. Misra** and S. Samanta (1988). A Mathematical Analysis of the Vibration Characteristics of the Human Tibia, *Computers and Mathematics with Applications* (UK), Vol. 16, No. 12, 1017–1026.
144. **J.C. Misra** and S. Samanta (1987). Effect of Material Damping on Bone Remodelling, *Journal of Biomechanics* (Oxford), Vol. 20, 241–249.
145. **J.C. Misra** and S.I. Singh (1987). A Study on the Nonlinear Flow of Blood Through Arteries, *Bulletin of Mathematical Biology* (England), Vol. 49, 257–277.
146. **J.C. Misra**, S.B. Kar and S. Samanta (1987). Stresses Generated in a Viscoelastic Solid due to a Heat Source in The Vicinity of a Spherical Cavity, *CSME Transactions* (Canada), Vol. 1, 87–94.
147. **J.C. Misra**, S.B. Kar and S. Samanta (1987). Distribution of Stresses in a Heated Non-homogeneous Rod, *Solid Mechanics Archives* (Oxford), Vol. 12, 423–438.
148. **J.C. Misra**, S.B. Kar and S. Samanta (1987). Effects of Mechanical and Thermal Relaxation on the Stresses in a Heated Viscoelastic Continuum with a Cylindrical Hole, *CSME Transactions* (Canada), Vol. 11, 151–159.
149. **J.C. Misra** (1987) Mathematical Modelling of the Physiological Problem of Brain Injury, *The Mathematics Student*, Vol. 55, 217–223.
150. **J.C. Misra** and S. Chakravarty (1986). Flow in Arteries in the Presence of Stenosis, *Journal of Biomechanics* (Oxford), Vol. 19, 907–916.
151. **J.C. Misra** (1986). Stresses in the Human Head Generated due to Thermogenesis, *Rheologica Acta* (Germany), Vol. 25, 201–205.
152. **J.C. Misra** (1986). Distribution of Stresses in a Pre-cracked Bone Specimen, *Rheologica Acta* (Germany), Vol. 25, 485–490.
153. **J.C. Misra**, G.C. Bera and S. Samanta (1986). Vibration of a Tubular Bone in Axial Planes, *Mathematical Modelling* (UK), Vol. 7, 483–492.

154. **J.C. Misra**, S.B. Kar and S. Samanta (1986). Dynamic Stresses in an Elastic Inhomogeneous Medium having a Spherical Cavity with its Surface Maintained at a Fixed Temperature, *Solid Mechanics Archives* (Oxford), Vol. 11, 103–112.

155. **J.C. Misra** and S.N. Maiti (1986). Thermal Stresses in an Infinite Non-isotropic Plate having a Penny-shaped Crack, *Forschung Im Ingenieurwesen* (Germany), Vol. 52, 33–36.

156. **J.C. Misra** and M. Mishra (1985). Stress-field in a Bone Medium Having a Star-shaped Crack, *Engineering Fracture Mechanics* (England), Vol. 22, 65–76.

157. **J.C. Misra** and S.I. Singh (1985). A Model for Studying the Stability of Thoracic Aorta, *Mathematical Modelling* (UK), Vol. 6, 295–306.

158. **J.C. Misra** and S. Chakravarty (1985). Dynamic Response of a Head-neck System to an Impulsive Load, *Mathematical Modelling* (UK) Vol. 6, 83–96.

159. **J.C. Misra** and K. Roychoudhury (1985). Response of a Blood Vessel Segment to Finite Strain with Small Sinusoidally Varying Incremental Strains Superimposed upon it, *Journal of Mathematical Analysis and Applications* (USA), Vol. 110, 200–211.

160. **J.C. Misra** and S.I. Singh (1985). Distribution of Stresses in the Left Ventricular Wall of the Intact Heart, *Bulletin of Mathematical Biology* (England), Vol. 47, 53–71.

161. **J.C. Misra** (1985). Stresses in a Tubular Bone Exposed to Heat Radiation from a Distant Heat Source, *Rheologica Acta* (Germany), Vol. 24, 520–533.

162. **J.C. Misra**, S.B. Kar and S. Samanta (1985). On the Thermally Induced Flexural Deformation of an Anisotropic Viscoelastic Plate Resting on an Elastic Foundation, *CSME Transactions* (Canada), Vol. 9, 228–232.

163. **J.C. Misra** and S. Chakravarty (1984). A Study on Rotational Brain Injury, *Journal of Biomechanics* (Oxford), Vol. 17, 459–466.

164. **J.C. Misra** and S.I. Singh (1984). Pulse Wave Velocities in the Aorta, *Bulletin of Mathematical Biology* (England), Vol. 46, 103–114.

165. **J.C. Misra** and S. Samanta (1984). Wave Propagation in Tubular Bones, *International Journal of Solids and Structures* (England), Vol. 20, 55–62.

166. **J.C. Misra** and M. Samantarai (1984). Stress Concentration in the Vicinity of Cracks in a Sandwiched Medium, *International Journal of Fracture* (The Netherlands), Vol. 24, 239–254.

167. **J.C. Misra** and S. Samanta (1984). Thermal Stresses in Rotating Discs of Thermorheologically Simple Solids, *Solid Mechanics Archives* (Oxford), Vol. 9, 259–267.

168. **J.C. Misra** (1984). Fredholm Equations for a Thermally Stressed Strip Having an Infinite Row of Griffith Cracks, *Rev. Roum. Sci. Tech. Mec. Appl.*, Vol. 29, 403–413.

169. **J.C. Misra**, S.B. Kar and S. Samanta (1984). Thermal Creep in a Spherical Shell Subjected to an Elevated Temperature Field, *Arch. Mech.* (Poland), Vol. 36, 299–306

170. **J.C. Misra** and M. Mishra (1984). Exterior Star-shaped Crack in a Bone Medium, *Engineering Fracture Mechanics* (England), Vol. 19, 101–112.

171. **J.C. Misra** and K. Roychoudhury (1984). An Analysis for the Flow of Blood Through Thick-Walled Vessels, Considering the Effect of Tethering, *Rheologica Acta* (Germany), Vol. 23, 548–555.

172. **J.C. Misra** and S. Chakravarty (1984). A Poroelastic Shell Model for Studying the Problem of Head Injury, *Journal of Mathematical Analysis and Applications* (USA), Vol. 103, 323–343.

173. **J.C. Misra** and K. Roychoudhury (1983). Effect of Initial Stresses on the Wave Propagation in Arteries, *J. Mathematical Biology* (USA), Vol. 18, 53–67.

174. **J.C. Misra** and V.V.T.N. Murthy (1983). A Model for Studying the Stress-field Around Simple Fractures in Human Patella, *Aeronautical Quarterly* (Royal Aeronautical Society London), Vol. 34, 303–313.

175. **J.C. Misra** and S.I. Singh (1983). A Large Deformation Analysis for Aortic Walls Under a Physiological Loading, *International Journal of Engineering Science* (England), Vol. 21, 1193–1202.

176. **J.C. Misra** and V.V.T.N. Murthy (1983). An Estimate of the Stress-field in an Osseous Medium Having a No-slip Interface Crack, *Engineering Fracture Mechanics* (England), Vol. 18, 1075–1086.

177. M. Mishra and **J.C. Misra** (1983). An Anisotropic Strip Weakened by an Array of Cracks, *International Journal of Engineering Science* (England), Vol. 21, 187–198.

178. **J.C. Misra** and S. Samanta (1983). Propagation of Torsional Waves in Tubular Bones, *Journal of Mathematical Analysis and Applications* (USA), Vol. 96, 313–319.

179. **J.C. Misra** and V.V.T.N. Murthy (1983). Surface Remodelling of Bones Induced by Intramedullary Nailing, *Rheologica Acta* (Germany), Vol. 22, 512–518.

180. **J.C. Misra** and K. Roychowdhury (1983). Effect of Inertia and Compressibility on the Stress- field in Blood Vessels, *J. Math. Phys. Sci.*, Vol. 17, 399–415.

181. **J.C. Misra** and V.V.T.N. Murthy (1983). A Mathematical Model for Studying the Physiological Process of Internal Bone Remodelling, *Bull. Tech. Univ. Istanbul*, Vol. 36, 67–80.

182. **J.C. Misra** and R.M. Achari (1983). Thermal Stresses in an Orthotropic Disk due to a Rotating Heat Source, *Journal of Thermal Stresses* (USA), Vol. 6, 115–123.

183. **J.C. Misra**, M. Mishra and S.N. Maiti (1983). Theoretical Stress Analysis for Non-isotropic Body of Cylindrical Configuration Containing a Row of Cracks, *Engng. Fracture Mechs.* (England), Vol. 17, 471–489.

184. **J.C. Misra** and S. Chakravarty (1982). Dynamic Response of Arterial Walls in Vivo, *Journal of Biomechanics* (Oxford), Vol. 15, 317–324.

185. **J.C. Misra** and S. Chakravarty (1982). A Free Vibration Analysis for the Human Cranial System, *Journal of Biomechanics* (Oxford), Vol. 15, 635–645.

186. **J.C. Misra** and K. Roychoudhury (1982). Nonlinear Stress-field in Blood Vessels Under the Action of Connective Tissues, *Blood Vessels* (Switzerland), Vol. 19, 19–29.

187. **J.C. Misra** and S. Samanta (1982). Thermal Shock in a Viscoelastic Half-space, *Journal of Thermal Stresses* (USA), Vol. 5, 365–375.

188. **J.C. Misra** and K. Roychoudhury (1982). A Study on the Stability of Blood Vessels, *Rheologica Acta* (Germany), Vol. 21, 340–346.

189. **J.C. Misra** and S. Chakravarty (1982). Effect of Solar Radiation on the Human Head, *International J. Engg. Sci.* (England), Vol. 20, 445–454.

190. **J.C. Misra** and S. Chakravarty (1982). Stability of Fluid-filled Shells—mathematical Models for Human Head, *Acta Mechanica* (Vienna), Vol. 44, 159–168.

191. **J.C. Misra** and S. Samanta (1981). Finite Creep in Thick-walled Cylindrical Shells at Elevated Temperatures, *Acta Mechanica* (Wien/New York), Vol. 41, 149–155.

192. **J.C. Misra**, M. Mishra and S.N. Maiti (1981). Pressure Necessary to Produce a Griffith Crack of a Given Shape in an Orthotropic Solid, *International Journal of Fracture* (The Netherlands), Vol. 17, 477–482.

193. **J.C. Misra** and S. Samanta (1981). Kriechverhalten Der Kugelschalen (In German), *Beton- und Stahlbetonbau* (Germany), Vol. 76, 143–145.

194. **J.C. Misra** and K. Roychoudhury (1981). A Mathematical Model for Studying the Role of Inertia and Compressibility on Large Deformations in Blood Vessels, *Ganit-Journal of Bangladesh Math. Soc.,* Vol. 1, 73–83.

195. **J.C. Misra** and R.M. Achari (1981). Thermal Stresses in a Viscoelastic Rod, *J. Math. Math. Phys. Sci,* Vol. 15, 123–131.

196. **J.C. Misra** and S.N. Maiti (1981). Integral Equations for Studying a Thermoelastic Problem of Fracture Mechanics, *Rev. Roum. Sci. Tech. Mec. Appl.* (Bucarest), Vol. 2, 531–543.

197. **J.C. Misra** and S.N. Maiti (1981). Distribution of Temperature Necessary for Maintaining a Crack in a Prescribed Shape, *Forschung Im Ingenieurwesen* (Germany), Vol. 47, 82–84.

198. **J.C. Misra** and V.V.T.N. Murthy (1981). Stress Concentration Around Cracks in Long Bones, *Forschung Im Ingenieurwesen* (Germany), Vol. 47, 37–40.

199. **J.C. Misra** and S. Chakravarty (1980). Study of Compressibility in Vascular Rheology, **Rheologica Acta** (Germany), Vol. 19, 381–388.

200. **J.C. Misra** and R.M. Achari (1980). On Axisymmetric Thermal Stresses in an Anisotropic Hollow Cylinder, *Journal of Thermal Stresses* (USA), Vol. 3, 509–520.

201. **J.C. Misra** and S. Samanta (1980). Creep in Spherical Shells, *Math. Forum,* Vol. III, 23–30.

202. **J.C. Misra** (1980). Thermal Stresses in a Non-isotropic Elastic Strip, *Arch. Bud. Masz,* Vol. 27, 219–225.

203. **J.C. Misra** and R.M. Achari (1980). Flexural Deformation of Plates Due to Moving Heat Sources, *Der Stahlbau* (Germany), Vol. 49, 23–25.

204. **J.C. Misra** and R.M. Achari (1980). Temperature Stresses in an Infinite Disc Having a Heat Source in the Vicinity, *Journal of Thermal Stresses* (USA), Vol. 3, 57–66.

205. **J.C. Misra** and S. Samanta (1980). Bending of a Heated Viscoelastic Plate on an Elastic Foundation, *Journal of Non-equilibrium Thermodynamics* (Germany), Vol. 5, 137–142.

206. **J.C. Misra** and R.M. Achari (1979). Stresses in a Heated Inhomogeneous Aeolotropic Rotating Annular Disc of Varying Thickness, *Forschung Im Ingenieurwesen* (Germany), Vol. 45, 80–82 (Springer).

207. **J.C. Misra** and V.V.T.N. Murthy (1979). An Analytical Estimate of the Stress-field in the Vicinity of a Crack in the Human Cranial Bone, *Medical and Life Sc. Engg.*, Vol. 5, 95–107.

208. **J.C. Misra** and S.N. Maiti (1979). Thermoelastic Stresses in a Long Cylinder Weakened by an Infinite Row of Cracks, *J. Math. Phys. Sci.*, Vol. 13, 311–323.

209. **J.C. Misra** (1978). Axisymmetric Vibration of Human Skull-brain System, *Ingenieur Archiv.* (Germany), Vol. 47, 11–19.

210. **J.C. Misra**, C. Hartung and O. Mahrenholtz (1978). Stresses in a Human Skull Due to Pulse Loading, *Ingenieur Archiv* (Germany), Vol. 47, 329–337.

211. **J.C. Misra** (1978). Response of a Human Head to an Impact, *Medical and Life Sci. Engg.*, Vol. 4, 142–152.

212. **J.C. Misra** (1978). Thermoelastic Stresses in an Infinite Slab of Transversely Isotropic Material, *Bul. Inst. Pol. Timisoara, Ser. Mechanica*, Vol. 23, 163–168.

213. **J.C. Misra** and S.N. Maiti (1978). Effect of the Presence of a Crack on Thermal Stresses in a Long-Insulated Cylinder, *Bull. Cal. Math. Soc.* (Springer), Vol. 70, 63–71.

214. **J.C. Misra** and R.M. Achari (1977). On the Thermal Stresses in a Solid Hemisphere Exposed to Sun's Rays, *Rev. Mec. Appl.*, Vol. 22, 687–694.

215. **J.C. Misra**, C. Hartung and O. Mahrenholtz (1977). Effect of Pulse Loading on Brain Injury, *Mechanics Research Communications* (UK), Vol. 4, 297–302 (Springer).

216. **J.C. Misra** and S.N. Maiti (1976). Thermal Stresses in a Finite Aeolotropic Cylinder Due to Thermal Crack, *Rev. Roum. Sci. Tech. Mech. Appl.* (Bucarest), Vol. 21, 339–351.

217. **J.C. Misra** (1975). Thermal Stresses in a Rotating Disc of Anisotropic Material, *Arch. Bud. Masz.* (Poland), Vol. 22, 138–144.

218. **J.C. Misra** and S.N. Maiti (1975). Thermal Stresses in an Aeolotropic Medium with a Cylindrical Cavity and an External Crack, *Rev. Fac. Sc. Univ. Istanbul. Ser. A.*, Vol. 40, 17–28.

219. **J.C. Misra** (1974). A Note on the Thermal Bending of a Thin Elastic Rectangular Plate Resting on an Elastic Foundation, *Pure and Applied Geophysics* (Switzerland), Vol. 112, 83–89.

220. **J.C. Misra** (1974). Thermal Stresses in a Semi-infinite Aeolotropic Material having a Source of Heat at a Point on the Plane Boundary, *Ind. J. Mech. Maths*, Vol. 12, 14–19.

221. **J.C. Misra** (1974). Thermal Stresses in a Finite Cylinder Having Temperature Varying Linearly Along the Length Prescribed on the Curved Surface, *Pure and Applied Geophysics* (Switzerland), Vol. 112, 90–95.

222. **J.C. Misra** and S.N. Maiti (1974). On Thermoelastic Stress Distribution in the Vicinity of an External Crack in an Infinite Solid of Transversely Isotropic Material, *Bull. Acad. Pol. Sci. Ser. Sci. Tech.*, Vol. 22, 567–578.

223. **J.C. Misra** (1973). A Note on the Thermal Bending of a Solid Elastic Circular Plate, *Ind. J. Th. Phys.*, Vol. 21, 35–39.

224. **J.C. Misra** (1973). Note on the Thermal Bending of a Simply Supported Rectangular Plate of Anisotropic Material, *Ind. J. Mech. Maths.*, Vol. 11, 33–36.

225. **J.C. Misra** (1972). Thermal Stresses due to an Internal Source of Heat in a Solid Hemisphere with Radiating Curved Surface, *Ind. J. Pure Appl. Maths.* (INSA), Vol. 3, 612–621 (Springer).

226. **J.C. Misra** (1972). Note on the Thermal Stresses in an Elastic Semi-circular Disc., *Rev. Mech. Appl.* Vol. 17, 1165–1173.

227. **J.C. Misra** (1971). Thermal Stresses in a Long Aeolotropic Cylinder Having a Source of Heat at a Point Inside it, the Curved Surface Being Exposed to Heat Radiation, *Ind. J. Pure Appl. Maths.* (INSA), Vol. 2, 143–153 (Springer).

228. **J.C. Misra** (1971). Note on Thermal Stresses in an Elastic Sphere Due to Constant Temperature and Uniform Normal Pressure Prescribed Over a Band Along the Equator, *Ind. J. Th. Phys.*, Vol. 19, 57–64.

229. **J.C. Misra** (1971). Thermal Stresses in a Long Circular Cylinder Horizontally Placed with its Curved Surface Exposed to Sun's Rays, *Ind. J. Th. Phys.*, Vol. 19, 91–96.

230. **J.C. Misra** (1971). A note on the thermal stresses in an elliptic plate due to a source of heat at the centre of the plate, *Bull. Cal. Math. Soc.*, Vol. 63, 135–141 (Springer).

231. **J.C. Misra** (1971). On the Bending of a Heated Rectangular Anisotropic Plate with Two Opposite Edges Simply Supported and Two Others Built in due to Different Temperature Distributions on the Plane Surfaces, *Bull. Cal. Math. Soc.*, Vol. 63, 183–190 (Springer).

232. B. Mandal, G.C., Shit and **J.C. Misra.** Thermal response during blood flow with magnetic manoparticles and drug targeting delivery.

233. R. Haldar, G.C. Shit and **J.C. Misra.** Oscillatory flow of a biomagnetic viscoelastic fluid in a channel with stretching walls.

(b) ***Communicated for Publication:***

234. B. Mallick and **J.C. Misra,** Thermal irreversibility in electroosmotically modulated micropolar fluid flow exposed to Joule heating.

235. M. Ferdows, M.G. Murtaza, **J.C. Misra** and E.E. Tzirtzilakis, Biomagnetic fluid flow on a nonlinearly stretching sheet with variable thickness in a magnetic environment.

236. M.G. Murtaza, **J.C. Misra,** E.E. Tzirtzilakis and M. Ferdows, A study on biomagnetic maxwell fluid flow past a nonlinearly stretching sheet with consideration of magnetization.

237. M. Dhange, S. Salgare, B. Shindhe, K. Chavan, N.A. Jaffar and **J.C. Misra.** Haemodynamic behaviour of blood mixed with dispersed nanoparticles of gold flowing on an oblique manifold stenosed vestel.

(c) ***List of Book chapters written:***

238. **J.C. Misra** and S.K. Pandey: Peristaltic transport of physiological fluids, In Biomathematics: Modelling and Simulation, World Scientific Publishing Company, London/USA/Singapore, 167–193, 2006.

239. **J.C. Misra,** S. Mukherjee and A.K. Das: Mathematical modelling of DNA Knots and links, In Biomathematics: Modelling and Simulation, World Scientific Publishing Company, London/USA/Singapore, 195–224, 2006.

240. **J.C. Misra** and S. Samanta: Modelling in bone biomechanics, In Biomathematics: Modelling and Simulation, World Scientific Publishing Company, London/USA/Singapore, 451–491, 2006.

241. **J.C. Misra** and S. Chakraborty: Modelling of head impact problems, In: Mathematical Models for Bio-Engineering and Probabilistic Systems, Narosa Publishing House, New Delhi, 1–26, 2005.

242. **J.C. Misra** and V.V.T.N. Murty: Mathematical models in fracture and remodelling of bones, In: Mathematical Models for Bio-Engineering and Probabilistic Systems, Narosa Publishing House, New Delhi, and 27–53, 2005.

243. **J.C. Misra**: Mathematical Theory of Thermoelasticity, In: Modern Applied Mathematics, Narosa Publishing House, New Delhi, 2005.

244. **J.C. Misra** and B. Pal: Some Problems in Newtonian and Non-Newtonian Fluid Dynamics Having Physiological Applications, In: Modern Applied Mathematics, Narosa Publishing House, New Delhi, 2005.

245. S. Mahapatra, S. Bhattacharyya and **J.C. Misra**: Computational Study of Separating Shear Flow Past a Surface-Mounted Hemispherical Obstacle, In: Applicable Mathematics—It's Perspectives and Challenges, Narosa Publishing House, New Delhi, 124–132, 2001.

Details of Books Published

Sl No.	Title	Authors/ Editors	Publishers	Year of Publi-cation	ISBN Number
1.	Mathematical Modelling of Nonlinear Systems, Vol. I: Nonlinear Systems and Mathematical Models	**J.C. Misra and S.B. Sinha**	IIT Kharagpur	1999	
2.	Mathematical Modelling of Nonlinear Systems, Vol. II: Mathematical Techniques and Application Areas	**J.C. Misra and S.B. Sinha**	IIT Kharagpur	1999	
3.	Applicable Mathematics: Its perspectives and Challenges	**J.C. Misra**	Narosa Publishing House, New Delhi	2001	8173194068
4.	Recent Trends in Mathematical Sciences	**J.C. Misra and S.B. Sinha**	Narosa Publishing House, New Delhi	2001	817319405 X, 9788173194054
5.	Uncertainty and Optimality	**J.C. Misra**	World Scientific	2002	9789812380821
6.	Applicable Mathematics in the Golden Age	**J.C. Misra**	Narosa Publishing House, New Delhi	2003	8173194874
7.	Mathematics and Mathematicians at IIT Kharagpur	**J.C. Misra**	Allied Publishers, New Delhi	2003	8177644653
8.	Computing and Information Sciences: Recent Trends	**J.C. Misra**	Narosa Publishing House, New Delhi	2003	8176463612, 9788176463614
9.	Computational Mathematics, Modelling and Algorithms	**J.C. Misra**	Narosa Publishing House, New Delhi	2003	8173194904, 9788173194900
10.	Industrial Mathematics and Statistics	**J.C. Misra**	Narosa Publishing House, New Delhi	2003	8173194882, 9788173194887
11.	Mathematical Models for Bioengineering and Probabilistic Systems	**J.C. Misra**	Narosa Publishing House, New Delhi	2005	8173194939
12.	Modern Applied Mathematics	**J.C. Misra**	Narosa Publishing House, New Delhi	2005	8173194920
13.	Biomathematics: Modeling and Simulation	**J.C. Misra**	World Scientific, Singapore/London/USA	2006	9812381104
14.	Achinpurer ak Pathik (in Bengali)	**J.C. Misra**	Kabitika Publishing House, Kolkata	2023	9788119564897
15.	A Traveller in an Unknown Land (Autobiography)	**J.C. Misra**	Allied Publishers, Noida	2025	9789348699770

Edited Books on the Author

Sl No.	Title	Authors/ Editors	Publishers	Year of Publi-cation	ISBN Number
1.	A Mathematics Wizard in Different Eyes	**H.P. Maity, M.N. Das, R. Nayek and B.L. Das**	Allied Publishers, Noida	2025	9789348699282
2.	Nana Chokhe ak Barenya Ganit-Sadhak (in Bengali)	**H.P. Maity, M.N. Das and B.L. Das**	Kabitika Publishing House, Kolkata	2023	9788119564439

The Archives: Recognitions and Roots

Author meets Mr. Walter Scheel, President of West Germany, Bonn, 1976

IIT Kharagpur Board of Governors Chairman Mr. Russi Mody (Chairman and Managing Director of Tata Motors) hands over the Silver Jubilee Research Award to the Author during Convocation 1984

Author receives Fellowship Certificate from President of Indian National Academy of Engineering (INAE), Dr. Anil Kakodkar, Chairman of the Atomic Energy Commission of India, 1999

Prof. Misra's Address after being Awarded INAE Outstanding Teachers' Award in the Annual Convention of INAE, Bhubaneshwar, 2013

Author delivers P.L Bhatnagar Memorial Lecture at ISTAM Congress, NIT Hamirpur, December 2001

Felicitation of the Author at the 46th ISTAM Congress held in Hamirpur, Himachal Pradesh

Author being Awarded 'Ram Mohan Puraskar' for
"Outstanding Contributions to the Field of Mathematics", 2004

Delivering Presidential Address in Mathematical Sciences Section (Including Statistics)
of the 94th Indian Science Congress, Tamil Nadu, 2007

With Renowned Astrophysicist Dr. Jayant Narlikar, Padma Vibhushan and Cricketer Sourav Ganguly

INAE President Mr. Baldev Raj hands over "INAE Outstanding Teacher Award-2013" to the Author

Author meets German President Joachim Gauck in Berlin, June 2016

Inaugural Session of the International Conference ICOMMONS, 1999. L to R: Author (Convenor), O. Mahrenholtz (Chief Guest) from Germany, Director A. Ghosh, S. Dattagupta (Guest of Honour), S.B. Sinha

Author along with his wife meets Japanese Delegates of ICOMMONS at IIT Guest House, 1999

Welcome Address of Convenor at the Inaugural Session of the International Conference ICRAMS 2000

Meeting with Foreign Delegates of ICRAMS 2000

Panel Discussion during ICRAMS 2000

Cultural Evening Programme by Rabindra Bharati University during ICRAMS 2000

As Convenor of ICRAMS 2000, Author felicitates the Artists from Rabindra Bharati University

Welcome Address of the Author (Co-ordinator) to the Delegates of UNESCO Sponsored Training Programme (for SAARC countries), January 2000

Informal Meeting with Delegates of Training Programme on Computer Applications in Mathematics Teaching

Inaugural Session of Mathworx-2K; Left to Right: Author (Convenor), A.S. Gupta, Swami Atmaprabhananda (Chief Guest), S.Kumar

Swami Sukdevananda, Principal, R.K. Mission V.C. College Rahara (3rd from Left), Inaugurates Mathworx-2k+1 convened by Prof. Misra, IIT Kharagpur

Welcome Address by the Convenor (Author), Mathworx-2k+1

With Principal, Sacred Heart High School, Father Malay, Chairman of the Valedictory Session of Mathworx-2k+1 (fourth from the right)

Inauguration of Mathematicians' Convention, 2001
Left to Right: D.N.Mitra, M.P. Jain, Director A. Ghosh, Author (Convenor)

AMPP 2001: Welcome Address by the Convenor (Author)

With the Delegates of AMPP-2001

Felicitated by Director, IIT at Maths Convention, IIT Kharagpur, 2001

With Mrs Shrabani Sengupta, Recipient of President's Award, 3rd September, 2024

The Author and his wife, with Prof. G. Sarojamma, HoD (Maths.), Later VC of SPM University, Tirupati, 2008

Lighting the Lamp by the Author (Chief Guest) during Inauguration of National Conference on Mathematics, Utkal University, 2009

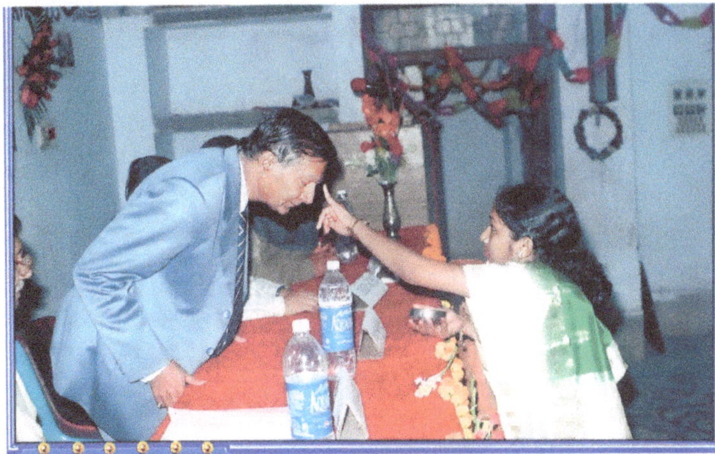

At the Inaugural Session of National Conference of Mathematics, NIT Warangal: Reception of the Chief Guest

Felicitation/Inauguration of First Edition of the Autobiography, Pratapdighi, 13th January, 2024
On Dais L-R: BDO Shri Sankha Ghatak, Author, Ananda Maharaj (Belda Yogashram),
Baman Maharaj (Chaitanya Ashram, Kharagpur)

Glimpses of the Grand Ceremony, Pratapdighi, 13th January, 2024

Address of the Chief Guest (Author) at the National Conference of Mathematics at Utkal University, Bhubaneswar

Address of the Chief Guest (Author) at the National Conference organised by Mathematics Department, NIT Warangal

With the Delegates of National Conference at NIT Warangal

At the Inauguration of the Maths Conference organised by Vidyasagar University, Midnapore on the Occasion of Reunion 2007. Author (sitting at the centre) as the Chief Guest

Vidyasagar Fest at Pratapdighi: Author was felicitated by various Organizations, 2014

With the Students and Faculty Members of Centre for Healthcare Science and Technology, IIEST Shibpur

With the HoD and faculty members of the Applied Maths. Dept. of Dhaka University, Bangladesh, 2022

L-R: Author, his Parents (with new-born Subhas in the lap) and Shorasi, 1970

On Father's Birthday, Sitting: Parents, Standing (Left-to-Right): Sudip, Author, Shorasi, Namita; On floor: Child 'Suman'

In Bhubaneswar

During a Tour in Winter

In IIT Quarters C1-63

Visit to Kerala Arts and Crafts Village, Kovalam, Kerala, on 15th October, during Engineers Conclave 2022

In IIT Quarters C1-63

Steamer Journey in Andaman and Nicobar Islands

Visit to Cellular Jail, Andaman and Nicobar Islands

Author's Mother with Three Successive Generations

At IIT Kanpur: With Subhas, Sulagna, Devarati and Devapratim

Devarati receiving DST Inspire Innovation Award, 2020-21

Devapratim holding Several Award Certificates. Principal, IIT Kanpur Kendriya Vidyalaya (left) was present

Devapratim greeted for Securing AIR 6 in Narayana Scholastic Aptitude Test (NSAT), 2023-24

Daughter Sumita's Family

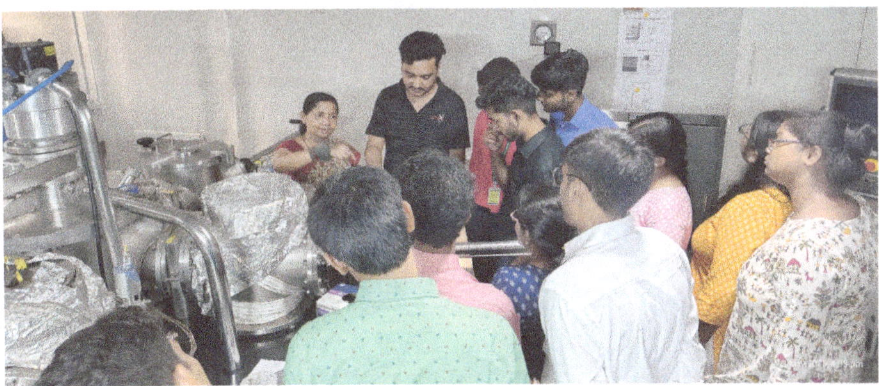

Sumita demonstrating Solar Cell Fabrication Facilities at IIEST Shibpur to Students of Academy of Technology, a leading Engineering College in West Bengal

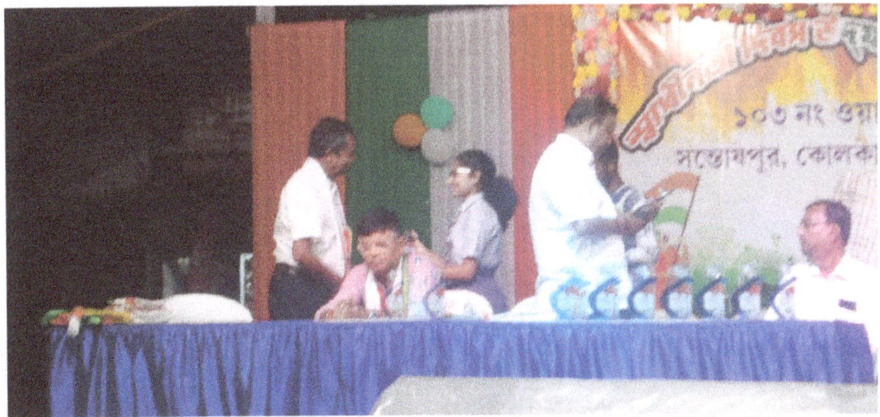

Granddaughter Supurna felicitated for Outstanding Performance in ICSE Class-X Exams

Author and his Wife with Sudip and his Family at Pisa (Italy), 2019

Devadeep receiving 'Young Scientist Award', Chennai, 2022-23

Devadrita with Award Certificates

Devadrita in a Dance Programme

Child Devadrita in a Music Class

Infant Devadeep receives the Author on his Arrival at Hamburg Railway Station, Germany, 2011

Grandson Devadeep in the guise of a 'Bangali Babu'

Grandson Devapratim in the guise of a 'King' during his Sacred Thread Ceremony

Sacred Thread Ceremony of Elder Son Subhas and Worship of Goddess Kali at ancestral home at Bagmari

Educational Tour with Children to Shri Mangueshi Temple, Goa

Educational Tour to Indian Parliament House in New Delhi

Educational Tour with Children in their teen ages at Raj Ghat, New Delhi

Author's Father with his Grandson Subhas

Performing Shradh of Ancestors at Gayadham (Bihar) in presence of Father-in-law, Shorasi, Debasish (Sibu) and Elder Sister

Author with Family in Nazi Party Rally Grounds, Nuremberg, Germany, 2019

Author with Family Members in Nuremberg (Germany), 2019

At Nuremberg Castle in Germany, 2019

At Prague Castle in Czech Republic, 2019

St. Vitus Cathedral, Prague's largest and most significant Church, 2019

At Nuremberg Castle Viewpoint, 2019

At Charles Bridge, Prague (Czech Republic), 2019

Inside the Hotel Room in Prague, 2019

Author with Family Members at Nuremberg Railway Station, 2019

Waiting for Train, Nuremberg Railway Station (Germany), 2019

At Stuttgart Railway Station (Germany), 2019

At Zugspitze (Highest mountain peak in Germany), 2019

With Mr. Saroj Nayek's Family at Nuremberg, 2019

Author with his Wife: Boat-Ride in Venice (Italy), 2019

Visit to Handcrafted Clothes Factories in Burano and Glass Factories in Murano, Venice, 2019

At Florence Railway Station, Italy

Sudip feeling happy with his parents in front of the Famous Colosseum of the Roman Empire, 2019

Inside St.Peter's Basilica, a Church in Vatican City, 2019

Outside St.Peter's Basilica, Vatican City, 2019

In front of the Eiffel Tower, Paris, 2019

In front of Louvre Museum, Paris, 2019

Author with his Family in Venice, 2019

During Travel in Metro at Nuremberg, 2019

At the Botanical Garden of Erlangen, 2019

Steamer Journey in Venice, Italy, 2019

In front of Murano Glass Factory, Venice, 2019

In Copenhagen, Capital of Denmark

A Visit to Mizo Huts (traditional, eco-friendly homes in Mizoram), Aizawl, 19th March, 2025

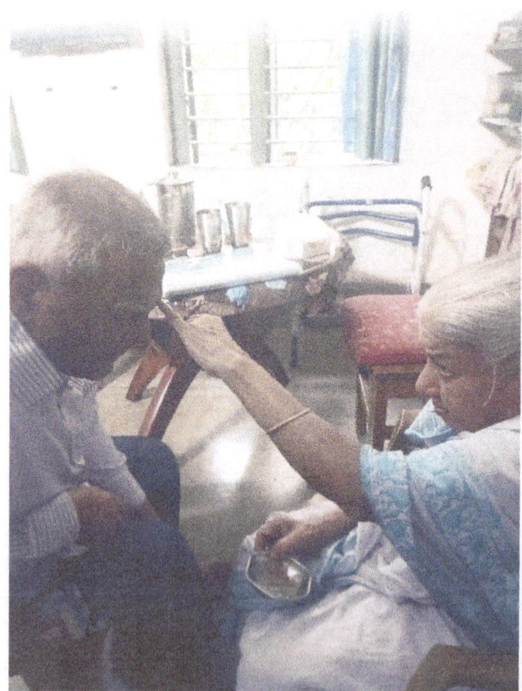
Elder Sister Durgarani showering blessings upon the Author during Bhaidooj, 2024

At R.K.Mission, Belgharia with Family Members, 19th April, 2024

President, West Bengal Academy of Science and Technology hands over Fellowship Certificate to the Author on his Election as FAScT, 2025

With Swami Devarajananda of Belur Math at Ramakrishna Mission, Belgharia, 2024

With Padma Shri Prof. Harish Chandra Verma, at Central University of South Bihar, 2025

Felicitation as an Eminent Retired Professor during Inaugural Ceremony of Platinum Jubilee Celebration, IIT Kharagpur on 18th August, 2025

Worshipping River Yamuna at Ayodhya in Sacred Memory of Parents and Younger Brother Dines on 13th October, 2025

With Ms. Kriti Yadav and her Supervisor, Prof. S.K. Pandey after conducting the Ph.D. thesis defence as External Examiner, Mathematical Sciences Department, IIT (BHU), Varanasi, 11th October, 2025

With Technology Icon Arjun Malhotra, 18th August, 2025

Friends of Sixty Plus Golden Life Association, Santoshpur, Kolkata Celebrating the Felicitation of the Author by I.I.T. Kharagpur, 7th September, 2025

Technology Durga Puja at IIT Kharagpur, 30th September, 2025

Speaking on Srimad Bhagavat Gita during a Religious Discourse as a part of Inauguration Programme of Shantiswari Kali Temple, Pratapdighi, East Midnapore, *Akshay Tritiya,* 30th April, 2025

With Dr. Bibhudhendu Pati and His Family, Bhubaneswar

An Evening in Varanasi During Winter

During a Visit to Lingaraj Temple, Bhubaneswar